TRANSCORTICAL APHASIAS

Transcortical Aphasias

Marcelo L. Berthier
Clinic University Hospital and University of Malaga, Spain

Psychology Press
a member of the Taylor & Francis group

BS

Psychology Press Ltd, Publishers
27 Church Road
Hove
East Sussex
BN3 2FA
UK

British Library Cataloguing-in-Publication Data

A catalogue record for this book is available from the British Library

ISBN: 0–86377–840–2 (Hbk)
ISBN: 0–86377–841–0 (Pbk)
ISSN: 0967–9944

Typeset by Graphicraft Limited, Hong Kong
Printed and bound in the UK by Biddles Ltd, Guildford and King's Lynn

11/21/02

This book is dedicated to the memory of my father,
Luis D. Berthier

Contents

vii

Series preface

From being an area primarily on the periphery of mainstream behavioural and cognitive science, neuropsychology has developed in recent years into an area of central concern for a range of disciplines. We are witnessing not only a revolution in the way in which brain–behaviour–cognition relationships are viewed, but a widening of interest concerning developments in neuropsychology on the part of a range of workers in a variety of fields. Major advances in brain-imaging techniques and the cognitive modelling of the impairments following brain damage promise a wider understanding of the nature of the representation of cognition and behaviour in the damaged and undamaged brain.

Neuropsychology is now centrally important for those working with brain-damaged people, but the very rate of expansion in the area makes it difficult to keep up with findings from current research. The aim of the *Brain Damage, Behaviour and Cognition* series is to publish a wide range of books that present comprehensive and up-to-date overviews of current developments in specific areas of interest.

These books will be of particular interest to those working with the brain-damaged. It is the editors' intention that undergraduates, postgraduates, clinicians and researchers in psychology, speech pathology and medicine will find this series a useful source of information on important current developments. The authors and editors of the books in this series are experts in their respective fields, working at the forefront of contemporary research. They have produced texts that are accessible and scholarly. We thank them for their contribution and their hard work in fulfilling the aims of the series.

CC and GH
Sydney, Australia and Birmingham, UK
Series Editors

Brain Damage, Behaviour and Cognition: Developments in Clinical Neuropsychology Titles in Series

Series Editors
Chris Code, University of Sydney, Australia
Dave Müller, University College Suffolk, UK

Cognitive Retraining Using Microcomputers
Veronica A. Bradley, John L. Welch and Clive E. Skilbeck
The Characteristics of Aphasia
Chris Code (Ed.)
Classic Cases in Neuropsychology
Chris Code, Claus-W. Wallesch, Yves Joanette, and André Roch Lecours (Eds)
The Neuropsychology of Schizophrenia
Anthony S. David and John C. Cutting (Eds)
Neuropsychology and the Dementias
Siobhan Hart and James M. Semple
Clinical Neuropsychology of Alcoholism
Robert G. Knight and Barry E. Longmore
Neuropsychology of the Amnesic Syndrome
Alan J. Parkin and Nicholas R.C. Leng
Clinical and Neuropsychological Aspects of Closed Head Injury
John T.E. Richardson
Unilateral Neglect: Clinical and Experimental Studies
Ian H. Robertson and J.C. Marshall (Eds)
Cognitive Rehabilitation in Perspective
Rodger Wood and Ian Fussey (Eds)

Series Editors
Chris Code, University of Sydney, Australia
Glyn Humphreys, University of Birmingham, UK

Transcortical Aphasias
Marcelo L. Berthier
Communication Disorders Following Traumatic Brain Injury
Skye McDonald, Leanne Togher, and Chris Code (Eds)
Spatial Neglect: A Clinical Handbook for Diagnosis and Treatment
Ian H. Robertson and Peter W. Halligan
Apraxia: The Neuropsychology of Action
Leslie J. Gonzalez Rothi and Kenneth Heilman
Developmental Cognitive Neuropsychology
Christine Temple

Preface

Transcortical aphasia is the term used for syndromes in which the ability to repeat language is relatively preserved despite marked disturbances in other linguistic domains. These kinds of aphasia were first described by brilliant German neurologists about a century ago, in the same era that pioneering research on language disorders were describing the classical aphasic syndromes (e.g. Broca's aphasia). Since then, the validity of the transcortical aphasias has nearly always been questioned and controversial; the initial popularity waned to the point of being either neglected in monographs or considered artefacts of language testing. Goldstein (1948) and Geschwind, Quadfasel, and Segarra (1968) among others revived the validity of transcortical aphasias, but the more contemporary history of transcortical aphasias is not radically different.

There are a number of well-known reference texts on language disturbances after acquired brain damage that uncover the syndromes of aphasia in a comprehensive and systematic fashion. In the past few years, for example, books solely dedicated to specific aphasic syndromes (e.g. conduction aphasia) or even to certain aphasic signs (e.g. agrammatism) have appeared within neuropsychological literature. However, although some instructive chapters dealing with transcortical aphasias have been published, this theme has been only superficially treated in major neurological textbooks and authoritative texts of clinical neuropsychology covering aphasic disturbances. A monograph on the different clinical, linguistic, aetiological, and neuroimaging aspects of transcortical aphasias has not been published, until now.

At first glance, it could be argued that the existence of a monograph on this topic is not only untimely because its publication coincides with the progressive decline in the use of standard diagnoses in the classification of aphasias, but also that this volume could be deemed "unnecessary", since the transcortical aphasias do constitute an uncommon language disorder. This is not the case, however. To continue to use the old symptom-complex approach to diagnose the "classical" syndromes of transcortical aphasias is not at odds with the subsequent fragmentation of the observed language deficits by using the cognitive neuropsychological model. In addition, the prevalence of transcortical aphasias range from approximately 4% to 20% of all aphasic syndromes due to cerebrovascular accidents, and one type of transcortical aphasia (the sensory class) is currently considered one of the most common types of aphasic disorders in the course of language dissolution experienced by victims of Alzheimer's disease and other cortical degenerative conditions.

In this book I do not intend to make a comprehensive review of all aspects of the transcortical syndromes. The reader should be aware that certain topics related to the transcortical pattern, such as reading and writing disturbances, apraxia, and conventional rehabilitation approaches, are only broadly outlined or not discussed at all. The topics selected are logically organised starting with two chapters dealing with the historical aspects and assessment of language deficits from a clinical and psycholinguistic perspective. The next three chapters are dedicated to the clinical phenomenology, aetiology, neural substrates, and linguistic mechanisms underlying each of the three established variants of the transcortical syndromes. The concluding chapters of the book present linguistic, behavioural, and motor issues related to the transcortical pattern that are generally grouped under the rubric of echophenomena as well as the contribution of the modern structural and functional neuroimaging techniques to our understanding of the relationships between language and cerebral structures among patients with transcortical aphasias.

This book is specifically addressed to advanced undergraduates, speech pathologists, linguists, neuropsychologists, cognitive neuropsychologists, neurologists, and behavioural neurologists. Detailed discussion of some of the topics in this volume is the result of my own research projects. My interest in the study of transcortical aphasias started at the beginning of the 1980s when I was working at the Department of Behavioural Neurology at the Dr Raúl Carrea Institute of Neurological Research and at the Center for Investigation and Rehabilitation of Aphasia (CIRA) in Buenos Aires. My first thanks must therefore go to Ramón Leiguarda and Silvia Rubio who have been especially influential in my development as a behavioural neurologist. At that time, through the encouraging counselling of Andrew Kertesz, who kindly authorised the translation to Spanish and utilisation of his Western Aphasia Battery, my colleagues and myself had the unique opportunity of assessing more than 100 aphasic patients, a number of whom showed a transcortical pattern of language deficits. Our major areas of interest were in the study of the neural basis of transcortical aphasias and examining the role of the right hemisphere in language repetition using, in selected cases, the Amytal (Wada) test and functional neuroimaging. I am indebted to

Adelaida Ruiz and Sergio E. Starkstein who actively participated in the assessment of such patients and in developing ideas presented in this book. I would also like to express my gratitude to the many other neurologists, linguists, neuropsychologists, and friends who generously allowed me to assess aphasic patients under their care as well as to the patients themselves, who were, as the name implies, very patient throughout the long testing sessions.

Since 1989, I have been working in Spain on the assessment of special patterns of transcortical aphasias, on the linguistic characteristics of residual repetition, on paralinguistic aspects (e.g. prosody) and in functional neuroimaging. I am very grateful to Jaime Kulisevsky from the Department of Neurology of the Sant Pau Hospital of Barcelona and to Ana Maria Fernández and Eugenio Martinez-Celdrán from the Department of General Linguistics at the University of Barcelona, who participated in these collaborative research projects while I was working as a research associate in the Clinic and Provincial Hospital there. I would also like to express my appreciation to my colleagues in Malaga, where I am working at present, who continually collaborate in research projects. They include Julian Hinojosa, Angel Posada, and Carmen Puentes.

The idea for this book was suggested by Chris Code, to whom I will be ever indebted for his encouragement in bringing my research together in a monograph. Chris Code and Andy Kertesz kindly read the first draft; they helped me to improve the quality of this manuscript. I much appreciate their lucid and encouraging comments. A special acknowledgement is also extended to Ruth Stoner, the only person to read all the draft chapters of this volume before submission, and who took great pains to refine more than a few awkward sentences. Of course, I would like to thank my wife Mabel and my daughter Carolina (Cuqui) for their enormous patience and continuous support during the writing process. Finally, I would also to thank the staff of Psychology Press for the efficient production of the book.

Marcelo L. Berthier
Malaga, June 1998

CHAPTER ONE

Historical aspects

INTRODUCTION

The modern history of aphasia undoubtedly begins with Paul Broca (1824–1880) (Benson, 1985; Geschwind, 1964b). Although the anatomist and phreno-logist Franz Joseph Gall (1758–1828) localised, as early as 1819, the "organs" for speech articulation and word memory in the orbital region of the frontal lobes, it was Broca who first revolutionised the medical community when he discovered that lesions in the posterior part of the third *left* frontal convolution induced expressive speech deficits, which he called *aphemia* (Benton, 1991). Thirteen years after Broca's discovery, Carl Wernicke (1848–1905), a young German neuropsychiatrist, generated a second major revolution in the under-standing of the cerebral localisation of aphasia when he published a mono-graph entitled *Der aphasische Symptomcomplex. Eine psychologische Studie auf anatomomischer Basis* (1874/1977). In his monograph, Wernicke described the salient features of sensory aphasia (now termed Wernicke's aphasia) that include grossly impaired auditory comprehension and fluent but paraphasic spontaneous speech.

Wernicke's contribution was by no means restricted to defining the clinicopathological characteristics of the sensory aphasia syndrome. He also developed a general schematic model to interpret anatomofunctional aspects of both normal language acquisition and aphasic disorders (Fig. 1.1) as well as a new classification of these disorders. Wernicke's hypothetical diagram of lan-guage function and his new classification of aphasias were rapidly accepted by other leading aphasiologists of the period preceding World War I, such as Bastian, Charcot, Lichtheim, Dejerine, and many others (Benson, 1985).

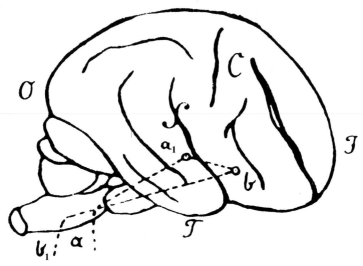

FIG. 1.1   Wernicke's (1874/1977) diagram for speech production, comprehension, and repetition. In this diagram *F, T, O* represent the frontal, temporal, and occipital lobes, respectively; *S* the Sylvian fissure; *a* the entrance of the acoustic nerve in the medulla oblongata; a_1 the central termination of the acoustic nerve in the cortex of the posterior temporal lobe; *b* the area of motor images in the frontal lobe; b_1 the centrifugal speech pathway emerging from the medulla oblongata. The association pathways a_1–*b* run subcortically through the Insula Reili.

WERNICKE–LICHTHEIM CONNECTIONIST MODEL

Wernicke (1874/1977) believed that language disturbances occurring after brain damage were the consequence of impairment in psycholinguistic functions (understanding spoken language, reading, writing, and so forth) that were represented in centres with specific anatomical locations. On creating his diagram of language representation in the brain, Wernicke was extremely conservative and made the effort to restrict the number of centres and their linguistic functions (Caplan, 1987, p. 54). He suggested that expressive language, including word and sentence repetition, was mediated by a "reflex arc" represented in the cortex surrounding the Sylvian fissure. He envisaged that incoming sounds were conveyed via the acoustic nerve (*a*) to the centre for acoustic images located in the cortex of the posterior temporal lobe (a_1). This sensory centre was connected by major subcortical fibre tracts to the centre for motor images located in the inferior frontal region (*b*) and its efferent pathways concerned with speech (b_1). Wernicke then suggested that these two speech centres and the commissure *a–b* were the first structures used in the normal acquisition of language through imitation of what the child hears. He went on to speculate that in subsequent stages of language development other fibre systems, independent of "sound images", were regularly used for spontaneous speech, a theory that was later accepted by Lichtheim (1885).

Wernicke (1874/1977) noted that two patients (Cases 3 and 4) of the 10 sensory aphasics he originally described had good auditory comprehension. By that time, he had become particularly interested in the analysis of milder cases of sensory aphasia. He found that in such cases, the symptom-complex was characterised by hesitant and laborious spontaneous speech and word-finding pauses in the presence of intact comprehension of spoken language. This combination of language deficits was termed commissural aphasia (*Leitungsaphasie* or *conduction aphasia*). Despite the fact Wernicke had pointed out that the interruption of the neural path linking the a_1 (centre for acoustic images) in the temporal lobe with b (centre for motor images) in the frontal lobe would induce conduction aphasia (Henderson, 1992), he failed to predict that repetition should be abnormal in this type of aphasia (Geschwind, 1964b). Lichtheim (1885) believed that the impairment of repetition may be one of the most relevant characteristics of the syndrome. He further argued that a lesion involving the fibre tracts interconnecting the motor and sensory speech centres at the level of either the Insula Reili or the superior longitudinal (arcuate) fasciculus, but sparing the major cortical speech centres would induce a combination of fluent paraphasic spontaneous speech, good auditory comprehension, and impaired repetition. In the same article, Lichtheim (1885) described a clinicopathological case study (patient JSB) who confirmed his prediction. For several years, Wernicke was reluctant to accept the characteristic triad of language deficits in conduction aphasia, until 1904, when his assistant, Karl Kleist, showed him a typical clinical case of conduction aphasia (Geschwind, 1963).

Lichtheim (1885) was profoundly influenced by the pioneer work of both Broca (1861 and 1863) and Wernicke (1874/1977) in his development of the localisationist concept of aphasia. He was particularly interested in the description of other types of aphasia which in his view could not be explained entirely on the basis of Wernicke's model, and which he believed resulted from the interruption of the pathways connecting major speech centres rather than from damage of the speech centres themselves (Caplan, 1987; Lichtheim, 1885). Based on previous models of language functioning and on the analysis of aphasic patients, Lichtheim complemented the schema of language representation in the brain drawn by Wernicke by including new centres and commissures. Following the same line of thought as Wernicke, Lichtheim developed his schema by starting with the acquisition of language by imitation (repetition). He first postulated the existence of specific centres for auditory images A and motor images M that were interconnected by a commissure completing a "reflex arc". The innovation of Lichtheim's schema was the incorporation of a new centre that he termed B, and which he viewed as the "part of the brain where concepts are elaborated" (Fig. 1.2).

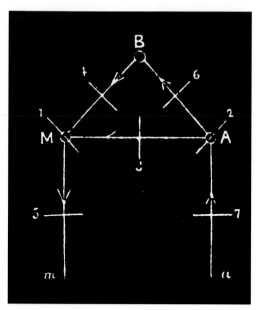

FIG. 1.2   Lichtheim's (1885) first diagram of speech centres, commissural pathways, and presumed sites of lesions that would cause aphasia. In this schema, *A* represents the centre of auditory images, *M* the centre of motor images, and *B* the centre of concepts (*Begriffe*). Lesions of commissures 4 and 6 would produce, in Lichtheim's view, inner-commissural aphasia (transcortical motor aphasia) and inner-commissural word deafness (transcortical sensory aphasia), respectively. Reprinted from Lichtheim (1885); by permission of Oxford University Press.

Based on the clinicoanatomical observations of Broca and Wernicke, Lichtheim assumed that the centre *M* was located in the inferior frontal convolution, centre *A* in the temporal convolution, and that the commissure linking *A–M* passed through the insula. While Lichtheim accepted that the "reflex arc" created by Wernicke was sufficient for simple language repetition and monitoring correct speech, he was convinced that other brain areas had to be used when less automatic aspects such as volition and intelligence are incorporated into language function. In other words, Lichtheim pointed out that when intelligence is required in the service of language, this function is accomplished through pathways linking the auditory centre *A* with various peripheral nonlanguage areas in which the concepts are elaborated (p. 436). Lichtheim also hypothesised the existence of pathways connecting the concept centre *B* with *M*, which he believed were necessary for volitional or intelligent speech. Although he was convinced that volitional speech relied on the commissure *B–M*, he additionally suggested that the phonological information used in verbal output is controlled by both the direct connections linking centre *A* with *M* and the indirect

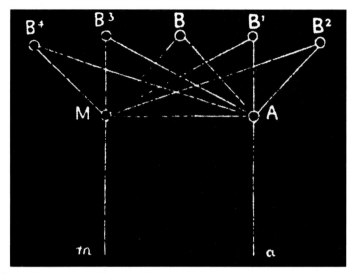

FIG. 1.3 Lichtheim's (1885) seventh diagram of the speech centres depicting the radiate set of commissural pathways linking the sensory centre *A* and the motor centre *M* with the centre of concepts *B* (*Begriffe*). Reprinted from Lichtheim (1885); by permission of Oxford University Press.

connection *A–B–M* (Arbib, Caplan, & Marshall, 1982; Lichtheim, 1885).[1] According to Lichtheim's model, the "concept centre" *B* (*Begriffe*) cannot be localised in a specific anatomical site, "but rather to result from the combined action of the whole sensory sphere" (p. 477). In addition, he indicated that the commissural pathways linking the concept centre *B* with the motor *M* and sensory *A* speech centres (commissures *M–B* and *A–B*) were not only two distinct and separate commissures, but a radiate set of converging fibre tracts coming from various unidentified regions of the cerebral cortex to the *A* and *M* centres. From a clinicoanatomical point of view, Lichtheim suggested that damage to these widely distributed commissures across the left hemisphere (*BM, B1M, B2M,* and so forth) would induce speechlessness and/or word-deafness (Fig. 1.3). He also suggested that simultaneous lesions in these commissures at their entrance to either centre *A* or *B* may induce the same language defects as if they had been damaged at more distant sites. He further hypothesised that since the motor

---

[1] Lichtheim believed that volitive speech was mediated by direct connections between the centre *B* and the motor centre *M*. The pathway *B–M* would produce normal spontaneous speech in sensory aphasia. This is not the case, however. Alternatively, Kussmaul (1877), who utilised a model similar to Lichtheim, argued that spontaneous speech, like repetition, took place via pathways which transmitted verbal information from centre *B* to *M* had to first pass by the centre *A*. Kussmaul's schema has been later adopted by other authors to explain the sparing of object naming in a patient with mixed transcortical aphasia (Heilman, Tucker, & Valenstein, 1976, p. 417).

centre *M* can be activated by two separate pathways, the disruption of either would induce different patterns of repetition (see further discussion in Butterworth & Warrington, 1995; McCarthy & Warrington, 1984).

LICHTHEIM AND THE INNER-COMMISSURAL APHASIAS

Inner-commissural aphasia

In 1885 Lichtheim, based on his own cases, first reported a variety of motor aphasia which he believed was the result of an interruption of pathways linking the concept centre *B* with the motor speech centre *M*. The resulting language impairment was characterised by loss of volitional speech and writing with preserved understanding of spoken and written language as well as copying, reading aloud, and repetition. This condition was termed *inner-commissural aphasia*. He interpreted language deficits as well as preserved language functions as follows: Spontaneous speech would be diminished because ideas stored in the concept centre *B* could not access the motor speech centre *A* necessary for verbal expression. By contrast, he interpreted that speech understanding would be preserved because both the centres *A* and *B* and their connections were spared. Finally, Lichtheim speculated that basic speech functions such as repetition and oral reading would also be spared because the centres *A* and *B* and their subcortical connecting pathways were intact. Wernicke accepted the clinical description of this novel kind of aphasia, but replaced the term inner-commissural aphasia by the now widely accepted transcortical motor aphasia. Lichtheim exemplified this type of aphasia by reporting a case of traumatic aphasia in an article entitled *On Aphasia* (1885) which was published in the prestigious neurological journal *Brain*. What follows is a summary of the most relevant clinical details of such case (pp. 447–449).

The patient, known as Dr CK, was an adult bilingual (German–French) man who had worked as a medical practitioner until he suffered a traumatic brain injury in a carriage accident. Following the accident Dr CK remained unconcious for three hours; on awakening it was noted that his speech was severely affected and he could say no more than "yes" and "no". He also had impaired swallowing and voluntary buccofacial movements, and a moderate hemiparesis with normal sensation was noted in his right limbs. Language examination in the ensuing days revealed that "whilst his vocabulary was still meagre, it was observed that he could repeat everything perfectly". CK could not write spontaneously, but his writing to dictation and copy were preserved. He was examined by Lichtheim six weeks after the accident. Neurological examination disclosed only a mild weakness in his right facial nerve and leg, and impaired recognition of objects palpated with his right hand. The profile of language impairment had also improved to the point that Lichtheim described CK's spontaneous speech as "copious", although he then stated that "he does not talk much, and speaks in a

drawing manner". During running speech, Lichtheim noted that the patient omitted words and produced paraphasias both in German and French. CK was aware
of the paraphasic distortions he produced during object naming and attempted
to correct himself. In this regard, Lichtheim commented "the auditory representation of words he cannot find were missing; he cannot name the number of
syllables of them". Although CK could comprehend and repeat these unnamed
words, he could not retain such words in his memory. Repetition was normal for
short but not long sentences. Auditory and written comprehension were both
normal. CK's narrative writing, like his spontaneous speech, was fluent but
replete with meaningless words. Copy and dictation were normal. Lichtheim
reported that one month later CK's language defects had improved considerably,
and only isolated deficits could be found in writing and naming.

Even though Lichtheim was unable to confirm the localisation of the responsible lesion in this case, he speculated that inner-commissural aphasia would result
from white matter lesions located at the base of the third frontal convolution
(p. 478). He arrived at such a conclusion after reviewing clinicopathological
details of some previous cases (p. 478): "Thus in the case of Farge, we find
that the patient had a right hemiplegia after a severe apopletic seizure. He could
say only a very few words; but could repeat correctly what was said, at least
the first words of a sentence . . . The autopsy revealed integrity of Broca's area;
but in the white matter beneath was found a patch of softening, the size of a
small egg."

The subsequent publication of a case of transcortical motor aphasia (inner-
commissural aphasia) associated with a small lesion of the white matter beneath the
motor speech region by Rothman (1906) provided further support for Lichtheim's
original formulation on the neurological basis of transcortical motor aphasia.

Inner-commissural word-deafness

Lichtheim (1885) also went on to predict that a lesion interrupting the commissures
between the centre of auditory images *A* and the concept centre *B* would provoke a sensory aphasia with fluent paraphasic speech, echolalia, and impaired
understanding of spoken and written language. While some symptoms were
coincidental with those described by Wernicke under the rubric of sensory aphasia, Lichtheim suggested that since the lesion would not interrupt Wernicke's
arc, the faculty of repeating words, reading aloud, and writing to dictation should
be preserved. He further commented, "Owing to the interruption of communication between A and B, there must be a complete loss of intelligence for what is
repeated, read aloud, written to dictation by the patient" (p. 453).

In his 1885 article, Lichtheim reported on a second aphasic patient who could
repeat language, but who had fluent oral expression and poor understanding of
spoken language. The patient, JU Schwarz, was considered to have *inner-
commissural word-deafness* (transcortical sensory aphasia):

Spoken Language—The disturbance in his power to understand it is very evident (verbal deafness). If one stands behind him and talks to him, he turns round and asks: "Do you speak to me?" The simplest request, to show his tongue, shut his eyes are answered by: "I don't know what one wants".

Speech—There is no deficiency in his vocabulary. He talks a good deal in a flowing manner: he seldom is short for a word; he occasionally uses a wrong or a mutilated one . . . He is in great difficulty when he has to name objects shown to him . . . Instead of "wine" he says "that is strong"; for "water", "that is weak", &c.

Repetition—He obviously could repeat correctly all that was spoken before him; but he apparently did not understand what he did repeat, as for instance the words, "My name is Peter Schwarz, and I am already 4 years old," which did not draw any signs of denegation on his part.

Written Language—He understands nothing printed, or handwritten. The simplest things placed before him he cannot read nor decipher. He knows the name of most letters, and gives it correctly; he only confounds the capital I.

Reading aloud—He can make up letters into words, and he can read aloud by spelling; but it was evident that the sense of the words remains closed to him. Out of sentence, "Will you have a glass of wine?" he goes correctly as far as "you" but has manifestly no idea of meaning.

Writing—His volitional writing is worse than his speaking—but he does write a few words correctly.

Writing to dictation was not tested at the very beginning. Later it was found that he could do it well if each word was given singly; whole sentences are rendered inaccurately, words being missed.

Copying—He copies perfectly, changing German into English characters, but does not understand anything of what he so writes.

In discussing the mechanism of inner-commissural word-deafness, Lichtheim (1885) referred to his own patient JU Schwarz as the only detailed clinical account of this type of aphasia. Since clinicopathological correlations were not possible in this case, Lichtheim cited a case study published by Broadbent in 1872, who had paraphasic speech and word-deafness but could could write to dictation, copy and repeat words, a pattern of language deficits very similar to inner-commissural word-deafness. Neuropathological examination in Broadbent's case revealed a small haemorrhage in the "white matter of the temporal lobe, between the posterior end of the Sylvian fissure and the lateral ventricle near the root of the cornu ammonis" (Lichtheim, 1885, pp. 478–479), thus favouring Lichtheim's viewpoint that the lesion spared major cortical speech centres, but damaged the connections between the centre for auditory images *A* and the more peripheral brain areas where concepts were elaborated (centre *B*).

Coexistence of inner-commissural aphasia and inner-commissural word-deafness

On discussing "total aphasia" (loss of speech with word-deafness), Lichtheim (1885, pp. 464–465), based on his clinicopathological observations, pointed out that the lesions provoked a combined damage to centres M and A and connecting pathways. Following this line of reasoning, he also predicted that the simultaneous damage of commissures $B–M$ and $B–A$ would provoke a combination of inner-commissural aphasia and inner-commissural word-deafness. Although he did not report patients showing this peculiar combination of symptoms (now generally classified under the heading of mixed transcortical aphasia), Lichtheim did discuss the important contribution made in a case report by Lordat describing a patient with reduced spontaneous speech and word-deafness but preserved word repetition. On interpreting this celebrated case, Lichtheim speculated that the causative lesion would provoke a simultaneous interruption of pathways $M–B$ and $B–A$, rendering the patient "speechless" and "word deaf" but able to read aloud, repeat words, and write to dictation because the connecting pathways between M and A centres were intact (pp. 465–466).

RIVAL THEORIES TO THE WERNICKE–LICHTHEIM MODEL

The combination of language deficits that characterised the transcortical aphasias (motor and sensory types) were, with some exceptions, widely accepted. However, several associationist authors (e.g. Bastian, 1887; Niessl von Mayendorf, 1911), although vigorous defenders of the connectionist diagrams, were unwilling to accept the neuroanatomical mechanism proposed by Wernicke and Lichtheim, and offered alternative interpretations to explain preserved repetition in aphasia.

Bastian (1887) was one of the pioneers in the development of the structural concept of aphasia. He conceptualised language disturbances in two main groups, amnesia and aphasia. Patients with amnesia had difficulty recalling words and disturbed thinking due to a lesion in the cortical speech centres, whereas patients with aphasia had normal thinking but difficulties in oral and written expression. Speech and writing deficits were explained as secondary to lesions in either "word centres" or "commissures between word centres" as Kussmaul, Lichtheim, and others had done (Henderson, 1992). But unlike these scholars of aphasia, he questioned the existence of a separate "centre for conceptions or ideas". Therefore, Bastian's rejection of the theory postulating an interruption of commissural fibres between the centre of concepts B and motor (Broca's) region M advanced by Lichtheim (1885) as the likely functional mechanism underlying transcortical motor aphasia is not surprising. He instead contended that in the case of "traumatic aphasia" (as he considered patient CK with transcortical motor aphasia described by Lichtheim), the dissociation between impaired spontaneous speech and preserved repetition and other expressive language functions such as oral reading depended upon different degrees of functional excitability of the speech centres. Bastian believed that transcortical motor aphasia was the result of incomplete damage to the motor speech centre which would produce an increased threshold of voluntary speech, but leave the remaining part of the speech area relatively intact and functional to strong externally generated auditory–verbal stimuli such as repetition (Bastian, 1887). He proposed a similar mechanism to explain the superiority of repetition over spontaneous speech in transcortical sensory aphasia or profound simple amnesia (as he termed this combination of impaired spontaneous and associational speech with normal imitative speech and fluent oral reading) (Bastian, 1887; Goldstein, 1948). Bastian theorised that a functional defect in the auditory speech centre would induce a discrete reduction of activity in speech centres restricted to "volitional" aspects of spontaneous speech, but that this centre might remain responsive to vigorous stimuli and also be capable of activating other anatomically connected centres. Thus, he interpreted language dissociation in transcortical aphasias as resulting from a "low functional state of the auditory speech centre . . . Words cannot be called up in it for spontaneous speech ('volitional'), though the centre responds to stimuli coming to it for imitative speech" (p. 935).

In contrast to these theoretical interpretations, Niessl von Mayendorf (1911) was the most important proponent of the theory that preserved language performances (repetition) in transcortical aphasias were mediated by the other cerebral hemisphere. He believed that if the language areas of the left hemisphere were destroyed, the preservation of repetition was the result of the activity of the homologous areas of the right hemisphere. Moreover, Niessl von Mayendorf and many other authorities, such as Pick and Foerster, rejected the idea of interpreting the transcortical motor aphasia as an independent form of language disturbance, alternatively considering that it merely represented a transitional stage in the recovery process of cortical motor aphasia.

A similar argument was advanced by Stengel (1936, 1947) to account for residual repetition and automatic echolalia in patients with severe reduction of verbal output and understanding. He accepted the clinical syndromes of transcortical aphasias described by Lichtheim (1885) and Goldstein (1917), and also considered echolalia and automatic completion of open-ended questions as integral components of the transcortical syndrome. However, in Stengel's later writings (1947) he claimed the that anatomical and physiological concepts used to create the term "transcortical" were obsolete. He acknowledged having had a few cases of transcortical aphasias, with only one patient who came to neuropathological examination. This case was of a woman with right hemiplegia and mixed transcortical aphasia featuring recurring utterances (te-te), poor understanding of spoken language, marked echolalia, automatic completion of open-ended phrases (e.g. "How did you sleep last . . . ? *night*"), and preserved counting and singing. Autopsy revealed a thrombosis of the left middle cerebral artery which caused a massive destruction of the whole speech area (Stengel, 1936). These clinico-anatomical observations led Stengel to agree with the dynamic concept of linguistic behaviour proposed by Hughlings Jackson (1874/1958), who had suggested that damage to the left hemisphere disrupted highly organised function and released the more emotional or automatic speech responses of the undamaged right hemisphere. Arguments of the same kind were advanced by Byrom Bramwell (1897), who on discussing dissociation between phonological and semantic information (word-meaning deafness) in a patient with transcortical sensory aphasia speculated that the ability to repeat language in the presence of severe word-deafness should depend on the right hemisphere (Bramwell, 1897, cited in Ellis, 1984, pp. 249–250).

> It is very difficult to explain the fact that the ability to repeat spoken speech (heard by the ear) was retained, considering the the word-deafness was so marked. The most likely supposition seems to be that the repeated (mere echo) speech passed through the right auditory speech centre (instead of through the left auditory speech centre, the usual channel) to Broca's centre in the left hemisphere.

Other authors, defenders of the holistic approach, attacked the localisationist conception of the transcortical aphasias. Some of them offered alternative functional interpretations (Freud, 1891/1953), while others minimised the importance of these kinds of aphasia, dedicating only a few lines in major textbooks to this topic (Brain, 1961; Weinsenburg & McBride, 1935). Others did not even include transcortical aphasias in their classification of acquired language disorders (Head, 1920, 1926; Marie, 1906).

One of the most significant studies opposing the classical connectionist approach of cerebral localisation of language function, including the Wernicke–Lichtheim schema, was published by Sigmund Freud (1891/1953). The monograph, entitled *On Aphasia: A critical study*, was first published in German in 1891, and translated to English and prologued by E. Stengel in 1953. Freud's work on aphasia was largely ignored until the structural diagramatic conception of aphasia began to vanish in the second decade of this century, and the ideas put forward by Freud were adopted by other scholars of aphasia (Caplan, 1987; Stengel, in the prologue to Freud, 1891/1953). In his monograph, Freud was the first one in the German-speaking neurological world to make a systematic critical analysis of the theory of brain localisation of the aphasias. Although nearly all of the leading authorities in the study of aphasia were criticised by Freud, he made a trenchant criticism of Wernicke's and Lichtheim's diagrams. Freud anticipated that his monograph would induce "a feeling of dissatisfaction in the reader's mind" because it contained a severe criticism to the currently accepted theory of aphasia. In his writings about aphasias, Freud's thinking was deeply influenced by Hughlings Jackson's teachings, and he also incorporated some of Bastian's conceptions, without accepting his ideas on the "physiological speech centres" (Stengel, in the prologue to Freud, 1891/1953).

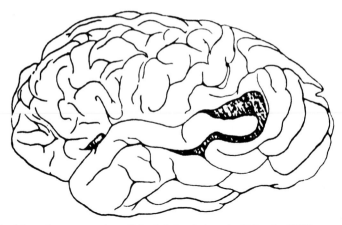

FIG. 1.4 Schematic representation of the left hemisphere in Hübner's (1889) case of mixed transcortical aphasia showing areas of softening involving posterior temporal and anterior frontal cortical regions.

Freud expressed major reservations with Lichtheim's theory of transcortical aphasias, dedicating almost one entire chapter to criticise it. Freud did not accept the utilisation of the anatomical label "transcortical" to refer to a disturbance of verbal behaviour, except in a case of transcortical motor aphasia published by Lordat (see later). He also rejected the existence of a centre of concepts (*Begriffe*), and the role of subcortical lesions in the pathogenesis of transcortical motor and sensory aphasias, proposed by Lichtheim, arguing alternatively that both clinical forms of transcortical aphasias may result from cortical lesions confined to either the motor area or sensory area. Stimulated by Bastian's hypothesis, Freud further argued that transcortical motor aphasia was the result of a "change in the functional state of the speech apparatus rather than a localized interruption of a pathway" (p. 29). The hypothesis put forward by Freud that the tract *B–M* for spontaneous speech did not exist was based on the pathological findings of single patients with transcortical aphasias reported by Hübner (1889), Magnan (1880), and others. For instance, in the case of Hübner (a patient showing a combination of motor and sensory transcortical aphasias after two successive cerebral insults), the neuropathological examination disclosed a yellow softening in the left hemisphere involving the posterior temporal gyrus, the supramarginal gyrus, and the gyrus parietalis inferior. The lesion was mainly cortical and encircled the Wernicke's area. There was a second small softening involving the third frontal convolution, corpus striatum, and claustrum, which in Freud's opinion was "insignificant" to account for the "enormous and profound disturbance of speech" documented in this case (Fig. 1.4).

Freud believed that the damage to the cortex of the sensory area was sufficient to impair understanding, and also to cause loss of spontaneous speech, because the pathways *B–M* and *B–A* were identical and because speech was generated only via the sound images. He took this finding as evidence against the existence of Lichtheim's *B–M* commissure. However, after a more careful review of other cases of transcortical aphasias with pathological verification, Freud was unexpectedly confronted with the fact that the lesion responsible for transcortical motor aphasia would also lie restricted to the motor speech area (Hammond, 1882; Magnan, 1880). The case described by Magnan (1880, pp. 120–122) was taken by Freud to illustrate this clinicopathological correlation:

> CATHERINE—, aged 61 years, was admitted on 18th of October, 1878, accompanied with a certificate from M. Lasègue, as follows: "Dementia, right hemiplegia, aphasia. Absolute inability to attend her needs.". She pronounced words or monosyllables without connection and could not name objects . . . She repeated words pronounced in her hearing, and even occasionally pointed to the object when the name was pronounced in the midst of others . . . She did not seem able to read . . . On postmortem examination . . . the tumour penetrating the left hemisphere like a wedge, separated and displaced the neighbouring parts, and its apex penetrated as low as the third frontal, and the anterior third of the upper border of the insula. The cortex of the posterior extremity of the third frontal, and upper margin of the first two *digitations* of the insula, had been, as it were, dissected and isolated by the tumour.

Freud used these cases of transcortical aphasias to refute the existence of some of the commissures hypothesised by Lichtheim, in particular the pathway *B–M*, stating: "it can be regarded as established that the occurrence of the so-called transcortical motor aphasia at any rate, does not prove the existence of a special pathway *B–M* for spontaneous speech" (p. 28).

Finally, Freud preferred the term *asymbolia* to transcortical sensory aphasia and, based on the famous case of Hübner (1889), he pointed out that asymbolia was the only form of transcortical aphasia that had a specific localisation, namely a pathological separation of the auditory area from its associations after posterior cortical damage. Alternatively he suggested that asymbolia could result from a transient functional impairment (e.g. epileptic) between the word associations and the object associations (p. 83).

Another antilocalisationist was Kurt Goldstein (1878–1965). He initially followed the ideas of his teacher Carl Wernicke (Henderson, 1992). Later, Goldstein separated himself from the diagram markers and was profoundly influenced by the ideas of Hughlings Jackson and Freud, to the point that the distinction made by Goldstein between central aphasias (conduction aphasia) and speech disturbances due to defects of the instrumentalities of language (transcortical aphasias) was derived directly from Freud's speculations on aphasia (Stengel, in Freud, 1891/1953). Although at first glance it seems that Goldstein rejected the diagramatic conception of aphasic disorders proposed by Wernicke and Lichtheim, careful analysis of his work on aphasia denotes that he had a paradoxical position in the history of aphasia. Since Goldstein adopted the more general principles of *Gestalt* psychology to explain the nature of aphasic disorders (Weisenburg & McBride, 1935, p. 39), he is often recognised as one of the most fervent opponents to the classical connectionist models (Geschwind, 1964b). At the same time it is evident that Goldstein was also interested in the anatomic localisation of aphasic disorders, accepting the classical tenets of connectionist classification, including certain aspects related to the transcortical aphasias (Geschwind, 1963, 1964b). Indeed, some of Goldstein's writings, for example on transcortical aphasias explicitly supported the connectionist view of aphasia, and on explaining their functional mechanism he incorporated the idea of "concept field" (*Begriffsfeld*) in his writings. He also concurred with Lichtheim in the representation of concept centre *B* as an extensive area of the brain located outside the central speech region. He went further by dividing the "concept field" into two functionally distinct zones; one anterior related to motor functions and another posterior related to sensory processes (Geschwind, 1964b; Goldstein, 1948). He was, however, more conservative than Lichtheim in some respects, denying the existence of "isolated connections of the motor and sensory speech area with the rest of the brain", and viewed the "instrumentalis and non-language mental performances—both motor and sensory—equally related with each other by a unitary performance which we call the concepts of words" (p. 299). Two forms of transcortical motor aphasia were outlined by Goldstein.

On interpreting transcortical motor aphasia, he was sympathetic to Bastian's theory of partial damage to the motor speech area as one of the pathophysiological mechanisms of the motor variant of transcortical aphasia (Goldstein, 1948, pp. 293–294). Notwithstanding, he also proposed other possible mechanisms to account for the symptom complex of reduced spontaneous speech with preserved repetition and auditory comprehension characteristic of transcortical motor aphasia. In fact, he tentatively described a second type of transcortical motor aphasia, which he believed resulted from a decreased impulse to speak (lack of intention, akinesis) due to a lesion in the frontal lobe. But after reviewing some previous cases, he was convinced that the most plausible mechanism underlying transcortical motor aphasia resulted from a "combination between a slight damage of intention (anatomically designated as a lack of the influence of the frontal lobe) and a slight defect of motor activities" (p. 295). Goldstein rejected the theory suggesting that preserved repetition in transcortical motor aphasia could result from the normal activity of the right hemisphere proposed by Niessl von Mayendorf, Bonhoeffer, and others. Instead, he argued that in most cases the left speech area was not so damaged as to assume that the contralateral cerebral hemisphere takes over the function of repetition. He also reasoned that if the right speech hemisphere can subserve repetition, why then, is it not also used for spontaneous speech.

Goldstein (1948) again used the connectionist model to explain the transcortical sensory symptom complexes. He had major reservations accepting that transcortical sensory aphasia was merely a subordinate form of Wernicke's aphasia.

He agreed that Wernicke's aphasia and transcortical sensory aphasia shared deficits in speech perception and in the instrumentalities of language, but he speculated that both functions were differently affected in these two syndromes. He argued that a lesion involving the left sensory speech area and the adjacent Insula Reili would provoke a sensory aphasia because the lesion induced a profound defect in perceptive function precluding both the understanding of spoken language and repetition, but not a transcortical sensory aphasia. Goldstein (1948) concluded that transcortical sensory aphasia was probably the result of a "combination of a slight damage of acoustic speech perceptions and a slight damage of the relation between the instrumentalis and the non-language mental performances" (p. 299).

Although the coexistence of simultaneous motor and sensory speech defects in the presence of preserved repetition had initially been predicted by Lichtheim (1885) and isolated cases were later reported by Hübner (1889), Stransky (1903) [cited in Goldstein, 1948, p. 304] and others, Goldstein was the first author to clearly define this new form of aphasia, which he termed "mixed transcortical aphasia" or "isolation of the speech area" (Geschwind et al., 1968; Goldstein, 1948). One of the first cases of "isolation" aphasia, published by Goldstein (1915/1948), had the following clinical characteristics:

The patient either *did not answer in an adequate way, . . .* or *repeated the questions echolalically, apparently mostly without understanding of the words. . . . He almost never speaks spontaneously.* If he is *addressed, he may speak a good deal . . . Very rarely were paraphasic distortions* of words observed. On simple demand, he never utters any of the *speech series*, but if one presents the first member of the days of the weeks . . . *he does so quite correctly*, but apparently *without any understanding* of the words.

He does not name any object, . . . On the other hand, he *selects* a number of everyday objects *correctly on presentation of the word.* But failures occur in this test, too, apparently because the patient did not understand the word he repeated correctly.

Repetition: patient repeats correctly letters, sound, nouns, words, also absolutely unknown and difficults words as "Bakairi," "Artilleriebrigade,"sentences like "Die Wiese ist gruen" (The meadow is green) . . . *He repeats without articulatory failures, without paraphasias, mostly in a typical echolalic way.*

Understanding: . . . *he does not understand a great number of words.*

The *autopsy* showed the following . . . *The left hemisphere appeared to be much larger than the particularly the region of the central convolutions, the part of the frontal lobes located before them, the gyri supermarginalis and angularis were elevated above the level of the rest of the brain . . .* There was *no localized* lesion to be seen . . . The enlargements of the hemisphere are due essentially to an *enlargement of the white matter . . .* there were small hemorrhages, but not in the region of Broca, in the temporal lobe and in the insula. The microscopic investigation showed a great number of encephalitic foci.

To explain this type of transcortical aphasias, Goldstein (1948) advanced a mechanism similar to the one already proposed in a less elaborate form by Lichtheim (Geschwind et al., 1968). He proposed that this type of aphasia was caused by extensive left hemisphere lesions strategically placed to spare the major speech centres responsible of motor and sensory aspects of speech. In addition, these lesions were ideally placed to isolate the classical speech area from peripheral parts of the brain important for non-language mental functions. This mechanism was called "isolation of the speech area" by Goldstein (1948).

CONCLUSIONS

Although many authors contributed to the consolidation of transcortical aphasias as new forms of acquired language disturbances, Lichtheim (1885) was the first writer to emphasise the clinical and theoretical significance of the transcortical syndromes. Lichtheim's work on transcortical aphasias was successful in at least three respects. The first merit of Lichtheim's work concerns his modification and expansion of Wernicke's original schema. Lichtheim's modification was, in great measure, introduced to explain the functional mechanisms underlying a new type of aphasias, the *inner-commissural aphasias*. His complex diagram contained different functional speech centres which were connected with each other through sets of fibre pathways. This diagram, which is now known as the Wernicke–Lichtheim model of representation of the language in the brain (Code, 1989, p. 5), is remarkably similar to information-processing diagrams recently proposed by cognitive neuropsychologists (Cipolotti & Warrington, 1995; Ellis & Young, 1988; McCarthy & Warrington, 1984). Second, Lichtheim's work had the merit of describing a new major type of aphasia, characterised by the preservation of some aspects of verbal production, most notably repetition. This pattern of language deficits combining impaired language abilities (spontaneous speech, auditory comprehension, or both) with the preservation of repetition and oral reading contrasted sharply with the well-known aphasias with repetition disturbance (motor, sensory, and conduction). Lichtheim's work on transcortical aphasias is also important because he predicted that his inner-commissural aphasias and inner-commissural word-deafness would have a different brain localisation than the traditional motor and sensory aphasias, with left hemisphere damage sparing the major speech centres but disrupting their connections with the rest of the brain.

After Lichtheim, the clinical profile of transcortical aphasias was widely accepted. The early pathoanatomical mechanism of a selective impairment of subcortical pathways linking the motor and sensory speech centres with the more peripheral parts of the brain, important for non-language mental functions, remains the most accepted account (Albert, Goodglass, Helm, Rubens, & Alexander, 1981; Benson, 1985, 1993; Geschwind et al., 1968; Goldstein, 1917, 1948; Rubens & Kertesz, 1983). However, the evidence also indicates that there must be at least two other mechanisms underlying preserved repetition in transcortical aphasias. One of them, which had already been discussed, though with less acceptance than Lichtheim's proposal, entailed transcortical aphasias with massive damage to the central language zone (Niessl von Mayendorf, 1911; Stengel, 1947) and residual repetition subserved by the undamaged right hemisphere. The other postulated hypothesis, superfically mentioned by Bramwell (1897) and more recently refined by Brown (1975), suggested that, after partial or total damage to the perisylvian language zone, residual repetition may be mediated by a cojoint activity of the remnant of undamaged left hemisphere structures and the right hemisphere. The more contemporary history of transcortical aphasias will be described in the following chapters.

CHAPTER TWO

Language testing

INTRODUCTION

The assessment of language in the transcortical aphasias (TA) can be done in a manner similar to other aphasias. Basically, there are three different levels to test language impairments in TA. First, the bedside method, which is routinely used in clinical settings. Second, TA can be assessed by using different standardised test batteries. Third, hypothesis testing tests (target-specific tests) which are currently used to assess theoretically relevant issues, for research purposes, and to organise language therapy programmes. In this chapter I will discuss these three methodologies.

BEDSIDE METHOD

The clinical testing of TA is in general similar to that reported for other types of major aphasic syndromes and it is generally used to briefly examine aphasia during the acute stage of illness. From a phenomenological perspective, the pattern of language deficits in TA is relatively similar to that observed in other aphasias, except that with TA the ability to repeat language is typically preserved. In the nonfluent types (transcortical motor and mixed transcortical aphasias) the profile of verbal expression is similar to that of Broca's and global aphasia, although patients with these two clinical types tend to show a decreased drive to speak (akinesia) and perseverations with no prominent phonemic and global paraphasias; they tend to have less articulatory and grammatical deficits than those observed in Broca's and global aphasia. It is evident that, although the nonfluent TA have poor drive to generate speech and may sometimes be mute at onset, oral expression in both types is clearly aphasic, except in dynamic aphasia (a subtype of transcortical motor aphasia) where overt signs of language disturbances such as paraphasias, word-finding difficulties, and object naming are conspicuously absent (but see further details in Chapter 3). In cases of nonaphasic mutism when the patient recover the ability to communicate orally the generated utterances, though short, contain linguistically and grammatically correct information (A.R. Damasio, 1991). In transcortical motor aphasia (TCMA), auditory comprehension ranges from normal at bedside testing (Freedman, Alexander, & Naeser, 1984) to discrete or moderate deficits when formal tests of comprehension are used (A.R. Damasio, 1991), whereas in mixed transcortical aphasia (MTCA) auditory comprehension is always severely impaired (Albert et al., 1981; Geschwind, et al., 1968; Whitaker, 1976).

The profile of spontaneous speech in transcortical sensory aphasia (TCSA) is usually described as fluent, copious, and marred by semantic and, less frequently, phonological paraphasias (Albert et al., 1981; Coslett, Roeltgen, Gonzalez Rothi, & Heilman, 1987). In cases of extreme severity, verbal paraphasias may be so prominent that although the flow of verbal information is abundant, the content of the message is irrelevant, giving rise to a semantic jargon (Kertesz, Sheppard, & MacKenzie, 1982). Cases with fluent, logorrheic spontaneous speech containing a mixture of semantic and phonological paraphasias may be seen in TCSA (Lesser, 1989). Unlike many patients with Wernicke's aphasia who show neologistic jargon, neologistic substitutions are not prominent in transcortical sensory aphasic patients (Buckingham & Kertesz, 1974; Lecours & Rouillon, 1976). In other cases of TCSA, little or no paraphasia is heard during spontaneous speech, utterances are mainly punctuated by difficulty finding words, and anomia has also been documented (Kertesz et al., 1982; Kremin, 1986). When the anomic pattern of spontaneous speech in TCSA is associated with mild deficits in the lexical–semantic comprehension of single words, the bedside procedure is not helpful in establishing a differential diagnosis with anomic aphasia (e.g. Albert et al., 1981; Sevush & Heilman, 1984). Spontaneous speech, in rare instances, is devoid of either phonological, semantic, or neologistic paraphasias, and, unlike patients with typical TCSA, utterances convey meaningful and coherent information (see Chapter 4). Regularly, there are little or no word-finding difficulties during spontaneous speech, and visual confrontation naming is also relatively preserved (Berthier, 1995; Heilman, Rothi, McFarling, & Rottmann, 1981). Thus, the pattern of oral expression in TCSA contrasts sharply with the neologistic jargon of Wernicke's aphasia, or the less abundant verbal expression of conduction aphasia which is primarily composed of phonological paraphasias and attempts at self-correction (*conduite d'approche*) (Goodglass, 1992).

Auditory comprehension in TCSA is impaired, but is not so marked as in Wernicke's aphasia. This results because the phonemic level of auditory processing, which is abnormal in Wernicke's aphasic patients, is usually spared in TCSA (Albert et al., 1981). In general, transcortical sensory aphasic patients retain their ability to understand conversational speech, yes/no questions, and simple one-step or two-step commands, but fail to understand syntactically complex material and the meaning of single words. Dissociated deficits in comprehension are not exceptional, with some patients showing isolated deficits in single-word comprehension (McCarthy & Warrington, 1987; Warrington, 1975), whereas others show the reverse pattern of performance (preserved single-word comprehension with impaired understanding of grammatically complex constructions) (Hier, Mogil, Rubin, & Komros, 1980).

The most distinctive linguistic feature of TA is the sparing of repetition for digits, words, nonwords, and sentences and the occurrence of echophenomena (Ford, 1989; Stengel, 1947). On standard examination of language functions, the examiner may note that the verbal expression of a given patient with TA, whether fluent or nonfluent, may be punctuated by the occurrence of echolalia, echo-answer, and completion phenomenon (for further details see Chapter 6). Among these, echolalia (automatic repetition by the patient of part or all of what is said by the examiner) is the most common and well-known phenomenon. The presence of echophenomena in an aphasic patient should immediately alert the clinician to the presence of a TA, since these abnormal automatic behaviours have been only rarely reported in aphasias with repetition disturbance (Broca's, conduction, Wernicke's). Nevertheless, echolalia may be observed in certain patients with aphasic profiles bordering between Wernicke's aphasia and TCSA, or between anomia and TCSA. The preservation of automatic speech (e.g. recitation of days of the week, alphabet) is more commonly observed in TA than in aphasias with repetition disturbance. Singing may be preserved in TA (Jacome, 1984), but also in aphasias with poor repetition such as Broca's aphasia (Yamadori, Osumi, Masuhara, & Okubo, 1977). Palilalia (repetition of the same word several times) accompanies the spontaneous utterances of nonfluent TA (Pick, cited in Goldstein, 1948; Wallesch, 1990). Other reiterative phenomena (e.g. contamination, recurring utterances) may be associated with TA (Code, 1989; Wallesch, 1990).

FORMAL TESTING WITH MULTIDIMENSIONAL BATTERIES

Although there are a good number of aphasia batteries, only a few of them have obtained a high rating of popularity by their clinical utility (see Beele, Davies, & Muller, 1984). Specifically regarding TA, only a few batteries explicitly test word and sentence repetition and give appropriate cut-off scores. These batteries are the Neurosensory Center Comprehensive Examination for Aphasia (NCCEA) (Spreen & Benton, 1977; Spreen & Strauss, 1991), the Western Aphasia Battery (WAB) (Kertesz, 1979), the Boston Diagnostic Aphasia Examination (BDAE) (Goodglass & Kaplan, 1983), and the Aachen Aphasia Test (AAT) (Huber, Poeck, Weniger, & Willmes, 1983; Huber, Poeck, & Willmes, 1984).

The NCCEA is a comprehensive battery designed to assess language abilities such as reading, writing and speech articulation, as well as basic visual and tactile functions. The NCCEA has not been specifically designed to obtain a taxonomic diagnosis of the aphasia typology, but is useful for investigating in some detail the pattern of language abilities and disabilities. Moreover, although the NCCEA is a battery specially designed to test language deficits in aphasic or in other related linguistic problems, it is not a useful test instrument to assess language function in normal individuals or well-educated neurological patients with mild language problems because these latter populations tend to obtain ceiling scores (Spreen & Risser, 1991). A shortened and modified battery related to the NCCEA is the Multilingual Aphasia Examination (MAE) (Benton & Hamsher, 1989). The MAE is composed of the following seven subtests: visual naming, sentence repetition, controlled oral word association (a measure of letter fluency), spelling, a short version of the Token Test, auditory comprehension of words and phrases, and reading comprehension of words and phrases. Interest-ingly, most of these tests (sentence repetition, controlled oral word association, spelling, and token test) have two or three alternate forms, thus reducing practice effects when reassessment is required.

The sentence repetition subtest of the MAE assesses the immediate oral repe-tition of sentences of increasing length. It contains 14 sentences that are gradu-ated in length from 3 to 24 syllables, thus enabling the assessment of meaningful verbal material from the extremely short (e.g. "Take this home") to the normal adult length (e.g. "The members of the committee have agreed to hold their meeting on the first Tuesday of each month"). In the sentence repetition subtest, there are two equivalent sets of sentences (Form I and II) composed of seven different linguistic constructions (e.g. positive declaration, negative interroga-tion), that allow testing of repetition not only under different syntactical vari-ations, but also favour the detection of subtle repetition deficits in patients without apparent impairments in communication abilities (Lezak, 1995).

The sentence repetition subtest of the MAE is highly correlated (0.88) with the repetition subtest of the WAB (Shewan & Kertesz, 1980). It seems to be especially useful for patients with TA (Davis, Foldi, Gardner, & Zurif, 1978) as well as for discriminating these aphasic patients from others who have impaired sentence repetition in the presence of good comprehension, and impaired atten-tion, memory, and reproductive speech (Crockett, 1977). Thus, this subtest can be used apart from the MAE battery when a more comprehensive assessment of repetition performance is desired, particularly among patients with aphasic disturbances. Normative data is available for children, adults, and older people (Spreen & Strauss, 1991).

Another subtest of the MAE that may be useful for administering to patients with TA is the Controlled Oral Word Association (COWA) (also known as "Word Fluency" and "FAS-test"). This subtest explores the subject's ability to produce words under restricted lexical search conditions and consists of the spontaneous generation of word lists beginning with a given letter (usually the *F*, *A*, and *S*) during a limited amount of time (one minute for each letter). In TA, the utilisation of COWA is particularly useful to assess the intrinsic genera- tion of lexical strategies in patients with nonfluent TA including the so called dynamic (or "adynamic") aphasia (Gold, Nadeau, Jacobs, Adair, Gonzalez Rothi, & Heilman, 1997; Robinson, Blair, & Cipolotti, 1998). Although frontal or frontal-subcortical lesions, regardless of side, tend to affect COWA perform- ance, lower word production is seen associated with left-sided and bilateral lesions (see Lezak, 1995; Stuss et al., 1998). Some researchers even suggest that effortful productions may reflect involvement of the left dorsolateral frontal convexity, whereas aspontaneity and reduced initiative to generate words most likely indicate involvement of the mesial frontal region of the left hemisphere (Perret, 1974; Walsh, 1985) (see Chapter 3).

The WAB was designed for clinical use and research purposes. It assesses repetition more comprehensively than other batteries. The WAB's repetition subtest starts with the repetition of single high-frequency words (A or AA Thorndike-Lorge frequency, 1968), followed by compound words, then goes on to numbers, word-number combinations, high-probability sentences (e.g. "The telephone is ringing"), low-probability sentences (e.g. "The pastry cook was elated"), and finally to sentences that increase in length with grammatical and phonemic complexity. Moreover, the naming section the WAB contains a subtest (sentence completion) that briefly assesses the completion phenomenon (e.g. "Roses are red, violets are . . . *blue*") usually documented among transcortical aphasic patients.

In order to avoid the confounding variable of verbal short-term memory, this section only includes a single long sentence. The classification criteria of the WAB for TA is based on a numerical range of scores on clinical subtests that are applied to classify the aphasic profile within the three clinically established varieties. Three oral language subtests are used to identify the type of TA, including fluency during spontaneous speech, comprehension, and repetition. According to the WAB rationale, patients with TCMA have a Fluency score of 0 to 4; a Comprehension score of 4 to 10; and a Repetition score of 8 to 10. Patients classified as having a TCSA have a Fluency score of 5 to 10; a Compre- hension score of 0 to 6.9; and a Repetition score of 8 to 10. Finally, patients with MTCA have a Fluency score of 0 to 4; a Comprehension score of 0 to 3.9; and a repetition score of 5 to 10.

The oral expression section of the BDAE has a variety of subtests aimed at assessing automatised sequences such as days of the week, months of the year, numbers, and the alphabet, as well as recitation of rhymes and singing. Testing of language repetition includes repetition of letters, words, numbers, and tongue twisters. At sentence level, the BDAE was the first battery that included repe- tition of high-probability and low-probability sentences. These sentences were carefully designed controlling the quantity of lexical information, variations in syntactic structure and grammatical words. The length of the sentences was graded using the subject–verb–object construction, and the amount of information was gradually increased by adding adjectives or adverbs. Short sentences contain five words (e.g. "The boy threw the ball"), while the long ones are composed of ten words (e.g. "The crowded liner steamed into port under a blue sky").

The task of sentence repetition of the BDAE is also to control the sequential probability and vocabulary of the sentence. It contains sentences in which the next word can be predicted from the preceding one (e.g. "The telephone is *ringing*"). The rationale is that the inclusion of a high-frequency word pertaining to the same semantic field as the preceding one may increase the probability of an accurate repetition. The BDAE also incorporates low-probability sentences, in which the successive word can not be predicted on the basis of the previous one (e.g. "The spy fled to Greece"). Some patients with conduction aphasia are unable to repeat low-probability sentences (Palumbo, Alexander, & Naeser, 1992), and these sentences are sometimes highly demanding for patients with TA (Berthier, Starkstein et al., 1991; Coslett, Gonzalez Rothi, & Heilman, 1985; Coslett et al., 1987; Kertesz, 1982) and even for normal subjects (Ardila & Roselli, 1992). For instance, among patients with TCMA errors during the repetition of low-probability sentences consist of omissions and changes in word order, thus suggesting that these are the result of mnemonic or attentional problems, rather linguistic ones (Ardila & Roselli, 1992).

The Aachen Aphasia Test (AAT) has been created for the clinical diagnosis of aphasias in the German-speaking population. It is composed of six subtests, namely spontaneous speech, token test, repetition, written language, naming on confrontation, and comprehension. The linguistic parameters used to assess repetition include single phonemes, monosyllabic nouns, loan and foreign words, compound nouns, and sentences. Patients' performance on repetition subtests as well as in the other linguistic parameters are scored on a four-point scale (from 0 = no similarity to the target, to 3 = correct response). The scoring criteria for the repetition subtest is based on the production of phonemic, morphological, and syntactic errors. To be classified as having a TA on the AAT, scores on the repetition task should be at least 60% correct (raw score = 90) and at least 20% higher than the score of the other subtests (e.g. token test, naming, written language, and comprehension) (Huber et al., 1983).

PSYCHOLINGUISTIC ASSESSMENT

The abovementioned multidimensional batteries, though useful for diagnostic purposes and clinical taxonomic classification of acquired aphasias, provide little or no information about the nature of abnormal language functioning in terms of information-processing models, necessary to guide therapy planning and to advance our understanding of language disorders (Byng, Kay, Edmunson, & Scott, 1990; Caplan, 1992; Cipolotti & Warrington, 1995; Ellis & Young, 1988;

Kay, Lesser, & Coltheart, 1992; McCarthy & Warrington, 1990; Shallice, 1988).
In the 1980s and 1990s, great effort has been made by cognitive neuropsychologists to create adequate testing tools for assessing the psycholinguistic aspects
of language impairments. Several authors created their own tests, as for example
the Psycholinguistic Assessment of Language (PAL) a 27-subtest battery outlined
by Caplan and Bub (1990, unpublished) [cited in Caplan, 1992, pp. 407–425].
Kay et al. (1992) also designed a battery of tests to examine language impairments within the cognitive neuropsychological framework. This is a useful research tool known as the Psycholinguistic Assessment of Language Processing
in Aphasia (PALPA), which is based on the logogen model and is available in
English, Dutch, and Spanish. While early versions of this model were developed
to explain experimental findings on word-reading experiments by normal individuals and aphasic patients (Morton, 1970, 1979), the models have been
expanded to include word processing during repetition, writing to dictation,
and oral and written picture naming (see Kay et al., 1992). A full explanation of
this model and of other cognitive models of language processing is beyond the
scope of this chapter, so I will examine the psycholinguistic testing of language
functions that are pertinent to TA.

Spontaneous speech is usually elicited by standard picture-based narratives
(Albert et al., 1981). The cookie theft scene from the BDAE, the picnic scene
from the WAB, and other complex scenes (Ellis & Young, 1988, p. 114) are
commonly used for this purpose, whereas fluency and lexical composition during discourse generation may be assessed by open-ended conversations and narrative story production (e.g. the Cinderella story) (Hadar, Jones, & Mate-Kole,
1987; Hadar, Ticehurst, & Wade, 1991). Naming is assessed with line drawn
objects (e.g. Boston Naming Test; Kaplan, Goodglass, & Weintraub, 1983) and
naming from verbal definitions (Coughlan & Warrington, 1978). Dissociated
patterns of performance between name retrieval and name recognition have been
reported in patients with TCMA and TCSA (Goodglass, Wingfield, Hyde, &
Theurkauf, 1986). Therefore, comparison of object and picture naming with
auditory single-word comprehension of these same targets may be useful to
detect possible dissociations in naming performance (Berthier, 1995; Heilman
et al., 1981; Kremin, 1986). Phonological discrimination is almost always preserved in TA, but syntactic and semantic comprehension is usually impaired
among patients with TCSA and MTCA (see Chapters 4 and 5). Syntactic comprehension may be assessed with the Token Test (parts IV and V; De Renzi &
Vignolo, 1962) or with tests specifically designed to assess grammatical comprehension (e.g. Bishop, 1989).

The assessment of semantic memory is of special interest, since its impairments can be readily observed in patients with TCSA due to acute lesions (Hart
& Gordon, 1990) or in the declining course of cortical degenerative conditions
(Hodges, Patterson, Oxbury, & Funnell, 1992; Snowden, Goulding, & Neary,
1989; Warrington, 1975). In broad terms, disorders of semantic memory are

characterised by a general dissolution of meaning for words and objects. From an aetiological point of view, these deficits have been increasingly recognised in the context of anomic aphasias, category-specific aphasias, and TCSA accompanying Alzheimer's disease, Pick's disease, and herpes simplex encephalitis (see Garrard, Perry, & Hodges, 1997 for review). Although there are as yet no standardised batteries to assess semantic memory (Cipolotti & Warrington, 1995), the general principle for assessment is to evaluate knowledge by means of tasks taping productive and receptive functions in both verbal and nonverbal domains. Neuropsychological tests currently used to evaluate semantic memory are those devised for other domains, including category (semantic) fluency (number of words generated in a particular category: animals, vegetables, clothes, body-parts, etc., in one minute), confrontation naming, naming from definitions, word definitions (e.g. vocabulary subtest of the WAIS); sorting pictures according to their category (e.g. living things *vs.* man-made things), word–picture matching tests (e.g. pyramids and palm tree test), and verification of semantic attribute questions (e.g. "does an elephant lay eggs?") (Garrard et al., 1997).

Repetition is not a unitary function. Rather, it must be conceptualised as a complex process that can be variously compromised by deficits of incoming auditory information, abnormal speech production, abnormalities in the central store of phonological information, or deficits in auditory–verbal short-term memory. Although the superiority of repetition performance relative to other linguistic functions (spontaneous speech, auditory comprehension, or both) is the hallmark of TA, some transcortical aphasic patients experience, for instance, difficulties with the repetition of word-lists of increased length or in repeating nonsense words. From this perspective, the precise characterisation of these abilities and disabilities in repetition tasks is crucially relevant for a better understanding of the stage of processing that is impaired or preserved among patients with TA (Gardner & Winner, 1978). Before advancing further in the discussion of the psycholinguistic assessment of repetition, it is important to establish how words and nonwords are repeated. As initially suggested by the Wernicke–Lichtheim model, current models of language processing also consider that repetition performance may be accomplished by different routines: lexical–semantic, lexical–nonsemantic, and nonlexical (Caplan, 1992; Katz & Goodglass, 1990; but see Glosser, Kohn, Friedman, Sands, & Grugan, 1997 for different arguments). The lexical–semantic process of repetition involves first the acoustic analysis of the speech signal and the activation of an entry in the phonological input lexicon, a module necessary for the recognition of familiar spoken words. Once the word is recognised as such, it accesses its meaning represented in the semantic system, which, in turn, activates an entry in the phonological output lexicon with the subsequent production of correct phonological responses. Lexical repetition can also be accomplished without semantic mediation, that is auditory information mapped on the phonological input lexicon is directly transmitted to the phonological output lexicon. This route becomes operative in pathological

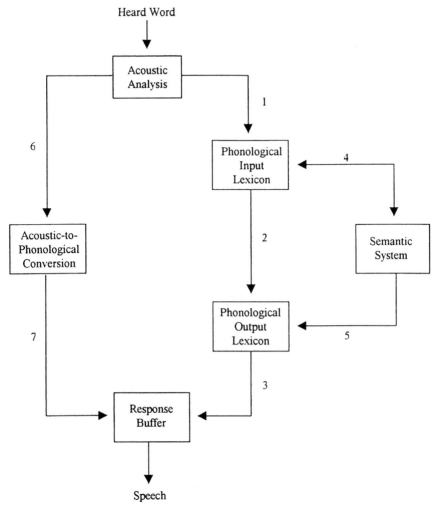

FIG. 2.1   Psycholinguistic model of repetition based on various sources (e.g. Caplan, 1992; Patterson & Shewell, 1987) showing the functional architecture of the three different processing routes. The lexical–semantic route is represented by arrows 1, 4, 5, 3. The lexical–nonsemantic route is represented by arrows 1, 2, 3. Repetition by the nonlexical route is indicated by arrows 6, 7.

cases where the access to the semantic system is disrupted by some kinds of lesion or when the semantic system is lesioned itself. Finally, the nonlexical route directly links the auditory input to the phonological output form without access to phonological lexical representations. This route is the only one that allows normal subjects and some aphasic patients to repeat nonwords. The functional architecture of the three different processing routes underlying repetition is shown in Fig. 2.1.

The assessment of repetition

Span performance

In general, the assessment of repetition begins with the testing of span performance, that is defined as the ability to reproduce a sequence of digits, letters, and words. These tests have been considered measures of attention capacity and/ or verbal short-term memory (Cipolotti & Warrington, 1995; Lezak, 1995), and span performance is thought to depend on a phonological store (Baddeley, 1986, 1996). The assessment of span performance requires the repetition of a progressively lengthening random sequence of numbers, letters, and words that the examiner reads at a stable rate. Immediate repetition of digits, letters, and words is useful because it allows for the differentiation between the repetition performance of patients with conduction aphasia as opposed to those patients with TA. Patients with conduction aphasia regularly have a very short span for immediate repetition of digits, letters, word lists, and sentences, generally producing phonological paraphasias on double digits, multisyllabic words and short phrases (Benson, Sheremata, Bouchard, Segarra, Price, & Geschwind, 1973; Kohn, 1992). In contrast, patients with TA have a normal immediate span for digits, single-word lists, and sentences (Berthier, 1995; Coslett et al., 1987; McCarthy & Warrington, 1987; Schwartz, Marin, & Saffran, 1979). Span performance may vary among transcortical aphasic patients, however. Some patients with TCSA were reported to have either a reduced digit span ($\leq$ five digits) or accurate number reproduction ($\geq$ five digits) but not in the correct serial order as well as impaired performance on repetition of four-word lists (Berndt, Basili, & Caramazza, 1987; Martin & Saffran, 1990). Moreover, Reis, Guerreiro, and Castro-Caldas (1996) reported that illiterate patients with TCSA did worse on digit span testing than literate patients with either motor or sensory variants. These authors suggested that illiterate individuals have inefficient phonological segmentation in the acoustic analysis of speech and that they rely on semantic processing to repeat digit strings.

Digit span and letter span.   Immediate digit repetition is regularly assessed with the Digit Span subtest of the intelligence and memory scales of the Wechsler batteries (Wechsler, 1945, 1955). Digit span subtests contain two parts: digit-forward and digit-backward. Since the latter test is more demanding than the forward condition and it may be impaired due to a range of variables (e.g. vigilance, mental control) other than memory and language (Weinberg, Diller, Gerstman, & Schulman, 1972), only the forward presentation in used to assess digit span performance (Bauer, Tobias, & Valenstein, 1993). The rate of presentation for digits is one per second, and the normal range of digits repeated by normal subjects is five to nine (Cipolotti & Warrington, 1995; Miller, 1956). As already stated, the assessment of digit span is usually a first step to differentiate the repetition performance between conduction and transcortical aphasic patients. In general, transcortical aphasic patients show normal digit span ($\geq$ five items), whereas conduction aphasic patients have extremely limited spans (Martin & Saffran, 1990; McCarthy & Warrington, 1984, 1987). Immediate letter repetition, also termed letter span, is almost identical to digit span (6.7 in the twenties age group and 6.5 in the fifties age group), experiencing a mild decline after age 60. Some authors suggest that letter span may be somewhat smaller than digit span (McCarthy & Warrington, 1990).

Word span and supraspan lists.   According to the classic article of Miller (1956), the immediate memory span is generally "seven, plus or minus two" irrespective if the repeated items are numbers, letters, or words. In adults the ability to repeat words remains relatively stable from age 20 to 60, except when the word list exceeds seven words (supraspan lists). There is a mild decline in word-list repetition after age 50 relative to younger people when lists containing between 9 and 11 words are used (Talland, 1965). Word span consists of the serial recall of auditorily presented words and is generally tested in a manner analogous to digit span. Thus, high-frequency words beginning a two-word list are initially presented, adding a word with each verbatim repetition. The test is discontinued after two successive failures. Low-frequency words, words of increasing length, or phonologically similar words can also be used (Waters, Caplan, & Hildebrandt, 1991). The assessment of supraspan lists consists of the repetition of word strings exceeding the individual word span. It is generally tested using word-list learning tests. According to Lezak (1995), most researchers use unrelated word lists such as those included in the Auditory Verbal Learning Test (Rey, 1964) or in the Selective Reminding procedure (Buschke & Fuld, 1974).

The testing of word span and supraspan word lists provide information on the functional structure of the auditory verbal short-term memory (AVSTM) in aphasia. Psycholinguistic investigations of aphasia have suggested that deficits in the AVSTM system are more related to language disturbances than memory problems (see Caplan & Waters, 1992; Martin & Saffran, 1990; Martin, Saffran, & Dell, 1996; Shallice & Vallar, 1990). Warrington and her colleagues (Shallice & Warrington, 1970; Warrington, Logue, & Pratt, 1971; Warrington & Shallice, 1969) first used specific testing procedures to detect impairments in AVSTM in three patients with conduction aphasia. These three patients had a marked reduction of auditory digit and word spans being unable to recall more than two items and also showed a reduced recency effect (poor recall of words at the end of the list) on auditorily presented tests of supraspan word-list learning. Although similar deficits in word span and supraspan lists have also been observed in other conduction patients (Caramazza, Basili, Koller, & Berndt, 1981; Martin & Saffran, 1990) as well as in some patients with TCSA (Berndt et al., 1987), the deficit in repetition of supraspan lists in the latter condition may be qualitatively different. Martin and Saffran (1990) described the case of a transcortical sensory aphasic patient (ST) who showed reduced word span (two items) and primacy effect (more difficult word-list retention for the initial than the final items) on a supraspan word list.

Word repetition

Single words.   A second important method for assessing repetition in TA is by using single-word lists. Since it is well known that lexical and semantic factors may influence the performance on oral language tests, the word lists are generally constructed using the two major categories of words: *content* words (nouns, adjectives, verbs, and many adverbs) and *function* words (articles, pronouns, possessive adjectives). These lists may also be organised according to other dimensions, namely concreteness (concrete–abstract), word frequency (high–low), length (monosyllabic–polysyllabic), imagery (high–low), and other attributes (e.g. emotional–nonemotional). Transcortical patients who repeat words relying on the lexical–semantic route show variations in performance with the concreteness of the word and its grammatical category, whereas those repeating by means of the nonlexical route are insensible to these parts of speech effects (Gardner & Winner, 1978; Katz & Goodglass, 1990; Martin & Saffran, 1990).

Nonwords.   The preserved ability to repeat complex nonsense verbal material is usually taken as evidence of normal functioning of the nonlexical repetition route. Since nonwords are not within the inventory of a language, some requirements for their construction are necessary. Nonwords should always follow the legal rules of language and must be pronounceable. They are usually derived from real words (e.g. replacement of a letter by another, addition or deletion of a syllable) and may or may not be homophonic with real words. In the classical subtypes of TA due to lesions outside the left perisylvian language cortex, the patient is able to repeat, sometimes in a compulsive fashion, extremely difficult words (e.g. *Artilleriebrigade*) (Goldstein, 1915) and nonsense words (Assal Regli, Thuillard, Steck, Deruaz, & Perentes, 1983; Coslett et al., 1987; Lesser, 1989; Whitaker, 1976). Recent evidence, however, indicated that nonword repetititon is not always spared in transcortical aphasic patients. Impaired nonword repetition with spared repetition of real words seems to be a frequent finding among patients with either TCMA, TCSA, or MTCA who have damage to the phonological system represented within the left perisylvian language cortex (Berndt et al., 1987; Grossi et al., 1991; Martin & Saffran, 1990; Trojano, Fragassi, Postiglione, & Grossi, 1988; see further details in Chapter 7).

Word lists.   Repetition of word lists is used to assess the influence of lexical semantic information (Berndt et al., 1987; Martin & Saffran, 1990; McCarthy & Warrington, 1984, 1987). Berndt and her co-workers (1987) used several four-word lists to assess repetition performance in a transcortical sensory aphasic patient (RR). Two of these lists were devised to assess lexical aspects; one was composed of high-frequency nouns and the other of grammatical function words. The other two lists were constructed taking into account the semantic relatedness of the words within the lists, so that one list contained semantically related words, while the other was in a random order irrespective of the semantic content. Patient RR's performance on the four-word list was defective, mainly due to poor recall of terminal items; his performance was unaffected by the lexical semantic variables. Similar word lists were used by Martin and Saffran (1990) in another transcortical sensory aphasic patient (ST). The patient had an almost intact performance on the repetition of single words and pairs of words, but he did poorly (producing neologisms) when he had to repeat low-frequency three-word lists and high-frequency four-word strings. RR and ST showed poorer performance on repeating word lists than sentences containing the same words, whereas another patient (NHB) with TCSA showed the opposite pattern of difficulties (see Case 3 in McCarthy & Warrington, 1987).

Some rather different word lists have been developed by McCarthy and Warrington (1987), who studied dissociation of performance on word-list repetition in two patients with conduction aphasia and impaired attention (digit) span, and in patient NHB with TCSA and preserved attention span. These authors constructed three types of three-word lists (verb, adjective, noun), which were composed of word strings of increasing meaningfulness, that is from nonorganised to organised semantic information. The first three-word lists consisted of random word combinations (e.g. walk, shiny, pools); the second lists conveyed loosely constrained meaningful information (e.g. crawl, slow, baby), and the third lists conveyed closely constrained meaningful information (e.g. eat, green, apple). McCarthy and Warrington demonstrated that while the two conduction patients could repeat satisfactorily only the triplets with meaningful word associations, patient NHB had a preserved span for words obtaining a similar performance on the three sets. This latter finding suggests that the meaningfulness of the to-be-repeated verbal material did not influence the patient's performance.

Sentence repetition

Clichés vs. novel sentences.   There is evidence that patients with TA have a superior performance on the production of automatic language such as series (e.g. counting, days of the week), overlearned phrases, proverbs, emotional utterances, conversational fillers, and clichés (Code, 1989; Lebrun, 1993) than aphasic patients with impaired repetition (e.g. conduction aphasia). McCarthy and Warrington (1984) compared the ability to repeat clichés (e.g. "On top of the world") with novel sentences (e.g. "She went to buy some milk") that had a comparable length and phonological and lexical complexity in two patients with conduction aphasia with a transcortical motor aphasic patient (patient ART). Since clichés are phrases or expressions spoiled by long familiarity, it has been suggested that this combination of multiple words is processed as single units because as a result of frequent utilisation, the meaning of a cliché may became independent of the semantic value of its constitutive lexical items (McCarthy & Warrington, 1984). Thus, the repetition of clichés may demand less processing than the repetition of novel nonclichéd sentences (Butterworth & Warrington, 1995), so that one can expect that patients who use on-line strategies for repetition such as transcortical aphasics should perform considerably better on cliché repetition than patients that repeat mainly using lexical mechanisms such as conduction aphasic patients. In support, McCarthy and Warrington (1984) found that in ART repetition of clichés was better than repetition of novel sentences, whereas the reverse was true for the two conduction aphasics.

Repetition of Well-formed and Deviant Sentences. Clinical studies of TA reveal that the preserved ability to repeat sentences is not always performed in an automatic or "parrot-like" manner (Geschwind et al., 1968; Rubens, 1975; Stengel, 1964). The first experimental studies designed to investigate the influence of syntactic and semantic variables on repetition performance were conducted by Whitaker (1976) in a single female patient (HCEM) with a slowly progressive MTCA occurring in the context of a degenerative dementing illness, and by Davis et al. (1978) in a small group of patients with unilateral cerebrovascular lesions of the left hemisphere who showed the three clinically defined varieties of TA (two patients had TCMA, one had TCSA, and another one had a MTCA).

Whitaker (1976) carried out a series of investigations on the repetition performance of patient HCEM. First, she was asked to repeat a series of syntactically and grammatically correct sentences (e.g. "The robber was chased by the police"). She repeated verbatim all stimulus sentences and was also able to reproduce adequately the interrogative intonation in some of them. Second, the patient was asked to repeat syntactically ill-formed sentences (e.g. "He *thinking* about you"). It was surprising that HCEM automatically corrected more than the half of the stimulus sentences (e.g. "He *thinks* about you") and produced verbatim repetition of the remaining ones. Spontaneous correction of anomalous sentences was not limited to syntactic errors, since she also corrected sentences with either phonemic errors in initial (e.g. "This is a gold *l*ing" ⇒ gold *r*ing) and medial (e.g. "This is a brown note*l*ook" ⇒ note*b*ook) consonants, and incorrect stress patterns in noun compounds (e.g. "físher mán" ⇒ fisherman), but she was unable to correct semantic anomalies (e.g. "The book is very happy") and repeated these stimulus sentences as produced by the examiner.

Based on previous descriptive work and on the interesting results of Whitaker's study of her demented mixed transcortical aphasic patient using a linguistic approach, Davis and colleagues (1978) designed a study to assess further the dissociation of functions between syntactic and semantic processing during repetition. These authors constructed a battery of sentences composed of the following four sets: (1) factually and grammatically correct sentences (e.g. "Russia is a big country"); (2) factually incorrect, but grammatically well-formed sentences (e.g. "The president lives in Boston"); (3) grammatically incorrect sentences with violations of selection restrictions (e.g. "The milk drank the cat"); and (4) grammatically incorrect sentences with minor syntactic errors such as number agreement (e.g. "The cats drinks milk") or pronoun usage (e.g. "The boy gave *she* a present").

Davis and co-workers found that patients with TA, even those with severe impairments in both auditory comprehension and spontaneous speech (MTCA), did not repeat experimental sentences verbatim except for set (1) which were composed of factually and grammatically correct sentences. The patients produced few modifications in sentence sets (2) and (3), but they automatically corrected certain aspects of sentences composed by ungrammatical material (e.g. errors of number agreement). Spontaneous correction of these errors were documented by the authors among patients with normal lexical–semantic comprehension (e.g. TCMA), but not in those patients with poor auditory comprehension. Transcortical aphasic patients with relatively spared comprehension were fully aware of the inadequacy of sentence sets (2) and (3), but were unaware of minor syntactic deviations contained in set (4). Patients with impaired comprehension, on the other hand, did not show any awareness of either syntactic or semantic anomalies in sentences.

This pattern of performance during sentence repetition has been replicated in subsequent studies of patients with TCSA (Berthier, 1995; Coslett et al., 1987; Heilman et al., 1981), MTCA (Assal et al., 1983; Pirozzolo, Kerr, Obrzut, Morley, Haxby, & Lundgren, 1981; Speedie, Coslett, & Heilman, 1984), and even in anomic aphasia (e.g. only access to syntax during repetition; Shuren, Greenwald, & Heilman, 1996), but not in transcortical patients with large lesions (Berthier, Starkstein et al., 1991, cases 3, 5, 12; Pulvermüller & Schönle, 1993) or diffuse hemispheric damage (Mehler, 1988) involving the cortex surrounding the sylvian fissure. This suggests that access to certain syntactic operations during repetition (e.g. those not driven by lexical knowledge) depends upon the integrity of some modular units of grammar which are represented within the anterior part of the central perisylvian language core. Dogil, Haider, Schaner-Wolles, and Husmann (1995) recently demonstrated preserved capacity for processing syntax during repetition in a patient who developed a TCSA in association with an extensive haemorrhage involving the anterior left perisylvian area. CT and SPECT scans revealed that the left perisylvian lesion selectively spared the mid part of the so-called "ventral frontal language region", an area thought to be important for grammatical processing (Deacon, 1990; Dogil et al., 1995).

The ability of transcortical aphasic patients to access syntax during repetition can be explored in a different way (Berndt, 1988). Berndt and colleagues (1987) examined the effects on syntactic variables in the repetition of sentences in their patient (RR) with TCSA by using two types of semantically reversible sentences of identical length and lexical composition. One set of sentences contained semantically reversible sentences with *subject*-relative centre-embedded clauses (e.g. "The car that follows the truck with the big wheels is red"), whereas the other set was composed of semantically reversible sentences with *object*-relative centre-embedded clauses (e.g. "The car that the truck with the big wheels follows is red"). The latter type is more difficult to understand because this kind of sentence contains two successive noun phrases (e.g. "car" and "truck") at the beginning. RR's performance on these tasks was significantly better for the repetition of sentences of the first set (17/32 correct) than for those of the second set (1/32 correct). Interestingly, errors in repetition were composed mainly of either omission of adjectives, replacement of target nouns by new lexical items, or reversal of the order of nouns. On the other hand, the syntactic structure of the sentences remained intact, thus reflecting RR's preserved appreciation of grammatical categories (Berndt, 1988). Martin and Saffran (1990) also assessed the potential beneficial effect of syntactic context during the repetition of sentences. They compared the performance of a woman (ST) with TCSA on the repetition of open-class word strings (e.g. "life" "woman" "state" "school") with her repetition of these words embedded in semantically anomalous sentences (e.g. "The *life* and the *woman* are *stating* the *school*"). They found that ST repeated significantly more accurately strings of three or four words when they were embedded in a syntactical frame even lacking semantic coherence than when these open-class words were presented in isolation. Therefore, the integrity of syntactic structure, though dissociated from semantics, is one variable that may benefit item recall during repetition performance in transcortical aphasic patients, perhaps by providing the order of items in the utterance (Martin & Saffran, 1990).

Completion of sentences

Stengel (1947) noted that in certain cases of aphasia with echolalia (e.g. TA) when the examiner uttered the initial part of a popular expression without completing it, the patient tended to automatically fill out the rest of it instead of echoing the beginning or the entire sentence (Lebrun, 1993). The "completion phenomenon" as described by Stengel has been viewed as an involuntary and often compulsive response that can be generated by the patient without understanding its meaning. By contrast, other patients appear totally unable to refrain from completing unfinished sentences even in the presence of intact auditory comprehension (Rubens, 1975). The completion phenomenon has also has been interpreted by Whitaker (1976) as a noncreative linguistic behaviour, where the successful completion responses occur in a specific linguistic–conversational setting, only when nonterminal prosodic contours and high frequency overlearned verbal material are used. In recent years, sentence completion exercises have been used in language testing not only to assess the access to overlearned verbal material, but also the retrieval of appropriate morphological forms based on endogenous conceptual representations (see later).

To test the completion phenomenon in TA different verbal stimuli can be used. Whitaker (1976), for instance, tested completion performance with word formation from letter stimuli, where the patient is asked to produce a word beginning with that letter (e.g. "t" $\Rightarrow$ table). Other exercises used by Whitaker included completion of incomplete semantically correct sentences (e.g. "Can you sing a ..."), and completion of proverbs and well-known song titles. Another way to test completion phenomenon in TA is to use sentence completion stimuli for which there are norms for the final word (e.g. Bloom & Fischler, 1980). In a study that assessed auditory verbal short-term memory for word lists and sentences in two conduction aphasic patients and in a patient (NHB) with TCSA, McCarthy and Warrington (1987) used stimuli derived from Bloom and Fischler's material. These authors examined performance of these three patients on a typical sentence completion exercise composed of open-ended sentences (e.g. "London is a very busy ...") as well as their performance on repeating full sentences ending with a high probability completion word (e.g. "London is a very busy city") and full but semantically anomalous sentences ending with an inappropriate word (e.g. "London is a very busy *river*"). Major differences between the two aphasic groups were in the sentence completion exercise condition with patient NHB performing significantly better than the two conduction patients. This pattern of results indicates that sentence completion is one useful test to differentiate conduction from transcortical aphasic patients.

Recent research on aphasia shows that patients' performance of sentence completion exercises depends upon the predictability of the required completion (Berndt et al., 1987) and upon the grammatical class of the word (e.g. completion of verbs may be significantly better than noun completion; Berndt, Haendiges, & Wozniak, 1997; Breen & Warrington, 1994; Zingeser & Berndt, 1988). Thus, it is important to examine the patient's performance on sentence fragments with a highly predictable final word (e.g. "The colour of bananas is ...") as opposed to sentence fragments with a more open-ended, less predictable final word (e.g. "He is afraid ..."), and also to use sentence fragment cues that should be completed with verbs (e.g. "Mistakes made in pencil are easy to *erase*") and nouns (Berndt et al., 1997).

The issue of sentence completion phenomenon is discussed further in Chapter 6, but I would like to comment here that completion of overlearned material is commonly seen in the context of transcortical patterns, whereas when more demanding, less predictable words are required, or when the transcortical pattern is an integral part of the cognitive decline seen in cases of focal cortical temporal lobe degeneration (Nakagawa et al., 1993; Tanabe et al., 1993) or in subcortical degeneration as in progressive supranuclear palsy (Esmonde, Giles, Xuereb, & Hodges, 1996) performance on sentence completion exercises may be impaired.

CHAPTER THREE

Transcortical motor aphasia

INTRODUCTION

Transcortical motor aphasia (TCMA) is characterised by a marked reduction of speech output, in the context of relatively preserved auditory comprehension, object naming, and repetition (Goldstein, 1948; Lichtheim, 1885). In 1885 Lichtheim, based on his own cases, described for the first time a variety of motor aphasia, characterised by loss of volitional speech and writing but spared understanding of spoken and written language as well as normal copying, oral reading, and repetition. A second important contribution to the clinical phenomenology of TCMA was introduced by Kurt Goldstein (1917, 1948), who, in a comprehensive analysis of language impairments associated with TCMA, described different patterns of verbal expression. Goldstein (1948) maintained that the characteristics of speech output deficits vary depending upon location of the lesion within the left frontal lobe. Subsequent studies on TCMA corroborated the notion that deficits in oral expression are heterogeneous (Ardila & López, 1984; Lebrun, 1995; Luria & Tsvetkova, 1968; Rubens, 1975) and further demonstrated heterogeneity in other linguistic domains (e.g. auditory comprehension; Freedman et al., 1984). Therefore, I will review the different types of TCMA that have been reported to date—classical and dynamic aphasia—paying attention also to atypical patterns as well as the occurrence of TCMA in unusual circumstances such as anomalous language dominance. At the end of this chapter, I will discuss some of the available evidence indicating that pharmacological treatment using dopamine agonist makes an additional contribution to the conventional language therapy in selected patients with TCMA.

THE CLASSICAL PATTERN

In the literature there are a number of adequate clinical studies describing the "classical" presentation of the TCMA syndrome, but there are as yet few cases which analyse the neurolinguistic characteristics underlying disordered verbal expression (McCarthy & Warrington, 1984). In this section, I will discuss two aspects of classical TCMA. The first topic concerns the characteristics of TCMA from a phenomenological perspective. The second topic is partially related to the previous one and includes the details of a case study which was evaluated within the cognitive neuropsychological framework. This case study provides some new insights into the organisation of spontaneous speech and repetition in TCMA. The issue of anatomical distribution of lesions producing the classical pattern of TCMA and dynamic aphasia still remains controversial (Alexander, Benson, & Stuss, 1989; Alexander & Naeser, 1988; Lebrun, 1995), though available evidence suggests that both forms of TCMA may result from damage to the same neural structures. Therefore, I will consider the aetiology and pathophysiological mechanisms of these two clinical variants in the same section.

Clinical characteristics

Analysis of clinical aspects reveals that in the classical variant of TCMA the patient initially shows a total muteness or a marked reduction in spontaneous speech (Albert et al., 1981; Rubens & Kertesz, 1983). Mutism is usually transient (Goldstein, 1948) and is replaced in a short time by the emergence of nonfluent verbal output (Alexander & Schmitt, 1980; Masdeu, Schoene, & Funkenstein, 1978). When spontaneous speech returns, it is sparse and limited to single words or overlearned phrases. Effortful initiation, hesitation, and verbal perseveration are common (Luria & Hutton, 1977; Rubens & Kertesz, 1983) and the patient's responses are generally contaminated by perseveration and echolalic incorporation of fragments of the questions (e.g. *Question*: "What is your occupation?"; *Answer*: "My . . . my occupation is . . ."). As a result of the reduced production of utterances, patients featuring TCMA are sometimes erroneously judged as being demented or depressed because they use evasive and vague responses such as "I don't know" or "I can't remember" (Albert et al., 1981; Rubens & Kertesz, 1983).

Some patients do not attempt to communicate spontaneously (akinesia of speech) and only speak when addressed. When the difficulties in speech initiation are prominent they may be associated with reduced gestures, facial expression, and affective communication, a constellation of deficits indicative of a global reduction of motor and language activation (Stuss & Benson, 1986). On the contrary, in spite of having marked reduction in spontaneous speech some TCMA patients use volitional movements such as waving the hands or tapping the feet to prompt verbal output (Stuss & Benson, 1986). Speech articulation is usually preserved, but emissions are variously described as soft, sparse, hesitant, laboured, or hypophonic. Stuttering, stumbling, perseveration of syllables and words, and tremor of lips and tongue during speech are occasionally reported (Rubens, 1975). Serial speech (recitation of the days of the week, counting) can be easily elicited by verbal prompts and is much better than spontaneous speech. As fluency improves, verbal expression consists of short sentences pronounced with effort and contaminated by echolalia and perseverations (Rubens & Kertesz, 1983). These sentences, however, are usually informative and lack paraphasias, neologisms and grammatical errors (Bogousslavsky, Assal, & Regli, 1987), although occasional semantic and phonological paraphasias (Alexander & Schmitt, 1980; Freedman et al., 1984), or partial word contaminations resembling phonological paraphasias (Lebrun, 1995), may be heard during the production of spontaneous utterances.

Visual confrontation naming is considerably superior to spontaneous speech and, in some instances, it can be relatively spared (McNabb, Carroll, & Mastaglia, 1988). Long latency responses in naming tasks are mainly the result of decreased drive and less frequently occur due to word-finding difficulties. Wordlist generation of different semantic categories and letters is severely compromised in most patients, and these deficits usually persist as important sequelae of TCMA (Berthier, Ruiz, Massone, et al., 1991; Rubens & Kertesz, 1983). Repetition may be impaired during the initial phase of mutism. Indeed, Goldstein (1948) early noted that if the impairment in the impulse to speak (akinesia of speech) was severe, repetition could also be affected, as repetition is not totally automatic and it requires voluntary impulse by the patient. Once repetition returns, it can adopt an involuntary character (automatic echolalia) and patients may echo entire phrases. Later during the recovery stages only the final part of the phrase is involuntarily repeated (mitigated echolalia) (Benson, 1975; Ford, 1989; Stengel, 1947; see also Chapter 6). In most patients nonfluency contrasts sharply with a disinhibition of unwanted speech productions such as immediate echolalia, perseverations, and automatic completion of open-ended sentences. This pattern of speech dissociation between inability of spontaneously generated words and sentences and echolalic repetition was clearly evidenced in one of two TCMA patients reported by Rubens (1975). When this patient (Case 1) was asked to describe the weather, she could only reply "f-f-fine", but she was capable of repeating long sentences such as "It is a beautiful warm, sunny day outside" correctly. Even more surprising was the fact that this patient could repeat the sentence "how are you?" after this was mouthed silently in her view by the examiner. Repetition of words and sentences is almost always intact, but occasional semantic paraphasias and simplification of sentences due to omission of complex elements without modifying the sentence meaning have been reported during the repetition of low-probability sentences (Ardila & Roselli, 1992). Sentence repetition is not necessarily an on-line process, since patients may automatically correct minor syntactic anomalies (e.g. errors of tense, number agreement, pronoun usage) during repetition of ungrammatical sentences (Davis

TABLE 3.1
Characteristics of Spontaneous Speech and Repetition in Transcortical
Motor Aphasic Syndromes

	Classical	Dynamic Aphasia	Atypical
Spontaneous speech			
Fluency	Sparse, perseverative	Hesitant, telegraphic	Stereotyped, stuttering
Oral agility	Impaired	Relatively preserved	Impaired
Initiation	Effortful	Normal	Effortful
Articulation	Preserved	Preserved	Impaired
Grammar	Preserved	Occasionally impaired	Impaired
Prosody	Occasionally impaired	Preserved	Often impaired
Paraphasia	Occasional, semantic	Absent	Occasional, phonological
Repetition			
Digits (span)	Preserved	Preserved	Impaired
Words	Preserved	Preserved	Preserved
Nonwords	Preserved	Occasionally impaired	Impaired
Short phrases	Preserved	Preserved	Preserved
Sentences	Preserved	Preserved	Impaired

et al., 1978). The distinctive characteristics of spontaneous speech and repetition observed in patients with "classical" TCMA is shown in Table 3.1.

Other language functions are generally preserved. Spoken and written comprehension are relatively preserved except for syntactically complex and lengthy verbal material. (Freedman et al., 1984; Ross, 1980). The presence of a moderate impairment in auditory comprehension is not a typical feature of classical TCMA and may be indicative of either extension of the lesion to the basal ganglia and insular cortex in cases with lesions anterior or superior to the frontal operculum (Freedman et al., 1984) or reflect additional damage to the supplementary sensory area in the left mesial parietal lobe (Ross, 1980), although several patients with TCMA and similar lesion location fail to show deficits in aural comprehension (Bogousslavsky et al., 1987). Spontaneous writing is frequently affected in a fashion parallel to spontaneous speech. Writing with the right hand shows letter repetition, distortions, and omissions indicative of aphasic agraphia. Impaired writing with the right hand may also be attributable to grasp reflex that usually accompanies left mesial frontal damage. Writing to copy and dictation may be preserved.

The nature of linguistic deficits

As the nature of the functional deficits underlying TCMA is concerned I indicated at the beginning of the chapter that reported cases describing the linguistic aspects of the speech production deficits in the classical subtype are scanty. On investigating the possible functional models underlying speech production deficits in aphasia, McCarthy and Warrington (1984) contrasted the performance of a patient with TCMA on various experimental tests of word/sentence repetition and oral reading with the performance obtained from two patients with conduction aphasia. The transcortical patient, ART, was a 58-year-old right-handed art school lecturer who suffered an ischaemic infarction in the left parietal cortical region. He presented severe nonfluent aphasia characterised by halting and effortful spontaneous speech. He produced phonemic and, less frequently, phonetic distortions in both verbal productions and oral reading tasks. His auditory and written comprehension was less affected than his oral productions. He could repeat four digits in correct serial order and repeated polysyllabic words almost perfectly. Nonword repetition was not explored. McCarthy and Warrington argued that this pattern of dissociation (paraphasic spontaneous speech in the face of preserved repetition) is just the opposite (relative preservation of spontaneous speech in the face of paraphasic repetition) of what they observed in the two conduction aphasics. Therefore, several tests to assess language dissociation in more detail were administered to ART and to the two conduction aphasics.

McCarthy and Warrington initially compared single-word repetition and oral reading. ART's performance on repetition of words of increasing syllable length was significantly better than the oral reading of these words. McCarthy and Warrington's second point deals with the comparison of repetition of idiomatic phrases of English (clichés) (e.g. "On top of the world") *vs.* novel sentences (e.g. "It was a fine evening"). The rationale for performing such an experiment was that the investigators considered that once incorporated into the individual language the cliché has a constrained syntactic and lexical structure and the meaning becomes independent of the semantic referents of its individual lexical constituents, so that it can be processed as a polysyllabic word using a single lexical entry. On the contrary, they considered that the repetition of novel sentences required the utilisation of more demanding cognitive operations. In other words, repetition of clichés is probably more automatic and hence less demanding than the repetition of novel sentences. ART repeated clichés considerably better (73% correct) than novel sentences (53% correct), whereas the two conduction aphasics showed the opposite pattern of deficits (better repetition of novel sentences than clichés). In a subsequent experiment, McCarthy and Warrington examined ART's semantic processing during the repetition of two types of sentences that had the peculiarity of having both a terminal low-frequency three-syllable word, but differed in the meaning of one previous word, which rendered the sentence "sensible" (e.g. "The scope *was* limited") or "nonsensible" (e.g.

"The scope *go* limited"). The authors compared ART's performance on the repetition of both sentence types with the repetition of the last word (e.g. "limited") in isolation. Once again, ART showed a pattern of performance that was the opposite of both the conduction aphasics, namely better repetition of the last word in the isolated condition than when it was embedded in a sentence. To rule out the possibility that the failure demonstrated by ART in repeating the last word of a sentence may rely on a concomitant deficit in verbal short-term memory, in a further experiment McCarthy and Warrington simply asked ART to listen to the full sentences and then repeat them. The repetition set again included the two types of sentences, "sensible" and "nonsensible". Responses were scored by taking into account the repetition of the full sentence and the target word occurring at the end of the sentence. ART showed a trend for repeating "sensible" better than "nonsensible" sentences and he always repeated the final word better than the whole sentences.

Although there have been no additional cases of TCMA assessed using a similar testing methodology that confirm the patterns documented in ART, McCarthy and Warrington's findings are interesting in many respects. The authors first suggested that in ART the speech production deficits are specific to particular task demands and were not the direct consequence of global disruption of output mechanisms, impaired word perception, word comprehension, or auditory short-term storage. The possibility that impaired speech production may be, at least in part, due to problems in speech initiation were not excluded, however. McCarthy and Warrington indicated that ART's performance on speech production tasks (repetition) was hampered by those tasks that maximised active semantic processing (e.g. repeating sentences for meaning). Like Wernicke (1874/ 1977) and Lichtheim (1885), the authors interpreted this finding as resulting from a disruption of the processing route connecting the semantic system with the speech output mechanism. On the other hand, McCarthy and Warrington considered that the direct route which connects the auditory verbal input with the articulatory output mechanism, and is used for rapid and automatic repetition without semantic mediation, was intact, allowing in ART the verbatim repetition of most polysyllabic words and clichés. More research using the cognitive neuropsychological approach is needed to obtain further information of dissociation between spontaneous speech and repetition in TCMA.

DYNAMIC APHASIA

Clinical characteristics

Kurt Kleist (1934) discussed one of the two types of TCMA (e.g. nonfluent spontaneous speech with normal articulation) already described by Goldstein (1917) and coined the term *"Antriebsmangel der Sprache"* (reduced drive of language) to refer to it. He suggested for the first time that the aspontaneity of speech, chiefly characterised by reduced word fluency, was a genuine language disturbance and not the consequence of generalised disorders of spontaneity or thought. Luria (1970) accepted Kleist's position and introduced the term dynamic aphasia (DA) "to refer to the patient whose spontaneous propositional speech output is severely reduced, yet at the same time the patient is able to comprehend language and use language in nominative (e.g. naming and reading) types of task". Luria described several subtypes of DA, but he never clearly delineated the differences from one another. In a recent re-elaboration of Luria's work on DA, Lebrun (1995) distinguished three different neurolinguistic syndromes. The first neurolinguistic syndrome he discussed is probably a replica of the classical profile of TCMA, so that it will not be elaborated further here. The neurolinguistic features of the second syndrome described by Lebrun are easily accommodated to Luria's original description of DA as well as to more recent considerations of the syndrome (Costello & Warrington, 1986; Gold et al., 1997; Lanoe, Pedetti, Lanoe, Mayer, & Evrard, 1994; Robinson et al., 1998). In this section I will focus specifically on the linguistic and anatomical correlates of this second DA syndrome. Finally, the third neurolinguistic DA syndrome discussed by Lebrun refers to the lack of drive to generate language that usually occurs in the setting of a more global akinetic syndromes after frontal lobe lesions. This syndrome is reminiscent of the aforementioned condition of partial mutism (Brown, 1987; Damasio & van Hoesen, 1980) that sometimes takes place after lesions of the supplementary motor area (SMA). Table 3.1 shows the characteristics of spontaneous speech and repetition in patients with DA.

Many of the cases described by Luria and colleagues under the heading of "frontal DA" encompassed more than just the classical syndrome of TCMA (see Lebrun, 1995). Patients with this type of DA usually present marked reduction in spontaneous speech, being able to produce only sparse and slow verbal output, but when the speech utterance is finally elicited, its phonological, syntactical, and logico-grammatical organisation remains largely spared (Luria & Tsvetkova, 1968). Transient aphonia may also be seen during the first hours or days (Tonkonogy, 1986). Patients are often unable to generate whole sentences during a free conversation, but show a tendency to echolalia and easily complete open-ended sentences. Auditory comprehension is unimpaired in most cases, but instances of poor understanding may be observed among cases in which general akinesia or language aspontaneity is severe. In general, if auditory comprehension deficits are present, they are transient and recover faster than verbal expression. Repetition for words and sentences is preserved, but nonword repetition may be impaired (Lebrun, 1995). Some patients are also unable to describe pictures, whereas others less severely affected can describe simple but not more complex pictures (Luria, 1970). Spontaneous speech may show a telegraphic style and mild to moderate agrammatism can be manifested by rare utilisation of small words and a tendency to use substantive uninflected words (Lebrun, 1995; Tonkonogy, 1986). Letter fluency is severely compromised and the ability to generate verbs and nouns may be differently affected. Patients with severe DA, for instance, are totally unable to generate either verbs or nouns instead producing only verbal perseverations, whereas a relative preservation of fluency for nouns but not for verbs may be observed in both less severely affected patients and during the recovery phases of DA (Luria & Tsvetkova, 1968).

Another important aspect of the deficit in speech output concerns the impaired production of spontaneous utterances. This obviously depends on the severity of aphasia and milder cases may produce conversational speech fairly well, but exhibit problems when they have to construct a story or during narrative. Luria and colleagues emphasised that in severe cases the inability to generate phrases is usually so prominent that patients cannot construct a sentence when specific words such as "cart" and "horse" are orally presented in isolation (Luria & Tsvetkova, 1968). In response to the presentation of these single words, DA patients often produce either echolalia or overused phrases instead of constructing a novel sentence. At times, lack of responses due to aspontaneity, or instead, the emission of complex verbal perseverations are observed. In an effort to overcome aspontaneity and perseverations, Luria and Tsvetkova demonstrated that external cues favoured the emission of utterances. For instance, when a DA patient was given nonverbal cues (e.g. pictures related to the meaning of the sentence) in an equal number to the main words composing the required sentence, and asked to point to the pictures and then construct a sentence, a beneficial effect on the phrase construction was seen. Based on these findings, Luria and co-workers argued that the fundamental functional deficit in DA resides in the predicative function of inner speech leading to an inability to achieve a "linear scheme of the phrase". They excluded intentional (or planning) deficits of verbal initiation or disturbances in the "final expression" of speech as responsible for the verbal adynamia.

The nature of linguistic deficits

Costello and Warrington (1986) reported a detailed neurolinguistic study of a modern case of DA. They argued that Luria's concepts cannot be applicable to explain their case and instead suggested that DA results from selective impairments in verbal planning. The patient (ROH) described by Costello and Warrington was a 42-year-old right-handed male who, following the surgical removal of a left medial frontal lobe malignant astrocytoma, developed epileptic seizures, right hemiplegia and marked expressive dysphasia. On formal language assessment, ROH showed a striking difficulty in speech initiation, impaired ability to generate sentences, extremely poor letter and semantic fluency and word definition, long latency to respond to questions and occasional instances of lack of response. However, in the few occasions that ROH could generate spontaneous or responsive speech, he produced fluent utterances; speech articulation, grammar, and prosody were all normal and there were no paraphasic errors. Other language functions such as visual naming for pictures representing nouns and action verbs, auditory comprehension, and repetition were almost normal. Costello and Warrington pointed out that the occasional occurrence of normal expressive language (either spontaneously or during responsive speech) clearly distinguishes DA from classical TCMA, in which the integrity of language function is only demonstrable during repetition tasks.

Based on a meticulous experimental investigation of ROH's expressive language difficulties, Costello and Warrington presented several arguments to support the contention that his deficits selectively compromised the planning of language, and were not the result of deficits in inner speech as initially proposed by Luria. First, although ROH could easily complete sentences in which the last word was deliberately omitted (e.g. "The boat passed easily under the . . . = *bridge*"), he had serious difficulties in completing sentences with a second phrase ("*The old lady* . . . was struggling across the road") as well as in generate sentences when a single word stimulus ("Ran", "Phone") was presented in isolation by the examiner. Moreover, when ROH was presented with a stimulus sentence (e.g. "Joe had fallen and twisted his ankle") and asked to generate a thematically related sentence (e.g. "He was taken to hospital for an X-ray") he responded by either producing grammatically correct sentences or a lack of response. By contrast, when the presented stimulus was a picture or a series of pictures (e.g. picture arrangement subtest of the WAIS), he could in most instances generate long (14-word) sentences. The preserved ability to generate a spoken narrative after a pictorial stimulus in RHO was used by Costello and Warrington to demonstrate that, within certain contexts, such patients can maintain a continuity between initial thought and extended verbal output. Moreover, the dissociation between preserved narrative speech responses after a pictorial stimulus presentation and severely impaired speech responses after a verbal stimulus material suggests that in RHO the left frontal lobe damage induced material-specific verbal planning deficits. Second, in the few sentences in which ROH was able to generate utterances spontaneously, there were no errors of word order and the utilisation of propositional language was always normal. According to Costello and Warrington, this evidence goes against the argument advanced by Luria that in DA there is a defective "linear scheme of the phrase". They argued that defective performance of RHO on sentence generation when all constituent words were provided by the examiner cannot be explained by Luria's hypothesis.

Gold et al. (1997) recently reported another case of "adynamic" TCMA in a patient (CO) who, after recovering from a right hemiparesis and slurred speech, suddenly developed new problems in oral expression together with apathy, incontinence, and unsteady gait. A CT scan disclosed bilateral striatocapsular infarcts. On neurological examination, CO appeared alert and oriented, but his oral expression was restricted to single words and short phrases produced with normal articulation and grammar and devoid of phonological or semantic paraphasias. However, CO's fluency improved during picture description and he was able to produce several short utterances. Auditory comprehension, visual naming, and repetition were preserved, but verbal short-term memory was impaired. Performance on language subtests of the Western Aphasia Battery (Kertesz, 1982) in CO were consistent with the diagnosis of TCMA. Impaired conversational speech and apathy in CO contrasted with echopraxia and perseverative responses while performing go–no–go and tactile inhibition task. He also showed impaired performance in other executive tests susceptible to frontal-subcortical dysfunction such as the Trail-Making test (parts A and B) and the Wisconsin Card Sorting Test. Nonverbal and verbal memory were preserved, but serial position on the word recall subscores of the California Verbal Learning Test demonstrated greater than normal primacy and recency effects.

Gold and his colleagues carried out a number of experiments in CO to examine the functional mechanisms underlying DA. These included: assessment of verbal akinesia through measurements of processing speed (latencies) during object naming, action naming, and naming to definition; a procedural discourse task (CO was asked to generate verbal descriptions of procedures such as making a cup of coffee) with or without the aid of verbal cues (e.g. "the first step is"); assessment of semantic knowledge of objects by using object naming, naming to definition, word-to-picture matching, semantic association, and sorting by categories tests, letter, and category fluency tasks; lexical priming; semantic categorisation tasks (e.g. the ability to sort semantically related items into different classes). The patient did not have impairments in speed of verbal processing (e.g. latencies to object naming, object to definition, and action-naming tasks were faster than in normal control subjects), attention, and semantic knowledge. Major deficits were found in several cognitive domains, namely, verbal fluency, verbal description of simple procedures, serial position in word-list recall, and "frontal" executive function.

Abnormal performance on letter and category fluency, concept formation, and mnemonic strategy were interpreted by Gold and co-workers as resulting from defective lexical and semantic search strategies. Gold et al. suggested that the coexistence of decreased verbal fluency, impaired problem-solving ability and planning strategies, and deficits in alternating and sequential motor tasks in CO resembled the key features associated with damage to the "dorsolateral prefrontal circuit" (Alexander, DeLong, & Strick, 1986; Cummings, 1993). They further argued that bilateral striatocapsular lesions may have selectively interrupted this frontal-subcortical connectivity, thus preventing the normal implementation of semantic strategies.

Robinson et al. (1998) recently reported a patient (ANG) who in association with a malignant meningioma involving the left frontal region (BA 45) developed a "pure" DA. The patient's spontaneous speech was markedly reduced, but there was no evidence of syntactical problems and other expressive language functions, namely object naming, repetition, and oral reading, were completely normal. Two different types of experimental investigations were carried out in

ANG. In the first investigation, she showed deficits in phrase and sentences generation while performing exercises of completion of open-ended sentences that should be completed by generating a single word (66/91 correct) or phrases (3/20 correct). ANG's performance in sentence completion with single words was apparently influenced by the number of potential response options. By contrast, ANG was able to generate meaningful and grammatically correct sentences for simple pictorial scenes (34/34 correct) selected from the PALPA (Kay et al., 1992), although she was totally unable to generate sentences when she was shown simple pictures (e.g. a doctor giving an injection to a young girl) and asked to generate sentences describing what might happen next. Her ability to rearrange isolated words (3 to 7 words printed on separate pieces of paper) to construct a meaningful sentences was preserved (14/15 correct), a pattern of performance that according to the authors ruled out the possibility raised by others researchers (Costello & Warrington, 1986) that DA was due to deficits in verbal planning skills. In the second investigation, Robinson and co-workers wanted to examine the hypothesis that DA in their patient was secondary to impaired ability to select the best verbal response whenever the stimulus activates other competing verbal options. Therefore, ANG was administered three different verbal generation tasks. In the first task ANG was asked to generate sentences from single proper nouns (e.g. IRA, Beatles) and single common words (e.g. sea, glass). Although her ability to generate sentences from proper nouns was almost intact (26/28 correct), she demonstrated severe problems in the generation of sentences from single common nouns (11/28 correct). The second task consisted of the generation of phrases to complete fragment of sentences with high and low response predictability. There were sentences with an unique response option for their completion (e.g. "The man bought a sandwich and . . .") and others which had many response options (e.g. "The man ate a sandwich and . . ."). ANG's responses were considerably better for generating phrases with high (9/12 correct) than low (3/12 correct) response predictability. The third task consisted of the generation of sentences from word pairs with high (e.g. "stairs–step") and low (e.g. "stair–carpet") association. Once again, ANG's responses were more accurate for the generation of sentences containing word pairs with high (22/30) than low (4/30) association. Robinson et al. suggested that the fundamental deficits in ANG were unrelated to the generation of appropriate strategy to complete phrases and sentences. They also confirmed their hypothesis that ANG was unable to select between competing verbal responses when the verbal stimulus activated many potential responses, but not when the stimulus activated a single response. The impaired selection of competing verbal responses in ANG was attributed to disruption of an executive controlling system that is presumably represented in the left prefrontal region (Robinson et al., 1998).

Esmonde et al. (1996) reported three patients suffering from progressive supranuclear palsy who presented, at the beginning, a disorder in verbal output resembling DA. All three patients had reduced verbal output in narrative and discourse situations and impaired performance on verbal fluency tasks (letters and categories) that contrasted sharply with almost normal ability in other oral tasks such as picture naming and naming from descriptions. Analysis of spontaneous speech showed occasional syntactic errors with omission of appropriate functor words, aborted phrases, and perseverations, but phonological paraphasias or articulatory problems were lacking. Repetition of words and sentences was preserved, though not formally tested. By contrast, formal assessment of completion tasks through single-word and phrase completions revealed prominent deficits in two patients. Errors were documented in both test conditions (words and phrases) and consisted mainly of perseverations of previous questions and the production of echolalic utterances. Mild impairments were noted in semantic and syntactic comprehension tests. The authors interpreted the unusual occurrence of DA in these three cases as resulting from dysfunction of frontal-subcortical circuits.

The neural substrate

The pattern of classical TCMA and DA have essentially been associated with two lesion sites; one involving the white matter anterolateral and superior to the left frontal horn and the other the mesial aspect of the left frontal lobe (see Rapcsak & Rubens, 1994 for a recent review). Occasionally, these two patterns of TCMA have also been found associated with pure subcortical lesions (Bogousslavsky, Miklossy, Deruaz, Regli, & Assal, 1986; Cappa & Sterzi, 1990; Cappa & Vignolo, 1979; De La Sayette et al., 1992).

Dorsolateral frontal lobe lesions

Lichtheim (1885) predicted that TCMA might occur after lesions involving the lower parts of the left frontal lobe just anterior to Broca's area. He further speculated that the lesion interrupted the fibres linking Broca's area with the anterior general concept centre. A few years later, the association of TCMA with lesions of the frontal subcortical white matter of the left hemisphere were first confirmed by Rothman (1906). On discussing the neuroanatomical aspects of this historical case, Goldstein (1948, p. 296) stated that the anatomical study disclosed "a small lesion in the white matter in the posterior part of the 3rd frontal convolution so located that it has apparently particularly severed the fibers originating from the frontal convolution without affecting severely the cortex of the frontal lobe and of Broca's area". Similarly, the syndrome of DA, as described by Kleist (1934) and Luria (1970), has classically been attributed to cortical lesions involving the lower parts of the left frontal lobe, just anterior to Broca's area (see Barraquer-Bordas, 1989). On studying the brains of war veterans, Kleist (1934) found that the lesions responsible for DA were placed in

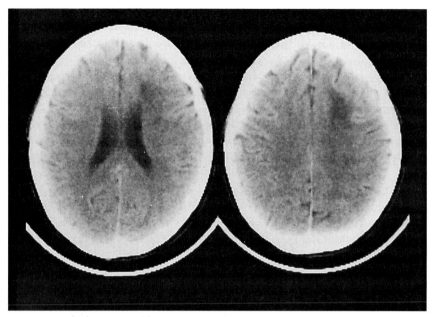

FIG. 3.1   CT scan showing an ischaemic infarction located outside the perisylvian language zone in a patient with "classical" transcortical motor aphasia. The low-density lesion involves the white matter anterolateral to the left frontal horn in the "watershed" territory between the anterior and middle cerebral arteries. The left hemisphere is represented on the right side of the figure.

the posterior margin of the second frontal convolution (BA 9) just superior to Broca's area, a pathologic distribution that, in his view, explained the pattern of verbal adynamia with normal articulation.

Modern studies of the neural basis of the classical pattern of TCMA using isotope brain scans (Kertesz, Lesk, & McCabe, 1977) and CT scans (Freedman et al., 1984; Naeser & Hayward, 1978; Naeser, Hayward, Laughlin, & Zats, 1981) have essentially corroborated this anatomic location. H. Damasio (1991), for instance, stated that in TCMA "Lesions are almost invariably located outside Broca's area, either anteriorly or superiorly, either deep in the frontal substance or in cortex" (pp. 56–57). Most authors agree that the classical pattern of TCMA usually results from vascular lesions in the "watershed" territory between the left anterior and middle cerebral arteries sparing the anterior perisylvian speech area (Kertesz et al., 1977; Naeser & Hayward, 1978; Fig. 3.1), although the syndrome has also been described in association with other pathologies (e.g. head trauma, neoplasm) placed in this anatomical region (Lebrun, 1995). Although a systematic analysis of lesion sites in series of patients with DA has not been performed, similar lesion locations were documented in single case studies (Costello & Warrington, 1986; De La Sayette et al., 1992; Robinson et al., 1998).

Mesial frontal lobe lesions

The classical pattern of TCMA and DA have both been associated with lesions in the left mesial frontal region including the SMA and the anterior cingulate gyrus. The aphasic syndromes has been variously reported after anterior cerebral artery occlusions and haemorrhages, traumatic brain injuries, surgical ablations, neoplasms, arteriovenous malformations, interhemispheric subdural empyemas, and haematomas (see references in Brust, Plank, Burke, Guobadia, & Healton, 1982; Rubens, 1975; Rubens & Kertesz, 1983). Focal cortical degenerative processes (corticobasal ganglionic degeneration) affecting the left superior frontal gyrus may also produce the syndrome (Lippa, Cohen, Smith, & Drachman, 1991).

Although various regions of the mesial frontal cortex are generally damaged by the lesion causing these two clinical variants of TCMA, the involvement of the SMA has been considered crucial for the clinical phenomenology of these syndromes. Therefore, a brief review of the SMA structure and function as well as of its neuroanatomical connections is of interest. The SMA is part of BA 6 and is situated on the mesial aspect of the cerebral hemisphere just anterior to the primary motor representation of the foot. It is limited anteriorly by the prefrontal cortex, posteriorly by the primary motor cortex (BA 4), ventrally by the cingulate gyrus, and laterally by the premotor cortex. The SMA is derived from the anterior cingulate-limbic periarchicortical proisocortex and is currently conceptualised as an extension of the limbic system (Sanides, 1970). Its functions are mainly related to both the intention to perform a motor act (Kurata, 1992) and speech initiation (Goldberg, 1985). Broadly defined as "one of the rare universally connected areas of the brain" (Kornhuber & Deecke, 1985), the supplementary motor cortex projects bilaterally to the striatum, anterior cingulate cortex, and frontal lobe (BA 4, 6, and 8) and receives information from all these structures, but not from the striatum (Damasio & van Hoesen, 1980). The SMA is also regarded as a cortical area of sensory convergence and it receives major connections from the primary sensory cortex (BA 3, 1, 2) and secondary somatosensory (SII) areas as well as from the posterior parietal association cortex (BA 5 and 7) (see Goldberg, 1985).

Knowledge on the role of the SMA in speech and phonatory behaviour comes from the pioneering studies of electrical brain stimulation in conscious epileptic patients carried out by Penfield and colleagues (Penfield & Roberts, 1959; Penfield & Welch, 1951) and others (Brickner, 1940; Erickson & Woosley, 1951). Stimulation of the SMA on either hemisphere induces long, drawn-out vowels, palilalic repetition of syllables, or meaningless combinations of syllables, but not forced emission of meaningful phrases. Speech arrest, hesitation, or slowing in the overall rate of speech are also observed after SMA stimulation, sometimes accompanied by bilateral mouth movements. Electrical stimulation experiments carried out in epileptic patients with intractable seizures (Fried et al., 1991;

Penfield & Welch, 1949) and functional neuroimaging studies with positron emission tomography in normal subjects (Colebatch, Deiber, Passingham, Friston, & Frackowiak, 1991) both suggest that the SMA is somatotopically organised in a rostral-caudal direction with the upper limb (arm–hand area) located caudal to the face area and rostral to the lower limb (leg–feet area) representation (Kurata, 1992). While various complex and sequential motor movements are located in lower and upper limb areas of the SMA, speech-related phenomena (e.g. vocalisations) only occur in sites rostral to the SMA face area (Fried et al., 1991; Penfield & Welch, 1951).

Vocalisations can also be elicited with stimulation of the anterior cingulate cortex at the level of the genu. Jürgens and von Cramon (1982) found that all cortical areas related to vocalisation in the primate brain receive afferent projections from the anterior cingulate cortex. In addition, these researchers suggested that the principal role of the anterior cingulate region is not the phenomenon of vocalisation itself, but instead the maintenance of an adequated threshold for vocalisations generated in any portion of the neural network. Thus, the SMA and the cingulate cortex seem to conform to a system that plays a supervisory role in speech and phonatory functions, particularly in volitive aspects of communication (Alexander et al., 1989). In support of this hypothesis, experimental studies on the monkey brain using horseradish peroxidase have shown strong reciprocal connections between the SMA and the anterior cingulate gyrus (Benjamin & van Hoesen, 1982). Dysfunction of these frontal-limbic connections is probably crucial for the occurrence of mutism and difficulties in speech initiation in classical cases of TCMA secondary to lesions of the left SMA (Alexander et al., 1989) to the extent that some authors consider this type of TCMA as an example of "limbic aphasia" (Rubens & Kertesz, 1983, p. 253).

Although the SMA and the anterior cingulate gyrus are interconnected cortical regions, some neurobehavioural manifestations (e.g. akinesia) associated with TCMA and DA seem to be more related to damage of the cingulate gyrus and its discrete subcortical projections than to the involvement of the SMA itself. Tonkonogy and Ageeva (1961; cited in Tonkonogy, 1986 as Case 7) reported a pathologically verified case of DA associated with a recent infarction in the territory of the left anterior cerebral artery. The lesion involved the white matter of the anterior cingulate gyrus showing partial extension into the SMA and the anterior part of the paracentral lobule. In the right hemisphere, there were also old ischaemic lesions involving the white matter adjacent to the wall of the lateral ventricle, the head of the caudate nucleus, and the anterior limb of the internal capsulae. Since in this case, DA coexisted with general akinesia and signs of motor aspontaneity, Tonkonogy considered the language impairment as a "secondary disorder of speech initiation due to the general akinesia" caused by the predominant involvement of the cingulate gyrus (Tonkonogy, 1986).

Additional cases of DA with similar lesion sites showing "negative" phenomena such as verbal and motor akinesia, but also featuring "positive" symptoms such as utilisation behaviour and other complex comportmental disturbances, have recently appeared in the literature (Assal, 1985; Cambier, Masson, Benammou, & Robine, 1988; Degos, da Fonseca, Gray, & Cesaro, 1993; Shallice, Burgess, Schon, & Baxter, 1989), suggesting that the anterior cingulate cortex and its subcortical projection sites (e.g. caudate nucleus) are key structures in the pathophysiology of DA associated with general akinesia. Complementary evidence comes from a second case of DA (Case 8) reported by Tonkonogy (1986). As in his previous case of DA, neuropathological examination disclosed an infarction in the territory of the left anterior cerebral artery involving the SMA, the paracentral lobule, and the upper portion of the motor and sensory strip, but in Case 8 the anterior cingulate cortex was not involved by the lesion. In Tonkonogy's opinion the lack of pathological involvement of the anterior cingulate gyrus and its subcortically connected structures most likely explained the absence of general akinesia.

Alternative explanations to account for the disturbances in oral expression of classical TCMA and DA after damage to the SMA have been offered. Since lesions in the left mesial frontal lobe may course with no overt signs of language disturbances such as paraphasias, word-finding difficulties, or agrammatism, these deficits have not been considered a true aphasia and were variously termed "partial mutism" (Brown, 1987; Damasio & van Hoesen, 1980), "aphasia without aphasia" (Luria & Tsvetkova, 1968), "Aphasia sine aphasia" (Von Stockert, 1974). A.R. Damasio and Anderson (1993) even suggested that decreased verbal output after lesions of the SMA may occur irrespective of the side of the causative lesion, since both SMAs are mainly related to affective and motor control of speech but are unrelated to linguistic processing. At first glance, this seems to be a reasonable argument, as speech disturbances have also been described in right-handed patients after lesions of the right SMA (Brust et al., 1982; Caplan & Zervas, 1978). Nevertheless, early work by Penfield and Rasmussen (1949) demonstrated that the surgical ablation of the entire right SMA produced "no speech deficits" (see further discussion in Jonas, 1981) and clinical evidence indicates that mutism after damage to the right SMA is exceptional (Brust et al., 1982).

Alexander, Benson, and Stuss (1989) went a step further with the role of SMA in communication by suggesting that there are quantitative and qualitative differences between the speech-related deficits provoked by damage to left and right SMAs. First, patients with right SMA damage may show a long-lasting and pervasive reduction of speech output, but they do not have prolonged mutism as is regularly documented after damage to the left SMA. Second, damage to the right SMA induces abnormalities in the modulation of affective prosody, namely flat emission during spontaneous prosody productions with a relative preservation of repetition of affectively laden material (transcortical motor aprosodia; Ross, 1981), whereas similar prosodic deficits are probably less frequent among nonfluent aphasic patients with damage to the left SMA and surrounding regions

(Ross, Thompson, & Yenkosky, 1997). In any case, further research on the contribution of each SMA to speech-related processes as well as to emotional aspects of communication (e.g. prosody) is needed.

Deep subcortical lesions

The advent of modern neuroimaging techniques (e.g. CT and MRI) has made possible the detection of cases featuring either the classical pattern of TCMA or DA associated with pure subcortical damage or with lesions affecting the mesial frontal cortex and deep grey nuclei (e.g. head of the caudate nucleus). Transcortical motor aphasic syndromes with clinical profiles similar to those observed after damage to the SMA have recently been reported after focal vascular lesions in the territory of the left anterior choroidal artery with damage to the posterior limb of the internal capsulae (Cappa & Sterzi, 1990) or in the distribution of the lateral lenticulo-striate arteries with damage to striatocapsular regions (Gold et al., 1997). TCMA and DA may also follow thalamic lesions (Bogousslasky et al., 1986; Cappa & Vignolo, 1979; De la Sayette et al., 1992; Jonas, 1981) or lesions involving the anterior cingulate cortex and head of the caudate nucleus (Degos et al., 1993; Shallice et al., 1989).

These subcortical structures have important connections with the SMA-anterior cingulate system, which in turn projects to the thalamus (mainly intralaminar and dorsomedial nuclei; Degos et al., 1993) and the caudate nucleus, probably through the medial subcallosal fasciculus (Naeser, Palumbo, Helm-Estabrooks, Stiassny-Eder, & Albert, 1989). Alexander and his colleagues (Alexander, Benson, & Stuss, 1989; Alexander & Naeser, 1988; Alexander, Naeser, & Palumbo, 1987) attributed these profiles of language deficits to subcortical lesions that involved the left antero-lateral subcortical white matter with or without extension of the anterior limb of the internal capsulae or the caudate nucleus and suggested that the involvement of subcortical structures interrupt important connections from the SMA and anterior cingulate gyrus to the Broca's area, thus disrupting the limbic activation of speech. Perhaps more important than the interruption of a given pathway to account for DA or other forms of subcortical TCMA is the concept that these specific anatomical regions are integral components of parallel frontosubcortical circuits (Alexander, Crutcher, & DeLong, 1990; Alexander, DeLong, & Strick, 1986) and that the selective damage of any component of the circuit system may induce cognitive (e.g. language) disorders with a relatively similar pattern of deficits (Cummings, 1993). For instance, in the case of DA by Cappa and Sterzi (1990) the lesion in the posterior limb of the internal capsulae may have decreased verbal output by interrupting pallido-thalamic and thalamo-cortical connections, whereas in the case of TCMA reported by Bogousslavsky et al. (1986) damage to the intralaminar, dorsomedial, and ventral posterior nuclei may have induced a similar deleterious effect on language production by severing connections with Broca's area.

Further evidence for the importance of subcortical involvement in DA and for the influence of damage to the frontosubcortical circuits in its pathophysiology comes from a recent study of language disorders in three patients with progressive supranuclear palsy. Two of these patients came to neuropathological study, which disclosed pronounced neuronal loss, gliosis, and neurofibrillary tangles in subcortical structures (e.g. substantia nigra, subthalamic nucleus, basal ganglia) with less severe pathological involvement of the prefrontal cortex. Based on these clinicopathological correlations, Esmonde and co-workers (1996) speculated that the initial site of pathology was centred in the subcortical structures and that the breakdown at the level of language planning and initiation that characterised the verbal output of these three DA patients most likely resulted from the disruption of frontosubcortical circuits rather than from direct frontal cortical pathology.

ATYPICAL PATTERNS

The characteristics of spontaneous speech and repetition in patients with atypical TCMA is shown in Table 3.1. Freedman et al. (1984) reported on the clinicoradiological correlations of TCMA in 15 patients. Eight (53%) of their fifteen patients had an atypical pattern of language impairment. They noted three main atypical features in this population, namely, impaired speech articulation, stuttering, and impaired auditory comprehension. Freedman and colleagues used the expression "near variant" to distinguish these atypical features from the classical pattern of TCMA. Impaired speech articulation was documented in four (27%) of the fifteen patients. Speech was characterised by "awkwardness in the production of individual phonological elements, simplification of phonological blends, or consistent nonparaphasic sound substitutions". Among this group, impaired speech articulation was accompanied by variable deficits in visual confrontation naming, writing, oral reading, and reading comprehension of lengthy and complex material. Category fluency was always severely compromised. The lesion responsible for this variant of TCMA was located in the white matter anterolateral to the left frontal horn, as in the classical form, but there was additional involvement of structures previously implicated in the control of speech articulation (Schiff, Alexander, Naeser, & Galaburda, 1983) and phonation (Jürgens, Kirzinger, & von Cramon, 1982) such as the pars opercularis, the inferior prerolandic gyrus, or the white matter deep to those regions (Fig. 3.2).

The second pattern of speech production impairment in the patients reported by Freedman and colleagues was characterised by the presence of stuttering. Three (20%) of the fifteen patients presented a clinical profile quite similar to the classical pattern, except for the presence of "involuntary repetition, prolongation, or arrest of speech sounds". One of such patients (Case 12) additionally had a mild impairment in auditory comprehension. As far as anatomical

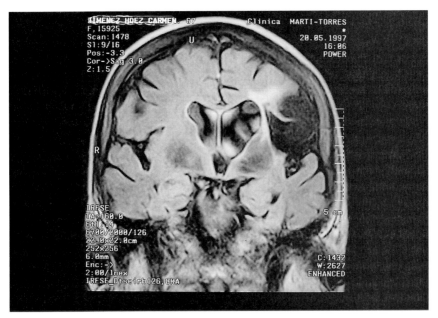

FIG. 3.2   MRI scan (coronal view) showing a perisylvian ischaemic infarction in a patient exhibiting TCMA with atypical features (dysarthria). The lesion involves the left posterior–inferior frontal gyrus (Broca's area), extending into the inferior part of the middle frontal gyrus and insular cortex. The left hemisphere is represented on the right side of the figure.

localisation of the causative lesion is concerned, all three patients had cortical lesions involving the left pars opercularis and the inferior portion of the premotor region. Freedman et al. (1984) suggested that due to the Rolandic location of the lesions, the occurrence of stuttering would be more related to aphemia (e.g. articulation impairment without language disturbances; Schiff et al., 1983) than to TCMA. On reviewing the literature on the anatomical bases of TCMA, I found that stuttering in TCMA may be associated with other localisations besides those reported by Freedman and associates. Stuttering has also been documented after infarction in the vascular territory of the anterior cerebral artery (McNabb et al., 1988, Case 1; Ross, 1980, Case 2) and in the deep territory of the left middle cerebral artery (Lanoe et al., 1994). Lanoe and co-workers (1994) recently reported a case of TCMA with atypical features including stuttering, hypophonia, semantic paraphasias, and impaired repetition of nonwords after a vascular lesion restricted to the the anterior corona radiata and centrum semiovale. A brain SPECT with Xenon 133 showed hypoperfusion of the anterior subcortical region coincident with the site of structural damage, but there was also a decrease of perfusion in the overlying anterior perisylvian language cortex area which probably contributed to the occurrence of "atypical" features.

The last "near variant" syndrome of TCMA described by Freedman and colleagues was characterised by auditory comprehension deficits. These comprehension deficits were not severe enough to classify these patients as having a mixed transcortical aphasia. Four (27%) of the fifteen patients had "deficit(s) in understanding oral verbal material at single-word or sentence-length level . . . (being) . . . most impaired on the more complex and lengthy verbal material" (Freedman et al., 1984). Two such cases (Patients 9 and 10) additionally had impaired speech articulation, whereas another case (Patient 12) also had stuttering. Auditory comprehension deficits were associated with lesions in the white matter anterolateral to the left frontal horn with lesions extending into the anterior putamen, head of the caudate nucleus, anterior limb of the internal capsulae, extreme capsulae, claustrum, external capsulae, and insula. The authors tentatively attributed mild comprehension deficits to either interrupted connections between the auditory cortex and head of caudate nucleus at the level of the internal capsulae, or damage of the short fibre tracts that connects Wernicke's area to Broca's area, in the extreme capsulae (Petrides & Pandya, 1988). Additional evidence indicates that damage to other subcortical structures such as the left thalamus (Cappa & Vignolo, 1979) may also induce TCMA with mild comprehension deficits most likely as a result of functional deactivation of posterior temporoparietal regions (Démonet, Puel, Celsis, & Cardebat, 1991).

It is interesting to note that there are some atypical cases of TCMA reported in the literature that do not fit well within the lesion sites reported by Freedman and associates. What follows is a brief summary of relevant clinicopathological details of three such patients.

Atkinson (1971)

The patient reported by Atkinson was a 38-year-old man who abruptly developed mutism and right hemiparesis. He remained speechless for the next 10 days, and then he regained a limited ability to utter single words. While some of the words were pronounced inappropriately, it was noticed that he could repeat long sentences such as "The office is on the twenty-fourth floor of the Merchant's Bank Building". On repetition tasks of the Schuell's Short Examination for Aphasia (Schuell, 1957), he correctly repeated all single syllable words (n = 22), multisyllable words (n = 10) and increasingly longer sentences. On the auditory comprehension task he identified only one of twelve pictures of objects named by the examiner and also misnamed eleven of twelve pictures of common objects. About one month later, re-evaluation with the Schuell battery revealed improvement in picture naming (11/12 correct responses) and auditory comprehension (11/12 correct recognitions). Spontaneous speech, however, remained abnormal and he was able to define only a few words ("bargain", "repair") from a list. By the next week, the deficit in spontaneous speech had improved to the extent that his utterances no longer sounded impaired. Subtle problems in the abstract use of language and concept formation including word-finding diffi-culty, poor word definition, and proverb interpretation persisted until death three months after onset.

On neuropathological examination, there was a frontal softening involving the convexity and mesial regions of the left frontal lobe. The lesion extended from the frontal and temporal poles back to the precentral sulcus in the lateral convexity and medially to the superior frontal sulcus. The frontal cortex includ-ing the Broca's area and its immediately subjacent white matter were also involved.

This case study was discussed by Harold Goodglass and the late D. Denny-Brown (see details in Atkinson, 1971). Interestingly, both experts agreed that the case contained some atypical features. Goodglass, for instance, was somewhat astonished by the fact that although the bulk of the lesion was found impinging on the Broca's area, repetition was preserved. He advanced the tentative explana-tion that "the amazing integrity of repetition in these instances depends not only on the sparing of certain structures but on the suppression of a control or inhib-itory function in other structures, to bring about a super-normal capacity to repeat" (p. 139). Denny-Brown was also struck by the fact that the patient had damage to Broca's area and he did not show the expected syndrome of phonetic disintegration. He attributed the language disorder to the effects of a hemodynamic failure that caused a circulatory insufficiency in the territory of the anterior and middle cerebral arteries. He speculated that as a result of diffuse disorder of the brain, "complex" linguistic functions (e.g. propositional speech) were impaired because they are more vulnerable than other "simple" automatic or reflex lin-guistic functions such as repetition of words and even complex sentences.

Patient O (Kertesz, 1979)

Kertesz (1979, pp. 138–142) described another case of TCMA with atypical clinico-pathological correlation. Patient O had a persistent nonfluent aphasia but he could repeat single words and phrases producing phonemic paraphasias only in complex sentences. Automatic speech was also preserved. Since he had a repetition score slightly below 8.0 (the cut-off point on the repetition subtest of the WAB that separates Broca's aphasia from TCMA) he was initially con-sidered a Broca's aphasic. In follow-up language evaluations (carried out three and nine months later), it was documented that although spontaneous speech remained nonfluent, the score in the repetition subtest had improved (7.9 and 8.0, respectively), placing him in the TCMA category.

On neuropathological examination there were multiple old ischaemic infarctions involving the left frontal lobe that resulted from an atherosclerotic occlusion of the left carotid artery and the proximal portion of the left middle cerebral artery. Gross examination of the brain revealed an extensive area of infarction that involved the inferior frontal cortex (BA 44 and 45 were partially preserved), precentral gyrus (BA 4), supplementary motor areas (BA 6, 8, and 9), and the anterior part of the superior temporal gyrus. The lesion extended superficially into the external capsulae, claustrum, and insular cortex, and deeply into the putamen and centrum semiovale, but spared the posterior superior temporal gyrus and the inferior parietal lobe. The right hemisphere did not show morphological abnormalities.

Kertesz concluded that the relative sparing of repetition makes this case atypical for Broca's aphasia, and he pointed out that the combined damage to both Broca's area and SMA explained the long-lasting course of language deficits. This case is also unusual in that a major involvement of the anterior perisylvian language zone (e.g. Broca's area, inferior precentral gyrus, insula) produced a nonfluent aphasia with a relative sparing of language repetition and not the expected typical Broca's aphasia with impaired repetition that usually follows extensive anterior perisylvian damage (Mohr, 1973). This suggests that in the chronic period Patient O probably had a reorganisation of language repetition in the intact right hemisphere (see also Chapter 7).

Racy, Jannota, and Lehner (1979)

Clinical and neuropathological findings from another case of atypical TCMA were reported by Racy, Jannota, and Lehner (1979). This case had the peculiarity that the ability to repeat was only partially preserved. The patient was a 62-year-old right-handed woman who suddenly developed nonfluent aphasia and right hemiplegia following an ischaemic infarction in the territory of the left anterior cerebral artery. The patient's history was noteworthy in that she had suffered a cerebrovascular accident 18 years earlier without residual speech problems that on autopsy was found to involve the left parietal opercular cortex and extended deeply into the subcortical parietofrontal white matter destroying the arcuate fasciculus. As a result of this combination of old and recent lesions, the "verbal output was nonfluent . . . [but] . . . she managed to complete the nursery rhymes given to her . . . [and] could correctly repeat short phrases . . . but failed on longer sentences". Serial speech was relatively preserved including recitation of the days of the week, alphabet or numbers from 1 to 20. Auditory comprehension was preserved for simple commands but she failed on more complex multiple-step commands. Reading and writing were also impaired.

The authors suggested that the last aphasic disturbance resembled only superficially the pattern of TCMA because, after the previous episode of aphasia caused by a left periopercular lesion, the language was probably reorganised in the right hemisphere rather than being mediated by undamaged left hemisphere structures. Thus, Racy and colleagues reasoned that auditory information from the left Wernicke's area was relayed through the corpus callosum to its homologous counterpart in the right hemisphere, from there to the right premotor association cortex, and finally to the left Broca's area via the anterior corpus callosum. Since the more recent lesion in the left mesial frontal lobe involved the anterior part of the corpus callosum, the authors suggested that this lesion partially abolished repetition by disrupting interhemispheric (right to left) connectivity. If this were the case, one would expect repetition being completely rather than partially impaired. Nevertheless, this patient even in the very early post-stroke period could complete open-ended rhymes and repeat short phrases well.

An alternative hypothesis that may explain the sparing of repetition of automatic speech (rhymes, serial speech, and short phrases) is that following the anterior interhemispheric disconnection this verbal material was repeated exclusively by the right hemisphere without participation of undamaged areas of the left hemisphere (Speedie, Wertman, Ta'ir, & Heilman, 1993). In support of this hypothesis, Berthier, Starkstein et al. (1991) have found in some mixed transcortical aphasic (e.g. Case 8) that after massive damage to the left perisylvian region, the isolated right hemisphere retained a limited capacity for subserving automatic aspects of language (e.g. counting days of week, and so forth), echolalia, and completion of open-ended proverbs.

Atypical patterns in patients with anomalous language dominance

Atypical patterns of TCMA may also be seen in left-handed patients with lesions involving the left perisylvian cortex. In a retrospective study of aphasia in 31 adult left-handers, Naeser and Borod (1986) classified four patients (Cases 2, 14, 19, and 20) as having an "Atypical TCM-like" pattern, because they show grammatical speech with word-finding difficulties, articulation problems with mild or moderate repetition problems and variable deficits in aural comprehension associated with lesions that mainly involved the pars triangularis and/or opercularis, lower part of the sensorimotor cortex, and periventricular white matter. A similar clinicoradiological correlation has been reported in an ambidextrous adolescent boy (Cranberg, Filley, Hart, & Alexander, 1987, Case 5). Atypical patterns may also be seen in patients with "crossed" TCMA and lesion involving the right perisylvian area (Angelergues, Hécaen, Djindjian, & Jarrié-Hazan, 1962; Tanridag & Öngel, 1989) and in individuals who presumably have a functional reorganisation of language function in either one or both cerebral hemispheres as a result of development lesions that take place before language acquisition (Lazar, Marshall, Pile-Spellman, Hacein-Bey, Young, & Mohr, 1997). A few years ago, I studied the language function, specifically word and sentence repetition, in a patient with a left frontal arteriovenous malformation (AVM) who developed TCMA during the course of a therapeutic embolisation (Berthier, unpublished observation).

The patient, AS, was a 40-year-old strongly right-handed male with 10 years of formal education without premorbid speech–language problems. He was referred to the neuroradiologist team for endovascular treatment of a serpirginous AVM that involved the Broca's area, the anterior insula, and the fronto-basal region of the left hemisphere. Before the endovascular embolisation, a brief neuropsychological evaluation showed no abnormalities in language function. Superselective angiograms and amytal injections in the major cerebral vessels feeding the AVM were performed to rule out the participation of brain areas surrounding the AVM to language processing (the amytal injection may elicit transitory—one to three minutes—clinical or electroencephalogram abnormalities if injected in an artery also supplying cortical eloquent areas) (see technical details in Berthier, Starkstein, Lylyk, & Leiguarda, 1990; Rauch et al., 1992; Viñuela & Fox, 1992). Since the injections of small dosages of diluted sodium amytal (30 mg) in major feeders did not induce either speech–language disturbances or electroencephalogram changes, the amytal test was considered negative. Unfortunately, this was an exceptional circumstance of a false negative superselective Wada test (10% of cases) (Rauch et al., 1992), since during the therapeutic embolisation procedure the patient suddenly developed nonfluent aphasia and right facial central weakness. An emergency CT scan ruled out the presence of haemorrhagic complications secondary to AVM rupture, but disclosed an extensive area of infarction involving the whole Broca's area and extending into the inferior and middle frontal gyri, anterior portions of insula, putamen, internal capsulae, corona radiata, and the head of the caudate nucleus. There was also evidence of embolic material scattered within the AVM nidus.

Formal language examination carried out two weeks after the embolisation revealed that AS's speech remained nonfluent and he could only utter echolalic or perseverative utterances (e.g. "eh-eh-eh"). Auditory comprehension was moderately impaired especially for long questions requiring a yes–no response or the execution of sequential motor acts. There was a remarkable fluctuation in the patient's comprehension deficits: he could not understand simple questions, but promptly answered some of the more complex ones. Object naming, word-list generation (animal naming), sentence completion, and responsive speech were severely affected, but his ability to repeat words and sentences was almost intact. Repetitions were performed with normal voice volume and speech articulation. In the ensuing days, repetition ability was examined in more detail. AS's performance on the digit span test was preserved, as he could repeat five digits forward in correct serial order. Repetition of lists of high- and low-frequency nouns, adjectives, verbs, and functors taken from the Frequency Dictionary of Spanish Words (Juilland & Chang-Rodriguez, 1964) was flawless. Nonword repetition was relatively preserved. Errors were few and consisted of omissions and reluctance to repeat the nonsense letter string. AS's performance on auditory lexical decisions indicated that he fairly reliably rejected nonwords (60%) and very frequently classified nonwords as real words (40%). On the other hand, he correctly classified real words as such (90%). There was no effect of syllable number in either the word or nonword that he failed to recognise. Also, there

TABLE 3.2
Patient AS: Performance on the Western Aphasia
Battery and List Repetition

Western Aphasia Battery	
Fluency (10)	0
Information Content (10)	1
Comprehension (10)	4.8
Repetition (10)	9.2
Object Naming (10)	6
Word Fluency (20)	3
Sentence Completion (10)	4
Responsive Speech (10)	4
Aphasia Quotient (100)	33.4
List Repetition	
High-frequency nouns (20)	20
Low-frequency nouns (20)	20
Adjectives (20)	20
Verbs (20)	20
Functors (20)	20
Nonwords (20)	16

was no effect of imageability or frequency in the few words that AS failed to identify on lexical decisions. The results of the WAB and list repetition are summarised in Table 3.2.

Sentence repetition was further assessed using the battery devised by Davis, et al. (1978) (see Chapter 2). The patient was required to repeat four types of sentence:

Type 1: 10 factually and grammatically correct sentences (e.g. "The dogs bark")
Type 2: 10 factually incorrect but grammatically correct sentences (e.g. "The cats neigh")
Type 3: 10 sentences that violated selection restriction rules (e.g. "The cheese ate the mouse")
Type 4: 10 sentences that violated minor syntactic rules, such as errors of number agreement (e.g. "The navigators leaves the boat"), or pronoun usage (e.g. "He gave she a present").

According to Davis and co-workers, the responses produced during sentence repetition were classified as follows.

(A) Exact repetitions.   Although in the original work of Davis et al. (1978) they used a relatively flexible classification since the production of literal paraphasias were considered exact repetitions, in the present studied a strict scoring criterion was adopted. Thus, the response was accepted as correct only when the entire sentence was repeated verbatim.

TABLE 3.3
Patient AS: Performance on Experimental Sentence Repetition Tests

Type of Response	Types of Sentence			
	Type 1	Type 2	Type 3	Type 4
Exact repetition	100	100	100	50
Corrective change	0	0	0	50
Noncorrective change	0	0	0	0
Auditory lexical decision (correct)	100	50	90	30
Auditory lexical decision (incorrect)	0	50	10	70

(B) Corrective change. This type of classification was only applicable to sentence types 2, 3, and 4. Changes in responses were used by the patients to correct ungrammatical sentences by applying different strategies such as addition, deletion, or substitution.

(C) Non-corrective change. This type of classification was used when the patient's repetitions were not exact replicas of what they heard, but the change did not render the sentence more grammatically or factually acceptable.

(D) Unintelligible sentences. Finally, clinical assessment with the WAB revealed deficits in language comprehension with difficulties in the processing of single words and sentences. Therefore, in order to investigate if errors during sentence repetition depended on deficit in auditory comprehension, AS was administered an auditory lexical decision task. The performance of AS in experimental sentence repetition and auditory lexical decision tests is summarised in Table 3.3.

AS's repetition of sentence types 1, 2, and 3 was verbatim. Syntactic errors were spontaneously corrected in half of type 4 sentences. His performance on auditory lexical decision tasks was excellent for sentence types 1 and 3, but moderately impaired for sentence type 2. Also, AS classified spontaneously corrected errors in sentence type 4 as normal, probably indicating that corrections were produced without conscious awareness. On the contrary, three of the five sentences repeated verbatim (without correction of syntactic errors) were classified by AS as anomalous. AS did not produce noncorrective changes or unintelligible responses.

Clinicoradiological correlations in AS indicate that the pattern of aphasia can be considered atypical because he had a nonfluent aphasia with impaired comprehension and preserved repetition, despite having extensive damage to the left anterior perisylvian speech area. Posterior cortical regions (e.g. Wernicke's area) traditionally linked with the processing of auditory information were largely spared in this patient. However, subcortical structures such as the anterior limb of the internal capsulae, head of the caudate nucleus, anterior putamen, external capsulae, extreme capsulae and insula, already considered responsible for the comprehension deficits among some patients with TCMA (Freedman et al., 1984), were severely damaged in AS. The exact pathophysiological mechanism under-lying poor language comprehension in AS as well as in other patients with atypical TCMA is unknown. Nevertheless, it has been suggested that damage to fibre tracts at the level of either the extreme capsulae or the anterior limb of the internal capsulae may interfere with the transmission of auditory information from the auditory cortex to the frontal lobe and caudate nucleus, respectively (Alexander, Naeser, & Palumbo, 1987). An alternative not mutually exclusive interpretation is that such patients often exhibit other behavioural problems, namely, apraxia, perseveration, inattention, or confusion of frontal lobe origin besides the decreased verbal output that could contribute to the apparent deficits in language comprehension (see further arguments in Chapter 7).

A second unexpected finding in AS was the sparing of repetition in the face of severe damage to the anterior perisylvian area and adjacent deep structures. Although severe Broca's or global aphasias should be the expected profiles of language impairment, repetition was largely spared for digits, words, nonwords, and sentences. AS repeated almost verbatim those sentences composed by gram-matically correct but factually incorrect material and those sentences that contained semantic inconsistencies. This pattern of performance has also been documented among other patients with typical TA. Moreover, evidence from other transcortical aphasics, and particularly from patient GS (a patient with TCMA who had a frontocallosal neoplasm), indicates that repetition is not always an on-line pro-cess, but also that such patients often modify grammatical errors during sentence repetition (Davis et al., 1978).

Given the growing body of evidence suggesting that damage to the left perisylvian speech area may selectively interfere with the processing of syntax in both comprehension and production tasks (Zurif & Caramazza, 1976), and based on the fact that some transcortical aphasics with extensive perisylvian damage fail to correct syntax during repetition tasks (Berthier, Starkstein et al., 1991; Mehler, 1988; Pulvermüller & Schönle, 1993), it could be anticipated that the access to syntax in AS during repetition tasks should be impaired. This was not exactly the case, however, since AS could automatically correct 50% of ungrammatical sentences during repetition, indicating that he had at least partial access to syntactic representations. Thus, it can reasonably be postulated that the anterior left perisylvian region and its adjoining cortical and subcortical struc-tures were critically responsible in AS for speech fluency but not for repetition and certain syntactic operations in production tasks. Furthermore, the fact that AS had a developmental malformation involving part of the anterior left per-isylvian area may be an indication that some linguistic functions, subserved in normal conditions by these regions, had been displaced, early during language acquisition, to other brain structures. Some support for this assertion comes from studies that examined the redistribution of higher cerebral functions among other patients with AVM.

Lazar and co-workers (1997) explored the redistribution of language functions in three patients with AVM using superselective amytal testing. Findings from one such case (patient 2) is relevant to the present discussion. This was a 47-year-old left-handed patient who developed transient aphasia due to AVM in the left temporal lobe. The AVM was surgically removed and a postoperative MRI disclosed left perisylvian damage involving the precentral and postcentral gyri and the lateral basal ganglia as well as a second, previously undetected, AVM in the right hemisphere. Superselective amytal injections in different branches of the right middle cerebral artery demonstrated variable deficits in language repetition ranging from mild impairment to mutism, whereas amytal injections in the left internal carotid artery revealed alexia but not language disturbances. Although the pattern of redistribution of cognitive functions in patients with AVM patients is often unpredictable (Lazar et al., 1997), the abovementioned data seems to indicate that residual repetition AS might be mediated by the undamaged right hemisphere.

COURSE AND PATTERNS OF RECOVERY

TCMA usually has a good prognosis (Kertesz, 1979). For instance, in Kertesz's series (1979) many patients with acute TCMA showed a complete recovery, whereas TCMA in other cases may evolve into either chronic anomic aphasia or residual speech (nonaphasic) problems. On the other hand, TCMA is sometimes observed as a chronic aphasia, since it may be the end-stage of the evolution of more severe nonfluent aphasias such as global and Broca's aphasias (Berthier, Porta, Posada, & Puentes, 1995; Kertesz, 1979). In rare circumstances, the pattern of TCMA may herald the onset of serious progressive diseases such as corticobasal ganglionic degeneration (Lippa et al., 1991), progressive supranuclear palsy (Esmonde et al., 1996), or Creutzfeldt–Jakob's disease (Shutterworth, Yates, & Paltan-Ortiz, 1985).

Among the nonaphasic residual speech problems, the most common deficit results from the persistence of word fluency difficulties, whereas deficits restricted to other aspects of communication such as prosody or speech articulation are less commonly seen. Impaired ability to generate lists of words belonging to specific letters or semantic categories may persist as the only language deficit in TCMA (Rubens & Kertesz, 1983), especially in those cases that have left frontal damage that spared Broca's area. Milner (1964) reported marked reduction of spontaneous speech characterised by a tendency to use isolated words to communicate or to respond to questions in patients who underwent surgical ablation of portions of the left frontal that spared the Broca's area. These patients did not show overt aphasia in the strict sense or decrements in verbal intelligence, but they had poor performance on tasks of verbal fluency. Subsequent studies revealed that patients with frontal lobe lesions showed greater impairment in verbal fluency tasks than do patients with lesions located elsewhere (Benton, 1968; Ramier & Hécaen, 1970) and also that left frontal lesions induced greater reduction of verbal fluency than right frontal lesions (Benton, 1968; Miceli, Caltagirone, Gainotti, Masullo, & Silveri, 1981; Milner, 1964; Perret, 1974; Ramier & Hécaen, 1970).

Reductions in word fluency performance are usually demonstrated in patients who have recovered from TCMA regardless of the cortical or subcortical localisation of the brain lesion. It has been suggested, however, that there are qualitative differences in the ability to generate word lists between patients with damage to the left dorsolateral frontal lobe (including Broca's area) and those with lesions involving the mesial aspects of the left frontal lobe (Walsh, 1985). Damage to the frontal convexity is associated with effortful productions, whereas lack of spontaneity and initiative as well as limited ability to use words at the level of abstract thinking (dynamic aphasia) usually follow lesions in the mesial aspects of the frontal lobe (Perret, 1974).

Anecdotal evidence suggest that subtle deficits in prosody and articulation can also be observed during the recovery process from TCMA. In exceptional circumstances, these deficits combine in a peculiar manner, giving rise to a foreign accent intonation (Berthier, Ruiz, Massone et al., 1991; Graff-Radford, Cooper, Colsher, & Damasio, 1986). In recent years, two patients with acute TCMA who developed the so-called foreign accent syndrome (Monrad-Krohn, 1947) have been described.

In 1986, Graff-Radford and co-workers described the case of a 56-year-old female who developed nonfluent, dysarthric, and sparse spontaneous speech, normal auditory comprehension, good object naming but poor writing in association with an ischaemic infarction that involved the left premotor region (BA 6) and the white matter antero-superior to the head of the caudate nucleus. Although clinical details on word and sentence repetition during the acute post-stroke period were not reported, the language deficit was classified as TCMA (see further discussion in Ardila, Roselli, & Ardila, 1988). Nonfluency cleared up in one month, and the patient's verbal productions were then fluent with rare paraphasic errors. Repetition, visual confrontation naming, and auditory and written comprehension were preserved but oral reading and writing were slow and laborious. The most striking feature of this case, however, was that on recovering speech fluency the patient's utterances were no longer pronounced with her premorbid midwestern accent, but with a foreign intonation. One month after the stroke onset, experimental segmental analysis of her voice revealed occasional vowel shifts (e.g. "till" ⇒ *teal*, "trip" ⇒ *treep*), grammatical errors, increased diphthongisation and tense speech posture. These phonetic misproductions were evident during spontaneous speech, repetition, and oral reading, and were associated with prolonged overall duration of speech utterances due to frequent insertion of pauses and word lengthening, improperly located emphatic stress, as well as deficits in the modulation of affective prosody during language production tasks. Graff-Radford et al. concluded that deficits in speech planning due to the left dorsolateral frontal lobe lesions were responsible for the foreign intonation.

In 1991, Berthier, Ruiz, Massone et al. reported a detailed study of foreign accent syndrome in four aphasic patients with cerebrovascular lesions. One of these patients initially had TCMA which evolved into a foreign accent syndrome during the recovery of speech fluency and communicative capacity. This patient (Case 4) was a 34-year-old right-handed woman who abruptly developed mutism without facial or limb weakness complicating a cerebral angiography. A CT scan revealed a small ischaemic infarction restricted to the posterior–superior margin of the left middle frontal gyrus. Two days later she began to utter nonsense word fragments (ma, . . . ma), and had effortful speech initiation. She automatically echoed the first words of the examiner's questions, and her repetition, though abnormal for long sentences, was better preserved than her spontaneous verbal output. Her auditory and reading comprehension were intact but writing was almost impossible. The pattern of language impairment was clinically interpreted as a TCMA. In the following weeks, language deficits greatly improved. Her spontaneous speech, however, remained moderately slow, hesitant, amelodic, and mildly dysarthric with staccato cadence. In parallel with the gradual improvement from expressive language deficit the patient developed a peculiar manner of intonation and accentuation that resembled a Slavic accent. The foreign accent resolved in three weeks along with the improvement of speech articulation. By that time, neuropsychological assessment revealed that the patient had an average intelligence (WAIS-R: verbal IQ = 96; performance IQ = 91) and a high-average memory performance (Wechsler Memory Scale, memory quotient = 113). On the language subtests of the WAB she obtained an aphasia quotient (85 points) slightly below the nonaphasic range. She had fluent spontaneous speech, which was syntactically complex and grammatically normal, but somewhat slow and monotonous. She rarely made word-finding pauses or phonemic paraphasias and had normal articulation but reduced verbal fluency (Controlled Oral Word Association Test = 20). There was no evidence of buccofacial apraxia.

Phonetic transcriptions of verbal material recorded two weeks after foreign accent remission failed to reveal abnormalities during spontaneous speech, oral reading, and repetition. By contrast, acoustic analysis of these utterances revealed a flat intonation in sentences that should be pronounced with different affective intonations (sad, happy, and angry), prolonged duration of utterances, inappropriate long pauses, and disorganised rhythm. Berthier et al. concluded that in this case of TCMA, the occurrence of a foreign accent was the consequence of a particular blend of discrete prosodic and segmental speech production deficits secondary to the damage of fronto-subcortical circuits implicated in the control of speech articulation and prosody.

Data from these two patients indicate that although language deficits in acute TCMA in general show rapid improvement, certain components of the language processing system (e.g. articulation, prosody), which cannot be properly explored in the acute stage because of the presence of nonfluency, may remain dysfunctional in the chronic stage constituting an important sequelae. Deficits in verbal planning as suggested by Graff-Radford et al. (1986) or the mixture of subtle articulatory and prosodic deficits as proposed by Berthier, Ruiz et al. (1991) may account for the rare occurrence of foreign accent among patients with recovered TCMA.

PHARMACOLOGICAL TREATMENT

Pharmacological approaches to the treatment of aphasia have shown promising results, particularly as an adjunct to speech and language therapy. Different types of drug have been reported to produce benefits, including intravenous amobarbital sodium, propranolol, d-amphetamine, and bromocriptine (see Small, 1994 for a recent review). Improvements were documented in verbal fluency, hesitation, and speech initiation and in nonverbal cognitive functions such as attention, motivation, socialisation and mood. Given that problems in initiating speech and verbal fluency are the main deficits in spontaneous speech of TCMA, pharmacological treatments using dopaminergic agonists (bromocriptine) have been performed in this clinical type of aphasia (Albert, Bachman, Morgan, & Helm-Estabrooks, 1988; Bachman & Morgan, 1988; Gupta, Mlcoch, Scolaro, & Moritz, 1995; MacLennan, Nicholas, Morley, & Brookshire, 1991; Sabe, Leiguarda, & Starkstein, 1992; Sabe, Salvarezza, Cuerva, Leiguarda, & Starkstein, 1995). All but three (Gupta et al., 1995; MacLennan et al., 1991; Sabe et al., 1995) of these studies reported improvements of language and speech deficits.

Albert and co-workers (1988) reported the first case study of pharmacological treatment of TCMA with dopaminergic agonists. These authors hypothesised that problems with speech initiation (akinesia of speech) among patients with TCMA and mesial frontal lobe damage may result from a selective disruption of the dopaminergic mesocortical projection system. Following this line of thought, they reasoned that pharmacological augmentation of brain dopamine with dopaminergic agonists such as bromocriptine (a postsynaptic dopamine agonist with affinity for D2 receptors commonly used to treat Parkinson's disease and other hypokinetic movement disorders) might help to improve the motoric aspect of language in aphasic patients. Albert and his colleagues treated a patient who had chronic TCMA secondary to a left frontal haemorrhage suffered 3.5 years before with different doses of bromocriptine (ranging from 15 to 30 mg). Semantic fluency, pause duration during conversation, response latency on visual naming, and responsive naming tasks improved during bromocriptine treatment and diminished after discontinuation of the drug.

In a subsequent study, Bachman and Morgan (1988) compared the language performance of Albert et al.'s patient while on bromocriptine with that obtained from two patients who had other types of chronic nonfluent aphasia (one had Broca's aphasia and the other had a mixed type). The authors found that bromocriptine was effective for improving speech and language performance in the patient with TCMA but no improvement was noted in patients with other clinical types of nonfluent aphasia, suggesting that dopaminergic agonists may be effective only for those patients who have nonfluent verbal expression characterised by impairments of speech initiation (Liebson, Walsh, Jankowiak, & Albert, 1994).

Similar results have recently been reported by Sabe et al. (1992) in an open-label trial of bromocriptine in seven patients with chronic nonfluent aphasia due to left hemisphere stroke lesions (but see Sabe et al., 1995 for different results). Sabe and her colleagues (1992) found that high doses of bromocriptine (15 to 60 mg/day) benefitted patients with TCMA of moderate severity, whereas severely impaired patients with either TCMA or other varieties of nonfluent aphasia did not improve. In accord with previous reports, these authors found that major areas of improvement were on spontaneous word production during the description of WAB picture, letter-controlled word fluency, pauses, and production of high-frequency words. However, in five of the seven patients bromocriptine induced painful hemidystonia on the paretic side (Leiguarda, Merello, Sabe, & Starkstein, 1993).

Other researchers reported less impressive results in the evolution of nonfluent aphasia after treatment with bromocriptine (Gupta & Mlcoch, 1992; Gupta et al., 1995; MacLennan et al., 1991; Sabe et al., 1995). After three months of bromocriptine, Gupta and Mlcoch (1992) documented that improvement was circumscribed to verbal fluency, while changes could not be demonstrated in other aspects of language function. In a subsequent double-blind, placebo-controlled study, Gupta et al. (1995) failed to obtain beneficial effects of bromocriptine on speech fluency, language content, and overall degree of aphasia severity in twenty men with chronic nonfluent aphasias, seven of whom showed a transcortical motor pattern. MacLennan and colleagues (1991), in an elegantly designed single-case study of the therapeutic effects of bromocriptine in aphasia, failed to find a beneficial effect of the drug on a patient with chronic TCMA. The design of this case included baseline measures, single-blind placebo and bromocriptine phases, and withdrawal periods. During all phases the patient was evaluated with the same test battery that included visual reaction time, measures of auditory comprehension, comprehension naming, word fluency, connected speech, and a questionnaire of communication and mood devised by the authors. There were no substantial changes in simple visual reaction time, Token Test, and on a short version of the Boston Naming Test, and only a modest improvement was documented during the placebo phase in word-fluency tasks. In connected speech there was an increase in the number of words and connected speech units produced by the patient during the bromocriptine phase as compared to the performance during placebo and withdrawal phases.

MacLennan and co-workers noted, however, that although bromocriptine increased the number of words in connected speech, there was a simultaneous increment of both informative and noninformative words. On the communication and mood questionnaire, the patient reported much improvement in questions that assess speech initiation, communicative ability, volunteer information, and interest in socialising, whereas the patient's wife reported that the patient only improved his interest in socialising with others during bromocriptine and withdrawal phases of the study. MacLennan et al. indicated that "data to support the effectiveness of Bromocriptine are weak and inconclusive . . . [and] . . . side effects are likely to occur even with low dosages". They concluded, however, that further research on the effects of bromocriptine on speech and language is warranted.

A case of dynamic aphasia treated with bromocriptine: Patient BS

Although pharmacological interventions in the treatment of aphasia are considered at present an adjunct to language therapy, current evidence suggests that some types of nonfluent aphasias characterised by a decreased drive to initiate communication such as TCMA may be amenable to pharmacological treatments. To examine the potential role of agonist dopaminergic drugs, I assessed the efficacy of bromocriptine in a patient who developed dynamic aphasia and global akinesia due to bilateral striatocapsular ischaemic infarctions.

BS was a 61-year-old woman who had two thromboembolic cerebrovascular accidents in the course of one year. The first vascular episode occurred one year before language evaluation and was characterised by transient right central facial weakness with no limb weakness or speech/language disturbances. Seven months later, BS sustained a second vascular event that caused a transient left hemiparesis but permanent "speech problems and decreased motivation". BS was referred five months later for language and cognitive evaluation because her deficits failed to improve with conventional speech therapy.

BS's past history was unremarkable, except for the presence of poorly controlled hypertension. She was a right-handed bilingual (Danish–English) retired teacher. She had lived with her husband in Malaga (Spain) for the past 10 years, residing in a small Danish community. Since she did not learn Spanish, language assessment was carried out in English.

Although BS had no motor weakness, her husband reported that since she had suffered the second stroke, she was partially dependent on activities of daily living. An interview with BS's husband revealed that she could spend almost the entire day speechless, refusing to engage in conversation, and only responded to questions with monosyllables or by moving her head. Akinesia was not limited to speech since she had reduced facial expression, body movements, and gestures during conversation. She was almost immobile most of the day and could

TABLE 3.4
Patient BS: Language Performance at Baseline and During Bromocriptine Treatment

Language Test	Max.	Baseline	Bromocriptine
Fluency	10	2	6
Information Content	10	4	7
Comprehension	10	9.3	9.5
Repetition	10	8	9
Object Naming	60	50	57
Word Fluency	20	11	18
Sentence Completion	10	10	10
Responsive Speech	10	10	10
Aphasia Quotient	100	62.4	84
Boston Naming Test	60	48	57
Letter Fluency (F.A.S.)		14	15
Connected Speech (total words in 2 minutes)		6	53

initiate motor or linguistic responses after a long delay. Her husband reported that she could perform motor acts under concentration or in response to vigorous external stimulation, but that when the stimulus was discontinued she remained motionless like a "cement block". BS also displayed low mood, social withdrawal, loss of energy, and poor concentration. On formal testing, the profile of her language impairment was classified as TCMA on the WAB (Table 3.4).

BS was alert and attentive but made no attempts to initiate conversation. Her verbal expression was nonfluent with sentences formed by no more than two or three words. Spontaneous speech was hypophonic and mildly dysarthric and lacked melody. There was a marked slowness in narrative speech. On description of the complex picture from the WAB she could only produce a few high-frequency words in two minutes (see later). During spontaneous speech and picture description, she needed continuous prompts because she stopped talking after every word. Only some of these long pauses were due to word finding difficulties. There were no phonological or semantic paraphasias. Automatic speech was considerably superior to her spontaneous verbal productions, and palilalia, echolalia, or other echophenomena were never present. Repetition of words, nonwords, and short sentences was intact. Auditory and reading comprehension were preserved. Visual naming for objects was relatively preserved but she had reduced word-list generation. Writing and oral reading were slow but normal in content. Her neurological examination failed to disclose motor weakness. An MRI scan of the head disclosed discrete infarctions involving the head and body of the caudate nucleus and its immediately adjacent white matter on the left hemisphere, whereas the right hemisphere lesion involved the head of the caudate nucleus, the anterior limb of the internal capsulae and part of the putamen (Fig. 3.3).

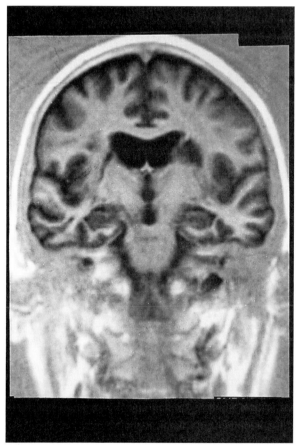

FIG. 3.3   MRI scan (coronal view) showing bilateral striatocapsular infarcts in a patient (BS) with dynamic aphasia. The left hemisphere is represented on the right side of the figure.

Based on the aforementioned studies documenting improvement in speech and language proficiency in cases of TCMA with pharmacological interventions, BS was offered treatment with bromocriptine. She was started on 1.25 mg of bromocriptine tid. The dosage was increased 1.25 mg every three days until a dosage of 20 mg was reached. In order to avoid disabling extrapyramidal side effects, dosages higher than 20 mg/day were not used. Formal language evaluations were performed at baseline and three months after the initiation of bromocriptine.

BS was administered a battery of language tests, including the language substests (information content, fluency, comprehension, repetition, and naming subtests) of the WAB (Kertesz, 1982) necessary to obtain the Aphasia Quotient

(AQ), word-fluency tasks for three letters (F.A.S.) (Controlled Oral Word Association Task; Borkovsky, Benton, & Spreen, 1967) and one semantic category (animals; Kertesz, 1982), and the 60-item Boston Naming Test (BNT; Kaplan et al., 1983). The total time for task completion was also measured. To assess connected speech, two speech samples (baseline and during bromocriptine treatment) were obtained from the spontaneous speech subtest of the WAB, including response to the first five questions and description of the complex picture (picnic scene). In the methodology described by other authors (e.g. Albert et al., 1988; Nicholas & Brookshire, 1993) speech samples were variously analysed for numbers of words, speaking rate in words per minute, number of correct information units (CIU; nonredundant content words that convey correct information about the stimulus), and percentage of CIUs (number of CIUs/number of words × 100). However, since BS did not produce redundant words, paraphasias, or perseverations during spontaneous speech, these indexes of lexical efficiency could not be examined. Finally, BS and her husband completed a questionnaire devised by MacLennan et al. (1991) to rate communicative ability, general speech, and mood. This questionnaire contained seven questions: Five of them were related to speech performance (e.g. "How often does he/she initiate conversation?") and two questions were related to mood (e.g. "How often is he/she interested in socialisation with others?). Scores ranged from 0 points (great difficulty) to 5 points (no difficulty). BS and her husband completed the questionnaire at baseline and every three weeks for a three-month period.

During bromocriptine treatment there was a considerable improvement in the overall language performance as reflected by an increment of 20 points in the AQ of the WAB. As expected, there were no substantial differences between baseline and drug period in the score of comprehension, responsive naming and completion phenomenon subtests of the WAB, most likely due to ceiling effects. Thus, it seems that the increment in AQ scores exclusively relied on the amelioration in subtests of verbal expression. BS demonstrated a considerable improvement in speech fluency and narrative capacity. Before treatment she could pronounce only six words in a two-minute period, whereas during bromocriptine treatment there was a marked reduction in response latency, hesitation, and pauses, and the number of words increased substantially. The following are examples of speech generated by BS during the description of the complex picture of the WAB at baseline and 12 weeks later while she was on bromocriptine.

Baseline.   "A house . . . and a family . . . boy" (120 seconds).

On bromocriptine.   "Is a family . . . on vacation . . . he is reading and she is drinking . . . and there's a boy who's playing with a dog . . . a boat with some people . . . and . . . a . . . a little boy who's playing and . . . there's a house . . . a car . . . I think . . . the people have a radio with . . . and they are sitting . . . on a mantle" (120 seconds).

Performance on visual confrontation naming tasks also improved as was demonstrated on the object-naming tasks of the WAB and BNT. Not only did BS improve on the number of pictures correctly named, but she also reduced the time to complete the BNT from 11 minutes in the baseline assessment to 5 minutes in the follow-up evaluation while she was on bromocriptine. At baseline, she had a long delay in her responses, and was sometimes also consumed with anomic pauses. On re-evaluation 12 weeks after starting bromocriptine, hesitancy, delay in responses, and pauses due to word-finding difficulty decreased. While these speech-timed measurements improved with pharmacological treatment, there were no important changes in BS's performance in word-list generation, as letter and category fluency tasks were essentially unchanged after bromocriptine treatment. Analysis of the communication and mood questionnaire showed that at the baseline, BS judged her own speech and mood as being more severely affected than her husband. Both agreed, however, that BS had great difficulties in oral communication, showing mainly problems in initiating conversation, effortful emissions, and poor motivation and socialisation. Four weeks after starting bromocriptine, both of them reported a considerable improvement and there was almost complete agreement on most items. Unfortunately, assessment of language, cognition, and motivation off bromocriptine could not be examined.

Bromocriptine treatment in BS favoured speech initiation, voice volume, production of content words, motivation, and social interaction. Considerable improvements in linguistic, motivational, and affective domains were obtained with low doses of bromocriptine (20 mg/day) and there were no side effects. Although post-withdrawal testing could not be done to rule out the placebo effect, it should be noted that features of DA and motivational deficits in BS had been unchanged during at least the five months previous to starting bromocriptine treatment. Interviews with her husband, consultant neurologist, and speech therapist confirmed that deficits had remained largely unchanged since the second cerebrovascular event. In addition, post-withdrawal testing is not always a reliable method to assess the drug effect among those treated with bromocriptine. In this context, Powell, Al-Adawi, Morgan, and Greenwood (1996) recently noted that brain-injured patients with motivational deficits of the kind documented in BS often continued enjoying the beneficial effects of low doses of bromocriptine (10 mg/day) on motivation and cognitive function (e.g. word span, verbal fluency) even after the drug was withdrawn.

The question that now arises is through which mechanism(s) bromocriptine exerts its beneficial effects on language, cognition, and motivation in BS? It has been suggested that the favourable effect of bromocriptine in nonfluent aphasia is only appreciable in patients exhibiting a transcortical pattern and improvements were indeed noted in measures of verbal output typical of the nonfluent transcortical syndrome, such as hesitancies and impaired initiation of speech (Albert et al., 1988; Bachman & Morgan, 1988; Sabe et al., 1992). Since patients with TCMA or DA usually have lesions in the left mesial frontal lobe (e.g. Costello & Warrington, 1986; Ross, 1980) or in its subcortically connected regions (Cappa & Sterzi, 1990; Gold et al., 1997; patient BS), it could be argued that these distinctive verbal output deficits may be caused by the interruption of mesocortical dopamine system at deep subcortical level or in its projection cortical target areas. Deficits in initiation, planning, and monitoring goal-directed responses after brain damage have been attributed to selective disruptions of mesolimbic and mesocortical dopamine systems and considerable amelioration occurred with low doses of bromocriptine (Powell et al., 1996). Analysis of lesion sites in the MRI scan of BS disclosed bilateral striatocapsular lesions (caudate nucleus, putamen periventricular white matter, and internal capsulae) that were well suited to disrupt the dopaminergic modulation of parallel frontal-subcortical circuits. The caudate nucleus component of these lesions may have damaged connections with the anterior cingulate gyri which in turn is reciprocally linked with the SMA on one side and with the ventral (limbic) striatum on the other (Cummings, 1993; Degos et al., 1993). The anterior cingulate gyrus-caudate nucleus complex together with the SMA constitute a system that probably plays a role in the initiation of motor and language routines including volitive aspects of speech and language (Alexander et al., 1989; Degos et al., 1993). Limbic influences, important in the initiation and energising necessary to maintain speech and language, may also depend upon the integrity of connections within the frontal-subcortical circuits (Alexander et al., 1989; Cummings, 1993; Damasio & van Hoesen, 1980; Sanides, 1970). Therefore, bromocriptine might have improved DA and decreased motivation in BS by augmenting dopaminergic activity within the components of the prefrontal-subcortical circuits.

CHAPTER FOUR

Transcortical sensory aphasia

INTRODUCTION

The syndrome of transcortical sensory aphasia (TCSA) is characterised by fluent spontaneous speech, and impaired auditory comprehension in the presence of preserved repetition (Albert el at., 1981; Goldstein, 1948; Lichtheim, 1885). Other language deficits (poor naming, preserved oral reading with impaired reading comprehension, and so forth) are, in general, integral components of the syndrome, but their presence is not essential to establish the diagnosis. In this chapter I will first discuss the clinical characteristics of TCSA. The emphasis is on differences in the patterns of verbal production and reception of language. The second part of this chapter discusses the neural substrate of TCSA; the first part of this section is dedicated to describing the association of the syndrome with focal brain lesions, whereas in the second part I will comment on the occurrence of TCSA in the context of progressive dementing illness (e.g. Alzheimer's disease). Near the chapter's end I will consider dissociation of language functions by reviewing data from some TCSA patients studied using the cognitive neuropsychological approach. I will conclude with a description of a special subtype of TCSA which is characterised by the preservation of word retrieval during confrontation naming in the presence of impaired name recognition of the same targets.

CLINICAL CHARACTERISTICS

Most studies have described the spontaneous speech component of TCSA as fluent but irrelevant without content due to verbal paraphasias. However, the disorder in the verbal output of transcortical sensory aphasic patients is not so simple, since it may take several different forms. Subtypes of oral expression have been described (Kertesz et al., 1982) and characterised depending on the type of errors (e.g. anomia, semantic paraphasias). It should be noted that although word-finding difficulties, phonological paraphasias, neologisms, and semantic paraphasias may coexist in the same patient (Lesser, 1989; Martin & Saffran, 1990), dissociations in the type of paraphasias that are produced during oral expression (spontaneous speech and naming) are not uncommon, to the extent that some researchers have attempted to correlate errors produced during fluent verbal productions with specific lesion sites (Cappa, Cavallotti, & Vignolo, 1981; Kertesz et al., 1982) (see later).

The most common pattern of verbal expression is perhaps represented by so-called "semantic" or "verbal" jargon (Alajouanine, Lhermitte, Ledoux, Renaud, & Vignolo, 1964; Kertesz, 1982; Lecours, Osborn, Travis, Rouillon, & Lavallée-Huynh, 1981), although some authors view it as a relatively rare form of jargon that occurs in some TCSA patients (Ryalls, Valdois, & Lecours, 1988). Although the syndrome of TCSA was not included in Head's nomenclature, on describing the semantic defects in oral expression of such cases, he stated: "These patients tend to talk rapidly as if afraid of forgetting what they wanted to say; at times this actually occurs and the conversation tails away aimlessly" (Head, 1926, pp. 257–268). A similar phenomenological observation has been more recently described by Kertesz (1982) who noted that these patients may appear more talkative than usual to the extent that pressure to keep talking may be observed in some. As a rule the meaning of utterances is lost due to the inclusion of numerous paraphasias, though articulation and intonation remain largely spared. Verbal output in semantic jargon consists of the frequent utilisation of proper words which are misused (Kertesz & Benson, 1970). The patient may substitute the target word (e.g. "cat") by another word that is semantically related (e.g. "dog") or by others without obvious semantic relatedness to the target word (Ryalls et al., 1988). Verbal paraphasias are also abundant and semantically correct verbs may be replaced by imprecise ones (e.g. "to be", "to have", "to put") or by the nonsense utilisation of predilection verbs (e.g. "to arrive", "to obtain"). Circumlocutions are frequent and they are filled with semantically weak adverbs (e.g. "exactly", "precisely") (Lecours & Rouillon, 1976).

Lecours and Rouillon (1976) stressed the presence of semantic jargon during conversation as the most characteristic feature of this subtype of TCSA and noted that there is a qualitative reduction in the utilisation of content words with recurrence of lexical segments within the same sentence, thus conferring the impression of "vagueness" and "emptiness". Sometimes the utilisation of predilection words and coined expressions are the only precise lexical segments recognisable in sentences. In the case that some lexical variety is achieved within the sentence, Lecours and Rouillon noted that the content of the sentences is always irrelevant. What follows is the transcription of a sentence produced by a patient with TCSA while discussing issues about ex-President Nixon's election (Lecours & Rouillon, 1976, pp. 132–133). (Note that, although some lexical variability is present, it does not guarantee a coherent meaning.)

> We took care of the internal part and we realized that, everywhere else, they put little peddlars and they were able, with a jacket – no, it is not a jacket – with powder – "powders and a jacket", I was going to say – with a peddled jacket of the best powder in order to form supreme judgements.)

Patients with TCSA featuring semantic jargon productions often appear anosognosic for the inadequacy of their discourse and they may also be unaware of their logorrhea (Lebrun, 1987), in particular when the auditory comprehension deficit is severe (Lecours & Rouillon, 1976). The logorrheic production of semantically irrelevant sentences is one of the reasons for which patients with TCSA featuring semantic jargon may be, at first glance, considered to be confused or manic (Kertesz, 1982). These logorrheic productions may also superficially resemble the output of patients with glosomaniac schizophasia (Lecours & Vanier-Clément, 1976; Ryalls et al., 1988).

The second pattern of spontaneous speech often encountered in TCSA is referred to as "anomic", since the enunciated utterances are empty and circumlocutory due to impaired access to content nouns and word-finding difficulties. According to Buckingham and Kertesz (1974) anomia in TCSA is generally manifested by pauses, hesitations and the replacement of unavailable words by indefinite articles (e.g. "a"), pronouns (e.g. "anybody", "somebody"), and filler words (e.g. "things", "stuff", "guy") at those places in the syntax where the context indicates that a content word should be used. In addition, spontaneous speech may give a halting impression in the case of "anomic" TCSA, a characteristic that is often conditioned by the frequent occurrence of word-finding problems. For instance, when the transcortical sensory aphasic patient (SD), described by Buckingham and Kertesz (1974) was asked to describe a picture (representing a field with children playing, ducks in a pond, and a kite stuck in a tree), he replied using indefinite pronouns and his description was marred by pauses and word-finding problems (p. 47):

> Well, find a couple of kids there playin' . . . there . . . playin' games . . . normal kids playing, I guess. This one guy (pointed to the duck) is – uh – . . . he's – uh – playing game with something and – uh – probably somebody else . . . He's got his kite in the . . .

A second case of TCSA (patient GC) briefly described by Buckingham and Kertesz (1974), produced pauses after the indefinite article "a" probably in an attempt to search for the correct word and used indefinite pronouns and short words as indefinites during the description of the same picture (p. 47):

There's a girl . . . and she's looking at a drawing or a . . . I guess you would call it a . . . She'd be looking after a . . . These things seem to look different. It must be the thing that's buggering me up.

Anomia during spontaneous speech in TCSA may be punctuated by the occasional occurrence of semantic paraphasias. This results because word-finding difficulties and anomia in TCSA regularly arise at the semantic level. In this subtype, semantic paraphasias are not prominent and may be selective for certain semantic categories (Goodglass et al., 1986), that is, such patients can name target nouns in some semantic categories but not in others.

Other patterns of spontaneous speech do exist in TCSA, but are less known. In my opinion, such patterns have been explored in less detail than the abovementioned subtypes because some of them are exceptional, as occurs in the so-called "transcortical sensory aphasia with relatively spared spontaneous speech and naming" (Heilman et al., 1981; patient AND in Kremin, 1986) (for further details see later), or because these patterns of spontaneous speech occur in cases of TCSA associated with lesions involving either the thalamus, putamen, striatocapsular region, or periventricular white matter. Since many authors (Basso, Della Sala, & Farabola, 1987; Cambier, Elghozi, & Graveleau, 1982; Crosson, 1985; Glosser, Kaplan, & LoVerme, 1982; Puel et al., 1984; Wallesch et al., 1983) state that subcortical aphasias had atypical language patterns that do not correspond to those associated with classical aphasic disorders due to cortical damage, this perhaps aroused less interest by researchers for the study of verbal output patterns. Despite the degree of phenomenological variability reported in subcortical aphasia (see Nadeau & Crosson, 1997 for review), the pattern of language impairment in some patients with subcortical lesions, whether of putamenal or thalamic origin, may resemble the profile of traditional aphasias including TA (Bogousslasvky et al., 1986; Cappa & Vignolo, 1979; Démonet et al., 1991; McFarling, Rothi, & Heilman, 1982). In general, the characteristics of spontaneous speech in subcortical TCSA include unintelligible, mumbling jargon speech in severe cases. Logorrheic speech with empty and/or paraphasic utterances supervene during evolution or is *de novo* presented in less severe cases. Hypophonia, mild dysarthria, echolalia, perseverations, and anomia with semantic paraphasias are almost constant elements of abnormal verbal expression.

The deficit in auditory comprehension is another component necessary to establish the diagnosis of a TCSA. Auditory comprehension is broadly described as "fragile" and "context-dependent" (Albert et al., 1981), but comprehension deficits are not as marked as those of Wernicke's aphasia, although cases featuring severe word-deafness are not exceptional (Bramwell, 1897; Goldstein, 1948; Lichtheim, 1885). On the other hand, patients with mild deficits in auditory comprehension have occasionally been grouped under the headings of "semantic aphasia" (Head, 1926; Hier et al., 1980) or "acoustic-amnesic dysphasia" (Luria, 1970).

Lichtheim (1885) considered that the fundamental deficit underlying poor comprehension in TCSA was due to the interruption of commissures linking the centre of auditory images with concept centre, rather than due to damage of these centres themselves, whereas others interpreted impaired comprehension along with other components (abnormal spontaneous speech and naming) of the TCSA symptom-complex as resulting from damage to the speech areas (Henschen, 1920–1922). This early distinction between lesions in the speech centres *vs.* lesions in fibre tracts connecting these major speech centres has some resemblance to the present conceptualisation of deficits in comprehension in TCSA within the impaired access-degraded store dichotomy. What appears clear is that there is still some controversy regarding the functional mechanisms underlying impaired auditory comprehension in fluent aphasias. In this connection, Berndt (1988) has recently stated that several types of impairments may be implicated in different transcortical sensory aphasic patients. Patients with TCSA usually have particular difficulty understanding lexical-semantic information and in manipulating complex syntactic information provided by grammatical morphemes; they also frequently show impairments in verbal short-term memory. Moreover, the coexistence of other linguistic deficits, sometimes termed "secondary" (Davis, 1983) such as jargon speech and logorrhea with impairments affecting non-language cognitive functions such as lack of awareness of jargon, amnesia, and agnosia would also relate specifically to auditory comprehension deficits usually observed in patients with TCSA (Alexander, Hiltbrunner, & Fischer, 1989; Kertesz et al., 1982; Lebrun, 1987).

This clinical evidence would lead one to postulate that impaired auditory comprehension nearly always results from the combination of various linguistic and nonlinguistic cognitive deficits (see Schulte & Brandt, 1989). But it is also true that qualitative differences in the type of auditory comprehension impairments in TCSA have also been described. For instance, patients with "semantic" aphasia (a mild form of TCSA) may display almost selective deficits in the understanding of grammatical structures (syntax) with relative sparing of vocabulary comprehension. Hier and associates (1980) reported the linguistic findings of three patients with semantic aphasia and posterior temporo-parietal-occipital haemorrhages who showed auditory comprehension deficits characterised by an extraordinary difficulty in grasping the meaning of words that embody spatial significance. All three patients failed to understand commands from part V of the Token Test (De Renzi & Vignolo, 1962), which contains the more syntactically complex commands and is the only part that includes prepositions (e.g. beside, under, behind, right, left, and so forth), and they also did poorly on the Logical–Grammatical Sentence Comprehension test (Wiig & Semel, 1974) demonstrating difficulty in grasping temporal, spatial, and passive relationships. On the other hand, the comprehension of other single words as assessed by the Quick Vocabulary test (Ammons & Ammons, 1962) was intact even for some low-frequency items (e.g. crystallised, saccharine, immature). Dissociated performance between the comprehension of syntax and lexicon was tentatively correlated by Hier and co-workers with distinct linguistic mechanisms presumably represented in different brain regions. Thus, the sparing of left temporal lobe sites accounted for the preservation of understanding of lexical units, whereas difficulties in understanding the grammatical structure of a sentence was interpreted as being related to focal damage to the temporo-parieto-occipital junction (Hier et at., 1980; see also Head, 1926; Luria, 1970).

Disturbances in auditory comprehension in cases of TCSA may be selective for the understanding of single words (McCarthy & Warrington, 1987; Warrington, 1975). Pure deficits in single-word comprehension, manifested by failures to correctly extract the meaning of objects and words are rare (see Hart & Gordon, 1990), since concomitant impairments in tasks assessing input phonological processing such as auditory lexical decision, where the patient is asked to distinguish real words from nonwords (lexical decision), are commonly seen (Lesser, 1989). When presented in isolation, deficits in single-word comprehension are seen in establishing synonym judgements (e.g. the ability to distinguish words that nearly have the same meaning—*gas* and *motor*) and categorical judgements (e.g. the ability to decide if pairs of words belong to the same semantic category or not—a *car* and a *bicycle*). Deficits are also seen in naming objects and living things from verbal definitions and in making property judgements by providing subordinate information (size, colour, and function) of objects and animals (e.g. "What has the same colour as a *skunk*—a *penguin* or a *pig*?" (Berndt et al., 1987; Hart & Gordon, 1990).

While the nature of pure deficits in word comprehension has been conceptualised as reflecting either selective impairments in the access to the semantic representations of words or, alternatively, degraded information in the central semantic store (Heilman, 1985; Heilman et al., 1981; Warrington, 1975), there are few studies in TCSA that have attempted to identify the level at which the processing of lexical-semantic comprehension is disrupted (Berndt et al., 1987; Martin & Saffran, 1990; McCarthy & Warrington, 1987; Schwartz et al., 1979; Warrington, 1975).

The contrast between deficits reflecting a breakdown in semantic knowledge itself and others due to impaired access to semantic representations has been explored in group studies and individual-case studies of patients with various cognitive disorders (see Shallice, 1988 for review). A number of operational criteria to differentiate one from the other have been suggested (Warrington, 1981; Warrington & McCarthy, 1983; Warrington & Shallice, 1979; for further discussion and criticisms see Caplan, 1987, 1992; Rapp & Caramazza, 1989). Selective impairments in single word comprehension due to "degraded store" disorders are characterised by: (1) poor effect of priming (cueing or prompting) to facilitate comprehension; (2) consistency of the success or failure to identify specific target words or pictures over testing sessions; (3) sensitivity to word frequency with poor recognition of low-frequency items but better recognition of high frequency items, since the former are probably more susceptible to deterioration due to less redundantly stored semantic representations; and (4) retention of superordinate categorical information because this type of knowledge is stored more firmly than subordinate attribute information.

Individual-case studies of patients who had single-word comprehension deficits attributable to a "degraded store" were first reported by Warrington (1975) under the heading of "selective impairments of semantic memory". She studied three patients with progressive dementing illness and linguistic deficits consistent with a subclass of TCSA that is characterised by difficulty finding words, impoverished vocabulary, good repetition of words (irrespective of whether their meaning is either lost or retained), and comprehension deficit selective for single words. Some findings from oral production tasks in two such patients (AB and EM) illustrate this topic. During a word definition task presented on two occasions seven months apart, EM showed a consistent pattern of performance in responding, since those words she was unable to define in the first evaluation were also unavailable to her in the second session. In addition, as a result of the progressive course of illness, both patients gradually lost information about individual objects and animals. This breakdown, however, was not widespread; it first affected the more vulnerable subordinate information of an item retaining the less fragile superordinate knowledge. When AB was, for instance, asked to define words like *hay*, *trumpet*, *needle*, and *cottage*, he replied "I've forgotten" or "No idea". Conversely, verbal definition of words whose meaning was spared like *supplication*, elicit the succinct yet accurate response "making a serious request for help" (Warrington, 1975; see also Shallice, 1988). The performance of AB and EM on defining the meaning of words was also heavily influenced by word frequency (high-frequency words were defined more accurately than low-frequency words).

Further studies in this class of TCSA, which examined the effect of cueing by means of sentence fragments (e.g. completion of open-ended sentences), found that words and proverbs, but not series speech (numbers, days of the week) had degraded semantic representations (Nakagawa et al., 1993). Lexical-semantic comprehension deficits were also interpreted in terms of a degraded store in other patients with TCSA because some operational criteria (consistency, word frequency, depth of processing) were met (Hodges et al., 1992; McCarthy & Warrington, 1987, patient NHB; Snowden et al., 1989).

The criteria for diagnosing "access" disorders, on the other hand, include: (1) priming and cueing facilitate the comprehension of the target word; (2) inconsistent performance in target recognition over testing sessions; (3) irrelevance of word-frequency for target recognition and less marked variability of frequency function than that usually evidenced in normal subjects; and (4) grasping of superordinate information of the target over subordinate information as occurs in cases with degraded store, although in this circumstance the recognition of superordinate information facilitates the access to its attributes. Finally, the rate of stimulus presentation as an additional criterion was proposed by Warrington and McCarthy (1983) to establish the diagnosis of access disorders. They noted that the introduction of an interval between the patient's response and the forthcoming stimulus presentation may improve performance.

The fact that patients with TCSA had deficits involving both comprehension and production has been taken as evidence of degraded information for that item in the semantic store. By contrast, cases of TCSA with lexical-semantic comprehension deficits due to "access" disorders may exhibit dissociation in performance between production and comprehension. Patients with TCSA featuring either "word-meaning deafness" (Bramwell, 1897) or the pattern of relatively spared spontaneous speech and naming (Heilman et al., 1981; Kremin, 1986) are good examples of this type of dissociation. These patients show relative sparing of spontaneous speech, repetition, word retrieval in naming tasks, and reading comprehension, thus suggesting that most components of the language processing system, in particular the semantic store and phonological output lexicon, are intact (Ellis & Young, 1988), but auditory word recognition is grossly impaired. The pattern of dissociation between "good" production and "poor" comprehension has been interpreted as a "unidirectional disconnection" or "dissociation" between intact phonological input lexicon and the semantic system (Ellis, 1984; Heilman et al., 1981; Kohn & Friedman, 1986). In the following sections of this chapter I will consider these disorders again, and I will also provide some data supporting the interpretation of these kinds of comprehension deficit in TCSA as access disorders.

THE NEURAL SUBSTRATE

Focal brain lesions

Posterior cortical lesions

The syndrome of TCSA has been generally associated with focal lesions in the left temporo-parieto-occipital junction, just posterior to Wernicke's area (Alexander, Hiltbrunner, & Fischer, 1989; Benson, 1988, 1993; Bogousslavsky & Regli, 1986; Buckingham & Kertesz, 1974; H. Damasio, 1991; Heilman et al., 1981; Kertesz et al., 1982). In a study of lesion localisation in 15 TCSA patients using CT and isotope brain scans, Kertesz et al. (1982) found two different cortical localisations. The most common lesion site for TCSA (n = 12) was in the areas covering the left parieto-occipital region and the occipito-temporal fasciculus but sparing the calcarine cortex. The major area of involvement in such cases was medially placed affecting the temporo-occipital region. All these lesions were of vascular origin and resulted from perfusion defects in the territory of the posterior cerebral artery or in the border-zone area between the middle and posterior cerebral arteries. This lesion localisation has been replicated in subsequent studies (Alexander, Hiltbrunner, & Fischer, 1989; Servan, Verstichel, Catala, Yakovleff, & Rancurel, 1995). In a smaller number of patients (n = 3), Kertesz and his colleagues (1982) found the lesions overlapping higher in the parieto-occipital convexity, a pattern of distribution that, with some variation, was also documented by other researchers (Ferro, 1984; Heilman et al., 1981; Sevush & Heilman, 1984).

H. Damasio (1991) has also described the neuroanatomical bases of TCSA. She found that the lesions usually involve either the posterior part of the middle temporal gyrus (BA 37), the angular gyrus (BA 39), or the white matter underlying these cortical regions, but sparing part or the whole primary auditory cortices (BA 41 and 42) and the posterior segment of the superior temporal gyrus (BA 22). H. Damasio considers that some overlap between TCSA and the other types of fluent aphasia (conduction and Wernicke) may really exist, but the core for TCSA occupies BA 37 in the middle temporal gyrus with variable extension into the visual association cortex and the angular gyrus. Alexander, Hiltbrunner, and Fischer (1989) agree with this lesion topography, but advance further considerations regarding the role of other structures in cases of TCSA with infarcts in the distribution of the left posterior cerebral artery. These authors propose that disturbances in semantic functions (e.g. lexical semantic comprehension, recall and recognition) may be the consequence of the involvement of the white matter underneath the temporal-occipital cortex together with the white matter periventricular to the temporal horn, including the posterior part of the temporal isthmus and the adjacent posterolateral thalamus. According to Alexander et al., this lesion topography is crucial for interrupting thalamo-cortical and cortico-cortical connections which converge in the posterior temporal association cortex (BA 37).

It seems obvious in the neuroanatomical data just reviewed that the involvement of the left superior temporal lobe (BA 41, 42, and 22) is not included in the list of cortical sites compromised in TCSA. Exceptions to the dogmatic view that the posterior perisylvian area is spared in TCSA really exist. To cite only some examples, Bastian (1887) and Goldstein (1948) considered that TCSA may also result from lesions that involved parts of the auditory word centre in the posterior temporal lobe (e.g. Wernicke's area). More recently, Kertesz, Harlock, and Coates (1979) found a patient with typical acute TCSA and a lesion involving the left Wernicke's area. Bando, Ugawa, and Sugishita (1986) also described the case of a right-handed patient with acute TCSA and a left posterior cortical ischaemic lesion that involved the Wernicke's area and its adjacent supramarginal gyrus. Moreover, some patients with TCSA, in whom language testing was carried out in the chronic period, did not have the usual lesion distribution with posterior cortical involvement sparing the Wernicke's area (e.g. Berndt et al., 1987; Martin & Saffran, 1990).

Anterior cortical lesions

Basso, Lecours, Moraschini, and Vanier (1985) described for the first time the combination of fluent TCSA with lesions of the left hemisphere that involved the anterior perisylvian language zone in two patients (Cases 18 and 19; see also Selnes, Rubens, Risse, & Levy, 1982). Subsequent cases confirmed these clinicoradiological correlations in right-handers with left hemisphere lesions (Berthier, Starkstein et al., 1991; Hadano et al., 1992; Willmes & Poeck, 1993; see further examples in Chapter 7) and in left-handers with right hemisphere lesions (Bolla-Wilson, Speedie, & Robinson, 1985; Berthier, Starkstein et al., 1991, patient 5). There is not yet a clear explanation linking anterior damage with fluent and copious spontaneous speech and poor comprehension. According to the classic language model outlined by the diagram-markers (e.g. Broca, Wernicke, and Lichtheim) and on further elaborations made by Geschwind (1965), these cases should be considered atypical because they showed fluent spontaneous speech and impaired comprehension after anterior lesions, and because language repetition was spared despite extensive damage to the perisylvian language zone. Interpretation of the cases applying a less strict reductionist framework do not seem to contradict the classical model in a straightforward fashion, but suggest a more dynamic conceptualisation of the pathophysiological mechanisms of preserved and impaired language functions in these cases. A number of factors such as diffuse representation of semantic representations, individual variability in the organisation of language networks, remote functional changes, mixed language representation, or premorbid language proficiency might account for the association between anterior lesions and TCSA (see further discussion in Chapter 7).

Deep subcortical lesions

The precise role of subcortical structures in language function is still debated and available evidence indicates that subcortical lesions may present the complete gamut of language deficits that have been traditionally described in association with cortical damage, unclassifiable patterns, or even no prominent aphasic deficits (see Nadeau & Crosson, 1997 for review). In addition, when language deficits are detected, the pattern of language impairments associated with subcortical damage is more heterogenous than the one reported after cortical involvement (Basso et al., 1987) and heterogeneity also prevails in cases with striatocapsular lesions as compared to others with thalamic involvement (Nadeau & Crosson, 1997).

Subcortical TCSA may result from striatocapsular or thalamic infarcts. The mechanism of TCSA associated with these two lesion locations seems to be wholly different. It has been repeatedly suggested that the basal ganglia (putamen and caudate nucleus) does not have a direct participation in language processes, and that after their damage language deficits would result from damage to adjacent white matter pathways (Alexander & Naeser, 1988; Alexander et al., 1987) or from remote deleterious effects (diaschisis) in the overlying cortical mantle (Demeurisse, Capon, Verhas, & Attig, 1990; Metter et al., 1986). On the other hand, some thalamic nuclei (e.g. pulvinar-LP) seem to be directly involved in language processing because they are connected with cortical language areas (Crosson, 1985; Nadeau & Crosson, 1997).

The pattern of TCSA is perhaps more commonly observed among cases with thalamic lesions than in others with striatocapsular lesions, since it has been suggested that extensive damage to the internal capsulae and basal ganglia would impair repetition due to pressure effects in the overlying perisylvian language cortex (Démonet et al., 1991; Ibayashi, Tanaka, Joanette, & Lecours, 1992; Nadeau & Crosson, 1997). This may not always be the case, since cases of TCSA associated with putamenal haemorrhages have been described, and some of them had "functional deactivation" (Cambier, Elghozi, Khoury, & Strube, 1980) demonstrated by PET scan in the entire overlying cortical mantle, probably indicating that preserved repetition was subserved by the right hemisphere (Berthier, Starkstein et al., 1991). The mechanism of TCSA after thalamic lesions may be different. Thalamic lesions may disrupt lexical-semantic aspects of language but spare its phonological and syntactical aspects (Raymer, Moberg, Crosson, Nadeau, & Gonzalez Rothi, 1997), a pattern of linguistic deficits that correlates well with the reduced perfusion found in SPECT studies involving the neural network linking the thalamus with the temporo-parieto-occipital association cortex (Démonet et al., 1991; Maeshima et al., 1992).

Diffuse and circumscribed atrophic cortical changes

Based on clinicopathological observations early authors (Henschen, 1920–1922) distinguished two main groups of TCSA: one associated with focal lesions involving the temporal lobes and another with generalised cerebral atrophy affecting predominantly the temporal lobes (Goldstein, 1948). In broad terms, this aetiopathogenic subdivision of TCSA is still valid. In fact, more recent studies on language impairment in progressive aphasia and degenerative demential have commonly encountered the pattern of TCSA among patients with Alzheimer's disease, Pick's disease, and other nonspecific forms of focal cortical degenerations.

Alzheimer's disease

Aphasia is a prominent feature of Alzheimer's disease (AD) with prevalence rates ranging from 60% (Chui, Teng, Henderson, & Moy, 1985) to 100% (Cummings, Benson, Hill, & Read, 1985) in cases without pathological confirmation, and reaching 80% in cases with a histopathological diagnosis (Price et al., 1993). In most studies, the performance on formal language tests strongly correlates with measures of cognitive decline, suggesting that the severity of language deterioration increases with the progression of dementia (Cummings et al., 1985; Hart, 1989; Selnes, Carson, Rovner, & Gordon, 1988). Although language impairment in AD is not associated with a pathognonomic clinical profile (Price et al., 1993), early dysfunction of language function usually begins with word-finding difficulty associated with other features of a fluent anomic aphasia (Appell, Kertesz, & Fisman, 1982).

It is generally held that language deficits in AD predominantly involve lexical-semantic abilities and pragmatic aspects of communication, whereas phonological and syntactic operations remain largely spared until advanced stages of the disease (Irigaray, 1973; Kemper, LaBarge, Ferraro, Cheung, & Storandt, 1993; Kempler, Curtis, & Jackson, 1987; Schwartz et al., 1979). Although various types of fluent aphasia have been described during the process of language deterioration in AD, it seems that the profile of TCSA is the most common. In a study of speech and language assessment of 30 patients with diagnoses of probable AD, Cummings and his co-workers (1985) found that through much of the course of the disease, the most consistent pattern of language deficit resembled TCSA. In support, Rapcsak, Arthur, Bliklen, and Rubens (1989) reported that five of their eleven AD patients, studied for writing difficulties, had the pattern of TCSA. Overall, AD patients featuring TCSA have fluent but empty spontaneous speech with semantic paraphasias, impaired naming and auditory comprehension, but preserved word and sentence repetition. Verbal expression is characterised by a relative preservation of phrase length, grammatical structure, and melodic contours of utterances, a pattern of spared language abilities that is also reported among patients with TCSA secondary to focal lesions of the left temporo-parietal association cortex (Albert et al., 1981; Kertesz et al., 1982; Rubens & Kertesz, 1983). However, unlike cases of TCSA secondary to focal vascular lesions, verbal expression among patients with TCSA due to AD tend to show less frequent neologistic paraphasia and echolalia. Spontaneous utterances are melodic and lack dysarthria, abnormalities of speech that are more commonly documented when TCSA occurs in the context of a multi-infarct dementia (Lesser, 1989; Powell, Cummings, Hill, & Benson, 1988).

Repetition performance in AD depends, as with other aspects of language, on what stage in the evolution of the degenerative process the linguistic skill is investigated (Hart, 1989). Repetition in mild AD is usually spared, particularly for phrases and sentences containing high-frequency words, but repetition performance is always significantly inferior to age-matched normal controls (Appel et al., 1982; Glosser, Kohn, Friedman, Sands, & Grugan, 1997; Holland, Boller, & Bourgeois, 1986). Variability in repetition performance is also more manifest in patients with mild and moderate AD than in controls, and longitudinal evolution of these patients reveals that not all show the same rate of progression in the dissolution of repetition abilities (Bayles, Tomoeda, & Rein, 1996). Moreover, several studies documented that the repetition of long sentences and others, not necessarily long but containing low-frequency items or meaningless word strings, entail great difficulty in mild and moderate AD patients (Bayles, Tomoeda, &

Rein, 1996). In support of this finding, Obler and Albert (1984, p. 248) reported that in the middle stage of the illness "these patients will have great difficulty with any low-frequency items and some difficulty with longer, high-frequency phrases beyond six words".

Patients with fluent, empty spontaneous speech and impaired comprehension, in whom repetition is only mildly impaired would be classified as having a TCSA (Cummings et al., 1985), whereas when repetition deficits prevail, the pattern of language impairment most likely resembles Wernicke's aphasia (Obler & Albert, 1984; Price et al., 1993). Automatic speech (e.g. the ability to recite overlearned verbal material) is minimally or not affected in the initial stages of AD. Patients are able to initiate series speech (counting, alphabet) without prompting but they often omit several items or produce incomplete fragments (Obler & Albert, 1984). In mid-stage AD, patients need prompts to start serial speech, and they frequently do not complete a series. Moreover, number of AD patients with TCSA also fail to complete open-ended sentences (Cummings et al., 1985).

Language comprehension is regularly impaired in AD patients with TCSA. Although the interpretation of comprehension deficits in AD is difficult because of the presence of other nonlanguage cognitive impairments such as episodic memory impairment, inadequate short-term memory, and perceptual disabilities (see Hart, 1989), mild to moderate semantic impairment may account for deficits in comprehension among AD patients (Chertkow & Bub, 1990; Diesfeldt, 1989; Grossman et al., 1996). In light of the fact that AD patients exhibit a relatively preserved comprehension of sentence syntax (Kemper et al., 1993; Kempler, Curtiss, & Jackson, 1987), deficits in comprehension appear to be selective for operations implying lexical-semantic processing (Garrard et al., 1997; Grossman et al., 1996). The semantic deficit in AD affects production and comprehension and in some patients it may selectively involve certain categories (e.g. living things) (Silveri, Daniele, Giustolisi, & Gainotti, 1991; Robinson, Grossman, White-Devine, & D'Esposito, 1996).

The transcortical profile of language deficits in AD has been associated with a specific distribution of histopathological changes in the posterior temporal-parietal-occipital association cortex (Chui, 1989). Functional brain imaging in AD patients with aphasia, alexia, and agraphia document metabolic changes in posterior association areas, which are believed to be critical for lexical-semantic operations. Conversely, metabolic activity in the central perisylvian language zones, necessary for syntax and phonological processing is relatively spared. While the diagnosis of AD must be suspected in cases of slowly progressive TCSA with or without associated dementia, cases of progressive dementia with features of TCSA have been reported in patients with AD and atypical localisation of neuropathological changes (Benson, Davis, & Snyder, 1988; Levine, Lee, & Fisher, 1993) as well as in cases with non-Alzheimer forms of dementia (Hodges et al., 1992; Neary, 1990; Snowden et al., 1989).

Posterior cortical atrophy

In 1988, Benson et al. described a progressive dementing illness characterised by neurological and neuropsychological deficits indicative of dysfunction of
posterior cortical association areas. These patients showed initial alexia, visual
agnosia followed by elements of Balint's and Gerstmann's syndromes as well as
by constructional apraxia, spatial disorientation, and TCSA. While visual problems are prominent early in the course, memory function, general behaviour, and
language may be relatively preserved for months (Victoroff et al., 1994, Case 3)
or years (Croisile et al., 1991). Since three of the five patients in Benson et al.'s
original series had radiological evidence of degenerative cortical changes, they
coined the terms "posterior cortical atrophy" (PCA; Benson et al., 1988) or
"progressive posterior cerebral dysfunction" (Victoroff et al., 1994) to name this
syndrome, whereas other researchers preferred the term "progressive biparietal
atrophy" (Mackenzie Ross et al., 1996). Given that disorders of complex visual
processing are prominent symptoms early in the illness in a patient who was
found to have histopathological changes typical of AD, some neurologists
described this syndrome as a "The visual variant of Alzheimer's disease" (Levine
et al., 1993).

Language impairment typically starts with word-finding difficulty in the presence of intact auditory comprehension and repetition. By this time, spontaneous
speech though fluent may be punctuated by anomic pauses and semantic paraphasias (Victoroff et al., 1994). Echolalia may also be present during the anomic
phase (Berthier, Leiguarda, Starkstein, Sevlever, & Taratuto, 1991). Confrontation naming is severely compromised but other naming modalities are preserved
and can be the only available channel for object recognition. As the disease
progresses, the pattern of language impairment is consistent with a TCSA. Spontaneous speech, though fluent, may sound paraphasic, and perseverations and
echolalia may get worse. Auditory comprehension deficits become evident and
anomia worsens but word and sentence repetition remain relatively preserved.
Later on in the clinical course, impairments in the phonological aspects of language and auditory–verbal short-term memory are often prominent, most likely
reflecting the extension of pathology from the inferior and superior parietal
lobes to the adjacent perisylvian language areas (Mackenzie Ross et al., 1996).

Neuroimaging studies with CT and MRI scan reveal selective atrophy of
posterior parietal cortical areas with gross sparing of mesial temporal lobe structures (hippocampus) (Berthier, Leiguarda et al., 1991; Mackenzie Ross et al.,
1996). Functional brain imaging with SPECT and PET performed in a few cases
demonstrated a decrease of metabolism in the temporo-parieto-occipital junction
areas (Benson et al., 1988; Croisile et al., 1991), an anatomical localisation that
has been implicated in cases of TCSA associated with focal lesions (Kertesz
et al., 1982; Rubens & Kertesz, 1983). Atrophic changes in the cerebral cortex
may be asymmetric. Metabolic studies in cases with early visuospatial impairment

(e.g. topographical agnosia, dressing apraxia) have shown more marked hypo-metabolism in the right temporo-parieto-occipital cortex (Croisile et al., 1991), whereas cases featuring initially visual agnosia and TCSA have a predominant involvement of the left hemisphere (Kertesz, 1993; Kertesz, Polk, & Kirk, 1992). One of these TCSA cases (Patient MF; in Kertesz et al., 1992) exhibited a marked dissociation of language functions with preservation of phonological and syntact-ical aspects of language (verbal production and repetition) and selective impair-ment of those linguistic functions dependent on visuoverbal semantic processes such as naming, description of visual and auditory stimuli, categorisation, and comprehension.

While the constellation of well-defined cognitive deficits secondary to poster-ior cortical dysfunction makes PCA a clinically homogeneous syndrome (Benson et al., 1988; Mackenzie Ross et al., 1996), brain biopsies and pathological exam-ination of postmortem brain tissue showed a variety of underlying pathologies. Few cases have come to neuropathological examination, yet the histopathological diagnosis was different in most of them. Alzheimer's disease was the most com-mon diagnosis (Berthier, Leiguarda et al., 1991; Levine et al., 1993; Mackenzie Ross et al., 1996; Victoroff et al., 1994), whereas other neuropathological dia-gnoses such as progressive subcortical gliosis (mainly involving the white matter of the parieto-occipital regions), and Creutzfeldt–Jakob disease (Heidenhain vari-ant) were carried out in the remaining patients. In summary, symptoms of TCSA are more likely to occur in relationship to other cognitive deficits indicative of pathological involvement of posterior cortical association areas. While this clinicopathological correlation is usually due to AD, it should be noted that progressive TCSA can also be observed in typical cases of AD with widespread generalised atrophy as well as in cases of temporal and frontotemporal "semantic" dementias associated with either no distinctive histopathology or changes typical of Pick's disease (Hodges et al., 1992; Snowden, et al., 1989).

Semantic dementia

The term semantic dementia (SD) has recently been introduced by Snowden et al. (1989) to describe a dementing illness characterised by a progressive breakdown of semantic knowledge involving language, memory, and object recog-nition. The first description of this condition was by Warrington (1975) who reported three patients exhibiting slowly progressive anomia with impaired word comprehension and preserved repetition under the heading "selective impair-ment of semantic memory". Hodges and his colleagues (Hodges, Patterson, & Tyler, 1994; Hodges et al., 1992; Patterson & Hodges, 1992) recently suggested that SD is a clinically recognisable syndrome. They proposed a number of clin-ical criteria for its diagnosis, including the following: (1) selective deterioration of semantic memory causing anomia with impaired lexical-semantic comprehen-sion for single words and reduced verbal fluency in different semantic categories;

(2) relative preservation of other aspects of oral production and comprehension (syntax and phonology); (3) normal visuospatial skills, frontal "executive" functions and nonverbally based problem solving; (4) relative sparing of both autobiographical and episodic memory; and (5) a pattern of oral reading consistent with surface dyslexia (e.g. better reading of words and nonwords than of irregular words).

Progressive fluent anomic aphasia may be seen in the early stages of SD. As the disease progresses, the full-blown profile of TCSA becomes apparent (Hodges et al., 1992). Spontaneous speech is fluenty effortless and syntactically correct but vocabulary is impoverished. Although a casual conversation may be judged to be normal, information content is reduced and contaminated by echolalia, repetitions and stereotyped phrases such as "You're nice, Yes, you are, very nice" (Snowden et al., 1989, Case LB, p. 176). Sometimes, spontaneous speech is described as circumlocutory due to loss of nominal terms. Verbal paraphasias are very frequent but phonological or neologistic errors are rarely heard. Automatic speech, including the recitation of nursery rhymes and completion of overlearnt material is largely preserved (patients grouped with profile B in Snowden, Neary, Mann, Goulding, & Testa, 1992) as well as repetition of polysyllabic words, sentences, and clichés (patient 5 in Tyrrell, Warrington, Frackowiak, & Rossor, 1990). Immediate digit repetition is usually preserved. Some patients also exhibited automatic corrections of syntax without comprehending the meaning of the sentences. For instance, when questioned "What do you stir your tea with?" one of the patients (SL) described by Snowden and his co-workers (1989) replied incorporating part of the question into the response "What do I stir *my* tea with?".

Loss of semantic information is not limited to spontaneous speech, since it is also documented in naming tests. Most patients are unable to name objects, digits, and body parts during either visual presentation or verbal descriptions. Naming failures are not benefited by phonological or semantic cueing. Word list generation is only mildly impaired for letter fluency (F.A.S.) but is markedly impoverished for different semantic categories. Single word comprehension (recognition) of the same targets is also abnormal and parallels the defect seen on confrontation naming. Errors in name recognition are predominantly within-category semantic confusions (e.g. "door" $\Rightarrow$ chair). Thus, patients with SD have a two-way deficit with naming and recognition being equally involved. This finding coupled with a consistent pattern of performance over testing sessions, preservation of superordinate knowledge and word frequency effect, and lack of improvement in the production or comprehension of target nouns with cueing, suggest that the locus of involvement in this type of degenerative TCSA resides in the semantic component of the word processing system (Garrard et al., 1997; Hodges et al., 1992; Nakagawa et al., 1993; Warrington, 1975).

Neuroimaging in cases of SD disclosed focal atrophy of the inferior portion of the temporal lobes with sparing of the hippocampus, and functional neuroimaging studies essentially confirmed this lesional topography (Hodges et al., 1992). However, lack of correlation between visible zones of cortical atrophy in CT or MRI and functional neuroimaging is not rare, since marked functional involvement of the structurally spared frontal lobes was found in two of the three patients originally described by Snowden et al. (1989). Little is known about the pathology underlying SD, as few cases have come to neuropathological examination. Available pathological data suggest that histopathological changes in this kind of circumscribed form of lobar atrophy are heterogenous, showing either nonspecific degeneration or ballooned cells and argyrophilic inclusion bodies compatible with Pick's disease (see references in Garrard et al., 1997).

DISSOCIATIONS OF LANGUAGE FUNCTION

The concept that brain damage may selectively impair certain linguistic functions but spares others as a result of lesions involving separate anatomic arrangements is not a new one (Bramwell, 1897; Kleist, 1934; Lichtheim, 1885; Symonds, 1953). During the past two decades, dissociation of performance in language testing in TCSA has also been documented in clinical (Hier et al., 1980; Kertesz et al., 1982) and psycholinguistic (Warrington, 1975) studies. Further analysis of language function in TCSA using the cognitive neuropsychological approach has revealed a number of dissociations. The most common type of language dissociation is concerned with the presence of a major breakdown in semantic but not phonological or syntactic processing. This pattern of dissociation has been demonstrated among single patients. In the following paragraphs I briefly discuss this pattern of dissociation in four patients. These TCSA patients were examined using a single-case study approach and include a case of slowly progressing dementia of degenerative origin (Patient WLP in Schwartz et al., 1979), a case of subacute multi-infarct dementia with predominant involvement of the left hemisphere (Patient TF in Lesser, 1989), and two cases of cerebrovascular accidents with ischaemic infarcts involving the left perisylvian language zone (Patient RR in Berndt et al., 1987; Patient ST in Martin & Saffran, 1990).

In these four patients spontaneous speech was fluent and clearly articulated, but frequently punctuated by anomia, circumlocutions, and phonemic and semantic paraphasias. Occasional neologisms were produced by ST and TF. Visual confrontation naming for objects and pictures was severely impaired in all four patients and, in keeping with their abnormal features in spontaneous speech, the more common errors in naming tasks included omissions, circumlocutory responses, and word substitutions that were visually similar to the target. As has been demonstrated in other patients with anomia and lexical-semantic comprehension deficits (Benson, 1988; Gainotti, 1987), these four patients did poorly on tasks requiring the matching of spoken words to pictures or objects, and in tasks that required knowledge of the meaning of words. The most common type of error in word-picture matching tasks was in discriminating the target picture from various semantically related distractors.

Repetition of words was preserved in all patients, but their performance on nonword repetition tasks was variable. Nonword repetition was faultless in TF, moderately impaired relative to word repetition in RR and ST, and not tested in WLP. Repetition of lengthy sentences was performed withour errors in WLP and TF, whereas RR and ST showed superior performance on repetition of sentences when compared to word lists (see data from patient NHB in McCarthy & Warrington, 1987 for the opposite pattern) and, in general, both patients demonstrated a preservation of syntactic structure during sentence repetition. However, in sentence repetition RR and ST appeared unaffected by semantics, since both patients repeated sentences they failed to understand although they did not reproduce the content verbatim.

While dissociations of language functions in these four patients were assessed using not exactly the same linguistic tasks, the patterns of symptom dissociation were similar. All showed impaired lexical semantic processing affecting both production and comprehension. These patients showed major deficits in naming objects and pictures, in matching spoken words to objects and pictures, in providing definitions of words and names of objects from their verbal descriptions, in completing low-predictable open-ended sentences, in detecting semantic inconsistences in sentences (e.g. "Cats have six legs") in spite of producing verbatim repetition of these anomalous sentences, in making semantic discriminations (e.g. words vs. nonwords), and in other tasks that require access to word meaning.

The impairment in lexical semantic processing contrasted sharply with the preservation of phonology and syntax in all four patients. In this connection, Berndt et al. (1987) rightly pointed out that if the phonological processes implicated in the repetition of nonwords is excluded, it could be assumed that phonology in patient RR would be preserved. The intactness of phonology was demonstrated in RR (and in the other three patients) by the nearly verbatim repetition of sentences of up to seven words in length and by the rare production of phonological paraphasias during spontaneous speech and naming tasks.

The second type of dissociation in these TCSA patients concerns the partial preservation of syntactic competence in the presence of impaired semantic processes. The syntactic characteristics of spontaneous speech and comprehension were investigated in more detail by Schwartz and her colleagues (1979). With regard to syntactic processing during production tasks, WLP could only produce irrelevant statements when she was required to complete short paragraphs that constrained the syntactic form of the response. Therefore, the researchers used a less demanding exercise, in which WLP had to introduce some modifications in sentences spoken by the examiner across diverse dimensions such as "negation" (e.g. *examiner*: "Tom has been ill"; *WLP expected response*: "Tom has not been ill"), "singular–plural" (e.g. *examiner*: "I have one tooth"; *WLP expected response*: "I have lots of teeth"), and "present tense–past tense" (e.g. *examiner*: "Today I am cooking dinner"; *WLP expected response*: "Yesterday I cooked dinner"). WLP was able to modify the sentences in most instances, failing in only 6 of 100 trials, and produced no ungrammatical responses. According to Schwartz et al. (p. 293) this pattern of performance on productive syntactic operations demonstrated a preserved "capacity to generate a variety of linguistic structures requiring such operations as pronoun substitution, insertion and fronting of the auxiliary, and the application of derivational and inflectional affixes".

With regard to syntactic processing during auditory comprehension, Schwartz et al. (1979) explored this function by using a series of semantically reversible sentences composed of subject-action-object, in which the reversal of the subject and object nouns in the phrase did not modify its meaningfulness (e.g. "The boy kisses the girl"). They used four different types of sentences, including constructions in active voice (e.g. "The cow kicks the horse"), passive voice (e.g. "The car is pulled by the truck"), comparative adjectives (e.g. "The man is older than the woman"), and spatial prepositions (e.g. "The square is over the circle"). The design was a sentence–picture matching task where, after listening to the semantically reversible target sentence, WLP was required to select from two pictures the one that depicted the action. Her performance was good for sentences construed using active and passive voices with a similar number of errors on each, and excellent for comprehension of spatial preposition and comparative adjective constructions. Error analysis revealed few failures, and all of them were lexical, rather than syntactical. Auditory comprehension deficit that was not specific to syntactic operations was also demonstrated in ST (Martin & Saffran, 1990), since she performed at chance level in reversible sentences containing active and passive constructions and considerably above chance in sentences containing simple active and locative constructions.

Dissociation of language function has also been documented in verbal production (spontaneous speech, naming, and repetition) in small series of patients with TA. A fine-grained analysis of the patterns of verbal expression in TCSA has been carried out in recent years. Heilman et al. (Heilman, 1985; Heilman et al., 1981) and Coslett et al. (1987) postulated that TCSA may have two different types of spontaneous speech and naming as well as a different performance in repetition tasks. Coslett and co-workers (1987) described two such subtypes in four patients with TCSA. Two patients (Group I; one case had a primary degenerative dementia and the other one had a left posterior parietal infarct) were found to repeat sentences using the lexical mechanism. The other two patients (Group II; one case had herpes simplex encephalitis with bitemporal involvement and the other one had a left subcortical haemorrhage involving the basal ganglia and thalamus) were found to have an impaired lexical route, repetition performance relying only on the nonlexical mechanism.

Coslett and his co-workers (1987) quantified the number of phonological and semantic paraphasias using measures of spontaneous speech (picture description, responsive speech) and naming (naming subtest of the Western Aphasia Battery, Boston Naming Test, and Peabody Vocabulary Test), and reading. Repetition of words, nonwords, and phrases, and the ability to recognise and correct syntactic and semantic anomalies during sentence repetition, were also examined. Both groups of patients showed similar performance on certain language tasks (e.g. number of semantic paraphasias during oral production tasks, intact repetition of words and nonwords, and verbatim repetition of sentences with semantic anomalies they failed to recognise), but not in other linguistic domains. In fact, the two patients of Group II produced substantially more literal paraphasias in production tasks than did patients of Group I, also failing in correct syntactic errors during repetition and recognising the ill-formedness of these sentences. On the other hand, patients in Group I not only recognised the syntactic anomalies embedded in sentences but they could also correct syntactic errors during the repetition of these ungrammatical sentences.

According to Coslett et al. (1987) these observations support the subclassification of TCSA into two subtypes. Patients of Group I exhibit the "classical" pattern with relatively preserved syntactic and lexical mechanisms that were dissociated from the semantic system, whereas syntactical and lexical processing were impaired in patients of Group II thus suggesting that they really had a different type of TCSA. These authors proposed a similar schema to classify patients with other clinical varieties of TA (e.g. mixed transcortical aphasia) and predicted the occurrence of other patterns of TCSA (e.g. relative sparing of spontaneous speech with preserved repetition of words but not of nonwords), but the small number of patients included in each group precluded further speculations on clinicopathological correlations. In this context, it is interesting to note that impaired access to the lexical system during repetition of ungrammatical sentences has been documented in subsequent studies among patients with TCSA (Berthier, Starkstein et al., 1991; see also Chapter 7) and mixed transcortical aphasia (Pulvermüller & Schönle, 1993) in patients with extensive involvement of the language-dominant perisylvian language zone.

Word-meaning deafness

Variability in performance during auditory comprehension tasks from one situation to the next is a common feature in aphasic patients with impaired comprehension (see Riedel, 1981). In this context, occasional patients with TCSA intermittently fail to understand the meaning of spoken words that they can understand when read. This condition has been termed word-meaning deafness (WMD; Bramwell, 1897). This generally occurs in aphasic cases of mild severity where other language functions such us spontaneous speech, repetition, writing to dictation, oral reading, and reading comprehension are relatively spared. The original, and probably best description of WMD, was published by Bramwell (1897) in a case of TCSA. This patient (Case 11) was a young right-handed woman who developed complete deafness without expressive aphasia immediately after suffering a unilateral left-hemisphere vascular lesion presumably affecting the "auditory speech centre". Initially, the patient was unable to identify loud nonspeech sounds including music and she also failed to understand even simple words, but was otherwise almost free of aphasia, except for the occasional occurrence of word-finding difficulties and semantic paraphasias (e.g. "skin" ⇒ hair) during spontaneous speech. Repetition of words and sentences was preserved, but she echolalically repeated portions of the question most likely in an attempt to grasp its meaning. The outstanding abnormality was the inability to recognise words when spoken, whereas the patient's ability to understand short written questions was fully retained. Also, writing to dictation was preserved even for long sentences. Bramwell's original case has been republished and interpreted according to current models of language processing as a unimodal disconnection (partial or complete) between the phonological input lexicon and the semantic system (Ellis, 1984; Ellis & Young, 1988).

Kohn and Friedman (1986) attempted a further elaboration of the cognitive deficit underlying WMD and they also described two additional cases. These authors argued that writing to dictation is not a necessary component of the syndrome, but that to establish a reliable diagnosis of WMD the patients should have preserved reading comprehension of the words that cannot be understood when presented in the auditory modality. In other words, when the access to semantics by means of the auditory modality is disrupted, the way to demonstrate the intactness of semantic stored information is by accessing it through another input channel (reading). None the less, Kohn and Friedman suggested that the status of writing to dictation would indicate the level at which the disruption between intact phonological and semantic processing has occurred. According to their hypothesis, preserved writing to dictation in one of their patients (Case HN) indicates that the breakdown has occurred after the auditory information has accessed its lexical phonological representation (post-access deficit). This patient, who had a mild Wernicke's aphasia, resolved instances of faulty auditory recognition of words via his own writing, just as the original patients described by Bramwell (1897) and Symonds (1953) did. On the other hand, impaired writing to dictation was seen in their other patient (Case LL) implying that the phonological–semantic dissociation took place before auditory information accessed its lexical phonological representations (pre-access deficit). This patient had not only impaired writing to dictation but his spontaneous writing was also poor, so that he could only resolve instances of poor understanding of auditorily presented words when he was allowed to read words written by others. During the course of recovery, patient LL displayed the language features of Wernicke's, transcortical sensory, and conduction aphasias. I have seen instances of WMD associated with poor spontaneous writing (jargonagraphia) and impaired writing to dictation in two patients with TCSA who had relative sparing of spontaneous speech and confrontation naming. Further testing revealed preserved repetition, oral word reading, and written word–object matching but impaired single word comprehension (see later).

Gogi (word-meaning) aphasia

Dissociation in performance between phonology and semantics has also been documented in cases of TCSA occurring in Japanese patients. Imura (1943) described a form of TCSA, peculiar to Japanese speakers, characterised by a selective impairment of *kanji* processing (ideographic characters which are semantic in nature) with the sparing of the processing of *kana* (phonetic symbols) and other phonological and phonetic functions such as articulation and repetition of words and sentences. This syndrome has been designated Gogi (word-meaning) aphasia to denote the selective impairment of semantic processing of words in sentence formulation, visual confrontation naming, category fluency, word–picture matching, oral reading, and writing to dictation. Gogi aphasia is rare and has been reported after focal traumatic lesions of the middle and inferior temporal lobe (Sasanuma & Monoi, 1975) and associated with circumscribed cerebral atrophy of the anterior temporal lobes presumably due to Pick's disease (Nakagawa et al., 1993; Tanabe et al., 1993).

Dissociation between naming and comprehension

Occasional single case studies demonstrate that in TCSA naming is not always impaired (Heilman et al., 1981; Kremin, 1986) Although in most patients with TCSA, impaired confrontation naming is associated with poor recognition of the words that cannot be named (semantic anomia) (Benson, 1988), dissociations between naming and recognition have been reported. Goodglass et al. (1986) described cases of category-specific dissociations between word comprehension and word retrieval. In a group of 117 aphasic patients, these authors reported 13 patients who showed deficits in name comprehension across different semantic categories in the presence of preserved naming of letters, body parts, and colours. Most patients had fluent aphasia and in two of them the pattern of language impairment was consistent with TCSA. One patient (Case 40) was a right-hander with a left perisylvian stroke lesion who could name in the absence of recognition in fourteen (30%) instances, but was able to recognise a picture in the absence of naming on only one (0.2%) occasion. In the other patient (Case 98), a left-hander with a stroke lesion involving the left temporal lobe, the dissociation between naming and recognition was less dramatic than in the previous case since he could name in the absence of recognition on seven (11%) occasions, but was able to recognise pictures in the absence of naming in four (10%) instances. These findings were interpreted by Goodglass and his colleagues as reflecting either impaired access to intact semantic representations or selective involvement of one of the two independent (input and output) components of the lexicon.

   The occurrence of intact object naming in the absence of comprehension represents an exceptional type of language dissociation in transcortical aphasias

(TA). The first cases of intact naming with impaired auditory comprehension in TA were described in patients with the mixed type (Heilman et al., 1976; Kapur & Dunkley, 1984; see further details in Chapters 5 and 7). Heilman et al. (1981) reported the case of a patient who developed a TCSA with relative sparing of oral language functions (spontaneous speech, object naming, and oral reading) after an ischaemic infarction in the left posterior parietal region. The patient was able to name 34 of 50 (68%) objects correctly, but on a word discrimination test recognised only 16 (32%) of these same objects. Heilman and his co-workers explained intact naming (without comprehension deficits) with pre-served semantic–phonemic pathways (accounting for intact object naming and spontaneous speech), or right hemisphere compensatory mediation.

Kremin (1986) reported two additional patients (AND and ORL) featuring TCSA and intact naming. In both patients, naming of visually presented targets (objects, figures) was much better than comprehension of spoken and written words. Patient AND showed comprehension deficits restricted to pictures and single words, which were explained by Kremin as due to impaired access to the semantic system. The other patient (ORL) showed impairments in compre-hension involving all tasks regardless of the modality of input, which were explained as due to impairment in the central semantic system. Kremin argued that intact object naming may be explained by the existence of a visual non-semantic naming route which would link input and output lexicons bypassing the semantic system. While this hypothesis could certainly explain preserved naming without comprehension in patient ORL who showed empty spontaneous speech and semantic impairment in comprehension, the preservation of oral speech production (spontaneous speech and naming) in patient AND suggests that object naming was, at least partially, controlled by semantic information. One limitation of Kremin's study is that both patients had bilateral cerebral damage. When tested one year after onset, AND showed memory problems, left hemianopia, left visual neglect and left hemiparesis as residual deficits from bilateral frontal and brain stem traumatic injury, while ORL was a left-handed woman who developed a transient nonfluent aphasia, followed by disorientation and fluent, empty speech production in association with a left frontal lobe meta-stasis and bilateral brain swelling. Thus, the above cases of TCSA with intact object naming demonstrated differences in aetiology and lesion location (focal *vs.* diffuse pathology), as well as in the interval between brain lesion and lan-guage testing.

A study of intact naming with impaired comprehension

Here I will present data from a recent study by Berthier (1995) in which an effort was made to overcome the aforementioned methodological problems. This research was divided into two parts. The first study was designed to examine the pattern of language deficits in a consecutive series of patients with TCSA and intact naming after unilateral cerebrovascular lesions. Since recovery from TCSA (with or without preserved object naming) in patients with cerebrovascular lesions usually occurs during the acute stage (Heilman et al., 1981; Rubens & Kertesz, 1983), formal language assessment was performed in all patients before two months of evolution after the lesion using standardised and experimental language tests. The main aim of the second study was to examine the mechanism(s) of intact naming in TCSA. Thus relevant variables such as demographic factors, lesion location, lesion volume, and cerebral asymmetries were determined in four groups of patients: (1) patients with TCSA and intact naming, (2) patients with TCSA and impaired naming, (3) patients with anomia, and (4) patients with focal left hemisphere lesions without clinical evidence of aphasia.

Case 1. EV, was a 71-year-old right-handed housewife with 12 years of formal education who was admitted because of left frontal headache, nausea and vomiting, immediately followed by severe right-sided weakness and difficulty understanding conversational speech. On admission, she was alert, fully oriented and concerned about her condition. On neurological examination, she had a right hemiplegia (sparing the face), right hemisensory loss of the cortical type and right trimodal (visual, auditory, and somatosensory) extinction on double simultaneous stimulation. EV also showed a severe left ideomotor apraxia and an intense feeling of nonbelonging of the right arm. Intellectual and memory functioning were average, though she obtained better verbal than performance IQ scores (Table 4.1). A high-resolution CT scan revealed an ischaemic infarction involving the left inferior and superior parietal lobe. There was subtle additional ischaemic damage to the posterior-superior frontal white matter (Fig. 4.1).

Case 2. RQ was a 63-year-old right-handed linotypist with 12 years of formal education who noticed the sudden onset of left retro-orbital headache and dimness of vision in the right visual field. On admission, he was alert and well oriented and, although he showed appropriate concern about his symptoms, he did not report language problems. On neurological examination, he had a right homonymous hemianopia, a right hemispatial neglect, and a mild right arm paresis. He also showed rapidly regressive Gerstmann's syndrome, map-finding difficulty, loss of dreaming and mental imagery, as well as jargonagraphia and impaired writing to dictation. There was no evidence of ideomotor apraxia or ideational apraxia. RQ's verbal IQ was average, but he scored below average in performance IQ. Memory functioning was average (Table 4.1). A CT scan revealed a haemorrhage involving the left temporo-parieto-occipital junction (Fig. 4.2).

Case 3. RL was a 68-year-old right-handed retired professor of dentistry who suddenly experienced problems in manipulating objects with his right hand

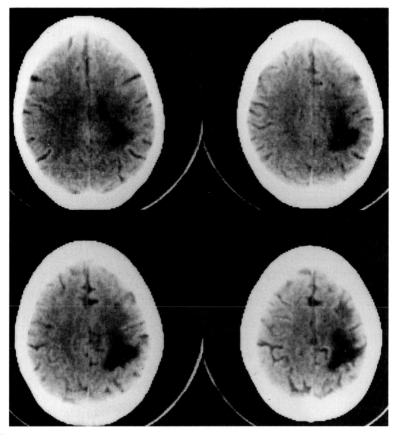

FIG. 4.1   CT scan of a patient (Case 1) with acute transcortical sensory aphasia due to an ischaemic infarction. The lesion involves the left posterior parietal region (but also note some extension into the frontal lobe). The left hemisphere is represented on the right side of the figure.

and difficulty in understanding spoken language. On admission, he was alert and cooperative but globally disoriented and with a tendency to minimise his deficits. On neurological examination, RL had a right homonymous hemianopia, right hemispatial neglect, and inaccurate reaching of objects with his right hand in both visual fields. He also showed rapidly regressive jargonagraphia with impaired writing to dictation, Gerstmann's syndrome, constructional apraxia, and severe ideomotor apraxia. Assessment of intellectual functions revealed a marked discrepancy between IQ scores obtaining better verbal than performance results and moderate decrement in memory abilities relative to his premorbid functioning (Table 4.1). The CT scan revealed a haemorrhage involving the inferior and superior parietal lobe.

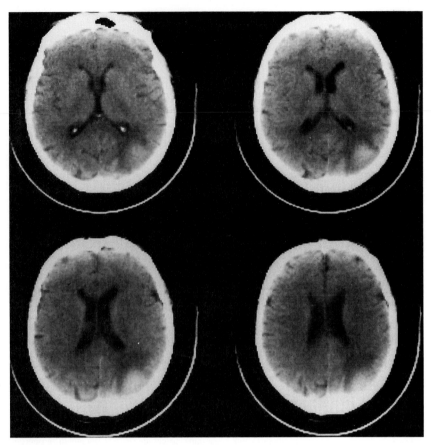

FIG. 4.2   CT scan showing a resolving haemorrhage in a patient (Case 2) with acute transcortical sensory aphasia. The lesion involves the left temporo-parieto-occipital region. The left hemisphere is represented on the right side of the figure.

Case 4.   OC was a 78-year-old right-handed housewife with seven years of formal education. She suddenly collapsed while walking and was admitted to hospital some hours later with right-sided weakness and aphasia. On examination, the patient was awake and alert but severely aphasic. She had a marked reduction of verbal output and could only comprehend simple questions and obeyed whole body commands. She had a right hemiplegia, a right hemisensory loss, and right visual and auditory inattention. Four days later, while still severely aphasic, the patient was able to echo most of the examiner's questions and also name common objects on confrontation testing. By that time her language impairment was interpreted as a mixed transcortical aphasia with preserved oral naming capabilities (Heilman et al., 1976). Although the auditory comprehension impairment remained almost unchanged during the following

TABLE 4.1
Language and Memory Test Scores

	Case				
	1	*2*	*3*	*4*	*5*
WAIS (age-scale scores)					
Verbal Scale IQ	98	98	111	NT	98
Information	10	12	13	NT	10
Comprehension	9	9	14	NT	9
Arithmetic	6	7	4	NT	4
Similarities	9	7	12	NT	10
Digit span	6	8	9	8	9
Vocabulary	9	12	13	NT	12
Performance Scale IQ	90	81	69	NT	84
Digit symbol	2	3	0	NT	8
Picture completion	8	5	9	NT	10
Block design	6	6	0	NT	5
Picture arrangement	6	6	2	NT	0
Object assembly	3	4	0	NT	2
Wechsler Memory Scale					
Memory quotient	106	100	92	NT	77

NT, not tested. Reprinted from Berthier (1995); by permission of Taylor & Francis Ltd.

days, her verbal output was considerably improved, and she was able to produce short meaningful sentences. A CT scan performed during the chronic period revealed an extensive low-density lesion involving the frontoparietal subcortical white matter.

Case 5.   HE was a 56-year-old nonfamiliar left-handed man, who suddenly became unable to understand his wife's speech. On admission, he was alert but was apathetic and unconcerned. He had a mild left hemiparesis, left hemispatial neglect, motor impersistence, impaired right–left orientation, and spatial disorientation. Assessment of general intelligence revealed that HE's verbal IQ score was average, but he obtained a below-average performance IQ score. Memory was moderately impaired in both verbal and visual domains (Table 4.1). There was no evidence of buccofacial and limb apraxia. Serial CT and MRI scans showed a large ischaemic infarction involving the right anterior perisylvian area. There was no evidence of left hemisphere involvement. Further clinical details are reported in Chapter 7.

Language Assessment with the Western Aphasia Battery (WAB) in all five patients with intact naming showed a profile of language impairment consistent with the WAB criteria for TCSA (Table 4.2). Spontaneous speech, however, did not show anomia or semantic jargon as in regularly observed in classical cases of TCSA. Indeed, oral expression was fluent, effortless, and well articulated, and patients uttered correct and meaningful sentences during free conversation, during description of the WAB picture, and in response to specific questions concerning their medical or occupational history. Oral expression was fluent and informative in two patients (Cases 2 and 3). The other three patients generated short phrases that were contaminated by echolalia and perseverations. These short phrases, however, had a well-organised syntactical and grammatical structure and contained content words, thus allowing the patients to convey coherent information. What follows are sentences generated by the five patients in response to one question ("Tell me a little about why you are here" or "What seems to be the trouble?") of the spontaneous speech subtest of the WAB:

Case 1 (EV).   "I was admitted because I felt bad and couldn't coordinate my speech . . . I felt a very strange sensation in my right arm, as if it weren't mine"

Case 2 (RQ).   "The reason that I came was that I had a stroke . . . and I believe that it was the result of some kind of pressure . . . since I felt a terrible pain in my head and I couldn't walk straight".

Case 3 (RL).   "I've suffered a confusional state . . . a confusional state . . . incoherence in certain expressions. I'm a professor of histology and I attribute this [the stroke] to a state of psychic tension . . ."

Case 4 (OC).   "My blood pressure went way up . . . a splitting headache . . . I thought I was going to die"

Case 5 (HE).   "I get nervous and nothing comes out and then I get even more nervous and I get stuck. I know it's difficult for me to explain . . . how hard it is to speak . . ."

Occasional word-finding problems, circumlocutions, and even less frequent paraphasias (semantic errors in Cases 1 and 4, and phonological errors in Case 2) were produced during running speech. In addition, four patients (Cases 1, 2, 3, and 5) scored at an average level on the vocabulary subtest of the Wechsler Adult Intelligence Scale (WAIS; Wechsler, 1955) (see Table 4.1) indicating that their definition of words of increasing difficulty was relatively preserved.

Auditory comprehension was moderately impaired although words and yes/no questions were understood better than sequential commands. Patients scored abnormally low on the auditory comprehension subtests of the WAB, and also showed impaired comprehension of syntactically complex material (Token Test, parts IV and V; De Renzi & Vignolo, 1962).

All five patients showed a relatively preserved performance on repetition and object-naming subtests of the WAB. Completion of open-ended sentences (e.g. "The grass is . . . *green*") and responsive speech (e.g. "What colour is snow?") scores ranged from mildly defective to normal. However, all five patients had

TABLE 4.2
Language and Reading Comprehension Test Scores

				Case		
	Max.	1	2	3	4	5
Western Aphasia Battery						
Information content	10	8	9	9	8	9
Fluency	10	9	9	10	9	8
Comprehension						
Yes/no questions	60	51	48	48	51	39
Auditory word recognition	60	41	46	42	50	50
Sequential commands	80	10	36	22	16	16
Repetition	100	9.4	9.6	9	9.8	8.9
Naming						
Object naming	60	58	58	60	60	60
Verbal fluency	20	2	5	5	5	6
Sentence completion	10	8	8	6	10	6
Responsive speech	10	10	8	8	8	10
Reading						
Sentence comprehension	40	14	22	14	4	18
Commands comprehension	20	8	12	7	9	16
Matching:						
1 written word–object	6	6	6	6	6	6
2 picture–written word	6	6	6	6	6	6
3 homoph. words–picture	10	9	7	8	8	9
Token Test	62	41	27	14	21	35

Reprinted from Berthier (1995); by permisson of Taylor & Francis Ltd.

impaired ability to generate words in a specific semantic category (animals). Reading comprehension was also moderately impaired but reading aloud was relatively preserved. Patients' performances on language and reading comprehension tests are shown in Table 4.2.

Experimental tests and results

Repetition.   Digit repetition, as assessed with the digit span subtest of the WAIS (Wechsler, 1955), was preserved in all five cases (e.g. they could repeat six or more digits forward in correct serial order) (see Table 4.1). All patients also showed a verbatim repetition of auditorily presented words and nonwords. The ability to correct syntactic and semantic errors during repetition of sentences with grammatical or semantic errors was also examined (Coslett et al., 1987; Davis et al., 1978;) Two patients (Cases 2 and 3) corrected all syntactic errors. In the case of Case 2 these corrections were produced without conscious awareness, while Case 3 could correctly indicate 70% of syntactic errors. Cases 1 and 4 automatically corrected 60% and 50% of syntactic errors, respectively. Case 5

TABLE 4.3
Performance on Visual Naming Tasks

		Case				
	Max.	*1*	*2*	*3*	*4*	*5*
Visual naming for nouns						
Object Naming (WAB)	60	58	58	60	60	60
Boston Naming Test						
Correct responses	60	51	49	43	48	54
Items failed		9	11	17	12	6
Type of error						
No response		4	3	9	4	2
Visual		1	0	0	0	1
Semantic		4	3	7	6	2
Phonemic		0	0	0	0	0
Circumlocution		0	3	0	1	1
Unrelated word		0	0	0	0	0
Rejection		0	1	0	0	0
Other		0	1	1	1	0
Phonemic cues (items passed)		8	10	17	11	3
Semantic cues (items passed)		0	2	0	0	1
Car parts	10	8	8	10	9	8
Body parts	10	9	10	10	10	9
Colours	10	10	10	10	10	10
Fruits	10	10	9	9	10	9
Visual naming for verbs						
Actions	10	10	9	10	9	10

Reprinted from Berthier (1995); by permission of Taylor & Francis Ltd.

was unable to correct any syntactic error. None of these five patients was able to detect semantic errors, and they repeated verbatim all semantically anomalous sentences.

Naming. Tables 4.3 and 4.4 show patients' performance across different modality-specific naming tests. Visual naming for *nouns* was assessed with the Boston Naming Test (BNT; Kaplan et al., 1983). According to normative data on the 60-item BNT for normal older adults (Van Gorp, Satz, Kiersch, & Henry, 1986), naming performance was average in four patients (Cases 1, 3, 4, and 5), and mildly defective in the remaining patient (Case 2). The distribution of error types was coded according to Zingeser and Berndt (1988). Error analysis indicated that naming performance was affected only by low frequency items (e.g. "igloo", "abacus"); errors were few and consisted mainly of failures to respond and, to a lesser degree, semantic paraphasias and perseverations of previous responses. Phonological paraphasias, unrelated words, and neologisms were absent. While semantic cues did not improve performance, phonemic cues (the

TABLE 4.4
Naming Performance Across Different Modalities of Input

	Max.			Cases		
		1	*2*	*3*	*4*	*5*
Tactile naming	20	10*	20	20	10*	20
Written naming	20	NT	0	0	NT	20
Auditory naming	10	9	9	8	10	10
Naming from description						
Correct responses	10–15	10	13	12	10	13
Type of error						
No response		4	2	3	5	2
Other		0	0	0	0	0
Semantic choice (items passed)		4	2	2	3	2

* Assessed for the left hand only; NT, not tested. Reprinted from Berthier (1995); by permission of Taylor & Francis Ltd.

first phoneme of the word) facilitated word retrieval. All five patients could correctly name nouns from different semantic categories (car parts, body parts, colours, and fruits). Visual naming for *verbs*, as assessed by the action-naming test (Nicholas, Obler, Albert, & Goodglass, 1985) was virtually intact.

Tactile naming was assessed by asking the patients to palpate and name a 20-item set of household objects without visual control. All patients could name without errors either 20 objects palpated with both hands (Cases 2, 3, and 5), or 10 objects palpated with the nonaffected left hand (Cases 1 and 4). Written naming was assessed in three patients, who were asked to write the names of 20 visually presented objects. Two patients (Cases 2 and 3) had jargonagraphia; therefore they were unable to spell any object name correctly. The other patient (Case 5), a left-hander, could write normally with either hand and performed flawlessly in the written confrontation naming task. Written naming could not be tested in the remaining two patients (Cases 1 and 4) because of right hemiplegia. Auditory naming was tested by asking the patients to listen and name 10 familiar environmental (nonspeech) sounds. All patients scored normally in this task. In addition, these patients were asked to name objects, parts of objects, and animals (15 items) from verbal descriptions (e.g. "What is the name of the bird that flies at night and hoots? = OWL") (Coughlan & Warrington, 1978). All five patients obtained scores well above the chance level (chance score = 5; maximum score = 15).

Finally, in order to test the unusual pattern of preserved object naming in the presence of impaired auditory comprehension, the patients' ability to point to objects and pictures (n = 60) after a verbal command was compared with their ability to name the same targets during visual presentation (Goodglass et al., 1986). Several items of different semantic categories (e.g. objects, line-drawings

TABLE 4.5
Auditory Word Recognition Versus Object and Picture
Naming

Cases	Auditory word recognition		Object/picture naming	
	No.	No. correct	No.	No. correct
1**	60	44 (73)	60	59 (98)
2***	60	46 (75)	60	60 (100)
3**	60	41 (68)	60	58 (95)
4*	60	50 (83)	60	60 (100)
5*	60	50 (83)	60	60 (100)

Values in parentheses are percentages. $*P < .001$; $**P <$ .0001; $***P < .00001$. Reprinted from Berthier (1995); by permission of Taylor & Francis Ltd.

of objects, geometric designs, colours, letters, numbers, furniture, and body parts) were chosen from the auditory word recognition subtest of the WAB. In order to compare performance across input and output modalities the 60 items were presented in separate sessions for naming and comprehension. Comprehension of the target word was presented in a within-category condition (forced choice from five semantically related distractors). All patients performed significantly better on the naming condition than on the comprehension condition (Table 4.5) and there were no instances of correct picture comprehension in the absence of correct naming.

Unfortunately, it was not possible to examine if the pattern of dissociation (preserved naming with impaired comprehension) documented in the verbal modality was also present in the visual modality. It should be noted, however, that two patients (Cases 2 and 3) could understand written words (9/9 correct), although they failed to comprehend when these words were presented in the auditory modality (6/9 correct). Moreover, all patients showed a flawless performance on other tasks of visual comprehension (written word–object and picture–written word matching) (see Table 4.2).

Reading comprehension.   While all five patients could read aloud well, they could not understand sentences from the reading section of the WAB. Written word–object and picture–written word matching reading subtests were normal in all five patients. To further assess reading comprehension we examined the patient's ability to match one of two homophonic words (e.g. "maśa" [mass] *vs.* "maza" [mace]), to a corresponding picture (Coslett et al., 1985). All patients scored better than chance (Table 4.2).

Oral reading.   Tables 4.6 and 4.7 summarise the patients' performance on the oral reading of words and nonwords. While one patient (Case 5) produced no

TABLE 4.6
Oral Reading: Words Versus Nonwords

	Words		Non-Words	
Cases	No.	No. correct	No.	No. correct
1**	60	51 (85)	20	10 (50)
2***	60	44 (75)	20	4 (20)
3****	60	60 (100)	20	6 (30)
4*	60	44 (75)	20	8 (40)
5	60	57 (95)	20	18 (90)

Values in parentheses are percentages. $*P < .004$; $**P < .001$; $***P < .0001$; $****P < .000001$. Reprinted from Berthier (1995); by permission of Taylor & Francis Ltd.

TABLE 4.7
Oral Reading: Words, Letters, and Nonwords

		Cases				
	No.	1	2	3	4	5
Words	60	85*	75	100	75	100
Concrete	40	85	77	100	75	100
High frequency	20	100	95	100	90	100
Low frequency	20	70	60	100	60	100
Abstract	20	85	70	100	75	100
High frequency	10	100	90	100	90	100
Low frequency	10	70	50	100	60	100
Verbs	20	95	90	95	80	100
Adjectives	20	85	90	95	90	100
Functors	20	80	80	100	80	100
Letters	40	100	50	100	80	100
Nonwords	20	50	20	30	40	90

* Values are % correct. Reprinted from Berthier (1995); by permission of Taylor & Francis Ltd.

errors on oral reading tasks, the other four patients read real words significantly better than nonwords. Though impaired, nonword reading was not totally abolished; omissions were few, and all four patients attempted to give a response. These responses, however, were composed of either nonsense letter strings or real words visually similar to the target (e.g. "lisiado" [crippled] ⇒ *elsiado*). Real word reading was intact in one patient (Case 3) but mildly impaired in the other three patients (Cases 1, 2, and 4). Errors were mainly visual and, less frequently, derivational, but there were no semantic errors. Further analysis of reading abilities disclosed that errors were more likely to occur in the reading of abstract than concrete words. Although this could reflect a concreteness effect, these errors were no more concrete than the target (e.g. "privación" [privation] ⇒ privacidad [privacy]). Residual word reading was not influenced by the grammatical class of the word. In two patients (Cases 2 and 4) the spelling of real words (*cabeza* [head] or nonwords *topifante*) was influenced by the spelling of a previously heard word (*alacena* [locker] ⇒ "alaBeza"), or nonword (*lontiso* ⇒ "lontisANTE"). Similar types of errors, but restricted to nonword reading, have been reported in a patient with developmental phonological dyslexia (Campbell & Butterworth, 1985).

Follow-up evaluations. Language and reading were re-examined in all patients about two months after the first evaluation. By that time none of the five patients could clinically be considered aphasic. In fact, all but one patient (Case 4) obtained aphasia quotients (AQ) on the WAB above the aphasic range (AQ: 93.6). Residual deficits in communication were mild and consisted of echolalia, reduced word-list generation and problems in the comprehension of long, syntactically complex sentences. Word and sentence repetition remained largely spared and the repetition of sentences with either syntactic and semantic anomalies improved dramatically and paralleled the recovery of auditory comprehension. When asked to repeat semantically anomalous sentences, all five patients fully appreciated the nature of errors and spontaneously corrected these anomalies or, more frequently, they refused to repeat these nonsense sentences. Object naming, sentence completion, and responsive speech remained largely spared and there was a moderate improvement, though not complete, in category fluency. Reading comprehension and oral reading improved considerably in two patients (Cases 1 and 2), whereas a moderate improvement in oral reading but not in reading comprehension was documented in two patients (Cases 3 and 4). A moderate improvement in reading comprehension was also documented in the left-handed patient with a right hemisphere lesion (Case 5). Only one patient (Case 4) still showed the dissociation between the oral reading of words and nonwords (96% *vs.* 40%) that characterises the syndrome of phonological dyslexia. In two patients (Cases 2 and 3) jargonagraphia had totally resolved and both patients obtained normal scores on the writing section of the WAB as well as in written naming.

In summary, I found that all patients showed a stereotyped profile of language deficits associated with TCSA. Language production (spontaneous speech and object naming) was relatively preserved, indicating that words can gain access to the phonological output lexicon form the semantic system (Ellis & Young, 1988; Heilman et al., 1981). On the other hand, language comprehension (word and sentence comprehension of spoken and written material) was moderately impaired, suggesting impaired access to semantics or a disruption of information represented in the semantic system (Berndt, 1988). Repetition of words, sentences, and nonwords was preserved and a relative preservation of

TABLE 4.8
Demographic and Lesion Characteristics

	TCSA-intact	TCSA-impaired	Anomia	Control
Number of patients	6	6	6	6
Age (mean years)	68	56	70	68
Sex (percentage females)	50	50	67	50
Education (mean years)	12	9	11	12
Handedness (percentage right)	83	100	100	66
Family history of left-handedness (percentage positive)	17	17	0	17
Time since stroke onset (mean days)	11.5	17	25.1	16
Lesion volume	13.6	7.7	6.4	2.1
Frontal torque	0.6	−0.15	1.8	15.1
Occipital torque	−3.2	−7.5	1.8	−6.1

Reprinted from Berthier (1995); by permission of Taylor & Francis Ltd.

syntactic but not semantic processing during repetition was demonstrated in four patients. Reading comprehension was impaired. Oral reading of real words was significantly better than reading of nonwords, and all patients produced derivational and visual errors, but not semantic errors. Follow-up evaluations revealed rapid improvement of language and reading deficits.

Twenty-four patients participated in the second part of this study: eighteen patients were selected from our population of 114 aphasic patients (Berthier, Starkstein et al., 1991); six nonaphasic patients were selected from a consecutive series of thirty patients with acute damage to the left hemisphere who had no clinical evidence of aphasia (AQ of the WAB ≥ 93.8). Twelve aphasic patients (six with TCSA and impaired naming and six with anomia) and six nonaphasic patients were matched for gender, age, education, and time since stroke onset to the patients with TCSA and intact naming. The study had a 2 × 2 design, with factors being the presence or absence of naming deficits, and impaired or preserved auditory comprehension. Therefore, four groups of patients were studied:

1. Six aphasic patients who met WAB criteria for TCSA, and had intact object naming (TCSA-intact).
2. Six aphasic patients who met WAB criteria for TCSA and had impaired naming (TCSA-impaired).
3. Six aphasic patients who met WAB criteria for anomic aphasia (Anomia).
4. Six patients with left hemisphere stroke lesions with minor speech problems (e.g. dysarthria) but no evidence of aphasia as assessed by the WAB (Control).

Analysis of demographic data failed to disclose significant between-group differences in age, sex, education, handedness, family history of left-handedness, and interval between aphasia onset and language testing (Tables 4.8 and 4.9).

TABLE 4.9
Lesion Location and Language Test Scores

Case	Age (years)	Sex	CT/MRI Lesion Location	PSI	EPSI	WAB		
						AQ	ON	C
TCSA with intact naming								
1	71	F	L parietal	–	+	78.6	58	5.1
2	63	M	L occipitotemporal, parietal	–	+	84.0	58	6.5
3	68	M	L parietal	–	+	82.2	60	5.7
4	78	F	L frontoparietal	–	+	81.2	60	5.8
5	56	M*	R frontotemporal	+	–	80.4	60	5.1
6	69	F	L frontal	–	+	84.0	58	6.6
TCSA with impaired naming								
7	76	M	L temporoparietal	+	–	65.8	45	6.5
8	67	M	L frontotemporal, parietal	+	–	43.2	3	3.2
9	62	F	L frontal. insula, basal ganglia	–	–	70.6	30	6.5
10	75	M	L putamen, PVWM	–	+	55.4	15	6.1
11	70	M	L temporo-occipital	+	+	60.6	38	5.6
12	70	F	L frontotemporal, temporoparietal	+	–	57.0	22	5.4

Anomia

13	39	F	L insula, putamen	+	–	81.4	54	8.3
14	71	M	L putamen, PVWM	–	+	84.4	51	8.2
15	67	M	L occipitotemporal, thalamus	–	+	86.2	25	9.5
16	71	F	L frontal	–	+	67.8	40	7.0
17	49	M	L occipitotemporal	–	+	80.2	29	7.7
18	41	M	L temporal, putamen	–	+	74.4	50	7.5

Control

19	72	M*	L parietal	–	+	94.0	60	9.7
20	55	F	L occipitoparietal	–	+	97.6	60	9.2
21	69	M	L putamen	–	+	98.8	60	9.7
22	58	F	L occipitoparietal	–	+	96.6	60	8.9
23	77	M*	L putamen	–	+	98.8	60	9.9
24	78	F	L frontal	+	–	96.2	58	9.1

CT = computerised tomography; MRI = magnetic resonance imaging; PSI = perisylvian involvement; EPSI = extraperisylvian involvement; WAB = Western Aphasia Battery; AQ = Aphasia Quotient; ON = object naming; C = comprehension.* Indicates left-handedness; PVWM = periventricular white matter. Reprinted from Berthier (1995); by permission of Taylor & Francis Ltd.

The TCSA-intact and TCSA-impaired groups obtained similar scores for the AQ, repetition, comprehension, and fluency subtests of the WAB. The TCSA-intact group performed significantly better on the object-naming subtest than the TCSA-impaired group ($P = .0001$), and the Anomia group ($P = .006$); performance was similar to the Control group ($P = .94$). Moreover, the TCSA-intact group had significantly better spontaneous speech (measured by the information content subtest of the WAB) than the TCSA-impaired group ($F = 16.7$, $df = 3.20$, $P = .0001$).

Neuroimaging studies (CT and/or MRI scans) were obtained for every patient two to six weeks after the stroke. Lesion volume, lesion sites, and measurements of cerebral asymmetries (frontal and occipital torques) were examined in all patients (see technical details in Berthier, Starkstein et al., 1991; Berthier, 1995). Volumetric analysis of lesions revealed that patients with TCSA (with either intact or impaired naming) had larger lesions than the anomia or the control groups. The TCSA-intact and the TCSA-impaired groups had similar lesion volume, but there was a trend towards differences in lesion location. In fact, five of the six patients (83%) of the TCSA-intact group had lesions outside the left perisylvian area, whereas four of the six patients (66%) of the TCSA-impaired group had lesions involving the left perisylvian area (Table 4.9). Four patients in the Anomia group (66%) and four patients in the control group (66%) had extra-perisylvian involvement, while the remaining patients had perisylvian damage. Finally, there were no statistically significant between-group differences in the measurements of cerebral asymmetries.

In summary, the second part of the study demonstrated that different performance in object naming tasks between the TCSA-intact and Control groups and the TCSA-impaired and Anomia groups was not related to differences in demographics factors, severity of auditory comprehension deficits, lesion volume, or cerebral asymmetries. These findings suggest that the sparing of object naming in TCSA may depend on other variables (e.g. lesion location, individual variability in the brain organisation of naming). The theoretical implications of these findings is discussed in more detail later. In the following sections I will discuss the status of the different linguistic components in these patients with TCSA and intact object naming.

The spontaneous speech component

The relative sparing of spontaneous speech and object naming in the presence of impaired comprehension documented in our patients differed widely from both the jargon speech productions and the semantically based anomia that have been classically reported in patients with TCSA (Benson, 1988; Rubens & Kertesz, 1983). Jargon speech productions and anomia with lexical comprehension disturbances in typical cases of TCSA have been interpreted as resulting from impairments at the semantic level (Berndt et al., 1987; Martin & Saffran, 1990; Schwartz et al., 1979). By contrast, the relative preservation of word retrieval during spontaneous speech and picture-based narrative (e.g. picnic scene from the WAB), object naming, naming from descriptions, and word definitions (e.g. vocabulary subtest of the WAIS) suggest that in these patients the semantic system was functional and able to activate spoken word forms in the phonological output lexicon.

The auditory comprehension component

Lexical comprehension deficits among patients with TCSA and preserved language production (spontaneous speech and/or object naming) have been variously interpreted as due to impaired access to semantics (Heilman et al., 1981; Kremin, 1986, Case AND), damage to the central semantic system (Kremin, 1986, Case ORL), or selective damage to the phonological representations necessary for word recognition (Goodglass et al., 1986; Margolin, 1991). These patients had a poor performance on standard tests of auditory comprehension and single-word semantic comprehension deficits. These deficits may have resulted from either disturbances in the semantic component of the word processing system or impaired access to a semantic store. Impaired semantic processing could be suggested, on the comprehension side, by the presence of single-word semantic comprehension deficits and, on the production side, by the occasional production of semantic paraphasias during visual-naming tasks and impaired ability to generate words in a specific category. It should be noted, however, that these linguistic deficits do not invariably reflect a deficit in the semantic system itself, since category-specific deficits have been conceptualised as impaired access disorders (Goodglass & Budin, 1988; Humphreys & Riddoch, 1987) and semantic paraphasias in naming tasks, as well as reduced verbal fluency for different semantic categories in patients presenting with mild anomia and comprehension deficits, have been attributed to a partial disconnection between intact semantic and phonological systems (Hadar et al., 1987, 1991). Therefore, impaired language comprehension may be interpreted in terms of impaired access to lexical items in a semantic store from the phonological input lexicon (Ellis & Young, 1988). Some support for a disruption of phonological–semantic information comes from the dissociated performance in comprehension of written as opposed to auditorily presented words in two patients (Cases 2 and 3). These two patients showed features of "word-meaning deafness" (Ellis & Young, 1988; Kohn & Friedman, 1986), since both had preserved language repetition and could understand written words they failed to comprehend when these words were presented in the auditory modality. A final point worth mentioning is that deficits in auditory word comprehension in the five patients reported here and in the case by Heilman et al. (1981) were transient. Based on previous data from anomic patients (Kay & Ellis, 1987), rapid recovery of vocabulary is more compatible with "re-accessing" the semantic representation of words than "re-learning" every "forgotten" word (Ellis & Young, 1988, p. 122).

The naming component

Further analysis of naming performance indicated that during naming of visually presented pictures there was no evidence of word length or grammatical class effect (nouns and verbs were named with equal proficiency). Word frequency, however, influenced naming performance since errors were mainly produced on low-frequency words. On the BNT (Kaplan et al., 1983) all five patients produced semantic paraphasias or omissions, which benefitted from phonological but not semantic cues. This pattern of performance suggests that the information from the semantic system did not activate lexical entries for low-frequency words in the phonological output lexicon (Ellis, 1985), and that phonological cues facilitated word retrieval by increasing the activation of entries to the phonological output lexicon (Howard & Orchard-Lisle, 1984). An impaired semantic activation could also be responsible for poor categorical word list generation (Hadar et al., 1987, 1991).

According to current information processing models of word retrieval, there are two different routes for visual naming: a route by which the visually presented target accesses the phonological output lexicon through the semantic system, or a direct nonsemantic visual-naming route which connects the input and output lexicons bypassing the semantic system (Diesfeldt, 1989; Kremin, 1986; Ratcliff & Newcombe, 1982; Shuren, Geldmacher, & Heilman, 1993; but see Shallice, 1987, 1988). The relative sparing of word production (for high-frequency nouns) during running speech, as well as the instances of correct naming and comprehension of objects and pictures, indicates a relative sparing of pathways linking the semantic system and the phonological output lexicon. The integrity of the semantic route, however, could not account for the instances of correct naming without comprehension. This naming–comprehension dissociation rather suggests that a visually presented target can directly access its lexical representations, bypassing the semantic system, by means of the direct nonsemantic naming route. In this regard Goodglass (1980, p. 653) speculated "that there are 2 major paths to the emission of a word—one proceeding automatically from stimulus to oral response and based on a one-to-one associative link between concept and output. The other occurring when immediate association fails, involving a search process and mobilization of peripheral semantic and phonological association ". Therefore, the present findings support the contention that although these two routes have independent functions, they tend to process parallel information (Shuren et al., 1993).

It is interesting to note that some patients of the TCSA-intact group shared a similar pattern of performance in other language tasks. Naming was preserved in tactile and auditory (verbal descriptions and nonverbal) modalities, but written naming was impaired. This dissociation in conjunction with evidence obtained from patients who showed the opposite pattern (better written than oral naming) (Bub & Kertesz, 1982; Hier & Mohr, 1977), supports the hypothesis that there are separate word stores for oral and written naming (Ellis & Young, 1988; Morton, 1980). Based on the evidence that previous case studies of TCSA with spared object naming (Heilman et al., 1981; Kremin, 1986) did not show the aforementioned dissociations of language function, one would predict that such patterns or preserved/impaired performances (e.g. preserved tactile but impaired written naming) would not necessarily be detected among individual patients with TCSA and intact oral naming.

The oral reading component

In four of the five patients included in the first part of this study, intact object naming coexisted with impaired phonological reading. Phonological dyslexia has usually been reported in association with aphasic disorders (see Friedman, Ween, & Albert, 1993; Sartori, Barry, & Job, 1984), including TCSA (Rapcsak et al., 1989; Sartori, Masterson, & Job, 1987), and in rare cases, it has also been documented in association with category and modality-specific aphasias (e.g. optic anomia and/or tactile anomia) (Beauvois, Saillant, Meininger, & Lhermitte, 1978; Goodglass & Budin, 1988; Rapcsak, Gonzalez Rothi, & Heilman, 1987). In these four patients the ability to read using the nonlexical phonological route was impaired, as shown by the poor performance on oral reading of nonwords (Beauvois & Dérousné, 1979; Friedman et al., 1993). By contrast, reading by means of the whole-word mechanism was preserved, as shown by the relative sparing of concrete word reading. During real word reading there were visual and derivational errors, but not semantic errors or concreteness effects suggesting that the semantic route was spared. The pattern of impairment in reading comprehension of sentences together with a normal matching of two homophonic words to the corresponding picture, and abnormal word–picture matching, suggests that residual oral word reading was carried out using mainly the lexical–nonsemantic (direct) route (Lytton & Brust, 1989; Newcombe & Marshall, 1981; Sartori et al., 1987) and, to a lesser degree, through the lexical–semantic route (Ellis & Young, 1988). Interestingly, reading by the lexical nonsemantic route has been associated with relatively preserved object naming and real word reading but impaired reading of nonwords (see Diesfeldt, 1991, for review).

Neural substrate and mechanisms underlying intact object naming

Results of the second part of this study did not reveal significant between-group differences in genetic (e.g. sex, handedness) or environmental (e.g. years of education, interval between stroke onset and language testing, aetiology) factors that could account for the double dissociation between naming and comprehension. Indeed, some patients showed impaired object comprehension and preserved object naming (the TCSA-intact group), while others showed a relative sparing of object comprehension but impaired object naming (the Anomic group).

There were, however, several findings that are worth mentioning. First, unilateral vascular lesions in the TCSA-intact group produced a selective impairment in object comprehension while leaving object naming relatively intact. The Anomic group showed the opposite pattern. Second, the left perisylvian language cortex was structurally damaged in most patients with TCSA and impaired naming, but spared in all right-handed patients with TCSA and preserved object naming. Third, although patients with anomia also had lesions that spared the left perisylvian language cortex, it should be noted that these patients had a predominant involvement of the temporal lobe, as is usually seen in anomic aphasics without lexical–semantic comprehension disorders (Coughlan & Warrington, 1978; Knopman, Selnes, Niccum, & Rubens, 1984), while patients with TCSA and intact naming had a predominant involvement of the parietal lobe. Lastly, although the occurrence of a semantically based naming deficit in TCSA has usually been related to damage to the posterior heteromodal association areas (Kertesz et al., 1982), particularly the angular gyrus (Benson, 1988), the patient reported by Heilman and colleagues (1981) with TCSA and intact object naming, as well as four of the six patients in the TCSA-intact group actually had lesions involving the angular gyrus and/or its subcortical projections. Taken together, these findings suggest a functional and structural independence of the neural substrates underlying object naming and comprehension. Therefore, these findings would not support a single anatomical "centre" or "system" responsible for object naming and comprehension but a distributed language network in which locally specialised brain regions and their interconnections participate in the naming process (A.R. Damasio, 1990; Mesulam, 1990).

The presence of deficits in single-word comprehension after involvement of the left posterior heteromodal association areas in the TCSA-intact group is in keeping with previous reports (Alexander, Hiltbrunner, & Fischer, 1989; Hart & Gordon, 1990; Mesulam, 1990) who view the left inferior parietal lobe as an integral component of the neural net responsible for semantic comprehension. On the other hand, the sparing of oral naming clearly demonstrates not only that the left inferior parietal lobe was not an essential component of the neural system specifically associated with naming, but also that oral naming in these patients depended upon the integrity of other structures. Based on previous reports from the literature, these regions may include the inferior-middle temporal (BA 37) and occipital areas (Alexander, Hiltbrunner, & Fischer, 1989; Benson, 1988; A.R. Damasio, 1990; Rapcsak et al., 1987), the frontal perisylvian region (Ojemann, Ojemann, Lettich, & Berger, 1989), the anterior temporal lobe (BA 20, 21, and 38) (Caselli, Ivnik, & Duffy, 1991; A.R. Damasio, 1992), or the thalamus (Ojemann, 1975).

The question that now arises is why a lesion involving the left inferior parietal lobe induces anomia in visual confrontation naming tasks with lexical comprehensive deficits in some patients with TCSA (e.g. Ferro, 1984; Sevush & Heilman, 1984), whereas in others it induces a selective impairment of lexical

comprehension but leaves naming relatively preserved. Although these dissociated patterns of naming performance may be the mere consequence of small
differences in lesion localisation, it is also possible that individual variability in
the organisation of the language processing system within the left hemisphere
may account for the preservation or impairment of naming functions (Caplan,
1987, 1992). In support of this hypothesis, marked individual variability in
cortical localisation of naming has been reported in aphasic patients (e.g. Knopman
et al., 1984), as well as during cortical stimulation mapping studies (Gordon
et al., 1990; Ojemann et al., 1989). Ojemann and co-workers (1989), for instance,
recently demonstrated that in some patients the electrical stimulation of the left
frontal (but not left temporoparietal) language cortex interfered with object
naming, while the reverse anatomical pattern (left temporoparietal but not left
frontal) was true for others. In this setting it is important to note that in the
TCSA-intact group four patients had lesions involving the parietal lobe, while
the frontal lobe was involved in the other two patients.

An alternative interpretation is that object naming in the TCSA-intact group
was mediated by the opposite hemisphere. Kapur and Dunkley (1984) and Fujii,
Yamadori, Fukatsu, Ogawa, and Suzuki (1997) reported right-handed patients
who developed "crossed" mixed transcortical aphasia with intact naming after
extensive damage to the whole right perisylvian area, thus suggesting that naming and repetition were mediated by the left hemisphere. Moreover, using bilateral intracarotid amytal injections, I have recently demonstrated that Patient 5
(a left-hander with a right perisylvian lesion) had spared language abilities
(spontaneous speech, repetition, and object naming) exclusively mediated by the
hemisphere contralateral to the lesion (see further details in Chapter 7). These
three patients had mixed language representation, so that the neuroimaging and
amytal findings may not generalise to the right-handed patients with TCSA and
intact naming after left hemisphere lesions described in this chapter. None the
less, a role for the right hemisphere in object naming has been demonstrated
in right-handers with left hemisphere language dominance by electrical stimulation mapping of the left perisylvian language cortex (Andy & Bhatnagar, 1984;
Bhatnagar & Andy, 1983), following focal brain lesions (Joanette, Gouler, &
LeDorze, 1988; Joanette, Lecours, Lepage, & Lamoureux, 1983), and in right-
handed epileptic patients with left hemisphere language dominance many years
after cerebral commissurotomy (Corballis, 1996; Gazzaniga et al., 1996).

CHAPTER FIVE

Mixed transcortical aphasia

INTRODUCTION

Lichtheim (1885), on characterising the inner commissural aphasias (the label he used to refers to those aphasic syndromes with preserved repetition; see Chapter 1), reported two aphasic patients who could repeat language; one had nonfluent speech but normal comprehension, a combination of symptoms consistent with the current profile of transcortical motor aphasia (TCMA), whereas the other patient had fluent and irrelevant spontaneous speech with poor comprehension, a profile concordant with the contemporary classification of transcortical sensory aphasia (TCSA; Albert et al., 1981). Lichtheim not only described these cases in some detail, but also predicted that the two syndromes might occur simultaneously, thus provoking a peculiar combination of nonfluent speech and impaired auditory comprehension in the presence of preserved repetition and other expressive capacities (e.g. writing to dictation). Unfortunately, Lichtheim was unable to examine such cases. A few years later, Hübner (1889) published the first clinical and neuropathological account of a combination of the motor and sensory varieties of transcortical aphasias (TA) in a patient who, after a cerebral insult, had spontaneous speech reduced to a few words ("ja", "jawohl", "nun ja") and impaired understanding of spoken language in the presence of echolalic repetition. On postmortem examination, there were three foci of softening in the left hemisphere together with mild generalised cortical atrophic changes. One area of softening was present at the temporo-parietal cortex just posterior to Wernicke's area, whereas other less extensive lesions were seen involving the left Sylvian edge of F3 and subcortical structures including the lenticular nucleus, caudate nucleus, and claustrum. After the publication of Hübner's patient, similar clinical cases were reported, usually under the heading of "echolalia", or misclassified as TCSA (see Goldstein, 1948, pp. 303–308) and variously attributed to degenerative dementia with predominant pathological involvement of the frontal lobe [Pick, 1898], senile dementia [Liepmann, 1900], vascular lesions [Stransky, 1903], and encephalitis (Goldstein, 1915). These cases were analysed and reclassified by Kurt Goldstein (1917, 1948) who coined the term "mixed transcortical aphasia" (MTCA) to label this unusual and complex form of language disorder.

On discussing the pathophysiology of MTCA, Goldstein (1948) theorised that its clinical features were the effect of abnormal interaction between the language centres and peripheral parts of the brain important for nonlanguage mental processes. He further proposed various possible mechanisms to explain not only the motor and sensory components of MTCA, but also to account for the preservation of repetition (see also Chapter 1). He thought that the combination of the motor and sensory types of TA resulted from partial damage to both the anterior and posterior speech centres (Broca's and Wernicke's areas). The second mechanism discussed by Goldstein considered that repetition was preserved despite damage to the speech centres, because it was mediated by the right cerebral hemisphere. Goldstein, however, was not absolutely convinced that these two mechanisms were important in the pathophysiology of MTCA. The main argument put forward by Goldstein against the role of the right hemisphere in repetition, was that he could not find a reasonable explanation by which the right hemisphere could mediate repetition in MTCA if it was totally unable to generate spontaneous speech. Goldstein instead posited that the anatomical region of the left hemisphere that mediated the elementary expressive and receptive components of language, although separated from other brain areas (isolation of the speech area), was incompletely or not damaged at all and could be utilised to subserve language repetition even in the absence of spontaneous speech, auditory comprehension, or both. He suggested that the lesion responsible for the deficit in auditory comprehension in MTCA lay in the temporal lobe and its connections with the parietal lobe, whereas nonfluency and lack of impulse to speak were secondary to lesions involving either the frontal lobe or its connections with the motor speech area.

Following these introductory historical considerations, this chapter will be concerned with the description of the MTCA syndrome from a phenomenological, linguistic, aetiopathogenic, and neuroanatomical perspective. I will also illustrate these themes by considering several modern single case studies, focusing mainly on the relationship between neurolinguistic features and the anatomofunctional status of different brain regions.

CLINICAL CHARACTERISTICS

Spontaneous speech in MTCA is characterised by a marked reduction of verbal productions. In the acute stage some patients are mute or their verbal productions are limited to either stereotyped single words (e.g. "yes", "no", "fine";

Brown, 1975, Case 2), incomprehensible expressions (e.g. "ja, jawohl, nun ja"; Hübner, 1889), incomplete short phrases (e.g. "Oh boy"; Speedie et al., 1984, Case 1), or overlearned phrases (e.g. "Oh my god"; Brown, 1975, Case 3). Paucity of spontaneous speech (Pirozzolo et al., 1981), or the generation of very short sentences containing no more than three or four words and semantic paraphasias, are found in certain instances (Bogousslavsky et al., 1988), whereas in others there are no phonological or semantic paraphasias, but verbal output is limited to incomplete phrases devoid of concrete nouns and verbs (Heilman et al., 1976). Although patients with MTCA are usually alert, some of them make no effort to communicate verbally, appear akinetic, and do not speak unless addressed (Heilman et al., 1976; Whitaker, 1976). Some patients produce isolated words only with the aid of completion cues (e.g. "Your name is . . . ?"; Brown, 1975), whereas others with no spontaneous verbalisations produce literal and verbal paraphasias in response to specific questions (Mehler, 1988). Spontaneous gesturing may also be reduced.

Verbal productions may be effortful but articulation and grammar are usually normal, particularly when the anterior speech area and the adjacent inferior motor cortex (Broca's area) are spared (Coslett et al., 1985; Ross, 1980). By contrast, effortful and laboured articulation may accompany cases of MTCA secondary to left perisylvian area damage (e.g. Hadano, Nakamura, & Hamanaka, 1998, Case 3). Nevertheless, differences in speech output depending on the location of the lesion should be viewed with caution until empirical work on verbal output anomalies is done (see later). Reduced voice volume (hypophonia) may also be observed among patients with subcortical lesions at the level of either the thalamus (Perani, Vallar, Cappa, Messa, & Fazio, 1987, Case 3), lenticular nucleus (Berthier, Starkstein et al., 1991, Case 19), or periventricular white matter (Cappa et al., 1993). In addition to nonfluency and meaningless utterances, speech output may be further contaminated by perseverations, palilalia, and echolalic responses. Echolalia is usually prominent in the early stage of MTCA, to the point that in the more severely affected patients, echolalic responses are the only formulated verbal sequences (see further details in Chapter 6). A transcript of the spoken output of a patient (TSM) with a MTCA secondary to a left medial frontoparietal cortex infarction (Berthier, Fernández, Martínez-Celdrán, & Kulisevsky, 1996, Case 1) clearly illustrates instances of palilalia and perseverations. In the following paragraph, patient TSM is trying to describe the picnic scene of the Western Aphasia Battery (WAB; Kertesz, 1982):

> . . . in the, in the . . . in the . . . government . . ., government . . . government . . . government . . . the comet . . . the comet . . . and the child reading the comet . . . and the man . . . the government, the government . . . I see . . . the government, the government . . .

Echolalia and palilalia were also abundant in her responses to other WAB questions:

Examiner:	What are the people doing?
Patient TSM :	What are the people doing?
Examiner:	What are the people doing?
TSM:	washing . . . washing, . . . washing . . . washing . . .
Examiner:	Where are they?
TSM:	the government, . . . the government . . . uh,uh,uh . . . the govern-ment . . .

The characteristics of oral expression may be somewhat different in other MTCA patients. The following are examples of recurring utterances generated in response to questions of the spontaneous speech subtest of the WAB by a patient (JDP) with MTCA secondary to a large perisylvian ischaemic infarction in the left middle cerebral artery territory (Berthier, Posada, Puentes, & Hinojosa, 1997, Case 4):

Examiner:	What is your occupation?
Patient JDP:	occupation? . . . eah,eah,eah,eah,eah . . . aviation
Examiner:	Tell me a little about why you are here?
JDP:	one . . . two . . . eah, eah, eah, eah, eah . . .

Comprehension is severely affected as in global aphasia. In most patients comprehension is nil, whereas some cases can intermittently comprehend simple commands only with the aid of nonverbal cues (Jacome, 1984; Speedie et al., 1984; Trojano et al., 1988). Some patients show preserved auditory comprehension only for "axial" or "whole-body commands" (e.g. "Close your eyes"), perhaps reflecting the limited comprehension capacity of the right hemisphere (Albert et al., 1981; Geschwind, 1965). When comprehension is less severely compromised, deficits are observed on a wide range of tests ranging from the execution of two-step commands to the understanding of syntax and single words. As a rule, nearly all patients are unable to follow even the simplest request of the Token Test (Bogousslavsky et al., 1988; Pulvermüller & Schönle, 1993).

Naming is usually severely impaired and the deficit encompasses naming and recognition of visually presented objects and pictures as well as naming from descriptions. In exceptional patients, however, object naming is preserved despite marked nonfluency and impaired aural comprehension. Intact object naming in MTCA has been reported in right-handed individuals with lesions in either the left hemisphere (Heilman et al., 1976) or the perisylvian area of the right hemisphere ("crossed MTCA"; Kapur & Dunkley, 1984; Fujii et al., 1997; further details in Chapter 4). Reading and writing are also severely affected, though some capabilities may be relative spared. Different patterns of impairments and dissociations in performance are found. Impaired reading comprehension may coexist with either poor oral reading but preserved writing in patients with lesions involving the white matter beneath the left angular gyrus (e.g. subangular dyslexia; Pirozzolo et al., 1981), good oral reading of words contrasting with impaired nonword reading and semantic paralexias (deep dyslexia), and inability to write spontaneously or to dictation (Coslett et al., 1985), or superior oral reading of words over nonwords (phonological dyslexia) but preserved writing to copy and dictation with features of surface dysgraphia (preserved nonword writing with errors in orthographically ambiguous words; see Patient CV in Chapter 6). Semantic agraphia (e.g. semantic jargon during spontaneous writing) has also been reported in patients with MTCA (Roeltgen, 1993).

THE NEURAL SUBSTRATE

The syndrome of MTCA has been described in association with either cortical or subcortical lesions of the left hemisphere. The most common causes of MTCA from cortical damage are lesions that involve the anterior and posterior border-zone areas. This peculiar anatomical distribution has been reported after severe hypoxia, cerebral oedema, and carbon monoxide intoxication (Benson, 1993; Geschwind, et al., 1968). Cases of rapid resolving MTCA have been reported after simultaneous left hemisphere infarctions due to left internal carotid artery occlusion affecting the anterior pial precentral-central artery territory (posterior–superior frontal region) and the watershed territory between the middle and posterior cerebral arteries (posterior parietal-occipital region) (Bogousslavsky et al., 1988). Occlussion of other major cerebral vessels such as the main trunk of the middle cerebral artery with damage to the whole perisylvian language zone (Berthier, Starkstein et al., 1991; Brown, 1975; Grossi et al., 1991; Pulvermüller & Schönle, 1993; Stengel, 1947; Trojano et al., 1988) (Fig. 5.1), the distal anterior cerebral artery with lesions affecting the supplementary motor and sensory areas in the mesial aspect of the frontoparietal cortex (Ross, 1980, Berthier, Fernández et al., 1996) (Fig. 5.2), or simultaneous occlusion of branches of both anterior and middle cerebral arteries (Hadano et al., 1998, Case 3) are associated with the language deficits characteristic of MTCA.

Subcortical MTCA can occur by large haemorrhages in the basal ganglia (Berthier, Starkstein et al., 1991, Case 19; Poeck, de Blesser, & von Keyserlingk, 1984) and thalamus (McFarling et al., 1982, Case 1) or after selective involvement of the left periventricular white matter (corona radiata and centrum semiovale) due to ischaemic lesions (Cambier et al., 1980; Cappa et al., 1993; Speedie et al., 1984, Case 1), encephalitis (Goldstein, 1948), or chronic arteriosclerotic demyelination (Binswanger's disease; Ali Cherif, Labrecque, Pelissier, Poncet, & Boudouresques, 1979). Severe closed head injury with anterior temporo-frontal bilateral damage or associated with diffuse axonal injury to the left cerebral hemisphere involving predominantly the subcortical white matter (Berthier, unpublished observation) can also cause MTCA. Finally, the symptom complex of MTCA has been described in dementing conditions such as Alzheimer's disease (Au, Obler, & Albert, 1991), frontotemporal degeneration (Whitaker, 1976), nonspecific degenerative dementia with perisylvian involvement (Mehler,

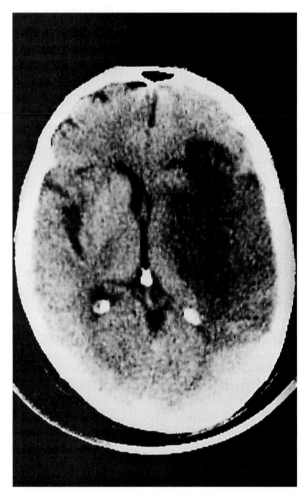

FIG. 5.1   CT scan showing an extensive perisylvian ischaemic infarction in a left-handed patient
with mixed transcortical aphasia. The lesion involves the territory of the left middle cerebral artery
and affects the fronto-temporo-parietal region extending deeply into the basal ganglia and internal
capsulae. This patient showed preserved repetition for words and short phrases but sentence repetition was impaired. The left hemisphere is represented on the right side of the figure.

1988), and Creutzfeldt–Jakob's disease (Kataki, Winikates, Kirkpatrick, &
Doody, 1996).

CLINICAL SUBTYPES

Heterogeneity in the clinical expression of aphasic disturbances is a common
finding (Basso et al., 1985; Willmes & Poeck, 1993). Given that heterogeneity
has been reported in aphasic syndromes with repetition disturbances such as

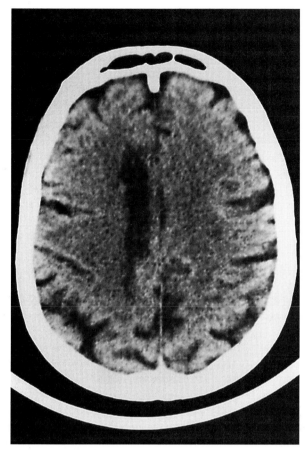

FIG. 5.2 CT scan of a patient with mixed transcortical aphasia and echolalia showing an ischaemic infarction in the territory of the left anterior cerebral artery with involvement of the mesial frontoparietal cortex.

conduction aphasia (Buckingham, 1992), it is not surprising to find different clinical patterns in the reciprocal disorders, TA. In Chapter 3, I reviewed data on the presence of heterogeneity in the verbal output of patients diagnosed as having transcortical motor aphasia (TCMA; Ardila & López, 1984; Körney, 1975; Lebrun, 1995; Luria & Tsvetkova, 1968). To recapitulate, some patients with TCMA aphasia show no spontaneous speech but automatic echolalia with normal articulation, whereas others instead have nonfluent, effortful articulation but no echolalia. Object naming may or may not be preserved in transcortical motor aphasic patients. I also outlined the different types of verbal output encountered in transcortical sensory aphasia (TCSA; see Chapter 4). Spontaneous speech is described as fluent, copious, and well articulated, but some patients show it composed of semantic paraphasias (Kestesz, 1982), others by anomia or neo-logistic jargon (Lecours & Rouillon, 1976), and still others show a relative pre-servation of spontaneous speech, lacking either word-finding difficulties, prominent paraphasias, or neologisms (Heilman et al., 1981). In the same setting, naming is virtually always impaired in TCSA (Berndt et al., 1987; Martin & Saffran, 1990), although exceptional cases with intact object naming but poor name recognition of the same objects have also been reported (Heilman et al., 1981; Kremin, 1986). Since the traditional description of MTCA viewed it as resulting from the coexistence of motor and sensory types (Goldstein, 1948; Lichtheim, 1885), it is reasonable to suppose that heterogeneity would also be detected among groups of patients featuring MTCA.

Goldstein (1948, p. 301) contemplated the possibility of heterogeneous patterns of symptoms in MTCA. In his experience, the verbal output and aural comprehension were often affected with different severity depending on whether the isolation of the speech area was complete or not. He also suggested that compulsive echolalia only occurred in severe cases when the intention to com-municate and speech understanding were totally abolished due to a complete isolation of the speech area. Partial isolation of the speech area in his view was associated with less severe expressive or receptive language deficits and echolalia was not observed. To further complicate matters, Goldstein considered that a distinct profile of language impairment in MTCA would be documented when the speech apparatus ("instrumentalities") is also damaged. He did not discuss patients presenting with this pattern of impairment, however.

More recently, Heilman (1985) also attempted to subdivide MTCA into three different types according to the patient's performance on object-naming tasks and on the correction of syntactic errors during repetition. According to Heilman, type I of MTCA is characterised by the preserved ability to correct syntactic anomalies with impaired object naming; in type II the ability to correct syntactic errors and to name objects are both impaired, and the opposite pattern, namely, preserved ability to correct syntactic errors and to name objects, characterises type III. Heilman indicated that only cases with types I and III of MTCA have so far been reported (Davis et al., 1978; Heilman et al., 1976; Whitaker, 1976). Recently, Pulvermüller and Schönle (1993) described a case of MTCA meeting the diagnostic criteria for type II, and Mehler and Rabinowich (1990) briefly reported data of five further patients confirming these three patterns of language dissociation.

The syndrome of MTCA is rare. It represented 3% of the 215 aphasic patients collected by Kertesz (1979) during the standardisation of the WAB and 1.3% of the 221 aphasic patients studied by Willmes and Poeck (1993) in a retrospective investigation of lesion sites in major aphasic syndromes using the Aachen Apha-sia Test. Berthier, Starkstein et al. (1991) found that 5 (24%) of 21 transcortical aphasic patients exhibited the combination of language deficits necessary to establish the diagnosis of TMCA. Therefore, a major drawback in the analysis of

MTCA is that only a few cases have been studied in some detail. Nonetheless, the paucity of reports allows in the present chapter a more fine-grained analysis of relevant cases. In the next section of this chapter, I will examine the profile of language disturbances in various well-known cases of MTCA grouped in their original publications under the label of "isolation of the speech area" (Assal et al., 1983; Geschwind et al., 1968; Whitaker, 1976). Other MTCA cases with adequate clinical and language descriptions but lacking radiological or pathological information or with good radiological data but reporting language abnormalities at very general level will not be analysed.

The pattern associated with isolation of the speech area

Goldstein coined the term "isolation of the speech area" to explain the neuronatomical mechanism underlying the pattern of impaired and preserved language abilities he found in cases of MTCA. He published his own cases and reviewed available publications on "echolalia" (the label used by that time to refer to MTCA). Of these reviewed cases, the patient described by Hübner (1889) is currently regarded, although not unanimously (Brown, 1975), as the first clinicopathological example of isolation of the speech area. Since the description of these early cases, the syndrome of MTCA was largely ignored until the publication of a seminal paper by Geschwind et al. (1968), describing clinical and neuropathological findings of an echolalic demented young woman who had survived a decade following a carbon monoxide intoxication.

Geschwind et al. (1968)

Patient description.   The patient was a 22-year-old woman admitted after carbon monoxide poisoning. After two weeks, neurological examination disclosed a paraplegia in flexion and her examiner noted that she could sing and echo verbal messages. When examined about one year after the onset, the neurological examination remained essentially unchanged, but Geschwind and his colleagues additionally found that she had motor akinesia of both arms most of the time and bilateral grasp reflexes. Cranial nerve examination was normal, and in particular there were no difficulties with hearing, phonation, and spontaneous tongue movements. She occasionally showed agitated behaviour and right-sided seizures that were controlled by antiepileptic medication.

Speech and language assessment.   Given that this patient was examined in the late 1950s, when bedside language testing was the most commonly used method to assess aphasia, the status of residual speech and language functions was examined through brief qualitative interviews during a 10-year follow-up. Spontaneous speech was lost except for the presence of a few noncommunicative exclamations, namely, stereotyped phrases (e.g. "So can daddy"), palilalia (e.g. "Hi daddy, Hi daddy, . . ."), expletives (e.g. "Dirty bastard"), or unrecognisable words. Responsive speech, object naming, and auditory and written comprehension were abolished. In contrast to her impaired ability to use expressive speech and to understand anything said to her, it was noticed that she automatically repeated verbal material, songs, and showed a relative preservation of verbal learning. The patient echoed questions without dysarthria and reproduced the melody correctly. Another surprising finding was her tendency to automatically complete open-ended sentences, proverbs, and songs. For instance, when the examiner said: "Close your eyes", she added "Go to sleep". The completion phenomenon was not only elicited by incomplete sentences and proverbs; the pronunciation of a simple word (e.g. "coffee") by the examiner would trigger a long response (e.g. "I love coffee, I love tea, I love the girls and the girls love me"). If the patient listened to a well-known song or musical commercial, she echoed these materials with correct articulation of words and melody and often continued singing the forthcoming lyrics even after the tape recorder was stopped. This prompted the authors to assess whether or not the automatic completion phenomenon favoured the learning of songs not previously known to her. They were astonished by the fact that after hearing songs novel to her a few times (e.g. songs composed after she had suffered the carbon monoxide intoxication) played on a tape recorder she could continue singing the lyrics and melody when the tape recoder was stopped, or only the lyrics if the examiner continued to hum the tune (see also Chapter 6).

Neuropathological examination.   A detailed neuropathological study revealed the pattern of widespread anoxic damage typically described among victims of carbon monoxide intoxication. There were extensive areas of laminar necrosis and subcortical myelin loss involving the frontal, temporal, parietal, and occipital lobes. The perisylvian language cortex, arcuate fasciculus, cingulate gyrus, parahippocampus, amygdala, and most of the hippocampus were largely spared bilaterally. At subcortical level, there was a bilateral cystic necrosis of the globus pallidus, myelin damage in the white matter of the frontoparietal regions, and gliosis with cell loss in both caudate nucleus and putamen. The brainstem and cerebellum were only mildly affected, and there was moderate enlargement of the lateral ventricles.

Comment.   Geschwind et al. performed a detailed pathological study in which they demonstrated the anatomical integrity of Heschl's gyrus, Wernicke's area, Broca's area, the lower third of the primary motor area, and the arcuate fasciculus, all structures previously implicated by Wernicke (1874/1977) in his "reflex arc", which he contended was necessary for language imitation (repetition). Therefore, in this paper Geschwind and his colleagues vindicated with empirical data the hypothesis put forward earlier by Lichtheim (1885) and Goldstein (1917, 1948) suggesting that transcortical aphasic syndromes result from strategically placed lesions that surround but spare the left perisylvian language zone responsible for repetition from the more peripheral anterior and posterior cortical regions which are essential for intention and meaning, respectively.

This single case study had a tremendous influence in reawakening the interest of clinicians to the study of TA to the point that after its publication, the syndromes of aphasia were reclassified and divided from an anatomical point of view into those due to perisylvian pathology as opposed to those with lesions sparing the central language zone; or when a linguistic criteria of classification was adopted, aphasic syndromes were grouped according to the preservation or impairment in the ability to repeat language (Albert et al., 1981; Benson, 1993; Benson & Geschwind, 1971; A.R. Damasio, 1992).

Geschwind et al.'s case study, although influential, also has some limitations. One such problem concerns the shallowness of language testing. In fact, while some aspects of verbal behaviour (song learning) were examined in a specially devised testing situation, other residual language functions such as repetition and completion phenomenon were succintly examined and no quantitative data were provided. Some reservation is also necessary with respect to the interpretation of clinicopathological correlations put forward by Geschwind and associates. The authors stated that the pattern of aphasic disturbances remained stable during the entire patient follow-up. Careful analysis of the case description, however, reveals that some aspects of the automatic verbal behaviour (singing and verbal learning) were present only early in the patient's illness and, more importantly, major features of MTCA (echolalia and completion phenomenon) disappeared long before the patient's death, rendering her with a global aphasia in the final two years. Geschwind et al. acknowledged the eventual disappearance of uninhibited repetition of verbal material and speculated that the superimposition of medical problems (fever, infections) on a static brain pathology, rather than the presence of an ongoing pathological process, accounted for language deterioration. In any case, it seems obvious that the interval between the evaluation of echolalic behaviour and postmortem examination limits the value of clinicopathological correlation put forward by Geschwind et al. A final point worth noting is that the patient's handedness was not mentioned, thus making uncertain which of either the left or right perisylvian language areas served echolalic repetition, singing, and automatic aspects of verbal function.

While only a limited language evaluation was possible in the mixed transcortical aphasic patient reported by Geschwind et al., subsequent studies examined residual speech and language abilities in more detail (Assal et al., 1983; Whitaker, 1976). The most comprehensive study of echolalic behaviour that appeared in the literature on psycholinguistic deficits associated with TA was published by Whitaker (1976), who reported a patient with MTCA occurring in the context of progressive degenerative dementia.

Patient HCEM (Whitaker, 1976)

Case description.   The patient, HCEM, was a 59-year-old woman with a diagnosis of presenile dementia and alcoholism. She had a positive familial history for progressive dementing illness and echolalic aphasia in her mother and two sisters. At the time of evaluation, HCEM had advanced dementia characterised by severe impairment in different cognitive domains, including attention, visual and auditory retention as well as planning and foresight. Performance in perceptual and motor tests, such as tactually guided behaviour and fine motor coordination, were less affected with the more prominent deficits observed on the right side, thus indicating a predominant left hemisphere dysfunction. The elementary neurological examination revealed increased muscle tone and hyper-reflexia in the lower extremities, but HCEM was able to walk without requiring assistance. There was mild tremor in the upper extremities. She was totally dependent in activities of daily living and had urinary incontinence.

Speech and language assessment.   HCEM had no spontaneous speech and never attempted to initiate conversations. Auditory comprehension, object naming, and responsive speech were virtually abolished. During clinical neuropsychological testing, it was noticed that she displayed palilalia and echolalia, to the extent that her echoes could not be suppressed even when she was instructed not to repeat. Whitaker administered a variety of experimental procedures to test repetition ability in her patient.

Repetition of words, nonwords, and foreign languages.   Whitaker found that HCEM could automatically repeat numbers, nonsense words (four to seven letters), and foreign languages well. She echoed only verbal stimuli that did not violate the English phonological constraints and remained silent when she heard nonsense and foreign words with unacceptable phonological sequences. Moreover, if a verbal stimulus was presented to her in a British dialect she switched the intonation of her echoes to her native American dialect.

Sentence repetition: Correction of syntactical and semantic errors.   HCEM echoed 10 syntactically and phonologically normal complex sentences (e.g. "Mary refused to talk to him") verbatim, and more surprisingly, she corrected all (n = 58) phonological or syntactical errors embedded in otherwise correct sentences, echoing the entire sentences (e.g. "Do you want *go movies?*" ⇒ "Do you want *to go to a movie?*") in 54 instances, or correcting only the abnormal fragment (e.g. "I have two *coat*" ⇒ "*two coats*") on 4 occasions. HCEM was also able to correct modifications in adjective–noun order (e.g. "I have *hair gray*" ⇒ "I have *gray hair*") and she also corrected phonemically erroneous medial consonants whether in initial (e.g. "This is a *pand*" ⇒ "*hand*") or median position (e.g. "The *petcil* is on the table" ⇒ "*pencil*") only if she could see the real object. By contrast, when HCEM heard semantically anomalous sentences she either remained silent or echoed without correcting the semantic anomalies.

Completion phenomenon.   The completion phenomenon was another relevant clinical feature of aphasia in HCEM. Her performance on a variety of completion exercises was fluctuating since she could not always complete the target verbal stimulus. She succeeded in completion mainly when the expected responses were high frequency nouns ("man", "girl", "bacon"), and occasionally when common adjectives ("hot") or verbs ("live") were preceded by predictable completion sequences (e.g. "Where do you . . ." ⇒ "*live*"). Not only did HCEM complete single words, she also completed longer overlearned verbal material such as familiar song titles and proverbs. However, when the context was semantically more open-ended, she produced words that were semantically unrelated to the target words (e.g. "can you tell me some . . ." ⇒ "*some nails*"). Whitaker pointed out that completion needed to be cued by a nonfinal intonation contour indicating that verbal information was forthcoming. Nonverbal sounds failed to elicit a completion phenomenon.

Linguistic prosody.   During a casual interview HCEM echoed all (n = 41) questions pronounced by the examiner, exactly reproducing the linguistic stress and intonational patterns (e.g. "Did you have a nice day yesterday?"). HCEM also corrected errors of linguistic prosody in all compound nouns (n = 22) deliberately pronounced by the examiner with abnormal stress patterns. Target words were presented in isolation (e.g. "vácuum cleáner" ⇒ "*vácuum cléaner*") or embedded in sentences (e.g. "The President lives in the White housé" ⇒ "*White hôuse*") (see futher details in Chapter 6). Perhaps Whitaker did not examine the ability to impart affective intonation during echoes because HCEM was studied several years before the concept of affective prosody became popular among neuropsychologists.

Neuropathological examination.   Postmortem macroscopic examination of the brain revealed a selective atrophy of the frontotemporal regions bilaterally, with slightly greater involvement of the right superior frontal gyrus, left temporopolar region, and orbital surface of frontal lobes on inspection of the convexity. Coronal sections, however, revealed that the atrophy of the frontotemporal cortex showed a knife-edge shaped gyri which was more marked on the anterior regions of the left hemisphere. Microscopic examination revealed nonspecific pathology with neuronal degeneration and gliosis involving the cerebral cortex, white matter, basal ganglia, and portions of the midbrain and cerebellum. Neuritic plaques, neurofibrillary tangles, and cortical Lewy bodies were not present.

Comment.   This patient was evaluated in the final stage of a progressive dementing illness of unknown aetiology which pathologically affected mainly the frontal and temporal lobes. In retrospect, HCEM's case would be classified as a case of frontotemporal dementia since she showed prominent behavioural changes (e.g. disinhibition, poor self-care, utilisation behaviour) and stereotyped language (for diagnostic criteria see Lund and Manchester groups, 1994).

In this case study, Whitaker attempted for the first time to interpret the functional organisation of residual aspects of verbal productions (echolalia and completion phenomenon) in HCEM using a top-down model of language production. She proposed a neurolinguistic model with hierarchical organisation, in which the first level corresponded to the basic input and output mechanisms of speech. This first level was intact in HCEM. The echolalic behaviour not only reflected her ability to process language auditorily, but also the absence of echolalia to nonlinguistic material (sounds) was taken by Whitaker as evidence that "her input mechanism is highly constrained to linguistic stimuli (p. 50)". The output mechanism was also preserved, since HCEM did not show articulatory deficits during the production of echolalic utterances. According to Whitaker, the indemnity of level I only permitted verbatim "parrot-like" repetitions. She suggested that HCEM's ability to monitor the input signal during repetition as demonstrated, for instance, by the modification of grammar, required the utilisation of level II. This second level corresponded to what Whitaker interchangeably labelled "automatic", "noncreative", or "nonvolitional" language and encompassed phonological organisation (phonemic patterns, stress, and intonational patterns), automatic overlearned aspects of grammatical organisation (e.g. rules of syntactic agreement, pronoun assignments), and probably some semantic features of late lexical operations alongside phonological operations, as well as certain overlearned phrases and speech automatisms. Whitaker considered that this second level of productive language organisation was largely spared in HCEM, because she could not only repeat language verbatim, but was also able to apply syntactical and grammatical rules suggesting that HCEM must have access to some aspects of the lexicon during automatic repetition. It seems, however, that access to a lexical storage was different, depending on the verbal or visual modalities of stimuli presentation. In the visual modality, for instance, she corrected phonemic errors in initial consonants (e.g. "a yellow *tencil*") during her echoed productions only when the actual object (e.g. "pencil") was placed in her visual field; when the actual object was outside of her visual field, she repeated the anomalous sentences verbatim. In the auditory modality, echolalia occurred in a specific conversational context, whereas the completion of open-ended phrases invariably required a prosodic cue (nonterminal intonational contour) to initiate every completion response.

The third level of functioning, which in Whitaker's opinion was dedicated to both cognitive-intellectual function as well as "creative" and "volitional" aspects of language, was severely affected. In fact, the ability to generate spontaneous utterances, participating in conversations, and to answer questions as well as to write spontaneously were lost. Moreover, HCEM was totally unable to make up a sentence when isolated words were given to her in a random order and she also demonstrated a lack of voluntary lexical retrieval during object naming tasks.

Patient NT (Assal et al., 1983)

Additional evidence favouring the neuroanatomical account of isolation of the speech area in MTCA was published by Assal and co-workers (1983), who reported the clinicopathological details of a patient with multiple ischaemic infarcts.

Case description. NT was a 60-year-old right-handed woman who learned to speak French at the age of 16 years. She was admitted in 1980 after suffering recurrent transient ischaemic attacks and seizures which left her with left homonymous hemianopia, gait instability, and impaired language functions. On a bedside evaluation of language functions, she demonstrated word-finding difficulty during spontaneous speech, impaired visual confrontation naming, poor auditory comprehension, pure alexia, and impaired constructional abilities. Serial CT scans showed a diffuse cerebral atrophy affecting cortical and subcortical regions, but there was no evidence of focal vascular lesions. EEG recordings carried out during the course of her illness disclosed bilateral abnormalities with generalised epileptic activity over the left hemisphere and slowing in the posterior cortical regions of the right hemisphere. During hospitalisation NT experienced a precipitous decline in her neurological condition, and she developed quadriparesis and cortical blindness.

Neuropsychological testing was carried out about eight months post-onset. Since NT had vigilance problems and she easily became fatigued, the evaluation of language functions had to be performed through numerous brief sessions. She had extremely poor auditory comprehension and her oral productions were almost exclusively composed of palilalia, echolalia, and automatic completion of utterances produced by the examiner. In fact, she had no spontaneous speech, except for some stereotyped interjections ("aïe, aïe, aïe"). Series speech was possible only with prompting, but it was restricted to a few items. Visual confrontation naming and naming from descriptions were abolished, but she could name some common objects by touch. Auditory comprehension was severely compromised for body commands and yes/no questions (9/30 correct). Reading was impossible to test and writing performance could not be examined due to severe motor deficits. Memory was severely affected. Therefore, Assal and his co-workers focused the evaluation of aphasia on the analysis of some linguistic aspects relevant to TA, namely repetition, echolalia, and completion phenomenon. The linguistic features of residual repetition capabilities in NT were examined according to the psycholinguistic experimental protocol devised by Whitaker (1976).

Repetition of words, nonwords, and phrases.   NT's performance on tests of word and nonword repetition was relatively preserved. She repeated 44/50 words (1 to 6 syllables) and 40/50 nonwords (1 to 4 syllables) flawlessly. Errors on word repetition were few and consisted of phonological transformations (e.g. "train" ⇒ "*tran*"), whereas errors in nonword repetition were almost exclusively lexicalisations (e.g. "flup" ⇒ "*flute*"; "sertikal" ⇒ "*vertical*"). Phrase repetition was largely preserved as NT could repeat phrases of 10 syllables errorlessly. She did not pay attention, however, to paralinguistic features of the message (intensity, prosody) and repeated these phrases devoid of linguistic and affective colouring.

Echolalia.   NT had severe echolalia mostly occurring when she was verbally addressed by the examiner. Only in certain occasions echolalic utterances were heard when the incoming auditory information was not directed to her (e.g. oral reading by another person, radio) but there were no instances of echolalia when the auditory stimulus was nonverbal (e.g. noises, music). Moreover, when NT heard a song, she echoed the verses (lyrics) but she did not imitate the melodic intonation. Further analysis consisted of the evaluation of syntactical and semantic influence on NT's echolalic behaviour. She could correct phonemic substitutions in words embedded in phrases (e.g. "J'écris avec un prayon [crayon] rouge" ["I write with a red pencil"]) in 16 of 20 occasions, and she also corrected errors of number agreement in 18 of 30 instances. On the other hand, she appeared totally unable to modify semantic inconsistencies in phrases (e.g. "Les fleurs arrosent le garcon") succeeding in 1 of 30 instances, and could only correct 1 of 20 semantically incoherent phrases (e.g. "Le pape habite à Moscou") [The Pope lives in Moscow]. Echolalic behaviour was also observed in phrases pronounced in English and German, but not for Italian expressions which were invariably echoed in a French-like way.

Completion phenomenon.   NT showed the completion phenomenon traditionally described among patients with TA. Formal assessment through several sentence completion exercises, however, revealed that she could manage to complete only certain exercises. On completion of proverbs, she did correctly on 9 of 25 and she could complete the title of 7 of 12 well-known songs. On another exercise which required the completion of 80 open-ended predictable sentences (e.g. "J'écris avec . . . [un zéro]" ["I write with a . . ."]) she produced 34 correct responses, 17 incorrect completions, and omissions on 29 occasions. Analysis of error profile revealed that NT's responses were heavily influenced by semantic variables. She failed to complete sentences in which the expected response implied animals (2/10 correct) and flowers (0/10 correct), but showed adequate performance on transformation in nouns from masculine to feminine in 20 of 30 phrases and vice versa, as well as from plural to singular (10/12 correct). She was also able to transform the tense of irregular and regular verbs (9/10 correct).

Neuropathological examination. The neuropathological study revealed extensive multifocal ischaemic infarctions. Gross inspection of the mesial surface of the cerebral hemispheres showed symmetric lesions from frontal through posterior parietal regions affecting the vascular territories of the distal anterior and posterior cerebral arteries. The extensive foci of infarctions were all suprasylvian and involved the anterior superior frontal regions (including BA 10, 11, 9, 8, and the supplementary motor areas), the upper portions of the cingulate gyri, the superior parietal regions and the occipital poles. Less extensive ischaemic changes were also seen involving the right basal ganglia, the left opercular cortex, the body and splenium of the corpus callosum, and the mesial temporal cortices (hippocampus formation) bilaterally. The central perisylvian cortices were largely spared and there were no pathological changes in the supramarginal and angular gyri.

Comment. The analysis of NT's language through her echolalic behaviour and automatic completion of sentence fragments is remarkably similar to the pattern of performance reported by Geschwind and associates (1968) and Whitaker (1976), although some new findings were also apparent. NT showed preserved repetition of words, nonwords, and sentences of increasing length, and she produced few errors that were phonologically related to the target words. She did not make semantic errors when automatically repeating single words and phrases. Thus, it seems that in NT the nonlexical phonological route for repetition, which directly links the auditory verbal input to the articulatory output, bypassing the conceptual or semantic representation, was spared as reflected by the preserved ability to repeat nonwords (Caplan, 1992; Ellis & Young, 1988; McCarthy & Warrington, 1984). In the same vein, the nonlexical route was probably used by NT for the completion of open-ended sentences with a highly predictable response (e.g. "The cat has four . . . *legs*"), because these phrases probably do not require a detailed semantic processing (Butterworth & Warrington, 1995; McCarthy & Warrington, 1984). The status of the lexical–semantic route of repetition in this case is more difficult to analyse, because the authors controlled the word lists for length only, but they did not mention if the experimental word lists were construed by taking into account other variables such as word frequency, and grammatical categories. NT had a preserved ability to complete some complex sentences and she also produced correct completions of more open-ended sentences occurring predominantly in certain semantic categories (colours, 40% correct), but not in others (flowers, 0% correct). Such a dissociation led Assal and his colleagues to conclude that correct responses had to be achieved by semantic mediation.

A surprising aspect of NT's performance was the discrepancy between the relative preservation of repetition of propositional language as compared to her poor ability to impart linguistic and affective intonation during sentence repetition. Assal et al. pointed out that impaired modulation of prosodic contours during repetition tasks was not due to inattention or indifference; they rather contended that NT had an inability to modulate linguistic and affective prosody properly. Indeed, although most sentences were repeated or echoed in a mono-tone, NT apparently attempted to modulate intonation as she could occasionally impart an uncoloured rising intonation during sentence repetition. These find-ings were replicated by Speedie et al. (1984) in two patients with MTCA and left hemisphere ischaemic lesions that spared the perisylvian language area (periventricular white matter in Case 1 and parieto-occipital region in Case 2). Based on the clinical perceptual rating of prosodic production, these two patients were found to produce flat intonations when they were asked to repeat semant-ically neutral sentences with different affective intonations. While Assal et al. did not discuss the pathophysiology of abnormal prosodic repetition, Speedie and co-workers (1984) suggested that the ability to repeat propositional language in their two patients was preserved because the left perisylvian area was intact. On the other hand, they argued that repetition of affective prosody was virtually impossible because the "isolated" perisylvian language area was disconnected from the right hemisphere which plays a dominant role in the modulation of expressive and receptive components of affective prosody. Clinicopathological correlations in NT seem to be in accord with the neuroanatomical model pro-posed by Speedie and co-workers to explain poor repetition of affective prosody in MTCA. Following the line of reasoning advanced by these authors, the anatom-ical integrity of both perisylvian language areas demonstrated in the neuropatho-logical study of NT allowed a relative preservation of propositional language during echolalic behaviour. Moreover, one could argue that her repetition of affective prosody was abnormal because the left and right perisylvian language areas, though anatomically spared, were disconnected from each other as a result of involvement of the corpus callosum and subcortical structures. In support of this hypothesis, some authors (Speedie et al., 1984; Starkstein, Berthier, & Leiguarda, 1988) have suggested that the integrity of the corpus callosum is crucial for the interhemispheric integration of propositional (left hemisphere) and affective (right hemisphere) components of language into a unified commun-icative behaviour (see Ross, Harney, de Lacoste, & Purdy, 1981 for different arguments).

Another possibility is that impaired modulation of linguistic prosody in NT may have been related to damage to the anterior cingulate gyri and supplemetary motor areas. In support of this interpretation, lesions in the anterior cingulate cortex were reported to impair the modulation of prosodic contours (Jürgens & von Cramon, 1982) and a patient with a haemorrhage of the anterior corpus callosum associated with swelling of the anterior cingulate cortex was found to have aprosodic spontaneous speech and repetition of phrases intoned with happy, sad, and angry intonations coupled with normal comprehension of affective prosody (Starkstein et al., 1988). In addition, Ross et al. (1997) recently docu-mented that impaired repetition of affective prosody in various aphasic syndromes, including cases of TA, is associated with lesions of the subcortical white matter just below the supplementary motor area that disrupt interhemispheric connections running through the corpus callosum. However, in the absence of additional evidence, it is difficult to determine if abnormal modulation of linguistic prosody during repetition tasks in NT was the direct consequence of bilateral mesial frontal lobe involvement by impairing the ability to impart emphatic stress and intonation at sentence level, essential to signal a question as opposed to declarative statements. In this regard, it is interesting to note that Geschwind et al.'s (1968) case, who apparently had some preservation of linguistic prosody during her echoes, had a remarkable preservation of both cingulate gyri.

The pattern associated with partial isolation of speech area

The cases of MTCA just described occurred in patients who had other cognitive deficits besides aphasia as a result of extensive, diffuse bilateral damage. Moreover, in most of these patients MTCA was diagnosed in the chronic period after an initial phase of global aphasia. Notwithstanding, the previously discussed cases of MTCA seem to fit well within the neuroanatomical requirements for a complete isolation of the speech area. This pattern of symptoms, however, has also been documented in patients who had radiologic evidence of a partial isolation of the speech area (Berthier, Starkstein et al., 1991, and Berthier, Fernández et al., 1996, Case 1; Pirozzolo et al., 1981; Rapcsak, Krupp, Rubens, & Reim, 1990; Speedie et al., 1984). Therefore, the analysis of some single case studies of MTCA with similar profiles of impaired and preserved language abilities to the patients just described, but in whom the aphasic syndrome was associated to less extensive left hemisphere lesions, is of interest.

Pirozzolo et al. (1981)

These authors reported the case of a 63-year-old male patient who suffered a large subcortical haemorrhage in posterior regions of the left hemisphere outside the perisylvian cortex which severely impaired his ability to speak and read. Upon neurological examination, the patient showed right hemiparesis and features of MTCA (paucity of spontaneous speech, impaired auditory comprehension, excellent repetition, and echopraxia) together with alexia without homonymous hemianopia or agraphia (subangular alexia), impaired naming, and colour agnosia. The CT scan disclosed a large haemorrhage located in the white matter underlying the left angular gyrus with mass effect and a questionable left thalamic lesion, but surprisingly did not show the expected involvement of the anterior (frontal) cortical areas. Pirozzolo and colleagues first studied the status of phonological organisation of language during repetition in their patient. The patient was capable of repeating difficult articulatory sequences and also corrected anomalous sentences with minor syntactical deviations (e.g. "This is a *sook*" ⇒ "*book*"). To prove that the repetition ability was not performed in an automatic "parrot-like" fashion, the authors presented foreign words and sentences to the patient. The presentation of German sentences (e.g. "Meine Mutter will ans Mer fahren") failed to elicit repetition and the hearing of Italian sentences that contained intermingled English words (e.g. "Il viaggio da Minneapolis at St Paul é non longo"), elicited the selective repetition of those words ("Minneapolis" and "St Paul") that aroused previously known phonological associations. Repetition performance was also susceptible to linguistic prosody. The patient corrected abnormal stress and intonational patterns of noun compounds embedded in sentences (e.g. "My mother was ba king' a cake"). Once the authors demonstrated their patient's intact access to phonological representations, they wanted to see if repetition performance was likewise susceptible to syntactic and semantic variables. They found that the patient corrected sentences with grammatical errors but not those containing semantic inconsistences, a pattern of dissociation previously reported among other MTCA patients with *complete* isolation of the speech area (Davis et al., 1978; Whitaker, 1976). Pirozzolo and co-workers explained the dissociation between phonological–syntactic and lexical–semantic operations in oral language (MTCA) and between reading and written (subangular alexia) as a "double disconnection syndrome", but they did not explain the unexpected finding of nonfluency without structural involvement of the anterior language regions.

Speedie et al. (1984, Case 2)

These authors reported a second case of MTCA associated with a single lesion involving posterior cortical regions of the left hemisphere. The patient (Case 2) was a 59-year-old right-handed man who had spontaneous speech reduced to automatic short phrases (e.g. "Oh boy"), poor auditory comprehension and naming, but spared ability to repeat sentences and to intermittently correct errors of tense and pronoun usage. The patient had, however, impaired ability to impart affective intonation during repetition. The CT scan disclosed a left parieto-occipital ischaemic infarction.

Rapcsak et al. (1990)

These researchers reported two patients featuring MTCA associated with extensive infarctions involving the Broca's area and surrounding frontal cortex in the left hemisphere. CT and MRI scans failed to disclose involvement of posterior cortical association areas, but in one of these two patients (Case 1) the SPECT demonstrated a decrease of perfusion not only in the anterior perisylvian regions, but also in morphologically intact posterior cortical regions. The authors suggested that a functional deactivation of anatomically connected areas may explain those cases of MTCA without anatomical isolation of the speech area.

Comment.   A lesson to be learned from the patients described by Pirozzolo et al. (1981) and Speedie et al. (1984) is that MTCA may be caused by single lesions in posterior regions of the left hemisphere. If these observations are viewed from an anatomical perspective, it appears that a partial (posterior) isolation of the speech area is, at least in certain cases, sufficient to induce not only the expected auditory comprehension deficit, but also nonfluent speech. Complimentary information from Rapcsak et al.'s patients also suggest that structural damage to anterior cortical regions may provoke nonfluency and also the unexpected impairment in auditory comprehension. Their SPECT findings in one such patients (Case 1) helps to explain how a single corticosubcortical lesion, whether anteriorly or posteriorly placed, can impair both expressive and receptive aspects of language. These observations are in agreement with the current conceptualisation of cerebral representation of language function, which view dichotomies of expression/reception and motor/sensory not only as more relative than previously thought, but additionally considers that production and comprehension of language are represented in different nodes of the same neural network (Mesulam, 1990).

The pattern associated with perisylvian damage

Geschwind and his colleagues (1968) clearly stated that the aphasic profile exhibited by their single patient fits well within the classical clinical description of MTCA, whereas the reported neuropathological findings were in accord with the model of isolation of the speech area earlier proposed by Goldstein (1917, 1848). Notwithstanding, since the publication of the seminal paper of Geschwind et al., the headings "isolation of the speech area" and "mixed transcortical aphasia" have been used interchangeably (Adams & Victor, 1989; Assal et al., 1983; Pirozzolo et al., 1981; Rubens & Kertesz, 1983; Vignolo, 1984; Whitaker, 1976), despite the growing body of evidence indicating that the classical theory of isolation of the speech area cannot provide a straightforward explanation for every case of MTCA (see Grossi et al., 1991 for a critical review).[2]

In contrast to what Hübner (1889) and Goldstein (1917) found, other early authors described patients who developed MTCA after damage to the perisylvian language zone (Niessl von Mayendorf, 1911; Stengel, 1947; Vix, 1910). Therefore, in these cases the sparing of repetition was interpreted as reflecting the mediation of the right hemisphere. While this pathophysiological mechanism

---

[2] Based on data reported here I believe that it would be appropriate to reserve the label of isolation of the speech area exclusively to denote the neuroanatomical mechanism underlying the clinical features of MTCA among patients who have both structural and functional neuroimaging evidence of indemnity of the perisylvian language cortex. Therefore, the term "isolation of the speech area" is used in this and other chapters to reflect one of the pathophysiological mechanisms underlying the syndrome of MTCA and not as synonymous of it.

has been largely neglected in recently published neuropsychological textbooks (Benson, 1985, 1993) and major review articles on aphasia (Damasio, 1992), during the 1980s and 1990s the classical theory of isolation of the speech area has been the subject of controversy (Berthier, Starkstein et al., 1991; Brown, 1975; Grossi et al., 1991). In the next section, I will examine several case studies of MTCA in which the pattern of impaired and preserved language abilities cannot be explained by the theory of "isolation of the speech area". Rather, clinicoanatomical correlations from these cases have aroused a renewed interest in the role of the right hemisphere in the mediation of residual language functions (e.g. repetition). At the end of the chapter, I will analyse possible similarities and differences in language performance between patients with MTCA and lesions sparing the perisylvian language zone and patients with MTCA and lesions involving it.

Brown (1975)

Early studies in MTCA (e.g. Hübner, 1889) as well as the more recent clinicopathological study by Geschwind et al. (1968) have been analysed by Brown in which he raised not only a number of critical remarks regarding the neuroanatomical mechanism of MTCA (e.g. isolation of the speech area), but also described two MTCA patients of his own to refute other rival theories.

Case descriptions.   Case 2, a 75-year-old right-handed man, suddenly developed "mumbling speech and weakness of the right arm". Spontaneous speech was restricted to the infrequent use of stereotyped short words such as "yes", "no", or "fine", or short well-articulated phrases such as "I don't know". Series speech was only partially possible and required prompting, but repetition was excellent. He repeated long phrases, jargon speech and foreign languages well. On sentence repetition, he could only echo the last words automatically. Completion phenomenon was prominent. Comprehension and naming were poor and he echoed verbal commands that he was unable to execute. On postmortem examination, there were two ischaemic lesions in the left hemisphere, one of which was recent and involved the posterior cortex of the middle temporal gyrus, whereas the other was an old cystic infarction in the inferior frontal lobe. This lesion encompassed the inferior and middle portion of the precentral gyrus and the opercular and pars triangularis of F3, and extended towards the anterior insula, extreme capsulae, claustrum, and white matter in the region of the arcuate fasciculus.

Case 3, a 78-year-old left-handed bilingual (Spanish–English) woman was admitted with right hemiparesis and mixed aphasia with spared repetition due to a left middle cerebral artery infarction. Spontaneous speech was mildly dysarthric and restricted to a single phrase "Oh Dios mio" ["Oh my God"]. Counting was impaired and recitation was possible only for well-known songs, but required verbal prompting. Repetition was preserved for words and phrases but impaired for nonsense verbal material. She demonstrated a tendency to produce echolalic utterances of commands that she did not understand and she was unable to modify pronoun usage during repetition.

Comment. Brown emphasised that his Case 2 was clinically similar to Hübner's (1889) original patient. Pathologically, both cases had involvement of anterior and posterior language zones, but in Hübner's case the posterior lesion was larger than the anterior one, whereas the reverse was true in Brown's patient, who had evidence of moderate involvement of the anterior perisylvian language zone. Brown also found similarities between his Case 3 and the patient reported earlier by Stengel (1947). While precise anatomical localisation was impossible in Brown's case (only an isotope brain scan could be done), he pointed out that in both, his patient and the neuropathological study of Stengel's case, lesions destroyed the whole left perisylvian speech area due to "thrombosis of the middle cerebral artery". Although data on language deficits in Brown's Cases 2 and 3 is limited, the bedside examination is probably sufficient to establish the diagnosis of MTCA in both cases. Moreover, after the publication of this paper, several reports have appeared in the literature supporting Brown's claim against the theory of isolation of the speech area in MTCA as the unique possible anatomical mechanism. The distinction between cases of MTCA with lesions sparing the perisylvian language zone from others with lesions involving it would be clinically and theoretically relevant and analysis of subsequent case studies may shed more light on the profile of language disturbances among patients with MTCA and perisylvian involvement.

Patient AP (Trojano et al., 1988; Grossi et al., 1991)

Case Description. The patient (AP) was a 69-year-old right-handed Italian woman who suffered a left hemisphere cerebrovascular accident which resulted in right hemiparesis, right hemisensory loss, and global aphasia. Formal language assessment carried out one month after onset confirmed a severe impairment in expressive and receptive language abilities but documented that AP could produce automatic speech, repeat words, and complete traditional Neapolitan and religious songs. Repetition, however, was not completely normal, since she could repeat only two digits forwards and fragments of sentences. Speech articulation was also impaired. A CT scan revealed an extensive area of infarction involving the frontotemporoparietal regions. Atrophic changes were also noted in the left hemisphere and an MRI scan additionally disclosed small areas of infarctions in the left occipital lobe and in the right periventricular white matter. A brain SPECT imaging showed marked hypoperfusion in the whole left hemisphere and higher than normal perfusion rates in the right hemisphere (see data in Grossi et al., 1991, Case 1).

Trojano and colleagues pointed out that the analysis of residual language functions in previous cases of MTCA was focused on echolalic behaviour and related aspects of automatic speech and that immediate word repetition had not been studied in great detail (except in the case of Assal et al., 1983, who reported some quantitative data). Trojano et al. were particularly interested in the possibility that the relative sparing of repetition in their patient depended on the activity of the phonological short-term store.[3] Therefore, they performed a fine-grained analysis of repetition of digits, words, and nonwords.

Repetition of words and nonwords.   The patient was required to repeat lists of words and nonwords. The word list consisted of 70 nouns and verbs balanced for frequency (35 high frequency and 35 low frequency) which varied in length from 4 to 8 letters. The nonword list consisted of 108 items that were balanced for length and phonemic distance from the words. On repetition of words, AP repeated 31 of the 70 (44%) words correctly. Her error responses were mainly phonological paraphasias (16/70, 23%) followed by errors in words beginning with a vowel (9/70, 13%) and incomplete repetition (end fragments of words) (4/70, 6%). The remaining type of errors consisted of repetitions unrelated to the target word (10/70, 14%). There was no effect of word frequency (high-frequency words = 19/35; low-frequency words = 12/35), or word-length effect (4 letter words = 5/14; 8 letter words = 6/14) in repetition performance. By contrast, on repetition of nonwords, AP's performance was poorer than for the repetition of words. She only repeated 29 of the 108 (27%) nonwords correctly, and again phonological substitutions were the most common type of errors. Finally, nonword repetition was clearly influenced by a length effect as the patient committed more errors on the repetition of polysyllabic nonwords (4 letter nonwords = 11/20; 8 letter nonwords = 2/22). Analysis of nonword repetition revealed that the production of phonological paraphasias was the most common type of error (35/108, 32%), followed by errors in nonwords beginning with a vowel (12/108, 11%), and then by incomplete repetition (6/108, 6%).

Comment.   Trojano and his co-workers concluded that repetition performance in their patient may have reflected a relative sparing of the verbal store and impairment of the rehearsal processes. The relative preservation of word and, to a lesser extent, nonword repetition documented in this MTCA patient, who otherwise showed a lack of productive and receptive language, was taken as evidence of the relative sparing of the short-term phonological store. Also, the authors argued that the automatic activation of the verbal store could account

---

[3] In a recent re-elaborated conceptualisation of working memory, Baddeley (1986, 1996) coined the term "phonological loop" to refer to the verbal component of the system. It comprises the phonological short-term store, a system capable of storing speech-based information over short time intervals and the articulatory rehearsal process, which is used to refresh memory traces in the phonological store by reactivating them in a serial, time-based manner.

for the patient's echolalic utterances. By contrast, the authors interpreted the reduced memory span for auditorily presented digits in their patient as indicative of impaired articulatory rehearsal mechanism. Given that the left perisylvian area was found to be structurally and functionally damaged the authors considered that the right hemisphere "seems capable to contribute in processing words and nonwords for the repetition" (Grossi et al., 1991, p. 210).

As a final comment, the authors pointed out that although their patient performance resembled other cases of MTCA in some respects, it differed from these previous cases in that AP had impaired repetition at sentence level (he could only repeat fragments of sentences), abnormal speech articulation, a digit span of only two items, and was unable to read aloud. Echolalia, though present, was restricted to automatic repetition of the last words spoken by the examiner. These distinctive features are worth noting, because other patients with MTCA secondary to vascular lesions (Pulvermüller & Schönle, 1993) or degenerative diseases (Mehler, 1988) involving the left perisylvian area have been described showing similar patterns of language deficits.

Patient KS (Pulvermüller & Schönle, 1993)

Case description.   KS was a 69-year-old right-handed businessman who suddenly developed a right hemiplegia, right hemianopia, and global aphasia due to a large left hemisphere ischaemic infarction in the carotid artery territory. A CT scan disclosed damage to the whole perisylvian language region. The lesion also affected the angular gyrus, occipital cortex, as well as subcortical structures such as the putamen, pallidum, and the adjacent periventricular white matter. One year after onset his score on the Aachen Aphasia Battery (AAB; Huber et al., 1984) was consistent with a severe global aphasia. By that time his AAB repetition score was poor (45/150). During the subsequent years the pattern of the aphasic impairment remained relatively stable, but about four years later it was noticed that his ability to repeat language had improved (AAB's repetition score = 119/150), and echolalia had appeared, so that KS was reclassified as having a MTCA.

By this time on a new language examination, he was able to repeat words, nonwords, and sentences (five to seven words). On lexical decision tasks he demonstrated a relative preservation of basic lexical abilities since he made correct decisions in 112/120 written words and in 40 nonwords. By contrast, other features traditionally described in MTCA were absent. Indeed, KS was not capable of completing sentence fragments and he could not modify sentences containing minor grammatical errors. He failed to correct grammatical errors in all of the 20 sentences construed with violations of subject–verb agreement and pronoun usage.

KS received intensive speech therapy tailored to improve impaired language abilites. The authors lucidly used the significant improvement of language repetition in the service of other still severely impaired language functions, namely spontaneous speech and auditory comprehension. Three weeks after starting language therapy, there was a significant improvement in verbal production and a tendency towards better auditory comprehension.

Comment.   Pulvermüller and Schönle documented the partial restoration of language functions in a globally aphasic patient four years after the occurrence of a massive left hemisphere cerebrovascular accident that destroyed the whole perisylvian language zone. They tentatively suggested that neuronal changes had taken place in the intact right perisylvian area as a result of intensive language therapy, allowing the amelioration of expressive and receptive language. They further speculated that at the onset of global aphasia, speech production (including repetition) and comprehension were abolished not only because both the phonological representation (stored in the left perisylvian zone) and semantic representation (stored in various extrasylvian cortical areas) were damaged, but also because the right hemisphere did not participate in the process of repetition before the stroke onset. The repeated stimulation provided by language therapy strengthened auditory-motor neuronal assemblies in the right perisylvian area favouring the late restoration of repetition and, to a lesser extent, of other language functions.

The pattern of repetition performance in KS is different to that described in cases of MTCA with isolation of the speech area (e.g. Davis et al., 1978; Whitaker, 1976) in that he did not correct syntactic errors during repetition of ungrammatical sentences and failed to show the "completion phenomenon". In addition, KS and AP (Trojano et al., 1988) had almost identical lesion locations, yet the profile of language repetition was somewhat different. AP showed discrepancy between word–nonword repetition and severely impaired phrase repetition, whereas KS showed a relative sparing of nonword and sentence repetition. It should be noted that differences in repetition performance between AP and KS may not necessarily reflect heterogeneity in the clinical expression of linguistic deficits of MTCA associated with perisylvian pathology. Rather, different stages of evolution in language deficits may account for the existing discrepancies. In fact, AP had *acute* MTCA with repetition skills only available for words and certain nonwords, whereas KS had *chronic* MTCA with better repetition for words, nonwords, and sentences most likely reflecting the beneficial effects of both spontaneous recovery and remodelling of right hemisphere phonological-semantic architecture.

Patient BO (Mehler, 1988)

Case description.   Patient BO was a right-handed man with a seven-year history of slowly progressing deterioration in cognitive functions including language, writing, and praxis skills. His problems started when he was 53 years old with impaired ability in spelling familiar words, manipulating common objects, and word-finding difficulties for common nouns during conversations. Visual confrontation naming, aural comprehension, calculation, and visual recognition of familiar faces became poor in the ensuing years, together with further deterioration in word-finding abilities as well as in spontaneous and imitative gesturing. Attention and selective verbal and nonverbal memory functions remained preserved during evolution. Serial CT scans performed through the seven years of follow-up disclosed a progressive focal atrophy involving the cortex of the left perisylvian area.

Language evaluation.   Mehler's report was mainly based on the results of language findings which he considered consistent with the diagnosis of MTCA. BO lacked spontaneous verbalisations and his responsive speech was described as "nonfluent, agrammatical speech with fluency improving during declarative speech". Speech articulation was normal, but serial speech perseverative. There were occasional verbal and literal paraphasias during spontaneous speech, and visual object naming tasks elicited literal paraphasias, omissions, as well as errors in name recognition. Naming was also impaired in other semantic categories (colours and fingers). Auditory and reading comprehension were both impaired. BO's repetition was intact, even for nonwords and foreign phrases. During repetition tasks, BO could repeat declarative and interrogative sentences said with different affective intonation, flawlessly, but he was poor at the auditory recognition (37%) and correction during repetition (25%) of ungrammatical sentences containing errors of number agreement and pronoun usage. Poor performance was also documented in the auditory recognition (45%) and correction during repetition sentences with semantic anomalies. In spite of having the clinical features of MTCA, BO did not echo words or phrases pronounced by the examiner, and he also failed to complete open-ended sentences. Reading comprehension was moderately impaired and oral reading showed a pattern of surface dyslexia. Writing was less affected than oral reading and the pattern of errors was consistent with a mild form of lexical (surface) agraphia characterised by correct spelling of nonwords, production of phonological plausible errors (e.g. "write" $\Rightarrow$ "*right*"), absence of word-class effect, and poor spelling of correct homophones.

Comment.   Mehler viewed the pattern of language impairment in BO's case "unusual" because most features traditionally described in MTCA such as echolalia and forced completion phenomenon were absent. Other unusual features included effortful, agrammatical speech, impaired correction of ungrammatical phrases, and preserved modulation of affective intonation during sentence repetition. Although the patient had cognitive decline besides the aphasia presumably due to a diffuse atrophic process involving both cerebral hemispheres, Mehler attempted to establish clinicoanatomical correlations and interpreted language as well as reading and writing deficits using the cognitive neuropsychological approach. For instance, deficits in verbal output were attributed to involvement of the left inferior frontal and precentral gyri, a presumed pathological distribution that in Mehler's view distinguished his patient BO from those cases of MTCA associated with infarctions in the anterior cerebral artery territory, which regularly display effortless articulation but akinesia of speech secondary to dysfunction of the supplementary motor area. Patient BO also failed to correct grammatical errors in sentence repetition tasks, a pattern of performance, that coupled with his excellent repetition of words, nonwords, and foreign words led Mehler to suggest that repetition was carried out nonlexically by privileged connections linking the auditory analysis system directly with the phoneme level. By contrast, lexical mechanisms were impaired in repetition, reading and writing.

The pathophysiological interpretation of language disturbances in BO advanced by Mehler is somewhat puzzling. BO had radiological evidence of progressive left cerebral atrophy with predominant involvement of the perisylvian cortex, but the author stated (p. 553) that "the pathological process resulted in a relative disconnection of integral frontal and parieto-occipital areas from adjacent perisylvian language zones", a conclusion that seems to imply that Mehler interpreted the features of MTCA in his case as resulting from isolation of the speech area. Taking into account data from the aforementioned cases (e.g. Pulvermüller & Schönle, 1993; Trojano et al., 1988), it could be argued that some features regarded as unusual by Mehler might readily correlate with the pattern of cortical degeneration of the perisylvian region itself, rather than being the direct consequence of disconnection of damaged frontal and parieto-occipital association cortices from the central perisylvian language cortex.

COURSE AND PATTERNS OF RECOVERY

Cases of aphasia presenting the set of features characteristic of MTCA are rare, to the extent that this symptom complex was not observed in various studies involving large samples of patients with vascular lesions of the left hemisphere that underwent formal neuropsychological assessment (see references in Bogousslavsky, Regli, & Assal, 1988). Therefore, there are isolated reports dealing with the longitudinal evolution of language deficits in these patients (Kertesz, 1982). As in other aphasic syndromes, the clinical course of MTCA depends on the nature of the lesion. In cases of degenerative dementia such as Alzheimer's disease (AD), frontotemporal degeneration (e.g. Pick's disease), and nonspecific dementia, MTCA may be observed in the late stage of evolution and is nearly always associated with severe cognitive decline (Mehler 1988; Whitaker, 1976). In this situation, MTCA is usually the end-stage of other clinical types of TA. For instance, nonfluent speech coupled with echolalia, palilalia, and perseverations, not incompatible with MTCA, are often documented among patients with late-stage AD (Sandson, Obler, & Albert, 1987). And patients with AD retain, even in the terminal stage, some repetition capacity (Hier, Hangelocker, & Shindler,

1985), a finding particularly demonstrable in those who produce echolalic utterances (Au, Obler, & Albert, 1991). In other dementing conditions (e.g. prion diseases) the mixed transcortical pattern may be an early symptom (Kataki et al., 1996).

Among patients with single event pathology (e.g. cerebrovascular accidents, encephalitis, neoplasms, traumatic lesions) the severity of MTCA is comparable to that observed among patients with global aphasia (Kertesz, 1982) and the transcortical pattern may be observed during the recovery process of global aphasia. Although Kertesz (1984) documented no cases of global aphasia evolving into MTCA during the evolution of 21 patients evaluated at one year post-onset, there are several single-case studies of MTCA, which at the onset of aphasia exhibited the pattern of severely nonfluent speech, poor auditory comprehension, and repetition characteristic of global aphasia (Geschwind et al., 1968; Pulvermüller & Schönle, 1993; Trojano et al., 1988; Willmes & Poeck, 1993). Some of these patients had a MTCA pattern in association with extensive damage to the left perisylvian language zone, others had large lesions restricted to basal ganglia structures, and still others had lesions that spared the perisylvian language area. While in most patients with extensive damage to the perisylvian region the syndrome of global aphasia is usually seen, some regain the ability of word and sentence repetition several months (Grossi et al., 1991) or even years (Pulvermüller & Schönle, 1993) after global aphasia onset. Interestingly, lesion size and location within the left perisylvian language cortex in patients with chronic global aphasia may be virtually identical to that observed among those global aphasics who experience a late recovery of repetition (Poeck et al., 1984). These observations raise the possibility that individual variability in the premorbid brain organisation of language functions may favour the reorganisation by the right hemisphere of originally left hemisphere functions in some patients. Grossi and colleagues (1991) using SPECT demonstrated higher than normal regional cerebral blood flow in the right hemisphere of patients with chronic MTCA and left hemisphere infarction of the entire middle cerebral artery territory. Further support for the hypothesis that the right hemisphere may play a major role in the restoration of repetition comes from patients with MTCA associated with left hemisphere lesions in whom a subsequent lesion in the right hemisphere abolishes repetition (Berthier, Starkstein et al., 1991, Case 19; Cambier, Elghozi, Signoret, & Henin, 1983, Case 1; Rapcsak, Krupp, Rubens, & Reim, 1990).

The syndrome of MTCA may also occur as an acute language disturbance (Berthier, Starkstein et al., 1991; Bogousslavsky, Regli, & Assal, 1988; Hadano et al., 1998; Jacome, 1984; Perani et al., 1987; Pirozzolo et al., 1981; Ross, 1980; Speedie et al., 1984). In contrast to the uniformly good prognosis of acute transcortical motor and sensory aphasias (Kertesz, 1982), the presence of an acute MTCA implies, in general, a poor prognosis. In cases with a favourable outcome, MTCA may evolve into a transcortical motor type or into a nonclassifiable combination of residual language deficits that, in general, includes reduced verbal output, object-naming problems with semantic paraphasias and moderate comprehension impairment, or only word-finding difficulties and semantic paraphasias (Bogousslavsky et al., 1988). The preservation of singing ability and prosody from the beginning might be an indicator of good prognosis (Jacome, 1984). Finally, cases of MTCA secondary to subcortical haemorrhage may improve to such an extent that only mild anomia and isolated paraphasias are discernible at the outcome (Berthier, Starkstein et al., 1991, Case 19).

CONCLUSIONS

I have addressed several key areas related to the language profile in the rare syndrome of MTCA. Similarities are evident among the cases reviewed above. Irrespective of the intrahemispheric localisation of lesions (extraperisylvian *vs.* perisylvian) within the left hemisphere, all cases presented the set of language deficits that characterises the profile of MTCA. The combination of nonfluent spontaneous speech, impaired auditory comprehension, and relative preservation of repetition was invariably present in every reviewed case. Nevertheless, on reviewing these data, it would appear that clinical and anatomical differences exist and that at least two subtypes of MTCA can be discerned. Analysis of these subtypes revealed differences in two linguistic domains, namely the pattern of speech production deficits and performance in repetition tasks. Before advancing in the discussion of potential differences, it should be noted that as a result of its rarity, only a handful of MTCA cases have been studied. Moreover, most studies on MTCA have approached the aphasic syndrome from a neuro-anatomical perspective (e.g. Geschwind et al., 1968), whereas cases interpreted within the cognitive neuropsychological model are rare and some of them focused on the analysis of cognitive functions in other linguistic domains (e.g. reading; Coslett et al., 1985). Thus, the differences described later should be viewed as preliminary and not generalised to all mixed transcortical aphasic patients until additional research using samples of adequately selected cases is done.

Analysis of speech production demonstrated that both subtype groups produced either no spontaneous utterances or their verbal outputs were limited to stereotyped phrases. Recurrent utterances with meaningless content have been reported, but not exclusively, among patients with perisylvian damage, whereas automatic utterances, sometimes expressed as aborted phrases containing "small words" (Goldstein, 1948, p. 302) but lacking verbs and nouns, prevailed among those with lesions sparing it. Agrammatism, by contrast, has only been described in association with perisylvian pathology (Alexander & Annet, 1996, Case 6; Kapur & Dunkley, 1984; Mehler, 1988). Many of the patients with MTCA and isolation of the speech area had a considerable reduction in the quantity of speech and did not produce phonological or semantic paraphasias during their spontaneous emissions (Assal et al., 1983), whereas others who were able to articulate short phrases tended to produce semantic but not phonological paraphasias (Bogousslavsky et al. 1988). Articulation, though difficult to assess due to severe nonfluency, is usually spared during spontaneous speech and echolalic repetition among patients with isolation of the speech area. Patients with perisylvian pathology showed the reverse: a variable impairment in speech articulation has been observed in most of them (Alexander & Annet, 1996, Case 6; Brown, 1975, Case 3; Davis et al., 1978, Case LG; Grossi et al., 1991; Hadano et al., 1998, Case 3; Jacome, 1984; Trojano et al., 1988). These cases with MTCA and perisylvian involvement also produced phonological paraphasias during spontaneous speech, a feature rarely documented among those cases with isolation of the speech area.

The other potential difference lies in the realm of repetition. Different per-formances in sentence repetition tasks have been pointed out by Heilman (1985) and Mehler and Rabinowich (1990) with some patients retaining a striking abil-ity to correct syntactic errors during repetition, while others showing on-line repetition of syntactically anomalous sentences. While these authors did not consider the potential influence of lesion location on the distinct patterns of performance in repetition, inspection of the cases reviewed here suggests that impaired syntactic processing during repetition in MTCA may be associated with large lesions that involve the perisylvian cortex (Mehler, 1988; Pulvermüller & Schönle, 1993). This clinicoradiological correlation is in agreement with data from TCSA that revealed a lack of ability to correct syntactic errors in un-grammatical sentences only in those cases showing extensive functional and/or structural damage to the left perisylvian language cortex (Berthier, Starkstein et al., 1991, Cases 3, 5, and 12). On the other hand, patients with MTCA and partial or complete isolation of the speech area can often spontaneously correct ungrammatical sentences during repetition, though the correction of anomalous syntax is generally restricted to certain aspects of grammatical organisation (e.g. rules of agreement; Davis et al., 1978; Whitaker, 1976). Although on clinical grounds, there is general agreement that patients with MTCA and isolation of the speech area can repeat everything they hear, including difficult words, non-sense words, nonverbal sounds, and semantically empty phonological sequences, there is yet little empirical evidence to maintain this assertion. Some of the MTCA patients with isolation of the speech area reviewed here could adequately repeat common words, phrases, and even long sentences verbatim, but unfortu-nately most patients were not tested for nonword repetition (Bogousslavsky et al., 1988; Geschwind et al., 1968; Pirozzolo et al., 1981; Ross, 1980, Case 1; Speedie et al., 1984). Two patients (Assal et al., 1983; Whitaker, 1976), in whom repetition of unfamiliar words and invented nonwords was tested, showed a relatively preserved performance. Word repetition was spared in MTCA patients with perisylvian pathology, but repetition of nonwords and sentences was moder-ately impaired. Two such patients (Grossi et al., 1991; Trojano et al., 1988) showed superior performance for the repetition of words over nonwords, whereas both word and nonword repetition, though less formally assessed, were preserved in other patients (Mehler, 1988; Pulvermüller & Schönle, 1993). Digit and word span may be reduced in both conditions, but available evidence indicates that major restrictions in immediate digit and word repetition prevail among patients with damage to the perisylvian language zone.

Finally, another potential source of evidence for possible differences is the patient's performance on related linguistic aspects such as echolalia, completion phenomenon, and automatic speech depending on the sparing or involvement of the perisylvian language cortex. While these linguistic aspects have not been studied in great detail, available evidence indicates that, at least in some patients with MTCA and isolation of the speech area, echolalia and completion of open-ended phrases is commonly documented. Automatic aspects of speech (e.g. counting, days of the week, recitation of overfamiliar rhymes and singing) are generally preserved, whereas the reverse may be true among those mixed transcortical aphasic patients with extensive damage to the perisylvian language cortex. Taken together, these differences, though preliminary, suggest that more than a single syndrome of MTCA really exist, and that lesions located within or outside the left perisylvian language cortex may induce different linguistic subtypes, each of them resulting from different linguistic mechanisms.

CHAPTER SIX

Echophenomena, automatic speech, and prosody in transcortical aphasias

INTRODUCTION

In this chapter I will discuss a variety of verbal and motor behaviours that are often encountered in patients with transcortical aphasias (TA). Some of these behaviours are imitative in nature and are usually grouped under the heading of echophenomena (EP). The imitation of another person's verbal and motor actions is constantly present during normal human development and probably plays an important role in the acquisition and consolidation of language and motor skills. Nevertheless, imitative behaviour of the kind I will describe here is always abnormal in adults. Although imitative behaviours are not pathognomonic of TA, and can often be documented in various neurological and psychiatric disorders which course without prominent language deficits (see later), the presence of EP in aphasia is virtually always associated with a transcortical pattern (Geschwind, 1964a; Stengel, 1947). The second type of behaviour I will discuss is not imitative and refers to automatic aspects of language. Part of this verbal behaviour is generally learned during infancy and childhood (e.g. counting, days of the week) and its utilisation during adulthood requires little effort, whereas other automatic language behaviours (e.g. social greetings, stereotyped expressions) are added to our vocabulary throughout our lives and are socially and culturally related (Code, 1989).

In contrast to EP, automatic speech is a normal component of language in the adult individual and usually remains spared among patients with TA and, less frequently, in aphasias with repetition disturbances (e.g. conduction aphasia). Towards the end of the chapter I will consider the status of linguistic and nonlinguistic (affective) prosody in TA, by describing recent evidence based on clinical and acoustic studies.

ECHOPHENOMENA

The term EP has been coined to refers to the strong tendency to imitate utterances and gestures performed by another person (Ford, 1989; Stengel, 1947). In normal conditions echoreactions, especially echoing words, inarticulated sounds, speech intonation, and gestures are commonly observed during the early stages of normal language acquisition, often before the child achieves a clear understanding of word meaning (Howlin, 1982; Stengel, 1947). By age two and three many children echo only the last words of sentences, although about 40% of children's utterances are exact or partial replicas of something they have heard before (Fay, 1967; see Locke, 1997 for a recent review). EP is subsequently inhibited in parallel with the progression of language and gesture development. It may reappear, for instance, during the learning of a second language where normal individuals use noncompulsive verbalisation and completion of open-ended sentences to reinforce auditory comprehension during the learning processes (Stengel, 1947).

In pathological conditions, EP has been reported in association with both neurologic and psychiatric disorders. It can be observed in a variety of early-onset conditions such as autistic disorder (Howlin, 1982; Kanner, 1946; Simon, 1975), Gilles de la Tourette syndrome (a developmental disorder characterised by multiple motor and vocal tics; Howard & Ford, 1992; Shapiro, Shapiro, Young, & Feinberg, 1988), and mental retardation (Trimble, 1981) as well as in processes with onset during adolescence or adulthood such as schizophrenia, delirium, and dementia (Ford, 1989). EP, including echolalia, echopraxia, verbigeration, and automatic obedience are major features of catatonia (Taylor, 1990). Echolalia, echopraxia, palilalia, and a wide range of other more simple involuntary vocalisations (e.g. guttural sounds) are often encountered in various movement disorders (see Tolosa & Peña, 1988 for review). Some of these symptoms (echolalia, coprolalia, automatic obedience, outbursts of aggressive behaviour) may also occur associated with exaggerated startle reactions in exotic culture-bound behaviours (e.g. Latah, Miryachit, and Jumping Frenchmen of Maine; Howard & Ford, 1992; Lees, 1985). Echolalia, and less frequently echopraxia, may accompany the end-stages of Alzheimer's disease (Cummings et al., 1985) and frontotemporal dementias (Gregory & Hodges, 1996; Grossman et al., 1996), whereas automatic and less compulsive variants of echolalia have been encountered during the restoration of consciousness after coma or epileptic attacks (Stengel, 1947).

In aphasia, a variety of repetitive verbal behaviours such as automatisms, recurring utterances, and perseverations have been reported in syndromes with abnormal repetition (Code, 1989; Lebrun, 1993; Sandson & Albert, 1987;

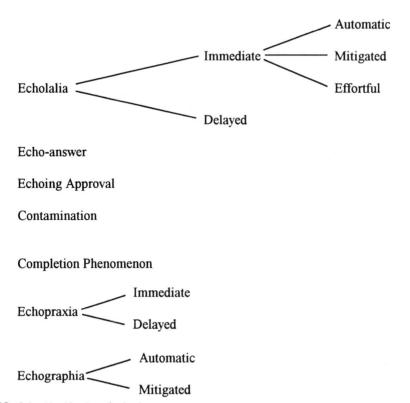

FIG. 6.1   Classification of echophenomena.

Wallesch, 1990). By contrast, patients with TA may display various reiterative phenomena from verbal material that they have heard from others (echolalia, echo-answer, contamination) or from themselves (autocontamination), or may produce stutter-like repetitions (Lebrun, 1995).

Echolalia

Echolalia is defined as the involuntary and noncommunicative repetition of words or utterances spoken by another person (Lebrun 1993; Stengel, 1936, 1947). Pick (1924) believed that among the echoreactions, echolalia was by far the most common symptom, because the imitation of spoken words plays a more important role in the acquisition of language than other forms of imitative behaviour (e.g. gestures, writing). There are various types of echolalia that, although they can occur in neurological and psychiatric disorders other than aphasia, have traditionally been associated with TA (Fig. 6.1).

The most common type of echolalia has been termed "automatic" or "involuntary echolalia" because the patients produce a compulsive "parrot-like" repetition of words and sentences which they fail to understand. This echolalic variant is usually seen in the early stages of TA as well as accompanying the end-stages of degenerative dementing illness. Patients with automatic echolalia do not appear inhibited by novel verbal information such as foreign languages and nonsense words, and they repeat this information verbatim immediately after it is pronounced by the partner. Occasionally the echo is just overlapped with the last words of the partner's utterance. Some authors label echolalia "complete" when the patient echoes the entire sentence verbatim and "incomplete" or "partial" when only a portion, generally the end, of the examiner's utterance is repeated (Ford, 1989). Automatic echolalia is virtually always generated when the patient is addressed by the partner. In exceptional circumstances, however, patients with TA repeat verbal information that is not directed to them but to other patients. Leiguarda, Berthier, and Rubio (1984) and Berthier (1993, unpublished observation) studied two transcortical sensory aphasic patients with left thalamic haemorrhages, who echoed questions (e.g. "How are you today?") and verbal commands (e.g. "Open your mouth and show me your tongue") that were directed to other patients. It is possible that this exceptional behaviour represents the verbal counterpart of the perseverative repetition of motor actions of right brain-damaged patients in response to stimuli directed to other patients described by Bogousslavsky and Regli (1988) under the heading "response-to-next-patient-stimulation".

Clinicoradiological observations indicate that there are two main types of automatic echolalia in TA (Ford, 1989). One type is associated with the two nonfluent types (motor and mixed). In transcortical motor aphasia (TCMA), depending on the severity of nonfluency, echolalic behaviour can be variously observed in patients who are initially mute, in others who have a marked reduced drive to speak spontaneously but can utter words when vigorously stimulated, and still in others who have nonfluent speech but produce phonological paraphasias, perseveration, and use few or no connective words. Transcortical motor aphasics display little or no control to suppress automatic repetition, to the point that they often repeat undesired verbal material (Schneider, 1938). The emotional reactions associated with irrepressible echolalia among these patients, who have otherwise normal auditory comprehension and full awareness of the involuntariness of their echoes, ranged from mood-congruent catastophic reactions (Rubens, 1975, Case 1) to incongruent feelings of satisfaction (Stengel, 1947), or even euphoria (Atkinson, 1971). In cases of TCMA, echolalia has been mainly linked to anterior lesions involving either the lateral or mesial aspects of the premotor frontal cortex with sparing of posterior auditory association area responsible for auditory comprehension.

Automatic echolalia coexists with nonfluency and severe deficits in auditory comprehension in patients with mixed transcortical aphasia (MTCA). In general, these patients appear unconcerned about their echolalic behaviour making formal evaluation of linguistic skills difficult (besides the echolalic behaviour) (Ross,

1980, Case 1). For instance, upon clinical testing of auditory comprehension (e.g. responses to yes/no questions), it is not possible to ascertain whether the patients' unresponsiveness totally depends on poor speech understanding, since they do not answer questions but merely echo them. There is agreement that in such cases the presence of automatic echolalia relies on the deficit in auditory comprehension that prevents an adequate monitorisation of echolalic responses. Echolalia in MTCA is associated with extensive cortical or deep subcortical lesions of the left hemisphere located outside the perisylvian language area. In general, echolalic utterances in nonfluent TA (motor and mixed types) are easily enunciated, though rare patients presenting with either atypical patterns of TCMA or MTCA due to lesions involving the perilsylvian language zone forcedly echo some of the words uttered by the partner in a slow and laboured way, a condition that has been termed "effortful echolalia" (Hadano et al., 1998).

The second type of automatic echolalia in TA is associated with fluent paraphasic speech, impaired auditory comprehension, and very often anosognosia for the speech deficits. This echolalic variety is typically observed among patients with transcortical sensory aphasia (TCSA) and appears in the context of reduced comprehension (Brown, 1975). It has been linked to lesions of the posterior temporo-parietal cortex (Ford, 1989) and subcortical lesions involving the thalamus or basal ganglia (Alexander & LoVerme, 1980; Lhermitte, 1984).

Longitudinal observation of the phenomenological characteristics of echolalia has revealed that there are various stages of echolalic behaviour besides the "automatic" type usually seen in the acute phases of TA. The evolution from uncontrolled "automatic" echolalia to less severe, and best monitored "voluntary" echo-responses is generally seen during the process of restoration of spontaneous speech and particularly with the improvement of language comprehension (Stengel, 1947). As a result of improvement in communicative abilities, some patients modify personal pronouns and verbal endings during their echolalic productions, a behaviour that is generally referred to as "mitigated echolalia" (Ford, 1989; Lebrun, Rubio, Jongen, & Demol, 1971; Stengel, 1947). In mitigated echolalia entire sentences may be echoed, but more frequently only isolated words of phrase fragments that sound ambiguous, equivocal, or are poorly understood are echoed. For instance, when Stengel (1947, p. 603) advanced the question: "Have you got any children?" to a hemiplegic and mentally retarded adult patient, he replied: "Children? I am not married". Whereas in automatic echolalia the echoed verbal information faithfully reproduces the linguistic intonation (e.g. declarative, interrogative) imparted in the target word or phrase, the intonational pattern is frequently modified in mitigated echolalia. For example, the transcortical sensory aphasic patient of Symonds (1953) when asked: "What is your name?" replied in an echolalic way: "My name! Charles Frederick Leale" (p. 4). Other patients, with mitigated echolalia, spelled the word heard instead of repeating it. The transcortical sensory aphasic patient of Yamadori and

Albert (1973), for example, when asked to point to the wall, said: "W-A-L-L, wall, W-A-L-L, wall" denoting his difficulty in understanding the meaning of words.

It is clearly appreciated that all the aforementioned varieties of echolalia share a common feature: the echoed words or utterances are reproduced *immediately after* they are pronounced by the partner, a condition that has been termed "immediate" echolalia. Although not examined in great detail some transcortical aphasic patients, instead of immediately repeating a heard word, tend to incorporate words, clichés, or short phrases into their discourse that are verbatim recall of something that they have heard before from other people or in communicative media. This has been referred to as "delayed echolalia". Delayed echolalia is a typical feature of autistic language (Simon, 1975) and it has also been frequently reported among patients with Gilles de la Tourette's syndrome (Tolosa & Peña, 1988). To take a common example, mentally retarded autistic individuals, in spite of having a limited vocabulary, occasionally use elaborate social greetings, generally out of context, previously heard in others, whereas others repeat what they have heard in school or on the radio hours or days later, when they are alone, often in a repetitive manner.

In TA, delayed echolalia has been reported in a case of chronic MTCA. Geschwind et al. (1968) described an unusual case of delayed echolalia in an adult patient with MTCA who suffered extensive bilateral brain damage after carbon monoxide poisoning (see further details in Chapter 5). According to Geschwind and his colleagues, in spite of the lack of oral expression and auditory comprehension, their patient was still capable of verbal and musical learning, as indicated by her preserved ability to sing new popular songs heard on the radio. This was tested in more depth using completion exercises in which the patient was cued with partial auditory information (e.g. the first stanzas of a song well known to her). The authors documented that the patient echoed the words and melody of the song and she could continue singing it when the radio was turned off. Even more surprising, was her ability to echo and then complete fragments of musical commercials and popular songs that were novel to her because they were composed some time after the onset of her illness. A detailed postmortem examination revealed widespread cortical damage with sparing of both perisylvian cortical areas, hippocampal formations, and some structures of the limbic system (e.g. cingulate cortex). On discussing the neural mechanism underlying verbal learning through echolalic singing, Geschwind et al. (1968) anticipated the existence of connecting pathways linking the hippocampus with the superior temporal cortex (e.g. Heschl's gyrus), later discovered by other researchers (Amaral, Insausti, & Cowan, 1983; Insausti, Amaral, & Cowan, 1987; Van Hoesen, 1985; Van Hoesen, Pandya, & Butters, 1972), and suggested that the sparing of these cortical regions and their interconnections could account for the remarkable learning and retention of new auditory information and (delayed) echolalic behaviour in their patient. Other aphasic patients exhibiting delayed echolalia can process the auditory stimulus from meaning and may exhibit self-repetitive verbal behaviour, resembling the "*conduit d'approche*" of conduction aphasia, probably in an attempt to rehearse every component of the auditory stimulus (Gardner & Winner, 1978).

The pathophysiological mechanism underlying echolalic behaviour is still poorly understood and it is not known whether one or more mechanisms are responsible for the various clinical subtypes of echolalia. In addition, there is no consensus about the neurological basis of echolalic behaviour. Pick (1924), for instance, viewed echolalia as resulting from loss of inhibition of speech impulses due to damage to the temporal lobes, whereas Goldstein (1948) considered that frontal lobe involvement is important in its pathogenesis. Denny-Brown (1956) interpreted echolalia as resulting from deficient frontal lobe control over other structures and Critchley (1964), sympathetic to this interpretation, considered echolalia as the result of faulty supralinguistic inhibition. Kleist (1934) was probably the first author who associated echolalia with lesions of the basal ganglia. Geschwind (1964a) classified echolalia along with other disorders of expression (mutism, palilalia) as "non-aphasic disorders of speech" because they differ clinically from true aphasic disorders caused by lesions of the classical speech regions. In his opinion echolalia generally occurs as a result of wide-spread brain lesions and most cases shared the same functional mechanism regardless of their etiology. Since Geschwind and colleagues (Geschwind et al., 1968) found echolalia associated with diffuse cerebral damage that spared the perisylvian language area, they postulated that its integrity in TA permits echolalia as well as other linguistic operations (e.g. application of syntactic rules) to occur. In contrast to what Geschwind found, Stengel (1947) was faced with a patient who had echolalia and automatic completion of open-ended questions despite massive damage of the whole speech area. This led Stengel to propose that both phenomena were the expression of right hemisphere function.

A more dynamic account of echolalia among patients with aphasia and left hemisphere lesions was adopted by other researchers (Brown, 1972, 1975, 1987; McFarling et al., 1982; Wallesch, 1990; Whitaker, 1976) who explained its pathophysiology according to the general ideas put forward by Hughlings Jackson regarding the hierarchical organisation of the nervous system. Briefly, Jackson (1874/1958) viewed language behaviour as a superposition of increasingly complex functions with successively higher levels developing later, but breaking down sooner in the course of language dissolution. He claimed that destruction of the more highly organised level not only prevents the utilisation of the voluntary or "superior" forms of language, but also suppresses the normal inhibition of superior over lower centres thus releasing the more "inferior" automatic, stereotyped, and stimulus-bound forms of language. Based on the findings from new cases, some researchers updated some Jacksonian ideas. Brown (1975) proposed that echolalia was determined by the "*combined performance of both residual left and intact right hemisphere capacity*" (his italics). Also, he maintained that the conceptualisation of echolalia as a linguistic regression sub-served by dynamic patterns in both cerebral hemispheres would also accommod-ate to explain cases of echolalia associated with bilateral pathology occurring during development such as mental retardation or infantile autism, or in the end-stages of degenerative processes such as dementing illness. In other words, using a hierarchical language-processing model (his microgenetic theory of lan-guage-brain relationships), Brown explained echolalia along with other aphasic disorders (e.g. TCMA) as the residual language capacity that results from the activity of intact areas of the brain (see Brown, 1982; Caplan, 1987 for further details). A similar argument was advanced by McFarling et al. (1982) to explain nonfluent speech and echolalia in two patients with acute TA secondary to ischaemic infarctions of the left thalamus. On interpreting the pathophysiology of language disturbances, these authors suggested that the thalamic lesions caused a loss of complex language functions (e.g. nonfluency) due to insufficient activa-tion of "superior" cortical language areas, but left the more automatic speech processes (echolalia) relatively spared. Wallesch (1990) and Whitaker (1976) also accept the neurological model that posits a hierarchical top-down organisa-tion of speech production, but based on the fact that some echolalic patients can apply syntactic rules, correct pronoun usage, and perform other linguistic opera-tions during their echoes, place the generation of echolalia at intermediate or high levels of this model.

Echo-answer

Echo-answer is a term coined by Lebrun et al. (1971) to denote an abnormal verbal behaviour linked with echolalia in which: "words from the question are superfluously repeated, as when the patient answers the question "Do you live in a flat?" with "*I live in a flat, yes*" (Lebrun, 1993, p. 229). Echo-answer and mitigated echolalia can be documented in normal individuals, but according to Lebrun their incidence is low. By contrast, Lebrun stated that the occurrence of these two verbal echoreactions are very frequent in aphasia. Although echo-answer and mitigated echolalia have been considered, at least in part, voluntary reactions, some echolalic patients are unaware of the incorporation of part of the examiner's question into their replies. Moreover, if these patients are requested to use short responses and asked explicitly not to repeat verbal material contained in the questions, they can often refrain from doing it (Lebrun et al., 1971).

Echolalia and echo-answer frequently coexist, but in some patients echo-answer predominates. Instances of isolated echo-answer were continuously docu-mented in a patient with TCMA reported by Brust and co-workers (1982). This patient could not repeat language when asked to do so and also failed to show echolalia in a strict sense; however, when she was asked: "Are you in the hospital?", she replied "*I am in the hospital*" instead of using the more economic response "Yes". In addition, patients with word-meaning deafness (WMD), a singular phonological–semantic dissociation deficit mainly reported in the context of TCSA (Ellis, 1984; Kohn & Friedman, 1986), usually exhibit echo-answer. Echo-answer in WMD is apparently designed to capture, ultimately, the meaning of words. Byron Bramwell (1897), on describing the details of the language impairment of his original patient (Case 11), clearly illustrated how the presence of mitigated echolalia and echo-answer favoured auditory comprehension. Bramwell stated (Ellis, 1984, p. 254): "When asked a question she often echoed the last part of it and then after repeating some of the words, seemed to understand their meaning . . . Thus when asked, 'Are you better?' She repeated the word 'better' obviously in an automatic, reflex way, then brightened up and said intelligently, 'Yes, better'".

Similar examples were later reported by Symonds (1953) in CL, a patient with presumed Pick's disease, who exhibited typical features of WMD in the setting of a TCSA. For instance, when CL was asked: "What is your surname?", he replied: "My surname—Charles Frederik Leale—is that you mean?" (p. 4). Also, when he was asked "Are you Charles Frederik Leale?" he replied: "I'm Charles Frederik Leale—Yes" (p. 4). Lebrun and colleagues (1971) rightly pointed out that echoreactions of this kind in patients like Bramwell's case result from an inability to grasp the content of auditory information.

There is little information regarding the issue of localisation of the lesion responsible for echo-answer in TA. Given that echo-answer may be a transitional stage in the recovery process of more automatic forms of echolalia, one could argue that both disorders have the same neurological basis. In support of this proposal, clear-cut examples of echo-answer have been described in association with the lesion sites traditionally implicated in the pathogenesis of echolalia (e.g. surface of the mesial frontal lobe, temporoparietal association areas) (Bramwell, 1897; Brust et al., 1982).

Echoing approval

Ghika, Bogousslavsky, Ghika-Schmid, and Regli (1996) have described a new form of verbal EP, which they termed "echoing approval", in two transcortical motor aphasic patients featuring impaired speech initiation, reduced verbal fluency and stuttering, but preserved repetition. Both failed to show echolalia in a strict sense (they did not repeat parts or the whole sentence produced by the partner), but during a short dialogue or in replying to questions they imitated the affirmative or negative syntactical construction of questions or their intonational pattern. When they discussed their symptomatology with doctors they always replied to positive questions with exclamations such as "yes, yes", or "exactly", and used "no, no" or "absolutely not" to echo negative questions. As a result of this abnormal behaviour, both patients nearly always incurred in self-contradictory statements. What follows is a fragment of a dialogue between the examiner and Patient 2 illustrating this point.

Examiner: "Do you sometimes have cramps?"
Patient 2: "Exactly"
Examiner: "Real cramps, such that your muscle gets hard and hurts a lot?"
Patient 2: "Yes, cramps, I have cramps"
Examiner: "Where?"
Patient 2: "In the calf, cramps, yes"
Examiner: "But you don't have cramps, do you?"
Patient 2: "No, . . . no"
Examiner: "You know whats cramps are, do you?"
Patient 2: "Yes, yes, cramps, like a big pain in your calf, yes I have cramps".
Examiner: "But you just told me that you don't?"
Patient 2: "No, not even . . ."

In addition, when the examiner was engaged in discussing details of the neurological exam with a colleague in the presence of Patient 1 (a 62-year-old woman) using scientific terms which were unfamiliar to her, she made statements of agreement or disagreement about the scientific labels, which wholly depended on the syntactical structures of the sentence or of its intonation. The following example illustrates this point.

Attending physicians (dialogue): "We were impressed by the peculiar type of aphasia"
Patient 1: "Yes, yes . . . yes, exactly, yes, yes"
Attending physicians (dialogue): ". . . and we thought she had some kind of transcortical, predominantly motor aphasia . . ."
Patient 1: "Yes, yes, exactly, that's it"
Attenting physicians (dialogue): ". . . with no phonemic or semantic paraphasia . . ."
Patient 1: "No, no, absolutely not"
Attending physicians (dialogue): ". . . the only abnormal physical signs were bilateral grasping, echopraxia, and a right Babinsky . . ."
Patient 1: 'Yes, yes, that's right . . ., exactly . . ."

According to Ghika and colleagues, echoing approval was not caused by impaired auditory comprehension or reduced attention span nor was it the expression of confabulatory or perseveratory responses. It was, however, associated with EP (e.g. echopraxia, echomimia), other environment-driven behaviours (e.g. utilisation behaviour), and frontal-lobe cognitive deficits (impaired performance on "go-no-go" and Luria's alternating tasks). Neuroimaging disclosed a callosofrontal glioma in Patient 1 and leukoaraiosis with multiple subcortical lacunar infarcts (Biswanger's disease) in Patient 2. The anatomical sites involved by the lesions led the authors to conclude that dysfunction of frontosubcortical (orbitofrontal and frontomesial) circuits may explain the full clinical spectrum of language, behavioural, and cognitive deficits found in these two patients.

Contamination

Lebrun and co-workers (1971) used the term "contamination" to name the in-
advertent inclusion of a word just heard into the patient's response instead of the
one he or she wanted to say. Contamination may occur not only by the undesir-
able incorporation of words said by the partner, but some patients may also
contaminate their statements or replies with the inclusion of their own words
(autocontamination). At times, the utterances of patients with contamination
behaviour are not only influenced by the word just heard, but by their meaning. The following is an example of this type of contamination produced by a
patient with TCMA, verbal paraphasias, and mild deficit in auditory comprehension during a sentence completion exercise (Berthier & Hinojosa, unpublished
observation):

> *Examiner:* "When it rains we use . . .?"
> *Patient:*   "a building"
> *Examiner:* "When it's cold we wear . . ."
> *Patient:*   "an umbrella"

Completion phenomenon

Completion phenomenon (CP) refers to the patient's compulsive tendency to
complete the examiner's unfinished sentences. CP was first described by Stengel
(1936) in a 60-year-old woman who showed severe aphasia and right-sided
hemiplegia. Her spontaneous language was restricted to the nonmeaningful
recurring utterance "te-te" and her aural comprehension was almost totally abolished. The patient could not repeat language on request, but showed echolalia.
Stengel (1947) stated that in certain instances when his patient heard an incomplete sentence pronounced slowly, she tended to complete it instead of repeating
verbatim the unfinished word sequence. For instance, when Stengel asked his
mixed transcortical aphasic patient: "How did you sleep last . . .?", she immediately completed: "night", or "last night" (p. 599). CP was not only elicited by
open-ended interrogative sentences, but was also triggered by declarative statements (e.g. "You are a good . . . *woman*") (Stengel, 1947). Stengel considered
CP as a spontaneous reaction which shares its automatic and compulsive character with echolalia. While often discussed together, CP does not necessarily occur
during the production of echolalic utterances. Rubens (1975) demonstrated that
there are instances in which patients complete an open-ended sentence without
echoing it (Case 1), whereas in others the entire fragment is echoed without
completing it (Case 2). Still other patients echo the entire fragment and then
complete it (e.g. *examiner:* "The lemons are . . ."; *patient:* "The lemons are
sour" (Berthier & Hinojosa, unpublished observation).

Automatic forms of CP are generally demonstrable in TA mainly when
overlearned verbal material is used. The auditory presentation of fragments of

well-known nursery rhymes or proverbs are easily completed in an almost auto-matic way even without understanding their meaning. The patient's perform-ance, however, worsens on sentence completion exercises when the expected response involves a less predictable, low-probablity item (e.g. "He is afraid . . .") (Berndt et al., 1987). This suggests that patient's performance on sentence com-pletion tasks might variously depend upon the sentence fragment characteristics, the frequency of usage of the missed terminal word, and also on other character-istics of the target (see Robinson et al., 1998).

The pattern of performance on sentence completion tasks observed in a few single case studies and small clinical series tend to support this assertion. For instance, HCEM, a mixed transcortical aphasic patient described by Whitaker (1976), easily completed sentences when the target words were high-frequency nouns (e.g. "Do you like to write with a . . ."—"*with a pen*"), but failed when the expected response was more open-ended (e.g. "Put on my . . ."—no response). Completion of proverbs and song titles well known by HCEM, even though the target word was of low frequency, were rapidly completed (e.g. "A rolling stone gathers no . . ."—"*moss*"). Whitaker (1976) suggested that since the majority of adequately completed sentences are those composed by overlearned material, the "completion phenomenon is, like echolalia itself, a pathological process presumably triggered off by a specific linguistic-conversational context and the nonterminal intonation" (p. 53). A complimentary interpretation of successful completion of sentences well known by HCEM in the presence of severe com-prehension deficit would be that these are processed as whole units that require little access to semantic representations (Butterworth & Warrington, 1995; Code, 1997; McCarthy & Warrington, 1987).

Nakagawa et al. (1993) investigated CP in a series of patients (n = 22) featuring TCSA of various aetiologies (e.g. semantic dementia due to focal atrophy, Alzheimer's disease, dementia coexisting with motor neurone disease, vascular lesions, neoplasms, and herpes simplex encephalitis). Two types of completion exercises were used; one consisted of a proverb completion task and the other was a picture naming task. The authors found a total lack of CP for proverbs in the face of preserved completion for serial numbers and days of the week in all patients with semantic dementia (n = 8) who had a pattern of auditory comprehension deficit characterised by a selective impairment in the recognition of words. Conversely, these authors found a relative preservation of CP in the remaining patients, who showed global auditory comprehension defi-cits (e.g. not restricted to word meaning). Nakagawa and co-workers interpreted their findings in patients with focal atrophy as reflecting a selective disturbance of the meaning of words and proverbs in the semantic memory system. In the same vein, Assal et al. (1983) found that failures in CP may be category-specific; in fact their mixed transcortical aphasic patient (NT) showed marked difficulties completing open-ended exercises in which the target nouns were animals and flowers (see further data in Chapter 5). Studies such as those of

Assal et al. (1983) and Nakagawa et al. (1993) illustrate that different types of CP really exist and that the ability to complete might depend on the functional status of semantic representations for different language units.

Echopraxia

Echopraxia is defined as the involuntary imitation of gestures previously seen in other people. The involuntary imitation occurs as an almost automatic reflex that recurs during clinical testing even though some patients are fully aware of the bizarre nature of their motor behaviour (De Renzi, Cavalleri, & Facchini, 1996). Alternatively, echopraxia may be experienced as a premonitory urge to copy the executed movement, to the extent that some echopraxic patients may avoid looking at another person with exaggerated gestures or abnormal movements in order to prevent compulsive imitation (Shapiro et al., 1988).

Given that patients with TA demonstrate a strong tendency to repeat (imitate) language and nonverbal sounds, the hypothesis that such patients may be also prone to imitate gestures is intuitively appealing. This may be not exactly the case, however. On reviewing the literature I found that the coexistence of these two disorders in patients with *unilateral focal* brain lesions is by no means exceptional, since to my knowledge, echopraxia has been briefly described only in a patient who showed MTCA and alexia without agraphia after an extensive haemorrhage involving the left angular gyrus (Pirozzolo et al., 1981). Further analysis of published data revealed that transcortical patients without echopraxia instead showed a constellation of other abnormal limb movements including loss of bimanual coordination, ataxic automatisms, drifting movements, groping, grasping, intermanual conflict, utilisation behaviour, and the so-called "alien hand" sign (Brion & Jedynak, 1972; Della Sala, Marchetti, & Spinnler, 1991; Gasquoine, 1993; Goldberg, Mayer, & Toglia, 1981; Leiguarda, Starkstein, & Berthier, 1989; Lhermitte, 1983; McNabb et al., 1988; Starkstein et al., 1988).

One possible explanation for the paucity of studies reporting the coexistence on TA and echopraxia in cases of unilateral focal brain damage could be that aphasia is the result of left hemisphere lesions that involve cortico-subcortical regions and neural pathways which are likewise critical for the programming of skilled movements (Kertesz & Ferro, 1984). By definition, echopraxia entails the "correct" imitation of a motor act and available evidence indicates that TA often coexist with limb apraxia. It is well known that although patients with ideomotor apraxia show a performance on gesture imitation that is either comparable with or better than pantomiming to verbal commands (Heilman & Gonzalez Rothi, 1993), gesture imitation is usually abnormal. Moreover, occasional patients with MTCA may show a pattern of performance on praxis testing that is characterised by poorer performance on gesture imitation than on pantomiming after a verbal command (Mehler, 1987, 1988). This probably occurs because the causative lesions in TA are generally well suited to interrupt occipitofrontal and parietofrontal connections normally implicated in the imitation of skilled movements (Jones & Powell, 1970; Kertesz & Ferro, 1984; Pandya & Kuypers, 1969).

Another argument against the coexistence of TA and echopraxia in patients with unilateral focal brain lesions comes from the fact that the transcortical pattern may also be caused by focal damage to the supplementary motor area (SMA; Alexander, Benson, & Stuss, 1989; Rubens, 1975). The SMA is regarded as responsible for the preparation of highly integrated forms of motor behaviour (e.g. complex arm movements) (Talairach, Bancaud, & Geier, 1973), playing a role in the transcoding of praxic representations into the innervatory patterns that activate the motor cortex (Heilman & Gonzalez Rothi, 1993). Recent clinical evidence indicates that ideomotor apraxia can be observed among patients with focal vascular lesions (Watson, Fleet, Gonzalez Rothi, & Heilman, 1986) or degenerative changes affecting the SMA (Leiguarda, Lees, Merello, Starkstein, & Marsden, 1994). Watson and co-workers (1986) documented bilateral ideomotor apraxia for transitive limb movements (e.g. using a screwdriver) in two patients with TCMA and ischaemic infarctions involving the left SMA. These two patients did poorly on command and although motor performance improved during the imitation of transitive movements and both patients had perseverative movements, poor inhibition of motor responses and grasp reflexes, they did not show echopraxic responses. By contrast, De Renzi et al. (1996) recently described imitation behaviour (echopraxia) in patients with lesions involving the mesial and/or lateral aspect of the frontal lobe, but unfortunately, the presence of related language and cognitive deficits was not systematically examined.

The coexistence of TA and echopraxia has been described in the context of other EP, such as echolalia, echographia, and "frontal" release grasping and sucking signs among patients with *diffuse or multifocal* brain damage (Assal, 1985; Ghika et al., 1996; Schneider, 1938; Stengel, 1946). Stengel (1946) documented echopraxia in two young adult mentally retarded patients, who showed features of mixed receptive and expressive language disorder coupled with echolalia and forced CP, a pattern of deficits that might be interpreted in retrospect as developmental or early acquired forms of MTCA. Compulsive imitation of gestures and motor actions as well as completion of common actions initiated by the examiner, remarkably similar to Lhermitte's "utilisation behaviour" (Lhermitte, 1983; Lhermitte, Pillon, & Serdaru, 1986), were prominent features in both cases. In addition, TCMA and dynamic aphasia coexisted with echopraxia and/or related environment-driven motor behaviours in patients who had radiological evidence of extensive bilateral damage to the fronto-subcortical circuits (Assal, 1985; Ghika et al., 1996; Gold et al., 1997) as well as in patients with frontotemporal dementia (see Case 3 in Ames, Cummings, Wirshing, Quinn, & Mahler, 1994 and Case 4 in Gregory & Hodges, 1996). Findings from all these cases suggest that multifocal (bilateral) damage to the frontal lobes and their subcortical connections may cause a disinhibition of primitive and poorly differentiated reactions to the environment. The following case illustrates the coexistence of both disorders (TA and echopraxia) in a patient with frontotemporal dementia.

A case of echopraxia and mixed transcortical aphasia in frontotemporal dementia

In the last few years, Berthier and Goldar (unpublished observation) studied a 52 year-old right-handed woman (NLE) with advanced frontotemporal dementia who showed disruptive behaviour, echopraxia, echographia, and features of MTCA. When examined five years after the onset of personality change, NLE showed prominent behavioural changes including features of the Klüver–Bucy syndrome (sexual misconduct and persistent eating of nonedible substances; Cummings & Duchen, 1981; Klüver & Bucy, 1937). Her behaviour was socially inappropriate; she appeared excessively friendly with strangers, displayed undue cheerfulness, and continuously sang and danced to an obscene song she had composed. Her husband indicated that she had no insight into her abnormal behaviour and denied any problems. On examination, she appeared disinhibited, demanding and restless. She was noted to have a bilateral grasp reflex, but the remainder of the neurological examination was within normal limits. By that time, a CT scan disclosed marked bilateral frontotemporal atrophy. Language function was assessed with the Western Aphasia Battery (WAB; Kertesz, 1982). Information content was restricted to the use of reiterative speech and echolalic utterances and her fluency score was extremely poor (1/10). Auditory comprehension was less affected than spontaneous speech, however. She obtained low scores on subtests taping yes/no questions (15/60), auditory word recognition (35/60), and sequential commands (12/80). Repetition was mildly affected (62/100). Naming was severely affected for pictures (4/60), word fluency (0/20), sentence completion (2/10), and responsive speech (2/10). The aphasia quotient (AQ) score (26.4 points) and the profile of language impairment both fitted well with the diagnosis of MTCA. Writing was almost impossible to test due to lack of cooperation, but on writing to dictation she showed echographia (she automatically copied words just written). On the assessment of auditory comprehension of sequential commands (where the examiner would line up three objects on the table and exemplify some of the commands to the patient to ensure understanding of instructions) NLE automatically imitated the movement just executed by the examiner. Attempts to interrupt her echopraxic behaviour were unsuccessful. The severity of language impairment interfered with testing or other cognitive functions. However, on a brief assessment of frontal-lobe nonverbal functions NLE was unable to inhibit inappropriate responses on "go-no-go" tasks and she perseverated on drawing multiple loops and geometric figures (Fig. 6.2).

Like other patients with diagnosis of frontotemporal dementia, NLE showed a progressive dementing illness, characterised initially by prominent personality and behavioural changes that were followed by a nonfluent reiterative aphasia

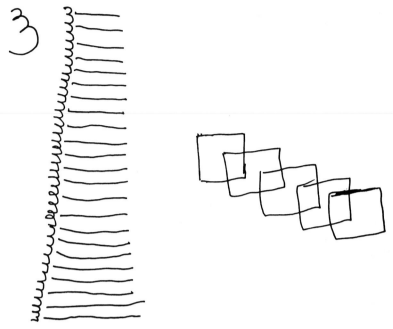

FIG. 6.2   Patient NLE: Examples of perseveration during drawing multiple loops and geometric designs.

with features of MTCA and EP (echolalia, echographia, and echopraxia) as well as poor inhibition of inappropriate responses on frontal-lobe tasks (e.g. gross perseveration on drawing multiple loops and geometric designs). The occurrence in NLE of restlessness, distractibility, disinhibition of sexual and oral tendencies coupled with the pattern of language changes as well as cognitive performance and neuroimaging findings are all indicative of frontotemporal involvement affecting functions mainly attributed to prefrontal, orbitofrontal, and temporal paralimbic cortices (Blumer & Benson, 1975; Cummings & Duchen, 1981; Mendez, Selwood, Mastri, & Frey, 1993; Mesulam, 1986; Neary, Snowden, Northen, & Goulding, 1988). Therefore, these findings suggest that global dysfunction of anterior frontotemporal regions play an important role in the pathogenesis of MTCA and related EP including echopraxia.

Echopraxia without aphasia

Analysis of echopraxia occurring in nonaphasic patients may shed more light on its underlying functional mechanism. For instance, immediate or delayed echopraxia in Gilles de la Tourette's syndrome have been related to dysfunction of either basal ganglia structures (Leckman, Walker, & Cohen, 1993; Shapiro et al., 1988) or anterior cingulate cortex-SMA system (Berthier, Campos, & Kulisevsky, 1996), whereas echopraxia and echolalia observed in encephalitis lethargica were associated with histopathological changes in both the basal ganglia and ventral tegmental area of the mesencephalon (Trimble, 1981). Similar lesion locations have recently been reported among individuals without tics (De Renzi et al., 1996; Gold et al., 1997), and, in exceptional patients, echopraxia may also be induced by highly focal lesions of the ventral midbrain tegmentum (Adair, Williamson, Schwartz, & Heilman, 1996). Adair and co-workers (1996) recently reported echopraxia and "frontal lobe symptoms" including decreased verbal fluency, abulia, and dysphoria in a nonaphasic patient who had MRI evidence of an ischaemic infarction involving the ventral tegmental area. The ventral tegmental area, which contains the majority of dopamine neuron cell bodies projecting to the basal ganglia and cerebral cortex, plays an important role in human cognition (De Kayser, Herregodts, & Ebinger, 1990; Weinberger, Berman, & Chase, 1988). Therefore, these findings taken together raise the possibility that damage of the ascending monoaminergic mesocortical system in either the midbrain tegmentum, basal ganglia, or in distant targets areas such as the frontomesial–cingulate region may induce compulsive echopraxia, decreased verbal fluency, and a "frontal lobe" pattern of cognitive deficits.

Echographia

Arnold Pick called attention to a peculiar echoreaction in which an aphasic woman echoed in writing all that she heard. On interpreting this singular phenomenon, he suggested "that the impressions on the auditory centre" stimulated "the writing centre". Initially, Pick (1900, cited in Pick, 1924) succinctly described two patients with this rare symptom, which by analogy with echolalia, he termed *echograhia* or *echo-writing*. His first patient was a nonaphasic, mentally retarded and illiterate individual, who echoed by writing very simple questions which he was unable to answer, whereas the second patient was a man with features of "sensory" aphasia (jargon speech, word-deafness) and "paragraphia" who during writing testing "copied everything, even sentences containing remarks grossly derogatory to himself" (p. 417). Several years later, Pick (1924) went into the problem more deeply and published a detailed clinicopathological study of echographia.

The patient was a 64-year-old Czech woman who developed aphasia and a rapidly resolving right hemiplegia due to thrombosis of the left middle cerebral artery that on postmortem examination was found to involve the foot of the first frontal gyrus, the opercular portion of the sensorimotor cortex, part of the first and second temporal gyri, and the anterior temporal pole. The supramarginal and angular gyri were spared. On language evaluation, the patient had fluent unintelligible jargon during spontaneous speech and naming with relative preservation of auditory comprehension for words, objects, simple sentences, and certain whole-body commands. She could repeat two or three words only, but intermittently was able to recite the Lord's Prayer flawlessly using adequate rhythm and intonational contours. Singing was possible with prompting, but lyrics contained jargon fragments and were enunciated with poor intonation. Oral reading was impossible. The most intriguing aspect of this patient's behaviour was her writing abilities. In spite of being profoundly aphasic, the patient appeared desirous for writing and frequently asked for writing paper. Spontaneously, she could write isolated words that she was unable to understand during reading. She was apparently aware of her writing errors and echoed words in an attempt to correct her misspellings. Written naming was severely impaired. Copy was largely preserved and she copied everything, particularly if these words were written in Czech. She was reluctant to copy German words, except when certain printed characters (e.g. addition of letters and accents) of the foreign words were deliberately modified to resemble a Czech word.

Pick interpreted the defects underlying echoreactions in aphasia as resulting from an imbalance between inhibition and release mechanisms. He believed that circumscribed damage of the temporal lobes decreased the influences of "diffusely arranged inhibitions" on the acoustico-speech reflexes, thus leading to a variety of echosymptoms. In his view, however, the release phenomenon could not enterily explain the "isolated" or "residual" echographia documented in his patient. Therefore, he interpreted this in complementary terms, indicating that since his patient's echo-writing was only observed when the patient was confronted with material written in her mother tongue (Czech), this behaviour may be a "voluntary action", and hence represent a clear example of "mitigated" or "selective" echographia. From a theoretical viewpoint, Pick concluded that this pattern of behaviour may by triggered by either the mere observation of the "word-picture itself" or "the acoustico-motor element of the 'inner word' whose existence can be inferred from the lip movements which accompany the attempt to read" (Pick, 1924, p. 427).

In recent years, echographia has been conceptualised as a form of reiterative agraphia and grouped along other disturbances of writing such as perseveration, paligraphia, and coprographia (Benson & Cummings, 1985). Unfortunately, since echographia is an exceptional disorder, additional case studies reported after early clinical (Stengel, 1947) and pathological descriptions (Pick, 1924) merely describe its occurrence. Echographia and other disorders of writing (e.g. impulsive graphic activity) have been reported in association with dynamic "frontal" aphasia (Cambier et al., 1988; Van Vugt, Paquier, Kees, & Cras, 1996). Berthier (1998) studied the characteristics of echographia and MTCA in an elderly woman who suffered a severe traumatic brain injury.

A case of hypergraphic jargon and echographia in mixed transcortical aphasia

The patient, CV, was a 76-year-old Spanish-speaking woman who suffered a closed head injury following a fall down the stairs. On admission to the emergency room, she was found confused and agitated, and showed a left hemiparesis.

An emergency CT scan disclosed haemorrhagic contusions in the anterior temporal lobes and a left frontotemporal subdural haematoma that was surgically evacuated. At operation, the left temporal pole was found to be contused and swollen, and some cortical necrotic tissue had to be resected. In the ensuing weeks, CV's agitation cleared and it was noted that she had nonfluent aphasia with impaired comprehension. Neurological examination disclosed four limb paratonia with extensor plantar responses and grasp reflexes bilaterally. She also had urinary and faecal incontinence. By that time, she also developed symptoms of the Klüver–Bucy syndrome (Lilly, Cummings, Benson, & Frankel, 1983; Klüver & Bucy, 1937). She appeared unable to recognise close relatives, was easily distracted, and developed a strong tendency to attend and react to every visual stimulus (hypermetamorphosis). CV also developed impulsive manual exploratory behaviour of available objects as soon as they were noticed. She continually picked up and scrutinised objects visually but did not attempt to use them (see later). She almost continually attempted to undress herself and also to remove the clothes of her family members and staff. She did not have increased appetite but once ate a large quantity of butter. A repeat CT scan three months after surgery revealed low-density lesions in both temporal lobes and left mesial frontal cortex.

By that time, her affect was described as "flat and devoid of emotions". CV appeared less active and showed a docile behaviour, but she still wandered around the house many hours a day and impulsively explored objects by touch. Her daughter informed me that CV's increased motor activity only abated when she was allowed to write.

Cognitive testing could not be performed due to distractibility elicited by irrelevant stimuli. However, she willingly cooperated in language, and particularly, writing tasks. Language testing with the WAB revealed that her verbal output was limited to echolalic utterances and to a few automatic sentences (e.g. "Do you want a cup of tea?") generally uttered out of context. At times, she used appropriate short phrases when upset (e.g. "Don't move the bed!"). Her fluency score was extremely poor (1/10). She rarely made spontaneous statements, but her oral communication increased during writing to dictation.[4] Auditory comprehension was severely impaired for yes/no questions (21/60), word recognition (28/60), and sequential commands (2/80), but repetition was relatively spared (70/100) as she failed to repeat only some words of the two long sentences. Naming was abolished for objects (0/60), word fluency (0 words in one minute), sentence completion (0/10), and responsive speech (0/10). Her AQ was 32.2/100, a score similar to the figure (mean = 31.8, SD = 16.4) reported by Kertesz (1979) among patients with MTCA. Reading comprehension was nil, but the

---

[4] The facilitatory effect of a motor task such as writing on verbal behaviour observed in CV has also been reported by Körney (1975) in a patient with TCMA in whom the elicitation of a grasp reflex augmented echolalic behaviour.

TABLE 6.1
Patient CV: Writing to Dictation

	No.	*No. Correct*
Nouns		
Concrete		
High frequency	40	36 (90%)
Low frequency	40	30 (75%)
Abstract		
High frequency	40	29 (72%)
Low frequency	40	21 (52%)
Verbs	20	15 (75%)
Adjectives	20	14 (70%)
Functors	20	18 (90%)
Letters	24	13 (65%)
Nonwords	40	34 (85%)
Ambiguous words	20	13 (65%)

pattern of performance on oral reading tasks was consistent with a *phonological dyslexia*, since she read real words (31/40) considerably better than nonwords (16/40). On writing to request CV failed to generate any word and was unable to name by writing any visually presented object, but she obtained ceiling scores on those subtests of the WAB that examine writing to dictation (10/10), writing to dictated or visually presented words (10/10), and dictated letters (5/5) and numbers (5/5). Copy was preserved, and she produced a single spelling error during sentence copy. Given the relative preservation of writing to dictation and the calming effect of writing on CV's behaviour, a more detailed evaluation of her writing was performed. On experimental writing tasks, CV's performance was consistent with a diagnosis of *lexical "surface" agraphia* (Beauvois & Dérousné, 1981; Lesser, 1989). She could write regular words (e.g. "mesa" [table]) considerably better than orthographically ambiguous words (e.g. "opinión" [opinion] ⇒ *opiñón*). She could also write most nonwords to dictation correctly; in fact more than 80% of these nonwords were written flawlessly, even some composed by long letter strings (e.g. "escamera") (Table 6.1).

CV's behaviour during writing was noteworthy. Her restless behaviour and object manipulation were almost constant and would cease only when she was allowed to write. Assessment of the influence of environmental cues on her behaviour was carried out. When 10 objects (e.g. glasses, spoon) were success-ively placed near to or far from her without comments for 10 seconds, she briefly manipulated and visually inspected all the objects, but never attempted to use them. Her manipulation of objects seemed, at least in part, to be unrelated to faulty visual object recognition, as on a spoken word–picture matching task she was able to point to 28 out of 60 items correctly. On the other hand, when a pen and paper were put in front of her, she began to write without instruction.

Writing could also be elicited by other kinds of stimuli. For instance, if during impulsive manipulation of objects, CV found a magazine and a pen on the table, she would copy the heading and advertisements, and then she would spend hours writing without hesitation, not paying attention to the presence of her astonished family members. This behaviour was so frequent that during a two-month period she produced an estimated 300 pages of unintelligible scrawl mainly composed by neologisms, perseverations, and letter reduplications (e.g. "m" $\Rightarrow$ *nnn*). Copy was also elicited by visuomotor stimuli. When the examiner wrote words or phrases in front of her, she invariably copied these writings, even though the examiner did not indicate verbally to do so. A combination of auditory–verbal and visual stimulation could also trigger writing in CV; at times she attempted to copy television information including both the spoken content of commercials as well as written messages. She copied very fast but at times became frustrated when she was unable to copy brief publicity spots. In this situation, if she did not have a piece of paper at hand she would start copying on whatever she could find and twice she wrote on a dish and a tablecloth.

Writing to dictation was also contaminated by echographia; she often wrote dictated words intermingled with other words she automatically copied from previous lines and paragraphs. At times, echographic behaviour adopted a prepotent character since she would interrupt dictation to copy previous words (e.g. "brilliant, brilliant, brilliant"). Immediately after the echographic intrusion, she paused, waiting for the forthcoming words, or when she did not remember the correct spelling of a word she often asked "What letter should I write?" CV's auditory span to dictated words did not exceed four words, so that she frequently missed the last words of the sentence. She then hesitated, asked "What else?" and waited for the interlocutor response to eventually complete the last fragment of the dictated sentence.

Further observation of CV's writing behaviour showed that if she had a pen at hand when the examiner asker her a question, she would begin to transcribe the content of the question verbatim, although she did not reproduce the few words or automatic phrases *she* produced during the interview. This phenomenon was so prominent that during the assessment of oral arithmetic calculation, when she was asked "I would like you to add 4 plus 4", she picked up a pencil and paper placed near her, then started writing the last portion of this simple number sum and continued responding to other arithmetical calculations by writing (Fig. 6.3).

In summary, CV had a MTCA coupled with a form of reiterative agraphia and environment-driven behaviours associated with extensive frontotemporal damage. Similar combinations of abnormal behaviours, albeit less severe, were described by Whitaker (1976) in her mixed transcortical aphasic patient (HCEM) with frontotemporal dementia. Whitaker (p. 25) noted that "when a sheet of paper was put in front of her and a pencil was put in her hand, she would start scribbling". Echographia was also evident during letter copy, but in contrast to CV, writing to dictation in HCEM was abnormal. On examining HCEM's

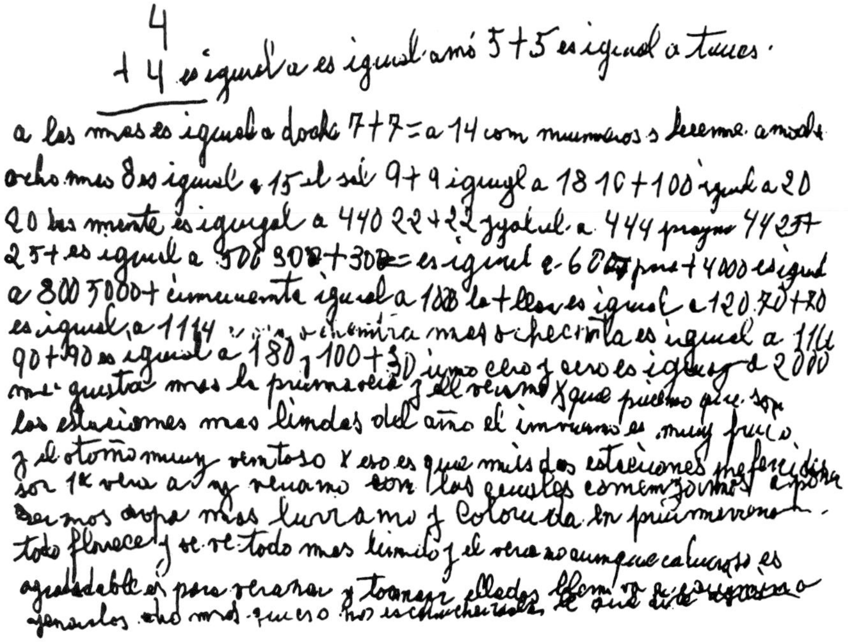

FIG. 6.3   Patient CV: Examples of hypergraphia elicited by auditory–verbal stimulation.

general behaviour, Whitaker stated (p. 16)"If there were objects lying on the table in front of her, she would pick them up, manipulate them briefly, and put them back", but purposeful utilisation of objects was not mentioned. The neuropathological study in Pick's patient showed left perisylvian damage with involvement of posterior temporal cortex, inferior frontal gyrus, and adjacent frontoparietal opercular cortex, whereas in CV and HCEM the bulk of lesions were in both frontotemporal lobes. This probably explain differences in the profile of aphasic impairments between Pick's case and CV and HCEM as well as the occurrence in these two cases of environment-driven behaviours other than echographia that were absent in Pick's case. Marked deficits in reading and writing comprehension with relative preservation of oral reading were found in CV and HCEM. Writing to dictation, and copy were severely impaired in HCEM and less compromised in CV. Analysis of these functions using the cognitive neuropsychological approach revealed that CV had a combination of lexical "surface" agraphia and phonological alexia. Similar patterns of dissociations have been discovered in other cases, and taken as evidence for the independence of distributed networks subserving spelling and writing (Roeltgen, 1993).

An interpretation of hypergraphic jargon and echographia in CV cannot be advanced in a straightforward way. Nevertheless, based on findings from CV and others patients with different types of EP (see Assal, 1985; Ghika et al.,

1996; Lhermitte, 1983; Van Vugt et al., 1996) one can drawn some inferences about the conceptualisation of these disorders as forms of environment-driven behaviours. It is possible that both hypergraphic jargon and echographia may constitute a form of utilisation behaviour, selective for writing skills (van Vugt et al., 1996). Utilisation behaviour, as described by Lhermitte (1983), is charac-terised by an exaggerated response to external stimuli that occurs in the absence of any specific instruction. The placement of objects in front of the patient immediately elicits their use, a subclass of utilisation behaviour that has been termed *induced* by Shallice et al. (1989) to distinguish it from the so-called *incidental* form, in which object utilisation occurs when the patient is engaged in cognitive, usually auditory–verbal, tasks (Eslinger, Warner, Grattan, & Easton, 1991; Shallice et al., 1989). At times, however, it seems that CV had a conscious intention to write; during spontaneous writing she paused frequently giving the impression of lexical search, and she voluntarily finished her writing signalling the end of the sentence with a bar to return the next day to just the same word. This resembled an additional form of utilisation behaviour, termed *spontaneous* by Eslinger and associates (1991), that is characterised by the execution of motor actions that take place without apparent external influence.

Impulsive object manipulation occurring in the setting of a Klüver–Bucy syndrome as was seen in CV can be ascribed to hypermetamorphosis, since she displayed a marked tendency to investigate the environment tactually and she did not use objects in a purposeful way (except for writing utensils). While this pattern of motor actions differed from the purposeful yet exaggerated motor activity exhibited by patients with utilisation behaviour, it is similar, though more dramatic, to some *incidental* forms of utilisation behaviour, namely the purposeless manipulative actions (*toying*) executed by frontal patients during cognitive testing situations (Shallice et al., 1989). It should be noted that some phenomenological overlap between hypermetamorphosis and certain forms of utilisation behaviour have been noted. Disinhibition, distractibility, and a strong tendency to react to every visual stimulus are integral components of hyper-metamorphosis and utilisation behaviour and both conditions are associated with lesions involving the frontotemporal cortices (e.g. Cummings & Duchen, 1981; Joseph, 1986; Lhermitte, 1983; Whitaker, 1976).

There is little previous data indicating what type of instrumental or environ-mental cues are necessary to trigger hypergraphia and echographia. In CV, for instance, copious unintelligible writing was elicited by the mere presentation of pen and paper, and, less commonly, it accompanied the culmination of echographic behaviour. A similar writing behaviour has been described in other brain-damaged patients. Joseph (1986) described the presence of ictal automatic writ-ing in a patient (Case 1) with history of multiple head injuries who had simple and complex partial seizures originated in the left temporal lobe. Neurological examination, presumably performed interictally, disclosed positive glabellar tap, bilateral grasp reflexes, and utilisation behaviour of common objects with the right hand only, probably reflecting additional dysfunction of interconnected structures in the frontal lobe. Eslinger et al. (1991) reported the case of a patient with reduced verbal fluency, echolalia, and "frontal lobe" type of utilisation behaviour associated with bilateral paramedian thalamic infarcts in whom the presentation of a testing set composed of paper, pen, and envelope elicited the writing of a coherent nurse's note and addressing the envelope to the examiner. Cambier et al. (1988) described a patient with a bilateral frontocallosal glioma, who exhibited dynamic aphasia, incessant graphic activity with meaningless semantic content, and echographia in conjunction with purposeless utilisation behaviour of objects. Echographia in Cambier et al.'s patient was elicited by the same kind of stimuli that I observed in CV. Both copied everything they saw, including their own writing. Also, CV and Cambier et al.'s patient both showed echographia as an *incidental* phenomenon. They copied the titles and advertisements of magazines and labels of envelopes that were placed nearby but not directed to them as well as reproducing all incoming auditory information through writing. Thus, they transcribed verbal questions, commands, and general remarks into writing, a behaviour not observed in the echographic patients originally described by Pick (1924).

Utilisation behaviour in other patients (Degos et al., 1993; Eslinger et al., 1991; Lhermitte, 1983; Shallice et al., 1989) was more global, in that it could be elicited by the presentation of different objects, including writing utensils. By contrast, in CV and Cambier et al.'s patient hypergraphia and echographia might be the predominant clinical manifestation of utilisation behaviour. Both patients showed impulsive object manipulation, but they never used these objects in a purposeful way. If these two patients really had instances of utilisation behaviour exclusively expressed through writing activities, this raises the possibility that in certain patients utilisation behaviour may be fractionated into various components depending on the type of stimulus. The report of an additional single case study provides some support for this argument. Assal (1985) reported the case of a patient who showed impulsive reading of information written in the objects (e.g. titles of magazines, ads printed on envelopes, clothing labels) she impulsively manipulated. She also read any other written material that come to her visual attention (e.g. names of streets, licence plates) and showed, albeit less severe, repetitive and purposeless ordering of objects placed in front of her. A CT scan revealed ischaemic infarctions in the mesial frontal and anterior cingulate gyrus bilaterally and in the posterior part of the right temporal cortex, a lesion distribution that in Assal's view interfered with the interplay of the right and left cerebral hemispheres, causing a disinhibition of the reading system in the left hemisphere. A similar argument was suggested by Yamadori, Mori, Tabuchi, Kudo, and Mitani (1986) to explain stimulus-induced writing among patients with hypergraphia due to right hemisphere lesions. In addition to changes in inter-hemispheric equilibrium, neuroanatomical and functional models propose that abnormal behavioural responses driven by environment cues (e.g. echographia, echolalia, hypergraphia, utilisation behaviour) are the result of lesions that suppress the normal inhibitory modulation of the temporal (Pick, 1924) and frontal lobes (Lhermitte, 1983; Shallice et al., 1989) over functionally dependent cognitive subsystems. Damage to the frontal-subcortical circuits in specific regions of the frontal lobe (Lhermitte, 1983; Lhermitte et al., 1986; Mesulam, 1986; Shallice et al., 1989), caudate nucleus (Eslinger et al., 1991), or thalamus (Degos et al., 1993) seems to be important on the pathogenesis of utilisation behaviour, whereas hypergraphia and echographia probably require additional damage to the temporal lobe (Pick, 1924, Patient CV).

AUTOMATIC SPEECH

On studying patients with aphasia, Hughlings Jackson (1874/1958) distinguished two types of speech, "propositional" and "automatic" (or "nonpropositional"). Propositional speech consists of voluntary combinations of words assembled to express ideas. Jackson called this ability "superior" in sharp contrast to emotional or automatic speech (AS) which he termed "inferior" because it comes "ready made, more holistically, without effortful formulation and are composed of invariant word sequences" (Code, 1989, 1997).

Code (1989, 1997) recently suggested that AS can be segregated into two types according to their propositionality. He proposed that AS with *low* propositionality includes the rote recitation of days of the week, arithmetic tables, counting, and other automatic activities that require little or no generation of new ideas or complex phonological and morphosyntactical linguistic features. On the other hand, expletives and emotional utterances are classified as AS of *high* propositionality.

Jackson believed that AS extended beyond the few utterances that patients with severe nonfluent aphasia could pronounce under certain emotional states. He also posited that the right hemisphere mediates automatic speech. Support for the right hemisphere hypothesis comes from instances of preservation of AS after complete left hemispherectomy (see references in Code, 1997), and from regional cerebral blow-flow (rCBF) studies. Measuring rCBF with 133-Xenon, Scandinavian authors (Ingvar & Schwartz, 1974; Larsen, Skinhoj, & Lassen, 1978; Ryding, Bradvik, & Ingvar, 1987) demonstrated cortical activation in both cerebral hemispheres during AS. Ryding et al. (1987) recorded cerebral activity in 15 nonaphasic patients, who had suffered transient ischaemic attacks involving either the left or right cerebral hemispheres, during AS and humming. The repetition of series of well-known words (e.g. days of the week) using a neutral, monotonous intonation induced a strong activation of cortical regions in the left precentral and inferior posterior frontal regions, and to a lesser extent, in the right postcentral gyrus. Measurement of cerebral activity in the same subjects while humming a well-known nursery rhyme (without words or mouth movements) activated both inferior frontal cortices. Therefore, despite the low spatial resolution of rCBF method used in these studies, these findings suggest that AS and humming are associated with activation of anterior cortical regions of both cerebral hemispheres (Ryding et al., 1987).

Further support for participation of the right hemisphere in automatic aspects of language comes from studies carried out in aphasic patients with lesions in the left hemisphere (see Code, 1997; Moore, 1989 for review). Cambier and co-workers (Cambier et al., 1983) reported two right-handed patients who clearly illustrated this clinicoanatomical correlation. The first case was a patient who suffered an extensive left perisylvian infarction and developed right hemiplegia and global aphasia. With the aid of speech therapy, the patient gradually recovered the ability to utter automatic series, complete sentences, and repeat echolalically isolated words. Two years after the initial left hemisphere lesion, the patient suffered a second infarction in right-sided perisylvian areas resulting in a total abolition of language. The second case described by Cambier et al. (1983) involved a patient who after suffering an extensive left hemisphere infarction affecting the territory of the anterior and middle cerebral arteries developed a severe global aphasia but retained the capacity to utter automatic series, recite a fable, and complete open-ended sentences. Data from these two patients indicate that the right hemisphere play a role in processing AS, but probably through different functional mechanisms.

In the first patient reported by Cambier et al. (1983), AS was abolished after the initial left hemisphere infarction, to reappear several months later. If one accepts the theory proposing that the right hemisphere exerts either a dominant role for the production of AS or a compensatory role for the mediation of AS only after left hemisphere damage, as originally proposed by Jackson (1874/1958), one possible explanation to account for language behaviour in Cambier et al.'s patient (Case 1) would be that the extensive left hemisphere lesion induced a functional deactivation of right hemisphere structures (transhemispheric diaschisis) due to interruption of interhemispheric connecting fibre tracts (Dobkin et al., 1989). Functional inactivation of the right hemisphere would not be per- manent, however, thus permitting the late restitution of AS in parallel with the recruitment of viable neurons in the right anterior perisylvian area (Heiss, Kessler, Karbe, Fink, & Pawlik, 1993; Pulvermüller & Schönle, 1993). An alternative explanation would be that the right hemiphere was not dominant for automatic aspects of speech production before the initial left hemisphere lesion, and that this originally left hemisphere language function, was eventually transferred to the undamaged right hemisphere as a result of speech therapy. This mechanism is compatible with Pulvermüller and Schönle's proposal that after massive left hemisphere damage, the right hemisphere has the neuronal "machinery" avail- able to slowly restore some linguistic capacities at the expense of new right perisylvian auditory-motor assemblies (see further details in Chapter 5).

In the second patient described by Cambier and his co-workers (1983) the functional mechanism seems to be wholly different, in that the production of AS was little or not affected by a massive left hemisphere infarction. In this case the right hemisphere, was most likely dominant for the mediation of AS. It is also possible that damage to the left hemisphere may have induced transhemispheric diaschisis accounting for the impairment of more complex aspects of AS, but leaving the more resistant low propositional aspects relatively spared.

A second source of evidence for a contribution of the right hemisphere to AS comes from occasional reports of nonaphasic patients with right hemisphere damage. Speedie et al. (1993) reported the case of a right-handed bilingual (Hebrew–French) patient who in association with a right basal ganglia haemorrhage lost his ability to produce AS, including overused phrases, recitation of rhymes, singing, and swearing. Comprehension of both automatic (nonpropositional) language and affective prosody were spared, but his ability to impart affective colouring to utterances was lost. Speedie and colleagues concluded that the basal ganglia lesions prevented the limbic signal to activate the speech processes necessary to produce automatic utterances. On the other hand, Ellis, Young, and Critchley (1989) reported the case of a recovered jargon aphasic patient (ML) (due to a left thalamic haematoma), who began to experience intrusive internal vocalisations containing early acquired overlearned material such as prayers, hymns, and musical fragments which she had learned by heart during childhood and that she described as a "nattering inside her", after suffering a right basal ganglia infarct. Recurrent vocalisations, which also consisted of recent thoughts or heard speech, were experienced by ML as internally generated and perceived in her own voice. This led the authors to not consider these "natterings" as symptoms typical of schizophrenia. Ellis et al. tentatively suggested that intrusive automatic (inner speech) vocalisations resulted from a peculiar combination of left and right hemisphere lesions that caused activation of early acquired overlearned material stored in the right hemisphere and dysfunction of the left hemisphere verbal working memory system. They also considered the case of ML as an example of intrusive, automatic inner speech activated by brain damage (Critchley, 1991).

The question that now arises is what is the status of AS in TA? Overall, in aphasia there is considerable variation in the patients' ability to generate automatic utterances (Ellis & Young, 1988, p. 252). For instance, while preserved AS is a feature of nonfluent aphasia, particularly of Broca's aphasia (Yamadori et al., 1977), this peculiar association is not invariably present in every nonfluent aphasic patient (Graves & Landis, 1985). The same variability in the frequency of dissociated performance between impaired propositional and preserved AS may be also true for transcortical aphasics. While anecdotal observations documented a relative preservation of AS in cases of TA irrespective of the clinical variant (motor, sensory, or mixed), careful analysis of published cases reveals that the situation regarding AS in TA is puzzling. To mention only one example, the acute transcortical motor aphasic patient (Case 2) described by Ross (1980) was unable to count from 1 to 20 or recite the alphabet after suffering a small vascular lesion in the left SMA, whereas automatic speech was found to be spared by Alexander and Schmitt (1980) in another acute transcortical motor aphasic patient (Case 2) with the same lesion location than Ross' patient. The literature is replete with similar examples not only in cases featuring the transcortical motor pattern, but also in sensory and mixed types.

PROSODY

Prosody refers to variations in rhythm, pitch, distribution of stress, and melodic contours in language. The term prosody was introduced by Monrad-Krohn to describe a third element of speech, in addition to vocabulary and grammar. Monrad-Krohn (1947, 1963) described four types of normal prosody encompassing affective (emotional and inarticulate prosody) and certain linguistic aspects of speech (intrinsic and intellectual prosody). Currently, there is a distinction between two major types of prosody, linguistic and affective.

Linguistic Prosody   also called nonaffective prosody, deals with the different modes used to convey a linguistic message and to introduce subtle nuances of meanings through variations in stress, pitch, and rhythm. For instance, the rising pitch on the last word of a sentence can indicate a question, whereas declarative sentences generally end with a falling intonation.

Affective Prosody   serves to impart emotional tone (anger, fear, pleasure) into sentences. For instance, sentences pronounced with a happy intonation are normally produced with a higher pitch, a greater intonation range and with more variability than are those enunciated with sad affective tone (Lieberman & Michaels, 1962). Inarticulate sounds, such as grunts and sighs, are also used to enrich affective communication (Ross & Mesulam, 1979; Weintraub, Mesulam, & Kramer, 1981).

Although there has been considerable research on prosodic deficits after lateralised brain damage, the hemispheric specialisation of speech prosody still remains a controversial issue (Heilman, 1993; Ross, 1988; Ryalls, 1988; Van Lancker & Sidtis, 1992). Some authors argue that affective prosody is strongly lateralised to the right hemisphere, whereas linguistic aspects of prosody are lateralised, but not exclusively, to the left hemisphere (Ross, 1988). On the other hand, based on the multifaceted nature of prosody and on instances of negative evidence (e.g. patients with spared affective prosody despite an appropriate right hemisphere lesion (Brådvik, Darvins, Holtas, Rosén, Ryding, & Ingvar, 1990; Lebrun, Lessinnes, De Vresse, & Leleux, 1985), some authors view prosody as a diffusely distributed communicative function without a specific pattern of brain organisation (Ryalls, 1988; Van Lancker & Sidtis, 1992). Finally, other researchers even suggest that the brain lateralisation of prosody may vary according to the affective or linguistic content of the message (Shipley-Brown, Dingwall, Berlin, Yeni-Komshian, & Gordon Salant, 1988).

Damage to the left hemisphere usually induces deficits in the production of prosody in addition to aphasia (Monrad-Krohn, 1947). However, since aphasia may mask concurrent prosodic production deficits, there are few systematic studies of prosody in aphasics. In these studies, the analysis of acoustic parameters was focused on the linguistic aspects of prosody in patients with various types of aphasia, including Broca's and Wernicke's (e.g. Cooper, Soares, Nicol, Michelow, & Goloskie, 1984; Danly & Shapiro, 1982; Gandour, Holasult-Petty, & Dardarananda, 1989; Kent & Rosenbek, 1982; Ryalls, 1982).

The prosodic features in TA have not been widely examined. Occasional reports included single patients, and since prosody was not the main focus of study, their results are mainly anecdotal and often contradictory. The mention of some examples of MTCA suffice to illustrate the discrepancies that exist in the literature regarding the modulation of prosody in TA. Whitaker (1976) reported the case of a demented woman (patient HCEM) with MTCA who, during echolalic performance, "maintained the stress and intonation patterns of the verbal stimuli" (p. 37). HCEM was also able to correct errors in stress patterns, but the modulation of affective prosody during echolalia was not evaluated. Mehler (1988) reported another case of slowly progressive MTCA who showed a preserved ability to repeat semantically neutral declarative and interrogative sentences with different affective intonations. Jacome (1984) reported a case of MTCA featuring exaggerated prosody, musicophilia and compulsive whistling. Conversely, other researchers reported cases of MTCA with impaired modulation of prosody in affective (Speedie et al., 1984) or linguistic contexts (Assal et al., 1983).

There are isolated reports dealing specifically with the evaluation of prosodic production of aphasic patients in affective contexts (Speedie et al., 1984; Ross, 1992). Ross (1992) evaluated the production of affective prosody in various clinical types of aphasia (Broca's, Wernicke's, and global), and compared the patient's performance on a quantitative verbal–articulatory task with those obtained from a group of right brain-damaged patients with aprosodia. Ross concluded that deficits in the production of affectively intoned speech in aphasics with left hemisphere damage are probably secondary to articulatory verbal disturbances and not due to deficits in affective prosody. Speedie et al. (1984) studied the perceptual correlates of repetition of affective prosody in two patients who had MTCA in association with lesions of the left hemisphere located outside the perisylvian language cortex (frontoparietal white matter in Patient 1 and parieto-occipital in Patient 2). These authors found that both patients could repeat propositional language verbatim, but they were unable to impart affective intonation and they repeated almost all sentences in a monotone. Based on perceptual judgements (acoustic analysis was not performed) and radiological findings, Speedie and colleagues hypothesised that these two patients could repeat propositional language because the left perisylvian area was intact, but that they were unable to repeat imparting affective tone because the intact left perisylvian area was disconnected from the right hemisphere, which is dominant for affective prosody.

Although TA is usually produced by lesions located outside the left perisylvian area (Rapcsak & Rubens, 1994; Rubens & Kertesz, 1983), in a recent review of the literature of acute TA Berthier, Starkstein and colleagues (1991) found that in a considerable number of patients it resulted from damage to the left perisylvian language area. Moreover, in three patients with TA and perisylvian damage bilateral amytal injections (Wada test) documented that word and sentence repetition were subserved by the contralateral hemisphere (Bando et al., 1986; Berthier, Starkstein et al., 1991). Therefore, while the mechanism of "disconnection" might explain the pattern of impaired repetition of affective prosody in Speedie et al.'s patients, it remains to be determined if the repetition of affective prosody is also disrupted in patients who develop TA after extensive damage to the left perisylvian region, and if these two TA groups (with or without left perisylvian involvement) have similar or different patterns of impairment in the repetition of affective prosody.

A study of affective prosody repetition in transcortical aphasias

In a recent study, Berthier, Fernández et al. (1996) investigated the perceptual as well as the acoustic correlates of affective prosody repetition in TA. Based on the results of a previous study (Speedie et al., 1984), one aim of the study was to examine whether impaired affective prosody repetition was present not only in MTCA, but also in the other clinical types of TA (TCMA and TCSA). Another aim was to explore whether impaired affective prosody repetition in TA was restricted to patients with lesions that spared the left perisylvian area, or whether it can also occur in those patients who have lesions involving this area.

Four right-handed aphasic patients with unilateral thromboembolic strokes participated in this study. Formal language examination was carried out in all patients using the WAB (Kertesz, 1982) and other language measures that included the shortened version of the Token Test (De Renzi & Faglioni, 1978) and experimental tests of word and sentence repetition (Berthier, Porta, Posada, & Puentes, 1995). According to taxonomic criteria of the WAB, two patients were classified as having TCMA (Patients 1 and 2), another patient as having MTCA (Patient 3), and the remaining patient as having TCSA (Patient 4). Language disturbances were studied in the acute period (within two months post-onset) in two cases (Patients 1 and 3) and in the chronic period in the remaining two cases (Patients 2 and 4). Demographic and language characteristics of patients are summarised in Table 6.2.

To examine the potential role of lesion location on repetition of affective prosody, two patients with lesions involving the left perisylvian area and two

TABLE 6.2
Demographic Characteristics and Language Test Scores of Patients with
Transcortical Aphasias

| | *Patients* | | | |
	1	*2*	*3*	*4*
Sex	Female	Male	Female	Male
Age (years)	68	38	71	66
Handedness	Right	Right	Right	Right
Education (years)	7	12	14	9
Months post-stroke onset	2	19	1	30
Western Aphasia Battery				
Information content	6	6	5	6
Fluency	4	4	4	8
Comprehension	8.4	5.8	3.7	5.9
Repetition	9.2	8.4	7.4	8
Naming	7.4	7	5.6	4.8
Aphasia quotient	70	62.4	48.4	65.4
Token Test (max. 36)	17	14.5	19	10
Word Repetition (120 nouns) (percentage correct)	92	97	87	96
Sentence Repetition (10 sentences) (percentage correct)	90	100	90	100

Reprinted from Berthier, Fernández et al. (1996); by permission of Taylor & Francis Ltd.

patients with lesions sparing it were selected. Lesion location was documented by CT and/or MRI scans (see methodological details in Berthier, Fernández et al., 1996). The two patients with perisylvian involvement had TCMA. One of these cases (Patient 1) had a large ischaemic infarction involving the frontocentral operculum and subjacent basal ganglia, while the other case (Patient 2) had an ischaemic infarction involving the whole perisylvian language area with extension into the basal ganglia and internal capsulae. One of the two cases with lesions sparing of the perisylvian language area (Patient 3) had a MTCA in association with an ischaemic infarction in the territory of the anterior cerebral artery involving the superior mesial frontoparietal region, while the remaining case (Patient 4) had a TCSA in association with two simultaneous but separate ischaemic infarctions involving the white matter anterolateral and superior to the left frontal horn and the temporo-parieto-occipital junction. None of the four patients had radiologic evidence of right hemisphere damage. Neuroradiological findings are shown in Fig. 6.4.

To assess the comprehension of affective prosody the four aphasic patients listened to 20 tape-recorded sentences read with either sad, angry, happy, or neutral intonation, and were asked to identify on a response card (with vertically arranged photographs of faces expressing these emotions and the word of each emotion typed underneath the corresponding affective face) which of the four

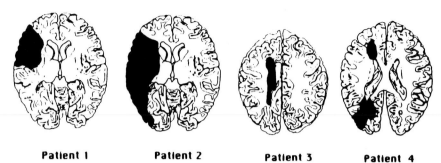

Patient 1   **Patient 2**   **Patient 3**   **Patient 4**

FIG. 6.4   Schematic diagrams of CT/MRI scans showing cross-sectional localisation of lesions in patients with transcortical aphasias. Reprinted from Berthier, Fernández et al. (1996); by permission of Taylor & Francis Ltd.

target affective intonations was most likely the sentence listened to (Heilman, Bowers, Speedie, & Coslett, 1984). Comprehension of affective prosody was abnormal in three cases (Patients 1, 3, 4) and was normal in the remaining case (Patient 2).

For the repetition of affective prosody task, patients were told that we were interested in how they repeated sentences imparting four different affective intonations (happy, sad, angry, or neutral). The four patients and two normal control subjects were instructed to repeat a set of 20 stimulus sentences. Target stimuli were semantically neutral sentences such as "Mañana voy a viajar a Málaga" ["Tomorrow I'm leaving for Malaga"] that conveyed mood to modulation of tone-of-voice. The four patients repeated most stimulus sentences verbatim. There were occasional instances of inadequate repetition of sentences due to aborted phrases, word perseverations, or paraphasias, but no dysarthric productions. Moreover, all patients had a normal performance on experimental tasks of word and sentence repetition (Table 6.2). The two normal control subjects repeated the 20 sentences flawlessly.

Perceptual judgements of affective prosody during repetition by the patients and control subjects were rated by five undergraduates from the Laboratory of Phonetics at the University of Barcelona using a four-point rating scale. The raters were required to assign one of the four affective tones: (1) happy, (2) angry, (3) sad, and (4) neutral to each sentence repeated by the patients and control subjects. Interrater agreement was calculated by using the following formula (total agreements/(total agreements + total disagreements) × 100) (Nicholas & Brookshire, 1993). As a group, the patients with TA were perceived to repeat sentences using correct affective intonations significantly less frequently than the control subjects. Interrater percentage agreement for the entire database was good for the aphasic patients and excellent for the controls (Table 6.3).

Acoustic analysis of sentences repeated with affective intonation were processed with a Computer Seech Lab (CSL) 4300 B (Kay Elemetrics, New Jersey)

TABLE 6.3
Perceptual Analysis

	TA Patients	Controls
Percentage of correct recognition	35	88*
Interrater percentage agreement		
Intonation		
Angry	62	95
Happy	73	95
Sad	73	80
Neutral	70	95

$* P < .001.$

at the Laboratory of Phonetics at the University of Barcelona. The following five acoustic parameters of the pitch plot were measured: (1) average fundamental frequency (F0); (2) F0 range; (3) adjusted F0 range; (4) F0 slope; and (5) duration (Fig. 6.5) (technical details in Ryalls, Joanette, & Feldman, 1987). Speech samples from the four patients were compared with similar data obtained from two normal adults (one male and one female). Aphasic patients and control subjects were monolingual native Spanish speakers with similar regional accents.

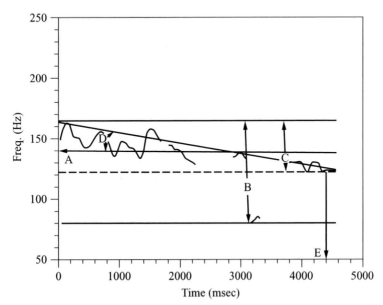

FIG. 6.5 Sample of speech plot illustrating acoustic measures: (A) average F0; (B) range; (C) adjusted range; (D) slope; and (E) duration. Reprinted from Ryalls et al. (1987); by permission of Masson S.p.A.

TABLE 6.4
Means and Standard Deviations of Acoustic Measures in
Patients with Transcortical Aphasias and Controls

Measure	Intonation	TA Patients	Controls
F0 (Hz)	Happy	170 ± 16	184 ± 30
	Angry	164 ± 25	170 ± 13
	Sad	164 ± 24	162 ± 14
	Neutral	168 ± 23	163 ± 20
Adjusted F0	Happy	78 ± 10**	113 ± 23
range (Hz)	Angry	70 ± 11*	97 ± 18
	Sad	80 ± 23	68 ± 0.7
	Neutral	73 ± 13	71 ± 8
Declination	Happy	7.4 ± 1.8*	11.5 ± 0.7
(degrees)	Angry	6.6 ± 2.7*	11.7 ± 0.1
	Sad	8.4 ± 3.6	8.9 ± 3.2
	Neutral	7.4 ± 1.7	9.7 ± 2.4
Duration (sec)	Happy	2.0 ± 0.5	1.4 ± 0.1
	Angry	1.8 ± 0.7	1.2 ± 0.2
	Sad	1.9 ± 0.6	1.3 ± 0.1
	Neutral	1.9 ± 0.6	1.4 ± 0.2

* $P < .03$; ** $P < .02$ (Mann–Whitney U-test). Reprinted from
Berthier (1995); by permission of Taylor & Francis Ltd.

Means and standard deviations of acoustic analysis variables in the four affective intonations for the TA patients and controls are shown in Table 6.4 (since values from F0 range and adjusted F0 range were identical, only data from the latter were included in the table). Pitch contours of sentences repeated with happy and angry intonations by the TA group showed a significantly narrower adjusted range of F0 and a less marked F0 declination than those repeated by the controls (Fig. 6.6). There were, however, no significant between-group differences in sentences repeated with neutral and sad intonations. Although the TA group showed a lengthening in the duration of segments relative to the normal control subjects, this difference failed to reach statistical significance. Within-group comparisons also failed to reveal significant differences.

The analysis of perceptual and acoustic correlates of affective prosody repetition in these four patients with TA yielded several important findings. First, all patients were impaired in the repetition of affective sentences, though the repetition of propositional language was relatively preserved. Second, impaired repetition of affective prosody was documented in all three clinically established varieties of TA (TCMA, TCSA, and MTCA). Third, poor affective repetition was present in TA patients with lesions *sparing* or *involving* the left perisylvian language area.

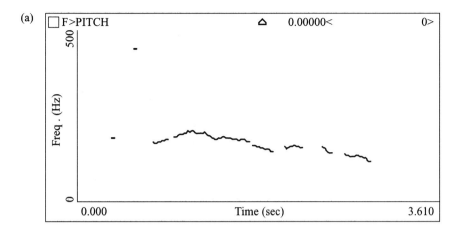

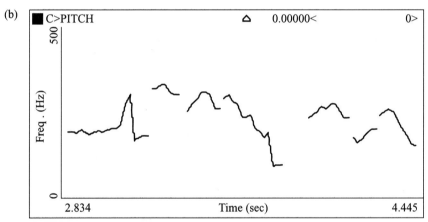

FIG. 6.6 Pitch plot of the sentence "Mañana voy a viajar a Málaga" ["Tomorrow I'm leaving for Malaga"] repeated with *happy* intonation by Patient 1 (a) and by a normal control subject (b). The sentence repeated by the patient shows a flat contour, while a normal contour is shown in the normal control subject. Reprinted from Berthier, Fernández et al. (1996); by permission of Taylor & Francis Ltd.

Speedie and her colleagues (1984, p. 270) reported impaired repetition of affective prosody in two patients with MTCA. Based on perceptual judgements, they found that "patients with transcortical aphasia employed neutral prosody in virtually all of their intonations (96%)". In agreement with these findings, the present results show that the four patients with different clinical types of TA repeated sentences with affective intonation significantly poorer than the normal control subjects. Moreover, acoustic analysis revealed significant between-group differences in the configuration of F0 contours (adjusted F0 range and declination) of sentences repeated with happy and angry intonations, but not in sentences repeated with either sad or neutral intonation. Acoustic analysis in normal speech conditions reveals that sentences intoned with happy and angry mood are usually pronounced with a higher pitch, a greater intonation range, and more variability of the speech curve than are sentences pronounced with sad or neutral intonations (Ladd, Silverman, Tolkmitt, Bergmann, & Scherer, 1985; Lieberman & Michaels, 1962). Therefore, when acoustical parameters of TA patients were compared with those from normal control subjects, differences were appreciable only in those sentences that require a greater modulation of prosody.

Another implication of this study was that repetition of affective prosody by patients with TA and left hemisphere lesions that *spared* the perisylvian area was not significantly different from the repetition of TA patients with left hemisphere lesions that *involved* the perisylvian area. These findings argue against the mechanism of "disconnection" between the intact left perisylvian area and the right hemisphere proposed by Speedie and co-workers (1984) to explain abnormal repetition of affective prosody in TA. Since the two patients reported by Speedie et al. had left hemisphere lesions that spared the perisylvian area, it could be argued that the functional mechanism suggested by these authors might be applicable only to those patients with TA caused by lesions located outside the left perisylvian area. However, recent studies using *in vivo* functional brain imaging (PET, SPECT) demonstrated that patients who develop TA after having left hemisphere lesions located outside the perisylvian area (whether cortical or subcortical) have a significant decrease of perfusion in morphologically undamaged sites of the left perisylvian cortex (see further data in Chapter 7). Thus, the present results suggest that the production of affective prosody is disrupted by anterior lesions of the left hemisphere. Moreover, these findings may indicate that after extensive structural or functional damage to the left perisylvian language area, the intact right hemisphere is inefficient to properly modulate affective prosody during repetition tasks.

Regional cerebral blood flow (rCBF) studies performed during automatic speech (number and word-repetition) and humming revealed a significant activation in both cerebral hemispheres involving the posterior–inferior frontal regions, the sensorimotor cortices, and supplementary motor areas (Larsen et al., 1978; Ryding et al., 1987). These findings, taken together with both the reported impaired production of affective prosody in recovered nonfluent aphasics with discrete left frontal damage (Berthier, Ruiz, Massone, Starkstein, & Leiguarda, 1991) and the results of the present study, suggest that in normal conditions the modulation of affective prosody may require a simultaneous processing in both cerebral hemispheres.

CHAPTER SEVEN

Neuroanatomical correlates of transcortical aphasias

INTRODUCTION

In the present chapter, I will examine neuroanatomical models which are mainly based on results obtained using structural neuroimaging (CT and MRI) and discuss some previous literature reviews which explain the sparing of repetition as resulting from preserved functions of the left perisylvian language cortex as well as the results of other studies which consider that preserved repetition is mediated by the intact right hemisphere. The starting point is based on the observation that despite the overall acceptance of the neuroanatomical account of "isolation of the speech area" in transcortical aphasias (TA), this model does not explain the preservation of language repetition in a number of cases published under the rubric of TA, so that other possible interpretations have been suggested. I will describe recent progress in the understanding of these alternative mechanisms which are thought to underly residual repetition in these aphasic patients. I illustrate this theme by presenting linguistic and structural neuroimaging data collected in a consecutive series of patients with acute TA and new information gathered using functional neuroimaging such as single photon emission computed tomography (SPECT) and positron emission tomography (PET). Therefore, in the second part of this chapter I will present a brief summary of some of the recent advances in the understanding of repetition abilities in both normal subjects and brain-damaged patients which have been performed using PET and functional MRI (fMRI) during cognitive activation. I then describe recent SPECT findings in a series of patients with TA, focusing on the functional status of the left perisylvian language cortex.

STRUCTURAL NEUROIMAGING

It has classically been considered that in TA, word and sentence repetition depend on the function of the spared left perisylvian language zone (Heschl's gyrus, Wernicke's area, Broca's area, inferior precentral gyrus, and their inter-connections) (Geschwind et al., 1968; Goldstein, 1948; Lichtheim, 1885; Rubens & Kertesz, 1983; Wernicke 1885–1886). In support of this neuroanatomical model, some neuropathological studies (Assal et al., 1983; Geschwind et al., 1968) and radiological studies (Kertesz et al., 1977; Naeser & Hayward, 1978) showed that TA resulted from acute brain lesions that surround but spare the central language zone, thus potentially disconnecting the intact perisylvian language cortex from the more peripheral brain areas that may play an import-ant role in conveying meaning and intention (Lichtheim, 1885).

Over the years, the neuronatomical model of "isolation of the speech area" (Geschwind et al., 1968; Goldstein, 1948) has been regarded as the likely model to explain the preservation of language repetition in TA. Alternative patho-physiological mechanisms, however, have been proposed. In this connection, early authors (Bastian, 1887; Goldstein, 1948; Henschen, 1920–1922; Hübner, 1889; Vix, 1910) reported cases of TA after lesions that partially involved the left perisylvian area, and it was Bastian (1887) who first suggested that partial damage to the major speech centres would impair the expression and under-standing of language but would spare repetition by increasing the excitability threshold of cortical speech centres to externally generated stimuli. In other words, Bastian stated that strong external stimulation guarantees that the act of automatic repetition remains largely preserved, but that internal stimulation is insufficient to arouse other linguistic functions. Although other early authors were sympath-etic with Bastian's proposal (Freud, 1891/1953; Henschen, 1920–1922), addi-tional cases were described in which the transcortical pattern of language deficits occurred in the setting of massive damage to the left perisylvian region (Niessl von Mayendorf, 1911; Stengel, 1947). These clinicopathological observations served to infer a right hemisphere participation in language repetition. Other researchers suggested that preserved repetition after left perisylvian damage was the result of the combined activity of left hemisphere structures unaffected by the lesion and the intact right hemisphere (Brown, 1975; Rubens, 1975).

The possible participation of the right hemisphere in repetition performance in TA also comes from more recently published studies (Bando et al., 1986; Basso et al., 1985; Berndt et al., 1987; Grossi et al., 1991; Hadano et al., 1998; Jacome, 1984; Kertesz et al., 1979, 1977; Martin & Saffran, 1990; Papagno & Basso, 1996, Case 1; Pulvermüller & Schönle, 1993; Rapcsak et al., 1990; Reinvang, 1987; Sartori et al., 1987; Selnes, Knopman, Niccum, & Rubens, 1985; Selnes, Rubens, Risse, & Levy, 1982; Trojano et al., 1988) which reported the case of patients, who despite having extensive damage to the central language zone, showed a relative preservation of repetition.

The neuroanatomical mechanisms of repetition in transcortical aphasias

Here I will present data from a clinicoradiological study reported by Berthier, Starkstein and colleagues (1991) which has been undertaken to examine the neuro-radiological correlates of TA and the mechanism(s) subserving language repetition.

This study was carried out in a consecutive series of patients who had an acute aphasia due to cerebrovascular accidents with a pattern of language deficits consistent with the three clinically established varieties of TA (motor, sensory, and mixed). Demographic information was collected in all patients. Language disturbances were studied with the Western Aphasia Battery (WAB; Kertesz, 1982) and, in order to investigate more closely the mechanism subserving repetition, some patients underwent further testing of language (frequency of paraphasias during object naming tasks, spontaneous correction of syntactic and semantic errors, and repetition of nonwords). The neuroradiological correlates of repetition were studied with CT and MRI scans (one patient also underwent a PET scan). Lesion volume and cerebral asymmetries (occipital and frontal torques or "petalias") were measured in both groups (see technical details in Berthier, Starkstein et al., 1991). Based on neuroradiological findings, TA patients were divided into two groups.

1   *Perisylvian group (PS).*   Patients included in this group were labelled PS to reflect the involvement of cortical and subcortical regions around the Sylvian fissure (fronto-temporo-parietal cortex (FTPC). Therefore, to be included in the PS group, patients had to have lesions involving one or more of the following brain areas: superior temporal cortex (STC; included Heschl's gyrus and Wernicke's area), inferior parietal cortex (IPC; infrasylvian supramarginal gyrus), inferior frontal cortex (IFC; Broca's area), inferior portion of the sensorimotor cortex (SMC), insula (INS), claustrum, or white matter tracts connecting these structures (arcuate fasciculus, extreme capsulae, and external capsulae).

2   *Extraperisylvian group (EPS).*   Patients included in this group were labelled EPS to reflect the involvement of either cortical–subcortical regions or deep subcortical structures located exclusively outside the perisylvian language region. These regions included the prefrontal cortex (PFC), frontoparietal cortex (FPC), IPC (angular gyrus), superior parietal cortex (SPC), temporo-occipital cortex (TOC), temporo-parieto-occipital cortex (TPOC), basal ganglia (BG), internal capsulae (IC), thalamus (TH), and periventricular white matter (PVWM; includes corona radiata and centrum semiovale).

Twenty-one of the one hundred and fourteen (18%) studied aphasic patients showed TA, a frequency quite similar to a previously reported series (Kertesz, 1982), in whom language disturbances were assessed using the same instrument (WAB). Within the PS group, five patients (55%), had a TCSA, three patients (33%) had a MTCA, and one patient (11%) had a TCMA. Similar frequency of type of aphasia was documented in the EPS, since nine patients (75%) had a TCSA, two patients (16%) had a MTCA, and one patient (8%) had a TCMA. This finding is important because it demonstrates for the first time in a consecutive series of patients that acute TA may occur regardless of the perisylvian or extraperisylvian location of lesions. In addition, PS and EPS groups were not significantly different in terms of background characteristics (e.g. age, gender, education), handedness, family history of left-handedness, and interval between stroke onset and language testing. Demographic information and radiological findings are shown in Tables 7.1 and 7.2.

Analysis of language deficits across the two groups revealed that although the PS showed significantly lower WAB scores (e.g. more severe aphasia) than the EPS group, the profile of language deficits was not significantly different between the two groups (Tables 7.3 and 7.4).

Further testing of language abilities was performed. The amount of phonological and semantic errors produced by the PS and EPS groups during the WAB object-naming subtest were examined in all 21 patients. The EPS group produced significantly more semantic paraphasias than the PS group ($P < .01$), whereas phonological errors predominated in the PS group but this difference failed to reach statistical significance. This finding is consonant with the notion that areas responsible for phonological processing are organised within the perisylvian language cortex and areas related to semantic processing may be organised in more peripheral brain regions (Cappa et al., 1981).

The ability to correct syntactic and semantic errors during repetition of sentences with grammatical or semantic errors (Berndt et al., 1987; Coslett et al., 1987; Davis et al., 1978) was examined in a subsample of nine patients with TCSA. Four of these patients were of the PS group and five of the EPS group. Six of the nine patients could correct syntactic errors spontaneously; four of them (Cases 14, 15, 16, and 17) had extraperisylvian involvement, whereas the other two patients, who also showed good syntactic processing (Cases 1 and 2), had perisylvian damage. The remaining three patients did not correct syntactic errors; two of them (Cases 3 and 5) had extensive perisylvian involvement, whereas the other had extraperisylvian damage, but a PET scan showing marked hypometabolism in the whole left perisylvian language zone. None of the nine patients with TCSA was able to detect semantic errors, and they repeated verbatim these semantic anomalous sentences. Finally, these nine TCSA patients could also repeat a list of nonwords (n = 20) flawlessly.

Analysis of neuroradiological data revealed a similar frequency of perisylvian or extraperisylvian lesions. Nine patients (43%) had perisylvian lesions and twelve patients (57%) had lesions limited to the extraperisylvian areas. The distribution of lesions in the PS group were the following: Two of the patients with TCSA (Cases 1 and 5) had ischaemic infarctions involving the anterior perisylvian area (IFC, SMC, and INS) with extension into the subjacent BG, IC, and anterior PVWM. Of the remaining three patients, one (Case 3) had a large

TABLE 7.1

Perisylvian Group: Demographic Information and Lesion Sites

Case	Age	Sex	Handedness	Family History of Left-handedness	Years of Education	Days Post-onset	Lesion Location[a]
1	62	F	Right	Negative	12	10	IFC, SMC, INS, BG, IC, PVWM
2	76	M	Right	Positive	7	7	STC, IPC
3	67	M	Right	Negative	18	20	FTPC, INS, BG
4	43	F	Right	Negative	14	10	FTC, TPC
5	56	M	Left	Negative	14	10	IFC, SMC, BG, IC, PVWM
6	35	F	Right	Positive	12	10	IFC, SMC, INS, BG, IC, PVWM
7	52	M	Right	Negative	16	40	FTPOC, INS, BG, PVWM
8	69	M	Left	Positive	18	40	FTPC, INS, BG, IC, PVWM
9	48	M	Right	Negative	18	10	IFC, SMC

[a] See abbreviations in text. Adapted from Berthier, Starkstein et al. (1991).

191

TABLE 7.2

Extraperisylvian Group: Demographic Information and Lesion Sites

Case	Age	Sex	Handedness	Family History of Left-handedness	Years of Education	Days Post-onset	Lesion Location[a]
10	70	M	Right	Negative	12	30	TOC
11	56	F	Right	Negative	7	15	BG, IC
12	75	F	Right	Negative	12	10	BG, IC
13	71	M	Right	Negative	7	10	IPC
14	63	M	Right	Negative	12	10	TPOC
15	71	F	Right	Positive	15	10	IPC, SPC, PVWM
16	78	F	Right	Negative	7	20	PVWM
17	68	M	Right	Negative	18	10	IPC, SPC
18	69	F	Right	Negative	8	10	PFC
19	54	M	Right	Negative	18	10	BG, IC
20	52	F	Left	Negative	12	10	FPC, BC, IC
21	52	F	Right	Negative	12	30	BG

[a] See abbreviations in text. Adapted from Berthier, Starkstein et al. (1991).

TABLE 7.3
Perisylvian Group: Results of the Western Aphasia Battery

Case	IC	F	Y/N	AWR	SQ	R	ON	WF	SC	RS	AQ	Aphasia Type
1	8	7	48	38	44	9.8	30	0	4	6	70.6	TCSA
2	4	8	48	53	29	8.4	45	5	2	8	65.8	TCSA
3	4	7	51	8	6	8.4	3	0	2	2	43.2	TCSA
4	4	7	54	46	8	8.9	22	0	6	4	57.0	TCSA
5	9	8	39	50	16	9.8	60	6	6	10	80.4	TCSA
6	0	0	26	26	0	7.0	12	0	0	0	26.8	MTCA
7	2	0	57	32	8	7.9	9	0	4	4	32.8	MTCA
8	3	0	52	20	2	5.2	7	0	6	0	26.4	MTCA
9	6	4	54	54	68	10.0	38	1	8	8	68.6	TCMA
GM	4.4	4.6	47.6	36.3	19.9	8.3	25.1	1.3	4.2	4.6	52.5	
SD	(2.8)	(3.6)	(9.6)	(16.0)	(23.0)	(15.4)	(19.5)	(2.3)	(2.5)	(3.6)	(21.0)	

IC = information content; F = fluency; Y/N = yes/no questions; AWR = auditory word recognition; SQ = sequential commands; R = repetition; ON = object naming; WF = word fluency; SC = sentence completion; RS = responsive speech; AQ = aphasia quotient; GM = group mean; SD = standard deviation; TCSA = transcortical sensory aphasia; MTCA = mixed transcortical aphasia; TCMA = transcortical motor aphasia. Reprinted from Berthier, Starkstein et al. (1991); by permission of Oxford University Press.

TABLE 7.4
Extraperisylvian Group: Results of the Western Aphasia Battery

Case	IC	F	Y/N	AWR	SQ	R	ON	WF	SC	RS	AQ	Aphasia Type
10	5	6	45	54	14	8.0	38	5	6	6	60.6	TCSA
11	4	7	39	42	12	8.4	20	1	6	6	54.6	TCSA
12	4	7	51	54	18	8.2	15	3	6	4	55.4	TCSA
13	6	8	50	50	30	8.0	51	6	10	8	72.0	TCSA
14	9	9	48	48	36	9.6	58	5	8	8	84.0	TCSA
15	8	9	51	41	10	9.4	58	2	8	10	78.6	TCSA
16	8	9	51	50	16	9.8	60	2	10	8	81.2	TCSA
17	9	10	48	44	22	9.0	60	5	6	8	82.2	TCSA
18	6	5	51	41	34	8.7	58	3	10	10	68.2	TCSA
19	0	0	45	34	4	8.0	0	0	0	10	24.0	MTCA
20	4	0	12	2	6	10.0	3	4	6	10	56.6	MTCA
21	6	2	60	57	60	8.6	41	5	10	10	64.0	TCMA
GM	5.7	6.0	42.2	42.1	21.8	8.8	38.5	3.4	7.1	7.5	63.2	
SD	(2.8)	(3.6)	(14.1)	(14.1)	(15.9)	(7.3)	(23.0)	(1.8)	(2.8)	(2.9)	(18.8)	

IC = information content; F = fluency; Y/N = yes/no questions; AWR = auditory word recognition; SQ = sequential commands; R = repetition; ON = object naming; WF = word fluency; SC = sentence completion; RS = responsive speech; AQ = aphasia quotient; GM = group mean; SD = standard deviation; TCSA = transcortical sensory aphasia; MTCA = mixed transcortical aphasia; TCMA = transcortical motor aphasia. Reprinted from Berthier, Starkstein et al. (1991); by permission of Oxford University Press.

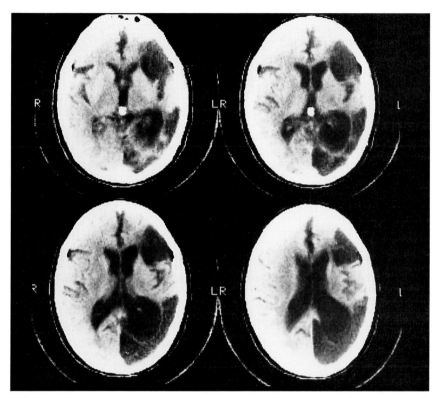

FIG. 7.1   CT scan showing two ischaemic infarctions in the left hemisphere of a patient (Case 7) with mixed transcortical aphasia and perisylvian involvement. The anterior lesion involves the posterior-inferior frontal cortex (Broca's area), inferior precentral cortex and anterior insula. There is mild extension into the putamen. The posterior lesion involves mainly the occipital, parietal, and temporal lobes. The posterior portion of the superior temporal cortex (Wernicke's area) is probably involved by the lesion.

ischaemic infarction involving almost the whole left perisylvian area (FTPC), a second patient (Case 4) had two separate ischaemic infarcts involving the left frontotemporal cortex (FTC) and the left temporoparietal cortex (TPC), and the remaining patient (Case 2) had a large haemorrhagic metastatic tumour involving the left STC and IPC (infrasylvian supramarginal gyrus), with only mild peritumoural oedema. One of the three patients with an MCTA (Case 8) showed a large ischaemic infarct involving the whole left perisylvian language area (FTPC); a second patient (Case 6) had a left ischaemic infarct involving the IFC, SMC, IPC, INS, and PVWM; and the third patient (Case 7) had two simultaneous left ischaemic infarcts, one anterior involving IFC, SMC, INS, BG (putamen), and the anterior PVWM, and the other posterior involving the TPOC region (Fig. 7.1). The only patient with a TCMA (Case 9) had an ischaemic infarct restricted to IFC and the adjacent inferior SMC.

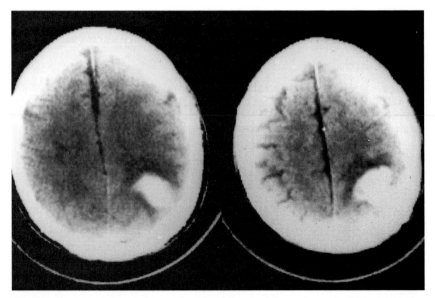

FIG. 7.2   CT scan showing a haemorrhage involving the left superior parietal lobe in a patient (Case 17) with transcortical sensory aphasia.

The distribution of lesions in the EPS group was the following: five of the nine patients with TCSA (Cases 10, 13, 14, 15, and 17) had left posterior cortical lesions (two haemorrhagic and one ischaemic IPC (angular gyrus) and/or SPC lesions, one TPOC haemorrhage, and one TOC ischaemic infarct) (Fig. 7.2); two patients (Cases 11 and 12) had left BG (putaminal) haemorrhages (one patient showed mild extension into the nearby temporal isthmus and IC); one patient (Case 16) had a large left parieto-frontal (PVWM) haemorrhage; and the remaining patient (Case 18) had a left ischaemic infarct in the PFC. One of the two patients with a MTCA (Case 19) had a large left BG (putamenal) haemorrhage with extension into the nearby IC and temporal isthmus, while the other patient (Case 20; a left-hander) had a right hemisphere ischaemic infarct involving the BG (head of the caudate nucleus and anterior putamen), anterior limb of the IC, anterior cingulate gyrus, and superior fronto-parietal PVWM. The only patient with a TCMA (Case 21) showed a haemorrhage restricted to the anterior portion of the left BG (putamen). Comparisons of lesion volume and cerebral asymmetries failed to reveal statistically significant differences between the PS and EPS groups.

Some further clinicoradiological correlations in single patients is worth mentioning. Repetition was further investigated in three patients using more specific testing methods of brain function such as the amytal test (Wada procedure) and PET scan. Details of these patients are now described.

Case 1. This patient was a 62-year-old right-handed woman, who was admitted because of fluent aphasia and right-sided weakness. Her spontaneous speech was mildly dysarthric and hypophonic, and fluency was frequently disrupted by word-finding pauses. The patient could only generate empty, circumlocutory and perseverative short phrases. Phonological paraphasias were abundant, but semantic errors and neologistic paraphasias were rare. On some occasions, fully formed sentences were produced in response to specific questions. Series speech and singing were preserved and remarkably superior than spontaneous speech. On both the WAB and the Token Test (De Renzi & Vignolo, 1962), auditory comprehension was moderately impaired (WAB comprehension subtest: 6.5/10; Token Test: 16/62). The patient could repeat words, nonwords, sentences, and nonverbal sounds flawlessly. During repetition she could correct 50% of syntactic errors but none of the semantic errors. During the language-testing session, she echoed most of the examiner's questions; these echoes were normally articulated but devoid of intonation. Object naming and word fluency were moderately impaired and there was a severe impairment in reading comprehension. She also showed buccofacial apraxia and a left arm ideomotor apraxia. On dichotic listening (Damasio & Damasio, 1979) she showed a left ear "paradoxic" extinction (0/110) and a normal right ear performance (104/110). An MRI scan showed an ischaemic infarction involving the left anterior perisylvian area. Injections of amytal in the right internal carotid artery caused a transient clouding of consciousness followed by a global aphasia. The patient remained mute for 90 seconds, and could not repeat simple, high-frequency words or name common objects. Auditory comprehension for simple questions was severely impaired. A left carotid artery injection could not be carried out.

Case 5. This patient was a 56-year-old nonfamilial left-handed man, who suddenly became unable to understand his wife's speech. His spontaneous speech was fluent, with normal articulation and prosody. Although sentences were short and often contaminated by echolalia and perseverations, they conveyed a meaningful message. There were no phonological, semantic, or neologistic paraphasias. Series speech and recitation of days of the week were flawless. Language comprehension was worse than oral expression. He scored abnormally low on the comprehension subtest of the WAB and in the Token Test (35/62). He frequently echoed the initial portion of questions and occasionally echoed entire sentences. Repetition of words, nonwords, sentences, and nonverbal sounds was intact. On a repetition subtest composed of semantically anomalous or ungrammatical sentences, he was able to repeat all the sentences correctly, but his performance had a "parrot-like" pattern, and he was unable to correct either syntactic (0/10) or semantic (0/10) errors. Except for a reduced word-list generation (animal naming: six words in one minute), naming was largely preserved (see further details in Chapter 4). While reading aloud was normal, he had impaired reading comprehension of the sentences of the WAB. He could write

normally with either hand and there was no evidence of buccofacial apraxia or
limb apraxia. On dichotic listening the patient showed complete left ear extinction (3/110) and normal right ear performance (107/110). An MRI scan showed
a large ischaemic infarction involving the right anterior perisylvian area. Injections of amytal in the right internal carotid artery did not change the pattern
of language impairment. During the period of effective narcosis, the patient
remained fully alert and spoke clearly, with fluent and meaningful sentences.
Naming of common objects, counting, and repetition of five four-word sentences
(e.g. "John drives the car") were intact. Auditory comprehension remained unchanged. Amytal injections in the left internal carotid artery caused a transient
loss of consciousness followed by a global aphasia which lasted two minutes.
During this period, the patient was totally unable to phonate or move his tongue
and lips, either on verbal commands or to imitation, rendering repetition impossible to test. He could not understand simple questions or one-step commands.

Case 12. This 75-year-old right-handed woman developed fluent aphasia
due to a left BG (putamenal) haemorrhage. Her spontaneous speech was fluent
but soft, dysarthric, and mainly composed of unintelligible, low volume "mumbling" jargon. At times, however, some utterances were punctuated by neologisms and recognisable paraphasic substitutions. Echolalia and perseverations
were prominent, but serial speech was intact, and she was able to sing without
prompting, using normal words and proper melody. Auditory comprehension
was good, but the patient followed simple commands only intermittently, and
achieved low scores on all the comprehension subtests of the WAB and on the
Token Test (15/62). She could repeat words, phrases, and even sentences composed of nonwords and foreign words fairly well. On the repetition subtest of the
WAB, she repeated all sentences flawlessly, except the longest one. On a further
repetition test composed of semantically anomalous or ungrammatical sentences
she corrected 40% of syntactic errors but none of the semantic ones. She had
impaired object and picture naming, and she performed poorly on sentence completion tasks. Oral reading and reading comprehension were severely impaired.
A PET scan showed significant decrements in metabolic activity over the whole
left fronto-temporo-parietal cortex, as well as in the deep grey nuclei (BG and
TH). There was also low metabolic activity in the cerebellar hemisphere contralateral to the left subcortical lesion (crossed cerebellar diaschisis). The results
of PET scan (asymmetry indexes) from patient 12 and normal control volunteers
is summarised in Table 7.5.

Further insight on the mechanism underlying repetition in TA comes from the
longitudinal evolution of one patient of the EPS group.

Case 19. This patient was a 54-year-old right-handed bilingual (Spanish–
English) man, who was admitted because of the sudden onset of aphasia and
right hemiplegia. Initially, he had no spontaneous speech, could only understand

TABLE 7.5
Regional Cerebral Glucose Metabolism:
Asymmetry Indexes

Region	Case 12	Normal Controls
Inferior frontal cortex	23.07*	1.00 (0.9)
Superior frontal cortex	39.35*	−1.90 (1.3)
Mesial frontal cortex	18.27*	5.00 (2.0)
Insular cortex	31.91*	1.00 (1.7)
Temporal cortex	28.26*	2.20 (0.7)
Parietal cortex	39.87*	0.20 (3.7)
Caudate nucleus	40.91*	−1.60 (1.7)
Lentiform nucleus	53.71*	0.71 (3.5)
Thalamus	56.26*	0.18 (2.3)
Cerebellum	−49.63	−2.05 (4.5)

* Lies beyond the 95% cut-off anticipated for the normal
distribution. Reprinted from Berthier, Starkstein et al. (1991);
by permission of Oxford University Press.

some simple questions and could point at a few common objects after a verbal
command. He was unable to follow one-step commands with his left hand and
to name common objects on confrontation testing. He could repeat words
and complex sentences flawlessly although his voice was hypophonic. A WAB
assessment was consistent with an MTCA (Table 7.6, Test 1). A CT scan showed
a large left BG (putamenal) haemorrhage. Three weeks later, there was marked
improvement in auditory comprehension and object-naming abilities. Speech
was mildly dysarthric, more fluent, and with better volume, but consisted almost
entirely of semantic paraphasias and neologistic distortions. Four months after
the acute event, a new language test showed that, although auditory comprehension and object naming had improved, he still had impaired comprehension
of complex sequential commands and deficits in word fluency, sentence completion, and responsive speech. Spontaneous speech had also improved to the
extent that only prominent deficits were isolated paraphasias and word-finding
difficulties. A WAB assessment was consistent with an anomic aphasia (Table
7.6, Test 2). One year after the acute vascular event the patient was readmitted
because of left-sided weakness and the gradual recurrence of incoherent speech
and comprehension problems. His language was considerably worse. Oral
expression was fluent and paraphasic and the continuous mixture of English and
Spanish made his verbal output impossible to understand. Auditory comprehension, repetition, and naming had also deteriorated, and the WAB assessment was
compatible with a Wernicke's aphasia (Table 7.6, Test 3). A CT scan showed
the old left putamenal lesion, as well as a recent haemorrhage involving the right
posterior BG (putamen) and the adjacent temporal isthmus.

TABLE 7.6
Case 19: Longitudinal Evolution of Language Deficits

	Test 1	Test 2	Test 3
Fluency	1	8	7
Information content	4	8	5
Comprehension	4,1	9,2	6,8
Repetition	8	10	6,6
Naming	0	6,3	2,5
Aphasia quotient	24	83	55,8
Type of aphasia	Mixed transcortical	Anomic	Wernicke

In this study, patients with TA showed a similar frequency of perisylvian (PS group) and extraperisylvian (EPS group) damage. PS and EPS groups were not significantly different in terms of background characteristics (e.g. age, sex, years of education), handedness, family history of left-handedness, and interval between disease onset and language testing. While the PS group showed a significantly more severe aphasia (e.g. lower Aphasia Quotient scores on the WAB), the frequency of type of TA (TCMA, TCSA, or MTCA), and the profile of language impairment were similar for both groups. Moreover, there were no significant between-group differences in either lesion volume or measurements of cerebral asymmetries. In summary, we could not find significant differences between the PS and EPS groups that might explain the presence of preserved language repetition in patients with extensive perisylvian damage. Therefore, in an attempt to explain these findings in the following sections I will advance a different interpretation of neuroanatomical findings.

Extensive perisylvian involvement with preserved repetition

Preserved repetition and extensive perisylvian involvement was found in 9 of the 21 TA patients. Indeed, patients of the PS group had lesions involving large portions of the perisylvian language area, demonstrating that the sparing of the language cortex is not necessary for repetition. In two patients (Cases 1 and 5), intracarotid amytal injections to the side contralateral to the lesion abolished language repetition. Moreover, in one of the patients (Case 5) the amytal injection in the carotid artery ipsilateral to the brain lesion did not worsen the patient's language deficits, thus excluding the participation of spared brain structures ipsilateral to the brain lesion in language repetition. Similar findings have been recently reported by Bando et al. (1986) in a right-handed patient who developed a TCSA after left temporoparietal infarction that included the Wernicke's area and supramarginal gyrus. Amytal injection in the right internal carotid artery abolished digit and word repetition, whereas a left hemisphere injection produced no changes in language performance.

While the right hemisphere actually subserved repetition of words, phrases, and long sentences in patients with TCSA (Bando et al., 1986; Case 1 of the present study), it should be noted that the right perisylvian area was not "ready" to operate the mechanisms necessary to process complex aspects of repetition performance (sentences) in the immediate post-stroke period in three patients of the PS group with MTCA and extensive left perisylvian damage (Cases 6, 7, and 8). This finding may be in accord with the theory proposed by Brown (1975) suggesting that the processing of repetition in TA requires the utilisation of multiple resources from undamaged structures of both cerebral hemispheres. An alternative theoretical framework for understanding individual differences in residual repetition would be that the compensatory neural resources of the intact right hemisphere to mediate some aspect of language production after major left hemisphere lesions may vary from person to person with some retaining the ability to repeat complex verbal material while others do not. To illustrate this point, Case 6, a right-handed woman with acute MTCA and extensive left anterior perisylvian damage, failed to show echolalia and had impaired repetition of long sentences, whereas the two patients described by Rapcsak et al. (1990) were, like Case 6, right-handers featuring an acute MTCA and left anterior (frontal) damage. But unlike our patient, these patients showed echolalic repetition of sentences four days after stroke onset. Interestingly, four weeks later one of them (Case 1) lost the ability to repeat after suffering a second infarct in the right perisylvian area.

Four of the five PS patients with acute TCSA (Cases 1, 3, 4, and 5) had fluent and paraphasic oral expression despite extensive damage to the anterior perisylvian area (e.g. Broca's area). Similar unexpected clinicoradiological observations have been reported by others (e.g. Basso et al., 1985) and attributed to anomalous intrahemispheric organisation (see the next section for further arguments on the same topic). In summary, although the direct participation of the contralateral undamaged hemisphere in repetition performance has been demonstrated in a limited number of patients, the present findings and those reported by Bando and co-workers (1986) are in favour of attributing an important role to the right hemisphere in repetition among patients with TA and lesions involving the perisylvian language zone.

"Isolation of the speech area" and preserved repetition

Preserved repetition and lesions outside the perisylvian language core were found in 12 of the 21 patients with TA. This is consistent with the classical hypothesis that sparing of language repetition is related to the integrity of both Broca's and Wernicke's areas as well as their interconnections, whereas the observed deficits in semantic processing, linguistic formulations, and production of volitional language result from damage to either cortical regions that are peripheral to the perisylvian zone or to subcortical structures (Gonzalez Rothi, 1997; Rapcsak & Rubens, 1994). Some data from the present study, however, seem to indicate that the mechanism of "isolation of speech area" may not be applicable to all patients of the EPS group. For instance, the finding of preserved repetition in one of these patients (Case 12), in spite of marked hypometabolism on the entire left cerebral cortical mantle, suggests a different mechanism underlying repetition among some patients with TA and deep subcortical lesions of the left hemisphere. Cambier et al. (1980) reported a patient who developed echolalic MTCA in association with extensive areas of infarction in the left hemisphere that involved the internal capsulae, head of the caudate nucleus, lentiform nucleus, corona radiata, and temporo-parietal white matter but the lesion spared the cerebral cortex. Ancillary testing revealed a complete right ear extinction on dichotic listening and greater activation of the left side of the mouth during repetition, thus indicating that the right hemisphere was implicated in the processing of incoming auditory information and repetition (Beaumont, 1983; Graves, Goodglass, & Landis, 1982). These findings taken together with functional data from PET in Case 12 (present study) and SPECT in Case 3 of Perani et al. (1987) indicate that extensive subcortical damage involving the basal ganglia and/or thalamus may induce a "functional deactivation" of the entire ipsilateral cortical mantle, suggesting that spared or residual language functions, such as repetition and echolalia, are carried out by contralateral hemisphere.

Different routes for repetition: Linguistic and structural considerations

The important issue to be addressed next is whether there are qualitative differences in repetition performance between patients with PS and EPS. Unfortunately, less than 50% of these patients could be assessed for repetition of words, nonwords, and anomalous sentences and only patients with TCSA were examined. Despite these methodological limitations, it is interesting to mention that there were no significant differences between the number of PS and EPS patients who corrected syntactic errors, suggesting that the lexical route was operative during repetition. By contrast, on-line repetition as indicated by impaired correction of ungrammatical sentences (abnormal processing by the lexical route), when present, was invariably associated with extensive structural and/or functional involvement of the left perisylvian cortex. This implies that, as suggested by Coslett et al. (1987) and other researchers, repetition in TCSA may be accomplished through three functionally different routes, lexical (semantic and nonsemantic) and nonlexical. In addition, all nine TCSA patients were able to repeat a short list of nonwords, indicating that the nonlexical route was intact. The preservation of nonword repetition in the EPS group is an expected result, but this finding among the PS group is intriguing because these patients had damage to structures represented within the left perisylvian area (e.g. Wernicke's and Broca's areas, arcuate fasciculus) that have been implicated in the repetition of words and nonwords.

Current models of language processing consider that nonword repetition is accomplished by a "direct" and "privileged" route between phonological input and phonological output mechanisms without lexical mediation (Butterworth & Warrington, 1995; Caplan, 1987, 1992; Coslett et al., 1987; Ellis & Young, 1988; Katz & Goodglass, 1990; McCarthy & Warrington, 1984; McCleod & Posner, 1984). The functional organisation of the nonlexical repetition route has some resemblance to the traditional acoustic–phonological transcoding process necessary for the automatic repetition of novel verbal material (e.g. nonwords) and nonverbal sounds, which is believed to be mediated by structures of the left perisylvian association cortex (Goldstein, 1948; Heilman, 1985; Wernicke, 1885–1886). In support, superior repetition of words over nonwords is reported as a constant feature in some perisylvian aphasias such as conduction aphasia and deep dysphasia (see references in Caplan & Waters, 1992; Katz & Goodglass, 1990). Therefore, the sparing of repetition of words, nonwords, and sentences in patients of the PS groups strongly suggest that such linguistic function should be mediated by structures located outside the central perisylvian cortex of the left hemisphere or, more likely, by the right hemisphere.

There is some evidence in the literature that acute nonfluent aphasia with impaired repetition (e.g. Broca's and global aphasias) associated with extensive damage to the left perisylvian can eventually resolve into TA (e.g. TCMA and MTCA) (see Berthier et al., 1995; Kertesz, 1979; Pulvermüller & Schönle, 1993). In these cases, the linguistic profile of TA does not become apparent until the chronic period, thus suggesting that neural networks of the right hemisphere were not devoted to language repetition immediately after the brain lesion (see further details in the next section). Thus, the recovery of language repetition in such cases must be functionally relocated in the right perisylvian area months or even years after the original left hemisphere insult. This was not the case in patients of the PS group, however, since the transcortical pattern was demonstrated in the early acute period, thus raising the possibility that the right hemisphere was involved in language repetition long before the brain damage. Following this line of reasoning, the final issue I wish to address in this section concerns the premorbid representation of language in the brain of patients with acute TA.

Premorbid language organisation in acute transcortical aphasias: Inferences for mixed representation of functions

The sparing of repetition in patients with massive damage to the perisylvian language zone and the abolition of repetition after amytal injections in the opposite hemisphere of two patients (Cases 1 and 5) suggests a major contribution of

both cerebral hemispheres in linguistic processes. Since bilateral cerebral dominance for language has been reported as a relative common finding in left-
handers as well as in right-handers with a family history of left-handedness
(Hécaen, De Agostini, & Monzon-Montes, 1981; Joanette et al., 1983; Rasmussen
& Milner, 1977), the occurrence of TA associated with damage to the perisylvian
area in two left-handed patients (Cases 5 and 8) and in two right-handed patients
with a family history of left-handedness (Cases 2 and 6), is not surprising. The
hypothesis of bilateral hemisphere participation in linguistic operations, however, is more difficult to apply to the right-handed patients with TA, since
Rasmussen and Milner (1977) found no evidence of bilateral language representation in a series of 140 right-handed epileptic patients in whom cerebral
dominance for language was determined using sodium amytal tests. It should
be noted, however, that amytal data obtained from epileptic patients is contradictory, since Mateer and Dodrill (1983) reported that four of their six
patients with bilateral language representation were actually right-handed. In
addition, bihemispheric language representation has also been demonstrated
using intracarotid sodium amytal tests in right-handed nonepileptic patients with
either "crossed" TCMA (Angelergues et al., 1962) or typical conduction aphasia
(Kinsbourne, 1971).

Further analysis of the subpopulation of right-handed patients with TA and
lesions involving large portions of the left perisylvian language area (Cases 1, 3,
4, 7, and 9) disclosed that they had spontaneous speech, naming, and auditory
comprehension mediated by the left hemisphere, since all these linguistic functions were disrupted by the lesion, and spared repetition might have been the
only language function carried out by the right hemisphere. This finding suggests that these patients had mixed language representation (e.g. both cerebral
hemispheres control speech production to varying degrees) rather than the seem-
ingly misconstrued concept of bilateral language representation where both
cerebral hemispheres subserve the same speech functions (Snyder, Novelly, &
Harris, 1990). Admittedly, mixed language representation seems to be a rather
capricious repartition of language functions in both cerebral hemispheres, but
consider the following arguments. First, impaired language repetition was the
main linguistic deficit found in nonlearned disabled right-handed patients who
developed "crossed" conduction aphasia after extensive damage to the right
perisylvian structures (Assal, 1982; Assal, Perentes, & Deruaz, 1981; Fournet
et al., 1987; Mendez & Benson, 1985, Case 3; Yarnell, 1981, Case 2). In the same
vein, Berthier, Posada, Puentes, and Hinojosa (in preparation) recently studied
an ambidextrous adult patient (JNR) with a Klippel–Trénaunay syndrome (Klipper
& Trénaunay, 1900; Kramer, 1972; Stickler, 1987)[5] and developmental dysgraphia,

---

[5] The Klipper–Trénaunay syndrome (KTS) is a rare congenital anomaly characterised by cuta-
neous port-wine hemangiomata, venous varicosities, and osseous and soft-tissue hypertrophy usually unilateral and involving a limb. Some patients also have associated central nervous system
(CNS) abnormalities, overlapping with those of the Sturge–Weber syndrome (encephalo-trigemial

who developed conduction aphasia after an extensive multifocal ischaemic infarction in the right perisylvian area. The cerebral angiography revealed a complete occlusion of the right middle cerebral artery and a SPECT showed widespread hypoperfusion in right hemisphere but normal perfusion rates in the left hemisphere. These findings raise the possibility that an early dysfunction of the left hemisphere caused not only both the mixed handedness and the disorder of written expression, but also it forced the right hemisphere to take over the processing of certain linguistic functions (Bryden, 1988; Locke, 1997). Further support for this proposal comes from cases of right-handed individuals, who after recovering from developmental language delays at the expense of a compensatory modulation of linguistic operations by the right hemisphere that would be previously carried out by the left hemisphere, become aphasic again after suffering a right hemisphere injury (Martins, Antunes, Castro-Caldas, & Antunes, 1995; see also Locke, 1997 for review). All this is not to say that the right-handed transcortical patients of the PS group had abnormal development of the left perisylvian area, but I believe that future studies in similar aphasic populations may explore other variables (e.g. environmental, developmental) than the ones investigated in this study, to search for cues indicating atypical patterns of brain organisation. In any case, taken together these findings favour the hypothesis that, at least in some right-handers, the perisylvian region of the right hemisphere may only mediate specific linguistic functions such as phonological processing and repetition (Alexander & Annet, 1996; Alexander, Fischette, & Fischer, 1989; Schweiger, Wechsler, & Mazziota, 1987).

FUNCTIONAL NEUROIMAGING

New brain imaging techniques, including PET, SPECT, and more recently fMRI, are providing valuable information about the functional organisation of the human brain, permitting the visualisation of specific cerebral areas during the execution of language tasks (e.g. repetition, word fluency) as well as the delineation of maps of functional connectivity (Habib, Démonet, & Frackowiak, 1996; Frackowiak, 1994; Sergent, 1994). In the past few years, these sophisticated neuroimaging techniques have been used to explore mainly the cognitive operations that take place in the *normal* human brain and, more recently, activation studies have began to be performed in brain-damaged patients (Belin et al., 1996; Ohyama et al., 1996; Weiller et al., 1995). A full discussion of this area is beyond the scope of this chapter (see Habib et al., 1996 for a detailed review). Thus, I will briefly discuss some functional neuroanatomical data obtained in normal subjects and brain-damaged patients during cognitive activation that may be relevant to TA (e.g. word repetition).

---

angiomatosis). CNS abnormalities in KTS include seizures, mental retardation, cerebral and spinal arteriovenous malformations, internal carotid artery aplasia, and cerebral infarcts (Smirniotopoulos & Murphy, 1992; Williams & Elster, 1992).

Functional neuroimaging correlates of repetition in normal and brain-damaged subjects

Recent studies of cerebral function in normal subjects with PET scanning during language activation tasks report marked increase of regional cerebral blood flow (rCBF) in the middle part of the left superior temporal cortex (just anterior to the classical location of Wernicke's area) and a decrease in the right perisylvian cortex during real word repetition (Howard et al., 1992). In another study repetition of single words produced a significant activation of the classic perisylvian language regions in both cerebral hemispheres (left greater than right) including the posterior–superior temporal cortex (Wernicke's area), posterior–inferior frontal cortex (Broca's area), and rolandic region (Ohyama et al., 1996). Repetition of nonwords in normal volunteers induces an asymmetrical (left greater than right) activation in both anterior portion of the superior temporal cortices. Modest increments are also seen in the right inferior frontal region (BA 44) (Weiller et al., 1995). Studies with fMRI in normal subjects during digit span tasks (e.g. five-digit repetition in the forward condition) report bilateral activation of posterior (Wernicke's area) and anterior (Broca's area) cortical regions with the anterior activation focus predominating in the left hemisphere (Pujol, 1996, personal communication) (Fig. 7.3).

Preliminary evidence seems to indicate that the pattern of cerebral activation is rather different in brain-damaged aphasic patients. Ohyama and co-workers (1996) studied the role of the nonlanguage dominant (right) hemisphere and undamaged cortical regions of the left hemisphere in a group of 16 right-handed patients with different types of aphasias (10 fluent and 6 nonfluent) due to vascular lesions involving the cortex of the left hemisphere. These authors found that in the resting state the rCBF was reduced in posterior–inferior and posterior–superior temporal cortices of the left hemisphere in patients with nonfluent aphasias (Broca's aphasia) as well as in those with fluent aphasic syndromes (anomic, transcortical sensory, and Wernicke's aphasias). The area showing significant rCBF reduction (at rest) in these patients was generally much broader than the area of structural damage documented in the MRI scans. Greater cortical activation during word repetition was found in the right posterior–inferior and posterior–superior temporal cortices in fluent and nonfluent patients than in normal control subjects. The nonfluent group had lower Aphasia Quotient scores of the WAB (Kertesz, 1982) (67.8 ± 10.9) (e.g. more severe aphasia) and greater lesion sizes (44.5 ml ± 35.6) than that in the fluent group (Aphasia Quotient: 78.2 ± 11.7; lesion size: 27.5 ml ± 18.1). Interestingly, the magnitude of activation in the right posterior–inferior cortex in these nonfluent aphasic patients was greater than that in fluent aphasics and the former recruited undamaged portions of the left posterior–inferior cortex during repetition tasks (Ohyama et al., 1996). These findings support the notion that the functional reorganisation of language function in the right hemisphere is more marked among severely aphasic

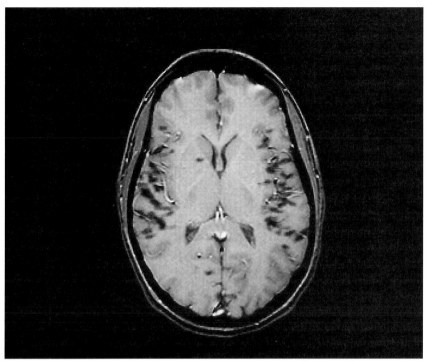

FIG. 7.3 Functional MRI scan performed during repetition of digits in a normal volunteer. Axial image section at the level of Broca's area showing activation of both posterior temporal cortices and left inferior frontal cortex (red areas). (Courtesy of the Centre Diagnòstic Pedralbes. Ressonancia Magnètica, Barcelona. Dr J. Pujol.)

patients with extensive involvement of the left hemisphere than in those with mild language deficits and less extensive lesions (Cappa & Vallar, 1992; Code, 1987, 1997; Gainotti, 1993).

Weiller et al. (1995) studied repetition of *nonwords* using PET in a group of six patients who showed near complete recovery from Wernicke's aphasia due to infarctions in the posterior branches of the middle cerebral artery with involvement of the posterior part of the left perisylvian language cortex. These authors found that nonword repetition significantly increases rCBF in right perisylvian cortical areas that were homotopic to the left hemisphere language zones, namely the superior temporal gyrus and inferior premotor and lateral prefrontal cortices; classical left frontal language areas spared by the structural lesion (e.g. Broca's area) were activated as well.

Belin et al. (1996) designed a PET study to examine the mechanisms of recovery from nonfluent aphasia in seven patients with extensive left perisylvian lesions (e.g. PET scan performed at rest showed hypometabolism of the whole perisylvian area). These authors found that repetition of unintoned words induced activation of the right superior temporal gyrus and inferior sensorimotor region coupled with a reduction of rCBF in the left inferior frontal cortex (e.g. Broca's area). Therefore, a converging interpretation of the findings reported by Weiller et al. (1995) and Belin et al. (1996) would be that word and nonword repetition in recovered aphasic patients activates both hemispheres when the structural involvement of the left perisylvian area is not extensive and confined to posterior cortical regions, whereas foci of activation are detected only in the right perisylvian area when its homotopic areas in the left hemisphere are either functionally or morphologically involved.

The contribution of the right hemisphere in the restoration of linguistic functions in some transcortical aphasics does not seem to be restricted to the ability to repeat words and nonwords. In normal volunteers, PET (Démonet, Chollet, Ramsay, Cardebat, & Nespoulous et al., 1992) and fMRI studies (Binder et al., 1995) carried out during different semantic tasks found activation of the left frontal and posterior polymodal areas inferring that the anatomy of the semantic processing system is lateralised and distributed in an anterior–posterior net. Other researchers even propose that in normal volunteers the execution of category judgement tasks activate the left posterior–superior temporal gyrus because this cortical region acts as the phonological input lexicon (Wise et al., 1991). Once more, the pattern of cerebral activation is different in aphasics, since data from a single right-handed patient featuring a TCSA due to an infarction in the left middle and inferior temporal lobe structures reveals that semantic information may be processed by alternative systems. Indeed, a PET scan performed while this patient performed a semantic category membership judgement task disclosed activation of the right angular gyrus instead of the left angular gyrus (the latter focus of activation was the usual pattern found in normal controls) (Grossman et al., 1993).

Functional neuroimaging studies in transcortical aphasias

Functional neuroimaging studies (PET, SPECT) studies carried out in aphasia have mainly examined patients with classical aphasic syndromes (Broca's, Wernicke's, and conduction aphasia) due to damage of cortical (Metter et al., 1989, 1990; Mlcoch, Bushnell, Gupta, & Milo, 1994) and subcortical structures (Baron et al., 1986; Demeurisse et al., 1990; Pappata, Mazoyer, Tran Dinh, Cambon, Levasseur et al., 1990). The most consistent finding has been diminished rCBF in the left temporoparietal cortex, regardless of the profile of aphasic impairment (Metter et al., 1990), with differences in rCBF in other cortical areas being related to the distinct type of aphasia (Kempler et al., 1988; Metter et al., 1989). These *in vivo* techniques have also been used to examine the functional correlates of atypical aphasic profiles due to subcortical damage to the left hemisphere (Démonet et al., 1991; Metter et al., 1986).

On the other hand, there have been few functional neuroimaging studies in TA and all of them have been focused on the evaluation of selected single cases (Berthier, Starkstein et al., 1991; de la Sayette et al., 1992; Dogil et al., 1995; Grossman et al., 1993; Lanoe et al., 1994; Perani et al., 1987; Perani, Papagno, Cappa, Gerundi, & Fazio, 1988; Rapcsak et al., 1990), or small groups of patients (Démonet et al., 1991). Most of these studies were performed in patients with TA caused by *subcortical* ischaemic or haemorrhagic lesions involving either the basal ganglia, thalamus, or periventricular white matter, and nearly always documented remote effects on the overlying cortical mantle. Striatocapsular and periventricular white matter lesions were reported to induce marked hypo-perfusion in the ipsilateral perisylvian language cortex among patients with either TCSA (Berthier, Starkstein et al., 1991, Case 12), MTCA (Perani et al., 1988, Case 2), or TCMA (Lanoe et al., 1994). Cases of TA resulting from thalamic lesions were mainly associated with reduced left hemisphere rCBF in the whole left perisylvian language cortex (Perani et al., 1987, Case 3) or restricted to the dorsolateral prefrontal and posterior parietal cortices with normal rCBF in the central perisylvian cortex (Démonet et al., 1991).

Considerably fewer studies using PET or SPECT have been performed in cases of TA associated with *cortical* lesions, and virtually all of them examined patients with either partial (Dogil et al., 1995; Rapcsak et al., 1990, Case 1) or complete involvement of the left perisylvian cortex (Grossi et al., 1991; Trojano et al., 1988). This is surprising since classical neuroanatomical theories of aphasia (Geschwind et al., 1968; Goldstein, 1948) posited that the TA resulted from damage to left hemisphere structures located outside the perisylvian langu-age core. According to this traditional view, the major speech centres (Broca's area and Wernicke's area) and their interconnections should be intact to guarantee the preservation of basic speech mechanisms (e.g. repetition), but separated from the anterior frontal cortex necessary for speech production, the posterior associa-tion cortex essential for lexico-semantic processing, or both.

Although the neuroanatomical model of isolation of the speech area earlier proposed by Goldstein (1948) and later championed by Geschwind and col-leagues (Geschwind et al., 1968) is by far the most widely accepted explanation to account for the preservation of repetition in TA, functional neuroimaging studies (PET, SPECT) are few in cases of TA with radiological evidence of structural *cortical* damage to left hemisphere regions that surround but spare the left perisylvian cortex (Grossman et al., 1993).

SPECT in transcortical aphasias: The functional status of the left perisylvian language cortex

Here I will present data from a recent study reported by Berthier et al. (1997), which was designed to examine the functional status of the left perisylvian cortex in a series of patients with TA and left hemisphere cerebrovascular accidents of different locations using SPECT. Therefore, four patients who had TA in association with structural lesions that involved portions or the whole left perisylvian cortex and four patients who had TA in association with corticosubcortical lesions that surrounded but spared this area were selected.

A new sample of eight aphasic patients with thromboembolic infarctions or intracerebral haemorrhages participated in the present study. Demographic information was obtained in all patients. Formal language examination was carried out using the WAB (Kertesz, 1982) and other tests including the Boston Naming Test (BNT; Kaplan et al., 1983), the 36-item short version of the Token Test (TT; De Renzi & Faglioni, 1978), and an experimental battery of word, nonword, digit, and sentence repetition. Language disturbances were studied in the acute period (within two months of evolution after the stroke lesion) in four patients, and in the chronic period in the remaining four patients.

MRI scans were performed in the same week the patients underwent both the language testing and SPECT. The MRI studies were carried out following the same protocol (Berthier, Kulisevsky, Gironell, & Heras, 1996) and the patients were classified into two groups, *perisylvian* (PS) and *extraperisylvian* (EPS) following the neuroanatomical criteria laid down in the morphological study described in the previous section (see abbreviations of cortical and subcortical anatomical regions in the previous section). The rCBF was measured with SPECT and 99 m TC-HMPAO in all patients and in four normal control (NC) volunteers (two males and two females) (see Berthier et al., 1997 for technical details).

The two patient groups (PS and EPS) showed similar demographic variables (age, sex, years of education, handedness, or interval between aphasia onset and language testing). At the onset of aphasia, two patients with chronic TA (MTCA and TCMA) had been classified on clinical grounds as having global aphasia. Within the PS group, two patients had a TCSA, one patient had a TCMA, and one patient had an MCTA. Within the EPS group, the four patients had a TCSA. The two groups obtained similar performances in language subtests of the WAB (fluency, comprehension, repetition, naming, and aphasia quotient), BNT and TT, but on the experimental tests of repetition the PS group did worse than the EPS in the repetition of nonwords. Demographic and language findings of both aphasic groups are shown in Table 7.7.

Analysis of MRI data from the PS group revealed that two patients (Cases 1 and 2) had acute TCSA associated with lesions that involved the left IFC and middle frontal gyrus, and the lower third of the SMC. The lesions extended into the anterior portions of the INS, BG (lentiform nucleus), and PVWM in both cases. Additional ischaemic damage was seen involving the right superior frontal gyrus in one of these patients (Case 2), whereas mild symmetric ischaemic changes were also observed in the PVWM in both patients. The STC (Wernicke's area) and the IPC (infrasylvian supramarginal gyrus) were morphologically spared in both cases. The other two patients (Cases 3 and 4) had chronic TCMA and MTCA associated with extensive damage to the whole left perisylvian language

TABLE 7.7

Demographic and Language in Data Patients with Transcortical Aphasias

	Cases							
	PS Group[a]				EPS Group			
	1	2	3	4	5	6	7	8
Sex/Age (years)	F.77	F.70	M.38	M.59	M.66	M.70	M.59	M.66
Type of aphasia	TCSA	TCSA	TCMA*	MTCA*	TCSA	TCSA	TCSA	TCSA
Months of evolution	2	3	12	16	1	3	1	32
Education (years)	7	7	12	9	8	6	9	9
Handedness	R	R	R	R	L	R	R	R
Fluency	8	6	4	1	6	8	7	8
Comprehension	6.7	6.6	5.8	6.5	4.8	6.9	5.6	5.9
Repetition	8.8	9.2	8.2	7.4	8.4	7.6	9.2	8
Naming	3.2	6.4	7	3.2	3.3	5.8	6.5	4.8
Aphasia quotient	67	66.4	60	32.2	45	70.6	66.8	65.4
Token Test	10.5	14	14.5	6	9	11	13	10
Boston Naming Test	11	13	31	16	27	NT	30	17
Word repetition (n = 260)	183	187	256	232	235	255	244	246
Nonword repetition** (n = 80)	16	38	57	42	69	75	72	64
Phrase repetition (n = 10)	8	9	10	9	10	10	10	10
Digit repetition	3	3	4	2	5	3	3	3

[a] See abbreviations in text. F indicates female; M male. NT not tested. * Classified as global aphasics during the acute stage. ** $P < .02$ (PS group vs. EPS group) (Mann–Whitney U test, two-tailed). Reprinted from Berthier et al. (1997); by permission of Rapid Science Publishers.

211

cortex involving the FTPC as well as the subjacent INS, BG, IC, and PVWM. In one of these two patients (Case 4) temporal lobe involvement was restricted to the subcortical isthmus area, and additional ischaemic damage was seen involving the left mesial frontal cortex. Schematic representation of lesion location in axial MRI images is shown in Fig. 7.4.

Analysis of MRI data from the EPS group revealed that two patients had TCSA associated with single lesions. Of these two patients, one (Case 5) had a large haemorrhage involving the left middle frontal cortex and the adjacent part of the SMC (the left IFC was spared), whereas the other (Case 6) had an ischaemic infarction involving the left IPC and SPC and the posterior part of the PVWM. Two other patients had TCSA associated with separate but simultaneous ischaemic infarctions involving anterior as well as posterior regions of the left hemisphere. Of these two patients, one (Case 7) had a large TOC lesion and a second, albeit less extensive, lesion involving the anterior cingulate cortex, the anterior corpus callosum, and the surrounding PVWM. The remaining patient (Case 8) had a large lesion in the TOC region and a second lesion was seen involving the BG (head of the caudate nucleus), the anterior limb of the IC, and the PVWM anterolateral to the frontal horn. There was also diffuse ischaemic changes in the left PVWM. Schematic representation of lesion location in axial MRI images is shown in Fig. 7.5.

Group and individual information of left-right rCBF ratios of patients with TA and NC volunteers are shown in Tables 7.8 and 7.9. The mean left-to-right asymmetry scores in the whole patient sample were significantly lower than in the NC group in six of the nine left-hemisphere regions of interest (ROIs) (the PFC, TH, and PVWM did not show between-group differences). Comparisons between the PS and EPS groups revealed that in the former reductions of rCBF were more marked in perisylvian and subcortical structures. As expected, the PS group had significantly reduced left-to-right perfusion ratios compared with the NC group in cortical regions that were morphologically damaged as well as in subcortical structures. Not surprisingly, analysis of individual scores in the PS yielded similar results, although in one of these patients (Case 2) there was also significant hypoperfusion in the morphologically intact STC. Comparisons between the EPS and NC groups showed that the EPS group had significant hypoperfusion not only in the posterior extraperisylvian region (IPC, TOC), but also in the posterior perisylvian (STC) cortex. Analysis of individual ratios in the EPS group yielded similar results with reduced rCBF in morphologically spared cortical regions such as the STC and SMC (Cases 5 and 8) and the IFC (Case 8; see Fig. 7.6).

When comparisons between the whole TA aphasic group and the NC group were performed excluding those ROIs that were structurally involved, the TA aphasic group still showed a statistically significant reduction in rCBF as compared to the NC group in ROIs placed on the STC and IPC. In summary, patients of the PS group had the most severe rCBF reduction in structurally

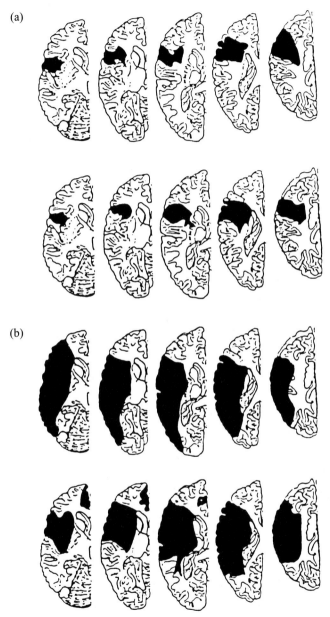

FIG. 7.4 Schematic diagrams of CT/MRI scans showing cross-sectional localisation of lesions in patients with transcortical aphasias and cortico–subcortical lesions *involving* the left perisylvian region: (a) Patient. 1; (b) Patient 4.

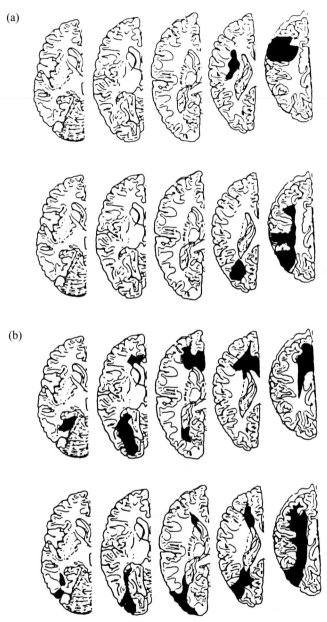

FIG. 7.5 Schematic diagrams of CT/MRI scans showing cross-sectional localisation of lesions in patients with transcortical aphasias and cortical–subcortical lesions *sparing* the left perisylvian region: (a) Patient 5; (b) Patient 8.

214

TABLE 7.8
Left–Right rCBF Ratios in Groups of Transcortical Aphasic Patients and
Normal Control Subjects

	Whole Sample (n = 8) mean (SD)	PS Group (n = 4) mean (SD)	EPS Group (n = 4) mean (SD)	NC Group (n = 4) mean (SD)
ROI*				
IFC	0.86 (0.17)$_a$	0.74 (0.11)$_{ef}$	0.99 (0.12)	1.03 (0.04)
PFC	0.89 (0.20)	0.77 (0.22)$_{fg}$	1.01 (0.06)	0.99 (0.00)
SMC	0.81 (0.16)$_b$	0.72 (0.09)$_g$	0.91 (0.16)	1.02 (0.04)
STC	0.85 (0.16)$_d$	0.76 (0.19)$_g$	0.93 (0.05)$_e$	1.02 (0.04)
TOC	0.83 (0.15)$_c$	0.80 (0.22)	0.86 (0.02)$_e$	1.00 (0.06)
IPC	0.85 (0.13)$_c$	0.81 (0.19)	0.90 (0.07)$_e$	1.01 (0.05)
BG	0.82 (0.24)$_b$	0.67 (0.27)$_g$	0.96 (0.06)	1.00 (0.01)
TH	0.90 (0.18)	0.77 (0.17)$_e$	1.02 (0.10)	1.01 (0.03)
PVWM	0.81 (0.24)	0.63 (0.23)$_{ef}$	0.99 (0.03)	1.00 (0.04)

* See abbreviations in text. All statistical comparisons are by Mann–Whitney U tests.
[a] $P < .05$ vs. NC group. [b] $P < .04$ vs. NC group. [c] $P < .01$ vs. NC group. [d] $P < .006$ vs. NC group.
[e] $P < .02$ vs. NC group. [f] $P < .02$ vs. EPS group. [g] $P < .01$ vs. NC group. Reprinted from
Berthier et al. (1997); by permission of Rapid Science Publishers.

TABLE 7.9
Individual Left-Right rCBF for Cortical and Subcortical ROIs

	Patients							
	PS Group				EPS Group			
	1	2	3	4	5	6	7	8
ROIs[a]								
IFC	0.87*	0.75*	0.58*	0.76*	0.93	1.17	1.00	0.87*
PFC	0.93	0.90*	0.44*	0.83*	0.98	1.11	1.00	0.98
SMC	0.85*	0.70*	0.63*	0.70*	0.81*	1.13	0.94	0.76*
STC	0.93	0.91*	0.50*	0.73*	0.87*	0.98	0.97	0.92*
TOC	0.99	0.91*	0.48*	0.83*	0.86*	0.89*	0.85*	0.84*
IPC	0.98	0.93	0.55*	0.80*	0.92*	0.98	0.94	0.79*
BG	0.92*	0.91*	0.44*	0.44*	0.96	1.06	0.96	0.89*
TH	0.95	0.91*	0.64*	0.61*	1.11	1.10	1.00	0.89*
PVWM	0.84*	0.82*	0.44*	0.42*	0.98	1.04	1.00	0.97

[a] See abbreviations in text; * indicates ratios at least 2 SD below the normal mean. Reprinted
from Berthier et al. (1997); by permission of Rapid Science Publishers.

(a)

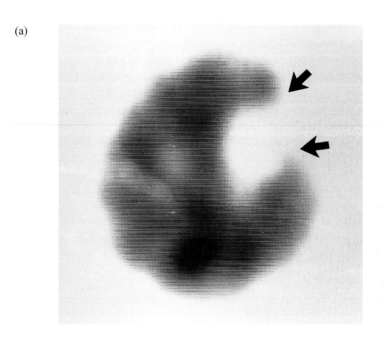

(b)

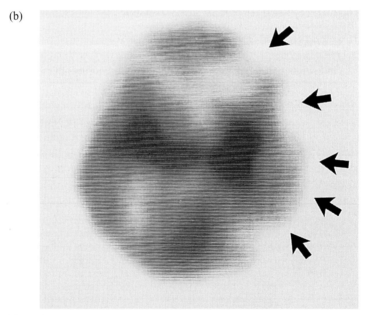

FIG. 7.6 Brain SPECT imaging from a patient (Case 8) with transcortical sensory aphasia showing marked hypoperfusion in the left dorsolateral frontal lobe (arrows in a) consistent with the site
of structural damage and in morphologically spared regions (posterior temporal cortex) of the left
perisylvian cortex (arrows in b).

damaged areas, although in one of these patients (Case 2) there was a significant decrease of perfusion in the morphologically intact STC (Wernicke's area). Two of the four EPS patients (Cases 5 and 8) had significant hypoperfusion in structurally undamaged regions of the left perisylvian area.

The results of the present SPECT study are not easily reconciled with the classical neuroanatomical interpretation of isolation of the speech area put forward by other authors (e.g. Assal et al., 1983; Geschwind et al., 1968; Goldstein, 1948) to explain the preservation of repetition in TA. In this study, repetition of words and sentences was preserved in spite of significant decrements of perfusion in various anatomical components of the language network represented in the left perisylvian language cortex. Both our findings and those of other research groups (Grossi et al., 1991; Pulvermüller & Schönle, 1993; Trojano et al., 1988) not only suggest that in certain subgroups of patients with TA (PS group and Cases 5 and 8 of the EPS group) the anatomofunctional integrity of the left perisylvian language cortex is not essential for repetition of words and phrases, but also permits inferences to be made about the role played by homologous regions of the right hemisphere in the mediation of residual aspects of repetition.[6] Furthermore, the abolition of repetition, echolalia, and automatic completion of well-known open-ended sentences in aphasic patients with left hemisphere damage after either a second lesion in the right hemisphere (Basso, Gardelli, Grassi, & Mariotti, 1989; Cambier et al., 1983; Rapcsak et al., 1990; Case 19 in the previous section), or following a right internal carotid artery injection of amytal (Bando et al., 1986; Case 1 in the previous section) provides direct evidence for a right hemisphere contribution to repetition processes.

The linguistic findings documented in the present sample are, in general, compatible with other recently published studies on TA (Berthier, 1995; Berthier, Starkstein et al., 1991), in that there were no significant differences in the language subtest scores of the WAB and in most experimental repetition tasks between the PS and EPS groups. In the current study, however, there were differences between the two aphasic groups in the repetition of nonwords, with the PS group performing significantly worse than the EPS group. Differences in nonword repetition between the previous work (see Berthier, Starkstein et al., 1991, and the previous section) and the present study were unrelated to differences in demographic variables, but might depend upon a range of other variables. First, differences in size and site of the brain lesions could account for the sparing of nonword repetition in the the first study and its impairment in the

---

[6] Most patients discussed in this chapter were scanned at rest, so that it is difficult to establish whether brain regions with normal anatomy but decreased rCBF (e.g. STC in the EPS group) still remained operating during the process of residual repetition. Therefore, further functional neuroimaging studies using cognitive activation paradigms are necessary to identify the regions and neural networks that participate in the process of language repetition and other linguistic functions among patients with TA.

second one. Second, it is possible that the existent discrepancies may rely on the fact that in the previous study (Berthier, Starkstein et al., 1991) patients featuring only TCSA (PS group = 4; EPS group = 5) were tested using a reduced number of nonwords (n = 20), whereas in the present study a longer list of non-words (n = 80) was used and two of the four PS patients had nonfluent speech (TCMA in Case 3 and MTCA in Case 4). Alternatively, given the reported anatomical and functional variability of some language functions (e.g. picture naming) in TA (Berthier, 1995), individual differences in the brain organisation of language functions, rather than methodological issues, might account for the distinct pattern of performance in nonword repetition.

Perisylvian involvement and nonword repetition

The finding of dissociated performance in the repetition of words relative to nonwords in the four patients of the PS group is in agreement with previous reports (Berndt et al., 1987; Grossi et al., 1991; Martin & Saffran, 1990; Trojano et al., 1988) who found better performance for the repetition of words than nonwords as well as reduced digit span in patients with TA and structural dam-age affecting the whole left perisylvian area (see Grossi et al., 1991 for SPECT data) or only portions of it (Martin & Saffran, 1990). Furthermore, the finding of significant decrements of perfusion in the structurally intact anterior left perisylvian cortex in one patient of the EPS group (Case 8) as well as in a patient with TCMA (Lanoe et al., 1994), both with impaired nonword repetition and damage to anterior subcortical regions (e.g. centrum semiovale), raises the possibility that decrements of perfusion in the left anterior perisylvian cortex exert the same deleterious effect on nonword repetition as does structural damage.

As already stated in this chapter, current models of language processing (Butterworth & Warrington, 1995; Caplan, 1992; Coslett et al., 1987; Ellis & Young, 1988; Katz & Goodglass, 1990; McCarthy & Warrington, 1984) propose that nonwords are repeated via the nonlexical route, which links the input phonological representations directly with the output phonology, bypassing the two lexicons. In addition to patients with TA and structural and/or functional involvement of the left perisylvian cortex reviewed here (Grossi et al., 1991; Lanoe et al., 1994; Trojano et al., 1988; Cases 1 to 4 and 8 in the present study), the nonlexical route has been found to be impaired in aphasic patients featuring either conduction aphasia (see Caplan & Waters, 1992) or deep dysphasia (Butterworth & Warrington, 1995; Duhamel & Poncet, 1986; Katz & Goodglass, 1990; Martin & Saffran, 1992; Michel & Andreewsky, 1983) due to damage to the left perisylvian language cortex. Data from patients with deep dysphasia (an aphasic syndrome analogous of deep dyslexia, characterised by the production of semantic errors during word repetition and poor repetition of nonwords) due to damage to the left perisylvian language cortex suggests that the impairment of the nonlexical repetition route is aggravated by a concomitant dysfunction of the short-term phonological store (Goodglass, 1992; Katz & Goodglass, 1990; Martin et al., 1996). In this regard, two PET studies of verbal working memory functions carried out in normal subjects revealed activation of various regions of the left perisylvian language cortex, and specifically localised the phonological store in the left supramarginal gyrus and the subvocal rehearsal process in Broca's area (Paulesu, Frith, & Frackowiak, 1993; Salmon et al., 1996). This converging evidence suggests that brain damage, whether structural or functional, to the left perisylvian language cortex in patients with TA may impair span performance and nonword repetition (Berndt et al., 1987; Grossi et al., 1991; Lanoe et al., 1994; Martin & Saffran, 1990; Trojano et al., 1988; Cases 1 to 4 and 8 in the present study) by disrupting the verbal components of the working memory system (Baddeley, 1986, 1996) and the process(es) underlying nonlexical repetition.

A further aspect that may be worth mentioning is the potential capacity of the right hemisphere to reorganise nonword repetition. Two patients of the PS group (Cases 3 and 4) with *chronic* TA achieved the best scores of the whole PS group on nonword repetition, despite having the most extensive structural and functional involvement of the left perisylvian language cortex. During the acute post-stroke period, both patients had global aphasia with impaired repetition which eventually evolved into TCMA (Case 3) and MTCA (Case 4). These findings lend additional support to the notion that after extensive left perisylvian cortex involvement, the undamaged homologous contralateral cortex is capable, at least in some individuals, of reorganising originally left hemisphere linguistic functions (e.g. Patterson, Vargha-Khadem, & Polkey, 1989; Rapcsak, Beeson, & Rubens, 1991). In this context, it has been argued that the right hemisphere supposedly contains distributed systems of interacting neurones available to slowly restore some phonological abilities at the expense of new right perisylvian auditory-motor assemblies (Pulvermüller & Preißl, 1994; Pulvermüller & Schönle, 1993). Further evidence for the role of the right hemisphere in the reorganisation of repetition comes from recent PET activation studies which demonstrated an increase of rCBF in the right perisylvian cortex during nonword repetition tasks among patients who had recovered from Wernicke's aphasia due to infarctions of the left posterior association areas (Weiller et al., 1995).

Unexpected intrahemispheric distribution of lesions in transcortical sensory aphasia

An intriguing finding of this functional neuroimaging study was that three patients showed the profiles of language deficits characteristic of TCSA (fluent paraphasic speech with impaired auditory comprehension and preserved repetition) despite having either structural/functional (PS group: Cases 1 and 2) or only functional damage (EPS group: Case 8) to the left Broca's area and surrounding corticosubcortical regions. This clinicoanatomical correlation has previously been demonstrated using CT and MRI scans (Basso et al., 1985, Cases 18 and 19; Hadano et al., 1992; Willmes & Poeck, 1993; see also Cases 1, 3, and 4 in the previous section) and the impairment in auditory comprehension due to Broca's area damage interpreted as resulting from atypical *intra*hemispheric language organisation (Basso et al., 1985) or "semantic confusion of frontal-lobe origin" (Hadano et al., 1992). Unfortunately, functional brain imaging studies have not been performed in these patients.

Brain SPECT imaging revealed that two such patients (Cases 2 and 8) had, in addition to hypoperfusion in the left IFC (Broca's area), decreased perfusion rates in cortical regions of the left hemisphere previously implicated in the phonological processing of heard words such as the STC (Heschl's gyrus and Wernicke's area) (Démonet et al., 1992; Selnes et al., 1985) and lexical–semantic comprehension such as the TOC (temporal-occipital cortex) and IPC (inferior parietal cortex) (Hart & Gordon, 1990). In the remaining patient with TCSA due to left Broca's area damage (Case 1) the SPECT showed normal perfusion rates in STC, TOC, and IPC. Although in this patient (Case 1) the cortical region corresponding to Wernicke's area was intact on MRI, sagittal views revealed a discrete involvement of the middle part of the left superior temporal gyrus (Heschl's gyrus), a cortical region important for spoken word recognition (Frith, Friston, Liddle, & Frackowiak, 1991; Howard et al., 1992). Moreover, in this SPECT study the STC was defined as a functional-anatomic region that resulted from the average of ROIs placed in Heschl's gyrus and Wernicke's areas across successive slices, so that ROI averaging may have masked decrements in perfusion rates in the STC. These results suggest that impaired auditory comprehension in cases of TCSA associated with *anterior* damage to the left perisylvian cortex results from a functional derangement of posterior neocortical association areas presumably due to interruption of reciprocal cortico-cortical projections. Some support for this argument comes from recent PET (Démonet et al., 1992) and fMRI (Binder et al., 1995) studies which demonstrated that the performance of semantic processing tasks by normal individuals activates frontal and temporo-parieto-occipital heteromodal cortical components of a neural net that is lateralised to the left hemisphere.

A second, likely, possibility is that damage to the *anterior* left perisylvian language cortex might be sufficient to alter the processing of incoming auditory information (Schäffler, Lüders, Dinner, Lesser, & Chelune, 1993), by disrupting the access from the frontal lobe sites to the posterior information store (Swinney, Zurif, & Nicol, 1989). Using cortical stimulation mapping of the left perisylvian cortex, Schäffler and colleagues (1993) documented that although in most instances electrical stimulation of the anterior left perisylvian cortex elicited speech arrest, besides the impairment of language comprehension, in selected electrodes the "stimulation elicited relatively selective comprehension deficit for the Token Test and two-step commands, but the patient was able to repeat questions given to him orally" (p. 713). This combination of impaired (auditory comprehension) and preserved (repetition) language abilities is similar to what we found in our patients with TCSA and anterior left perisylvian involvement.

Finally, these three TCSA patients and others reported in the literature (e.g. Basso et al., 1985) had structural and/or functional involvement of Broca's area, inferior sensorimotor cortex, basal ganglia, and anterior PVWM, yet their verbal expression remained fluent, copious, and paraphasic. While previous research suggested that nonfluency in aphasia requires extensive damage to the left frontal cortex extending well beyond the Broca's area to affect the insular cortex and adjacent white matter and possibly including the basal ganglia (Alexander, Benson, & Stuss, 1989), the present findings are in accordance with recent SPECT data which documented fluent speech in some aphasic patients with perfusion defects in Broca's area (Janicek, Schwartz, Carvalho, Garada, & Holman, 1993).

CHAPTER EIGHT

Conclusions

This volume presents a review of the transcortical aphasias (TA) and a recon-
ceptualisation of linguistic and neuroanatomical findings based on both previous
clinical and theoretical studies as well as in modern cognitive and functional
neuroimaging studies. Since Lichtheim's original description of TA (his inner-
commissural aphasia and inner-commissural word-deafness), these aphasic syndromes did not share the attention that was paid to the so-called "classical"
aphasias (e.g. Broca's aphasia). This perhaps occurred because the nosological
validity of the TA was questioned from the beginning to the point that some
authors did not even include TA in their classification of aphasias (Chapter 1).
During the following decades the different types of TA were steadily recognised
as clinical entities (TCMA, TCSA, and MTCA), but the number of articles
dealing with different aspects of TA waxed and waned and the TA never reached
the popularity obtained by the classical aphasias. Another factor that potentially
contributed to the paucity of research in TA lies in the dogmatic viewpoint that
these types of aphasia were rare. More recent research, however, demonstrated
that the TA are not so rare as previously thought and a number of studies have
been conducted to investigate several clinical and theoretical issues which may
be relevant to deepen our knowledge about TA.

While most studies (e.g. Bogousslavsky et al., 1987; Freedman et al., 1984;
Geschwind et al., 1968; Heilman et al., 1981; Kertesz et al., 1982; Ross, 1980;
Rubens & Kertesz, 1983) were carried out before the cognitive neuropsychological
approach become popular among researchers interested in the study of aphasias,
several modern cases have been examined using this methodology (e.g. Berndt
et al., 1987; Lesser, 1989; Martin & Saffran, 1990; McCarthy & Warrington,
1984, 1987; Sartori et al., 1987; Schwartz et al., 1979). These latter studies

usually employed quantitative and well-controlled procedures to tap language deficits (Chapter 2), and have provided us with a coherent theoretical framework which enables further progress in the psycholinguistic research on TA.

The interpretation of linguistic deficits and their neural substrate in TA is far from being an easy task. On reviewing the literature in TA, I found that one of the major problems concerns the issue of heterogeneity in the clinical presentation and neuroanatomical correlates. The implications of this problematic point in the interpretation of TA has been repeatedly discussed in various chapters of this book and will not be elaborated in great detail herein. Of central importance in the discussion of heterogeneity is to realise that some theoretical inferences on TA, which were based on discrepancy in the pattern of results, were elaborated ignoring important differences in the population of patients selected for study (e.g. effects of education, inclusion of patients with aphasias in different stages of evolution, differences in handedness, comparisons of linguistic deficits in patients with acute lesions with others showing slowly progressing diseases, and so forth) that themselves are sufficient to account for variability in previous reports in clinical and pathological findings. The variability in the literature as to what constitutes TA contributes to the wide variety of description and linguistic analysis of the patients, but the reader should also be aware that every variety of TA, namely TCMA, TCSA, and TCMA, may have more than one pattern of language deficits and different anatomical correlates.

The preservation of repetition is unanimously regarded as the key feature of TA, with variable deficits in other language functions (spontaneous speech and auditory comprehension) being also required to establish the taxonomic diagnoses of the transcortical syndromes (Albert et al., 1981; Benson, 1993; Kertesz, 1979). Overall, preserved repetition is associated with either nonfluent speech and preserved auditory comprehension in TCMA; with fluent paraphasic speech and impaired auditory comprehension in TCSA; and with grave deficits in both spontaneous speech and auditory comprehension in MTCA. However, at this elementary level of analysis one can reasonably say that these combinations of deficits are merely the "necessary ingredients" to establish the diagnosis of a given type of TA. But a more fine-grained linguistic dissection of every component of these major language functions (e.g. spontaneous speech, repetition, auditory comprehension) is mandatory to examine whether or not a further fragmentation of every clinical variety of TA into distinct subtypes may eventually illuminate the linguistic and pathophysiological mechanisms implicated in every subtype.

Several studies carried out in single cases (Berndt et al., 1987; Lesser, 1989; Martin & Saffran, 1990; McCarthy & Warrington, 1987; Schwartz et al., 1979; Warrington, 1975) or in small groups (Coslett et al., 1987; Mehler & Rabinowich, 1990) using the cognitive neuropsychological approach have been published, and some of these cases were indeed used to exemplify that different patterns of linguistic performance clearly exist. The mention of some examples suffice to illustrate heterogeneity. In Chapter 3, for instance, at least three different patterns of oral expression in TCMA were distinguished. Briefly, in the "classical" pattern the patient has sparse and perseverative spontaneous speech, effortful initiation, preserved grammar and repetition (words, nonwords, and sentences) and phonological or semantic paraphasias and poor prosody may also be observed (McCarthy & Warrington, 1984; Rubens, 1975; Rubens & Kertesz, 1983). Various atypical patterns of oral expression in TCMA have been described; their unusual features are chiefly composed of dysarthria, stuttering, and mild deficits in repetition (e.g. low-frequency words, nonwords, and sentences) (Freedman et al., 1984; Naeser & Borod, 1986). It has been noted that these two distinctive patterns of oral expression in TCMA are the result of a different topographical distribution of lesions within the left frontal lobe, being the "classical" subtype associated with lesions that spare the anterior perisylvian language zone (Broca's area, frontal operculum), and the atypical subtypes with lesions involving such cortical regions. The remaining pattern of oral expression in TCMA has been termed "dynamic aphasia" (Luria & Tsvetkova, 1968) and is characterised by markedly hesitant spontaneous speech, although some occasional spontaneously generated utterances as well as other channels for verbal expression (naming, repetition, and oral reading) are regularly normal both in form and content (Costello & Warrington, 1986; Gold et al., 1997; Robinson et al., 1998). Interestingly, available neuroimaging evidence suggests that the topographical distribution of lesions in dynamic aphasia (dorsolateral frontal cortex, mesial frontal cortex, or subcortical structures) is not radically different to that documented in patients exhibiting the "classical pattern" of oral expression in TCMA (Rapcsak & Rubens, 1994).

Similar heterogeneity apply not only to other linguistic components of the TCMA syndrome (e.g. naming, auditory comprehension), but also to the two other clinically established varieties of TA, namely TCSA and MTCA. While the pattern of repetition has not been extensively investigated in the TCMA literature (but see McCarthy & Warrington, 1984), in Chapters 2 and 4 I reviewed the contribution of contemporary psycholinguistic research to the delineation of three different routes to repeat language (Caplan, 1992; Katz & Goodglass, 1990) and, based on repetition performance, the recent description of two subtypes of TCSA. One of these subtypes is composed of patients who repeat using the "nonlexical" mechanism. They fail to correct syntactical errors during repetition of ungrammatical sentences and appear unable of recognising the ill-formedness of these sentences; the second subtype of TCSA is composed of patients who are capable of recognising syntactic anomalies embedded in sentences, and also to correct syntactic errors during repetition of these abnormal sentences. These latter patients are considered to repeat using the "lexical" mechanism. The two groups of patients show similar performance in other language tests, including preserved repetition of words and nonwords and verbatim repetition of sentences containing semantic anomalies they fail to recognise. Coslett et al. (1987), Heilman

(1985), and Mehler and Rabinowich (1990) proposed a similar schema to classify patients with MTCA, but the small number of patients studied by these authors precluded speculations on clinicopathological correlations. Although much research need to be done, there is empirical evidence suggesting that repetition using the "lexical" mechanism may be impaired after extensive lesions involving the perisylvian regions (Caplan & Waters, 1992; Duhamel & Poncet, 1986; Katz & Goodglass, 1990; Michel & Andreewsky, 1983) and reliance of on-line repetition by the undamaged contralateral hemisphere has been described in patients featuring TCSA or MTCA (Chapter 7).

The transcortical syndromes may also be regarded as heterogenous when the exceptional indemnity of certain language skills (object naming), other than repetition capacity, is taken in consideration. Word retrieval during spontaneous speech and object naming may be "intact" and dissociated from the auditory comprehension of the same targets in patients with TCSA (Heilman et al., 1981; Kremin, 1986) or MTCA (Heilman et al., 1976; Kapur & Dunkley, 1984; Fujii et al., 1997). Data from such cases have been taken to indicate that there is a direct nonsemantic naming route which connects the input and output lexicons bypassing the semantic system (Diesfeldt, 1989; Kremin, 1986; Ratcliff & Newcombe, 1982; Shuren et al., 1993). Other patients instead display the "classical" patterns of language deficits of TCSA or MTCA, but show "paradoxical" locations of lesions. This is exemplified by the unexpected anterior location of lesions in patients with TCSA (Basso et al., 1985; Hadano et al., 1992; Papagno & Basso, 1996; Sartori et al., 1987; Selnes et al., 1982) as well as by cases of MTCA associated with isolated lesions involving either anterior (Rapcsak, Krupp, Rubens & Reim, 1990) or posterior regions (Pirozzolo et al., 1981; Speedie et al., 1984). As stated in various chapters of this book, the interpretation of these diverse patterns of linguistic deficits and lesion sites is still elusive. Nevertheless, what seems clear is that heterogeneity is regularly observed in the three clinical varieties of TA, and that the salient linguistic features of these discrete subtypes can be observed in every variety of TA. For instance, consider again the case of "intact" object naming in TA. Preserved object naming has been described in patients featuring either TCMA (McNabb et al., 1988), TCSA (Heilman et al., 1981; Kremin, 1986), or MTCA (Heilman et al., 1976; Kapur & Dunkley, 1984). These findings are consonant with recent theories suggesting that the motor (TCMA, MTCA) and sensory (TCSA) varieties of TA are just the opposite extremes of a continuum of language deficits which result from localised dysfunction occurring at different levels of the same functional system (Heilman, 1991, cited in Gonzalez Rothi, 1997).

Very different mechanisms are possibly operating during the production and reception of language in patients with TA. This might explain the heterogeneity in linguistic features including, for instance, the variable status of repetition (e.g. some transcortical patients can repeat nonwords and long sentences, whereas others can not). From a neuroanatomical perspective, much emphasis has been put forth with respect to the mechanism of "isolation of the speech area" as the likely model underlying preserved repetition, but surprisingly little research has been conducted with functional neuroimaging techniques, perhaps because this mechanism was accepted in a rather straightforward fashion. Therefore, more research integrating cognitive neuropsychology and functional neuroimaging (e.g. fMRI) (i.e. exploration of whether or not the anatomically spared, but isolated left perisylvian language cortex is activated during repetition of different verbal stimuli) is warranted to test the validity of this neuroanatomical account.

The literature does not, however, unequivocally supports this traditional model. Ironically, rival theories to the classical model of "isolation of the speech area" have received considerable attention in recent years (Bando et al., 1986; Berthier, Starkstein et al., 1991; Grossi et al., 1991; Pulvermüller & Schönle, 1993; Trojano et al., 1988) and we are now witnessing the resurgence of historically neglected pathophysiological mechanisms (e.g. role of the right hemisphere in the repetition of TA patients). This is one of the reasons why, through several chapters of this book, I have attempted to provide a different interpretation of neuroanatomical findings. Within this framework, there is a limited but significant body of evidence from the structural and functional neuroimaging information reviewed in Chapter 7, which provides some support for the notion that the left perisylvian language zone may be structurally and/or functionally damaged in some patients with TA (see Grossi et al., 1991; Pulvermüller & Schönle, 1993). Thus, one can speculate that if the left perisylvian cortex is damaged, then repetition and other related linguistic operations (e.g. automatic speech) would be compensated by right hemisphere structures. This argument is supported by recent functional neuroimaging activation studies. Left-hemisphere damaged aphasic patients with either nonfluent or fluent spontaneous speech and variable deficits in auditory comprehension activate the right hemisphere more than the undamaged regions of the left hemisphere during the repetition of words (Belin et al., 1996; Ohyama et al., 1996) and nonwords (Weiller et al., 1995).

Available evidence, though limited, indicates that the right hemisphere participation in language repetition and other expressive functions may vary from one patient to another, but the factors influencing the degree of right hemisphere contribution remains to be determined. I have advanced a number of arguments to explain heterogeneity in TA in several chapters of this book, but it should be noted that the possibility of exploring some of these proposed mechanisms (e.g. individual variability in the organisation of language networks, premorbid proficiency in language, different availability of linguistic resources after brain damage) is still limited and awaits further research.

References

Adair, J.C., Williamson, D.J.G., Schwartz, R.L., & Heilman, K.M. (1996). Ventral tegmental area injury and frontal lobe disorder. *Neurology, 46*, 842–843.

Adams, R., & Victor, M. (1989). *Principles of neurology: Affections of speech and language* (4th ed., pp. 337–395). New York: McGraw-Hill Inc.

Alajouanine, T., Lhermitte, F., Ledoux, M., Renaud, D., & Vignolo, A. (1964). Les composantes phonémiques et sémantiques de la jargonaphasie. *Revue Neurologique, 110*, 5–20.

Albert, M.L., Bachman, D.L., Morgan, A., & Helm-Estabrooks, N. (1988). Pharmacotherapy of aphasia. *Neurology, 38*, 877–879.

Albert, M.L., Goodglass, H., Helm, N.A., Rubens, A.B., & Alexander, M.P. (1981). Dysphasia without repetition disturbance. In G.E. Arnold, F. Winckel, & B.D. Wyke (Eds), *Clinical aspects of dysphasia: Disorders of human communication* (pp. 92–106). Wien/New York: Springer-Verlag.

Alexander, G.E., Crutcher, M.D., & DeLong, M.R. (1990). Basal ganglia-thalamocortical circuits: Parallel substrates for motor, oculomotor "prefrontal" and "limbic" functions. *Progress in Brain Research, 85*, 119–146.

Alexander, G.E., DeLong, M.R., & Strick, P.L. (1986). Parallel organization of functionally segregated circuits linking basal ganglia and cortex. *Annual Review of Neuroscience, 9*, 357–381.

Alexander, M.P., & Annet, M. (1996). Crossed aphasia and related anomalies of cerebral organization: Case reports and a genetic hypothesis. *Brain and Language, 55*, 213–239.

Alexander, M.P., Benson, D.F., & Stuss, D.T. (1989). Frontal lobes and language. *Brain and Language, 37*, 656–691.

Alexander, M.P., Fischette, M.R., & Fischer, R.S. (1989). Crossed aphasias can be mirror image or anomalous: case reports, review and hypothesis. *Brain, 112*, 953–973.

Alexander, M.P., Hiltbrunner, B., & Fischer, R.S. (1989). Distributed anatomy of transcortical sensory aphasia. *Archives of Neurology, 46*, 885–892.

Alexander, M.P., & LoVerme, S.R., Jr. (1980). Aphasia after left hemispheric intracerebral hemorrhage. *Neurology, 30*, 1193–1202.

Alexander, M.P., & Naeser, M.A. (1988). Cortico-subcortical differences in Aphasia. In F. Plum (Ed.), *Language, communication, and the brain* (pp. 215–228). New York: Raven Press.

Alexander, M.P., Naeser, M.A., & Palumbo, C.L. (1987). Correlations of subcortical CT lesion sites and aphasia profiles. *Brain*, *110*, 961–991.

Alexander, M.P., & Schmitt, M.A. (1980). The aphasia syndrome of stroke in the left anterior cerebral territory. *Archives of Neurology*, *37*, 97–100.

Ali Cherif, A., Labrecque, R., Pelissier, J.F., Poncet, M., & Boudouresques, J. (1979). Encéphalopatie souscorticale de Biswanger. Étude d'un cas comportant une atteinte hémisphérique gauche nettement prédominante. *Revue Neurologique*, *135*, 665–679.

Amaral, D.G., Insausti, R., & Cowan, W.M. (1983). Evidence for a direct projection from the superior temporal gyrus to the entorhinal cortex in the monkey. *Brain Research*, *275*, 263–277.

Ames, D., Cummings, J.L., Wirshing, W.C., Quinn, B., & Mahler, M. (1994). Repetitive and compulsive behavior in frontal lobe degenerations. *Journal of Neuropsychiatry and Clinical Neurosciences*, *6*, 100–113.

Ammons, R.B., & Ammons, C.H. (1962). *The quick test*. Missoula, MT: Psychological Test Specialists.

Andy, O.J., & Bhatnagar, S. (1984). Right hemispheric language evidence from cortical stimulation. *Brain and Language*, *23*, 159–166.

Angelergues, R., Hécaen, H., Djindjian, R., & Jarrié-Hazan, N. (1962). Un cas d'aphasie croisée (thrombose de l'artere sylvien droite chez une drotière). *Revue Neurologique*, *107*, 543–545.

Appell, J., Kertesz, A., & Fisman, M. (1982). A study of language functioning in Alzheimer's disease. *Brain and Language*, *17*, 73–91.

Arbib, M.A., Caplan, D., & Marshall, J.C. (1982). Neurolinguistics in historical perspective. In M.A. Arbib, D. Caplan, & J.C. Marshall (Eds), *Neural models of language processes* (pp. 5–24). New York: Academic Press.

Ardila, A., & Lopez, M.V. (1984). Transcortical motor aphasia: One or two aphasias? *Brain and Language*, *22*, 350–353.

Ardila, A., & Roselli, M. (1992). Repetition in aphasia. *Journal of Neurolinguistics*, *7*, 103–113.

Ardila, A., Roselli, M., & Ardila, O. (1988). Foreign accent: An aphasic epiphenomenon. *Aphasiology*, *5*, 21–28.

Assal, G. (1982). Étude neuropsychologique d'une aphasie croisée avec jargonagraphie. *Revue Neurologique*, *138*, 507–515.

Assal, G. (1985). Un aspect du comportment d'utilization: la dépendence vis-à-vis du language écrit. *Revue Neurologique*, *141*, 493–495.

Assal, G., Perentes, E., & Deruaz, J-P. (1981). Crossed aphasia in a right-handed patient: Postmortem findings. *Archives of Neurology*, *38*, 455–458.

Assal, G., Regli, F., Thuillard, F., Steck, A., Deruaz, J.-P., & Perentes, E. (1983). Syndrome d'isolement de la zone du language: étude neuropsychologique et pathologique. *Revue Neurologique*, *139*, 417–424.

Atkinson, M.S. (1971). Transcortical motor aphasia associated with left frontal infarction. *Transactions of the American Neurological Association*, *96*, 136–140.

Au, R., Obler, L.K., & Albert, M.L. (1991). Language in aging and dementia. In M. Taylor Sarno (Ed.), *Acquired aphasia* (2nd ed., pp. 405–423). San Diego, CA: Academic Press.

Bachman, D.L., & Morgan, A. (1988). The role of pharmacotherapy in the treatment of aphasia: Preliminary results. *Aphasiology*, *2*, 225–228.

Baddeley, A. (1986). *Working memory*. Oxford: Oxford University Press.

Baddeley, A. (1996). The concept of working memory. In S.E. Gathercole (Ed.), *Models of short-term memory* (pp. 1–27). Hove, UK: Psychology Press.

Bando, M., Ugawa, Y., & Sugishita, M. (1986). Mechanism of repetition in transcortical sensory aphasia. *Journal of Neurology, Neurosurgery and Psychiatry*, *49*, 200–202.

Baron, J.C., D'Antona, R., Pantano, P., Serdaru, M., Samson, Y., & Bousser, M.G. (1986). Effects of thalamic stroke on energy metabolism of the cerebral cortex. *Brain*, *109*, 1243–1259.

Barraquer-Bordas, L. (1989). The aphasiology of A.R. Luria. *Journal of Neurolinguistics*, *4*, 1–18.

Basso, A., Della Sala, S., & Farabola, M. (1987). Aphasia arising from purely deep lesions. *Cortex, 23*, 29–44.

Basso, A., Gardelli, M., Grassi, M.P., & Mariotti, M. (1989). The role of the right hemisphere in recovery from aphasia: Two case studies. *Cortex, 25*, 555–566.

Basso, A., Lecours, A.R., Moraschini, S., & Vanier, M. (1985). Anatomoclinical correlations of the aphasias as defined through computerized tomography: Exceptions. *Brain and Language, 26*, 201–229.

Bastian, H.C. (1887). On different kinds of aphasia, with special reference to their classification and ultimate pathology. *British Medical Journal, 2*, 931–937, 985–990.

Bauer, R.M., Tobias, B., & Valenstein, E. (1993). Amnesic disorders. In K.M. Heilman & E. Valenstein (Eds), *Clinical neuropsychology* (3rd ed., pp. 523–602). Oxford: Oxford University Press.

Bayles, K.A., & Tomoeda, C.K., & Rein, J.A. (1996). Phrase repetition in Alzheimer's disease: Effect of meaning and length. *Brain and Language, 54*, 246–261.

Beaumont, J.G. (1983). Methods for studying cerebral hemispheric function. In A.W. Young (Ed.), *Functions of the right cerebral hemisphere* (pp. 113–146). London: Academic Press.

Beauvois, M.F., & Dérousné, J. (1979). Phonological alexia: Three dissociations. *Journal of Neurology, Neurosurgery, and Psychiatry, 42*, 1115–1124.

Beauvois, M.-F., & Dérousné, J. (1981) Lexical or orthographic agraphia. *Brain, 104*, 21–50.

Beauvois, M.F., Saillant, B., Meininger, V., & Lhermitte, F. (1978). Bilateral tactile aphasia: A tacto-verbal dysfunction. *Brain, 101*, 381–401.

Beele, K.A., Davis, E., & Muller, D. (1984). Therapists' view on the clinical usefulness of four aphasia tests. *British Journal of Disorders of Communication, 19*, 151–178.

Belin, P., Van Eeckhout, P., Zilbovicius, M., Remy, P., Guillaume, F.S., Chain, F., Rancurel, G., & Samson, Y. (1996). Recovery from nonfluent aphasia after melodic intonation therapy: A PET study. *Neurology, 47*, 1504–1511.

Benjamin, D., & van Hoesen, G.W. (1982). Some afferents of the supplementary motor area (SMA) in the monkey. *Anatomical Record, 202*, 15A.

Benson, D.F. (1975). Disorders of verbal expression. In D.F. Benson & D. Blumer (Eds), *Psychiatric aspects of neurological disease* (pp. 121–136). New York: Grune & Stratton.

Benson, D.F. (1985). Aphasia. In K.M. Heilman & E. Valenstein (Eds), *Clinical neuropsychology* (2nd ed., pp. 17–48). Oxford: Oxford University Press.

Benson, D.F. (1988). Anomia in aphasia. *Aphasiology, 2*, 229–236.

Benson, D.F. (1993). Aphasia. In K.M. Heilman & E. Valenstein (Eds), *Clinical neuropsychology* (3rd ed., pp. 17–36). Oxford: Oxford University Press.

Benson, D.F., & Cummings., J.L. (1985). Agraphia. In J.A.M. Frederiks (Ed.), *Handbook of clinical neurology. Vol. 1 (45): Clinical Neuropsychology* (pp. 457–473). Elsevier Science Publishers.

Benson, D.F., Davis, R.J., & Snyder, B.D. (1988). Posterior cortical atrophy. *Archives of Neurology, 45*, 789–793.

Benson, D.F., & Geschwind, N. (1971). The aphasias and related disturbances. In A.B. Baker & L.H. Baker (Eds), *Clinical neurology* (Vol. 1, pp. 1–26). Hagerstown, MD: Harper & Row.

Benson, D.F., Sheremata, W.A., Bouchard, R., Segarra, J.M., Price, D., & Geschwind, N. (1973). Conduction aphasia. *Archives of Neurology, 28*, 339–346.

Benton, A.L. (1968). Differential behavioral effects of frontal lobe disease. *Neuropsychologia, 6*, 53–60.

Benton, A.L. (1991). Aphasia: Historical perspectives. In M.T. Sarno (Ed.), *Acquired aphasia* (2nd ed., pp. 1–26). Academic Press: New York.

Benton, A.L., & Hamsher, K. de S. (1989). *Multilingual aphasia examination*. Iowa City: Aja Associates.

Berndt, R.S. (1988). Repetition in aphasia: Implication for models of language processing. In F. Boller & J. Grafman (Eds), *Handbook of neuropsychology, Vol. 1* (pp. 329–348). Amsterdam/ Oxford: Elsevier.

Berndt, R.S., Basili, A., & Caramazza, A. (1987). Dissociation of functions in a case of transcortical sensory aphasia. *Cognitive Neuropsychology*, *4*, 79–107.

Berndt, R.S., Haendiges, A.N., & Wosniak, M.A. (1997). Verb retrieval and sentence processing dissociation of an established symptom association. *Cortex*, *33*, 99–114.

Berthier, M.L. (1995). Transcortical sensory aphasia: Dissociation between naming and comprehension. *Aphasiology*, *9*, 431–451.

Berthier, M.L. (1998). Modality-specific utilization behavior: the case of echographia (EG) and hypergraphia (HG). *Journal of the International Neuropsychological Society*, *4*, 208.

Berthier, M.L., Campos, V.M., & Kulisevsky, J. (1996). Echopraxia and self-injurious behavior in Tourette's syndrome. *Neuropsychiatry, Neuropsychology, and Behavioral Neurology*, *9*, 280–283.

Berthier, M.L., Fernández, A.M., Martínez-Celdrán, E., & Kulisevsky, J. (1996). Perceptual and acoustic correlates of affective prosody repetition in transcortical aphasias. *Aphasiology*, *10*, 711–721.

Berthier, M.L., Kulisevsky, J., Gironell, A., & Heras, J.A. (1996). Obsessive-compulsive disorder associated with brain lesions: Clinical phenomenology, cognitive function, and anatomical correlates. *Neurology*, *47*, 353–361.

Berthier, M.L., Leiguarda, R., Starkstein, S.E., Sevlever, G., & Taratuto, A.L. (1991). Alzheimer's disease in a patient with posterior cortical atrophy. *Journal of Neurology, Neurosurgery, and Psychiatry*, *54*, 1110–1111.

Berthier, M.L., Porta, G., Posada, A., & Puentes, C. (1995). Preserved written expression in severe nonfluent aphasia. *Journal of the International Neuropsychological Society*, *1*, 205.

Berthier, M.L., Posada, A., Puentes, C., & Hinojosa, J. (1997). Brain SPECT imaging in transcortical aphasias: The functional status of the left perisylvian language cortex. *European Journal of Neurology*, *4*, 551–560.

Berthier, M.L., Posada, A., Puentes, C., & Hinojosa, J. (in preparation). Reorganisation of language function in the right hemisphere in a case of developmental dysgraphia.

Berthier, M.L., Ruiz, A., Massone, M.I., Starkstein, S.E., & Leiguarda, R. (1991). Foreign accent syndrome. Behavioural and anatomical findings in recovered and non-recovered patients. *Aphasiology*, *5*, 129–147.

Berthier, M.L., Starkstein, S.E., Leiguarda, R., Ruiz, A., Mayberg, H.S., Wagner, H., Price, T.R., & Robinson, R.G. (1991). Transcortical aphasia: Importance of the nonspeech dominant hemisphere in language repetition. *Brain*, *114*, 1409–1427.

Berthier, M.L. Starkstein, S.E., Lylyk, P., & Leiguarda, R. (1990). Differential recovery of languages in a bilingual patient: A case study using selective amytal test. *Brain and Language*, *38*, 449–453.

Bhatnagar, S., & Andy, O.J. (1983). Language in the nondominant hemisphere. *Archives of Neurology*, *40*, 728–731.

Binder, J.F., Rao, S.M., Hammeke, T.A., Frost, J.A., Bandettini, P.A., Jesmanowicz, A., & Hyde, J.S. (1995). Lateralized human brain language systems demonstrated by tasks subtraction functional magnetic resonance imaging. *Archives of Neurology*, *52*, 593–601.

Bishop, D.V.M. (1989). Test for the reception of grammar (2nd ed.). London: Medical Research Council.

Bloom, P.A., & Fischler, I. (1980). Completions norms for 329 sentence contexts. *Memory and Cognition*, *8*, 631–642.

Blumer, D., & Benson, D.F. (1975). Personality changes with frontal and temporal lobe lesions. In D. Blumer & D.F. Benson (Eds), *Psychiatric aspects of neurological disease* (pp. 151–170). New York: Grune & Stratton.

Bogousslavsky, J., Assal, G., & Regli, F. (1987). Infarctus du territorie de l'artere cèrèbrale antèrieure gauche. II: Troubles du language. *Revue Neurologique*, *143*, 121–127.

Bogousslavsky, J., Miklossy, J., Deruaz, J.P., Regli, F., & Assal, G. (1986). Unilateral left paramedian infarction of thalamus and midbrain: A clinico-pathological study. *Journal of Neurology, Neurosurgery, and Psychiatry*, *49*, 686–694.

Bogousslavsky, J., & Regli, F. (1986). Unilateral watershed cerebral infarcts. *Neurology, 36,* 373–377.

Bogousslavsky, J., & Regli, F. (1988). Response-to-next-patient-stimulation: A right hemisphere syndrome. *Neurology, 38,* 1225–1227.

Bogousslavsky, J., Regli, F., & Assal, G. (1988). Acute transcortical mixed aphasia: A carotid occlusion syndrome with pial and watershed infarcts. *Brain, 111,* 631–641.

Bolla-Wilson, K., Speedie, L.J., & Robinson, R.G. (1985). Phonological agraphia in a left-handed patient after a right-hemisphere lesion. *Neurology, 35,* 1778–1781.

Borkowski, J.G., Benton, A.L., & Spreen, O. (1967). Word fluency and brain damage. *Neuropsychologia, 5,* 135–140.

Brådvik, B., Darvins, C., Holtas, S., Rosén, I., Ryding, E., & Ingvar, D.H. (1990). Do single right hemisphere infarcts or transient ischemic attacks results in aprosody? *Acta Neurologica Scandinavica, 81,* 61–70.

Brain, R. (1961). *Speech disorders.* Washington: Butterworth.

Bramwell, B. (1897). Illustrative cases of aphasia. *The Lancet, I,* 1256–1259.

Breen, K., & Warrington, E.K. (1994). A study of anomia: Evidence for a distinction between nominal and propositional language. *Cortex, 30,* 231–245.

Brickner, R. (1940). A human cortical area producing repetitive phenomena when stimulated. *Journal of Neurophysiology, 3,* 128–130.

Brion, S., & Jedinak, C.-P. (1972). Troubles du transfer interhémispherique (*callosal disconnection*). À propos de 3 observations de tumeurs du corps calleux: la signe de la main étrangère. *Revue Neurologique, 126,* 257–266.

Broca, P. (1861). Remarques sur le siége de la faculté du langage articulé, suivies d'une observation d'aphémie (perte de la parole). *Bulletins de la Société d'Anatomie (Paris), 36,* 330–357.

Broca, P. (1863). Localisations des fonctions cérébrales. Siége du langage articulé. *Bulletins de la Société d'Anthropologie de Paris, 4,* 200–220.

Brown, J.W. (1972). *Aphasia, apraxia and agnosia.* Springfield: Thomas.

Brown, J.W. (1975). The problem of repetition: A study of "conduction" aphasia and the "isolation" syndrome. *Cortex, 11,* 37–52.

Brown, J.W. (1982). Hierarchy and evolution in neurolinguistics. In M.A. Arbib, D. Caplan, & J.C. Marshall (Eds), *Neural models of language processes* (pp. 447–467). New York: Academic Press.

Brown, J.W. (1987). *Mind, brain and consciousness: The neuropsychology of cognition.* New York: Academic Press.

Brust, J.C.M., Plank, C., Burke, A., Guobadia, M.M.I., & Healton, E.B. (1982). Language disorder in a right-hander after occlusion of the right anterior cerebral artery. *Neurology, 32,* 492–497.

Bryden, M.P. (1988). Does laterality make any difference? Thoughts on the relation between cerebral asymmetry and reading. In D.L. Molfese & S.J. Segalowitz (Eds), *Brain lateralization in children: Developmental implications.* New York: Guilford Press.

Bub, D., & Kertesz, A. (1982). Evidence for lexicographic processing in a patient with preserved written over oral single word naming. *Brain, 105,* 697–717.

Buckingham, H.W. (1992). Phonological production deficits in conduction aphasia. In S.E. Kohn (Ed.), *Conduction aphasia* (pp. 77–166). Hillsdale, NJ: Lawrence Erlbaum Associates Inc.

Buckingham, H.W., & Kertesz, A. (1974). A linguistic analysis of fluent aphasia. *Brain and Language, 1,* 43–62.

Buschke, H., & Fuld, P.A. (1974). Evaluation of storage, retention, and retrieval in disordered memory and learning. *Neurology, 11,* 1019–1025.

Butterworth, B., & Warrington, E. (1995). Two routes to repetition: Evidence from a case of "deep dysphasia". *Neurocase, 1,* 55–66.

Byng, S., Kay, J., Edmunson, A., & Scott, C. (1990). Aphasia tests reconsidered. *Aphasiology, 4*, 67–91.

Cambier, J., Elghozi, D., & Graveleau, P. (1982). *Neuropsychologie des lésions du thalamus* (Rapport de Neurologie au Congrés de Psychiatrie et de Neurologie de Langue Française) Paris: Masson.

Cambier, J., Elghozi, D., Khoury, M., & Strube, A. (1980). Répétition écholalique et troubles sèvéres de la compréhension: syndrome de dé-activation de l'hémisphère gauche? *Revue Neurologique, 136*, 689–698.

Cambier, J., Elghozi, D., Signoret, J.L., & Henin, D. (1983). Contribution de l'hémisphère droit au language des aphasiques. Disparition de ces langage après lésion droite. *Revue Neurologique, 139*, 55–63.

Cambier, J., Masson, C., Benammou, S., & Robine, B. (1988). La graphomanie. Activité graphique compulsive manifestation d'un gliome fronto-calleux. *Revue Neurologique, 144*, 158–164.

Campbell, R., & Butterworth, B. (1985). Phonological dyslexia and dysgraphia in a highly literate subject: A development case with associated deficits of phonemic processing and awareness. *Quarterly Journal of Experimental Psychology, 37A*, 435–475.

Caplan, D. (1987). *Neurolinguistics and linguistic aphasiology: An introduction.* New York: Cambridge University Press.

Caplan, D. (1992). *Language: Structure, processing, and disorders.* Cambridge, MA: MIT Press.

Caplan, D., & Waters, G. (1992). Issues arising regarding the nature and consequences of reproduction conduction aphasia. In S. Kohn (Ed.), *Conduction aphasia* (pp. 117–149). Mahwah, NJ: Lawrence Erlbaum Associates Inc.

Caplan, L.R., & Zervas, N.T. (1978). Speech arrest in a dextral with a right mesial frontal astrocytoma. *Archives of Neurology, 35*, 252–253.

Cappa, S., Cavallotti, G., & Vignolo, L.A. (1981). Phonemic and lexical errors in fluent aphasia: correlation with lesion site. *Neuropsychologia, 19*, 171–177.

Cappa, S.F., Perani, D., Bressi, S., Paulesu, E., Franceschi, M., & Fasio, F. (1993). Crossed aphasia: a PET follow up study of two cases. *Journal of Neurology, Neurosurgery, and Psychiatry, 56*, 665–671.

Cappa, S.F., & Sterzi, R. (1990). Infarction in the territory of the anterior choroidal artery: A cause of transcortical motor aphasia. *Aphasiology, 4*, 213–217.

Cappa, S.F., & Vallar, G. (1992). The role of the left and right hemispheres in recovery from aphasia. *Aphasiology, 6*, 359–372.

Cappa, S.F., & Vignolo, L.A. (1979). "Transcortical" features of aphasia following left thalamic hemorrhage. *Cortex, 15*, 121–129.

Caramazza, A., Basili, A.G., Koller, J.J., & Berndt, R.S. (1981). An investigation of repetition and language processing in a case of conduction aphasia. *Brain and Language, 14*, 235–271.

Caselli, R.J., Ivnik, R.J., & Duffy, J.R. (1991). Associative anomia: Dissociating words and their definitions. *Mayo Clinic Proceedings, 66*, 783–791.

Chertkow, H., & Bub, D.N. (1990). Semantic memory loss in dementia of the Alzheimer's type: What do the various measures measure? *Brain, 113*, 397–417.

Chui, H.C. (1989). Dementia: A review emphasizing clinicopathologic correlation and brain behavior relationships. *Archives of Neurology, 46*, 806–814.

Chui, H.C., Teng, E.L., Henderson, V.W., & Moy, A.C. (1985). Clinical subtypes of dementia of the Alzheimer type. *Neurology, 35*, 1544–1550.

Cipolotti, L., & Warrington, E.W. (1995). Neuropsychological assessment. *Journal of Neurology, Neurosurgery, and Psychiatry, 58*, 655–664.

Code, C. (1987). *Language, aphasia, and the right hemisphere.* Chichester, UK: Wiley.

Code, C. (1989). Speech automatisms and recurring utterances. In C. Code (Ed.), *The characteristics of aphasia* (pp. 155–177). Hove, UK: Lawrence Erlbaum Associates Ltd.

Code, C. (1997). Can the right hemisphere speak? *Brain and Language, 57*, 38–59.

Colebatch, J.G., Deiber, M.-P., Passingham, R.E., Friston, K.J., & Frackowiak, R.S.J. (1991). Regional cerebral blood flow during voluntary arm and hand movements in human subjects. *Journal of Neurophysiology, 65,* 1392–1401.

Cooper, W., Soares, C., Nicol, J., Michelow, D., & Goloskie, S. (1984). Clausal intonation after unilateral brain damage. *Language and Speech, 27,* 17–24.

Corballis, M.C. (1996). A dissociation in naming digits and colors following commisurotomy. *Cortex, 32,* 515–525.

Coslett, H.B., Gonzalez Rothi, L., & Heilman, K.M. (1985). Reading: Dissociation of the lexical and phonological mechanisms. *Brain and Language, 24,* 20–35.

Coslett, H.B., Roeltgen, D.P., Gonzalez Rothi, L., & Heilman, K.M. (1987). Transcortical sensory aphasia: Evidence for subtypes. *Brain and Language, 32,* 362–378.

Costello, A.L., & Warrington, E.W. (1986). Dynamic aphasia: The selective impairment of verbal planning. *Cortex, 25,* 103–114.

Coughlan, A.K., & Warrington, E.K. (1978). Word-comprehension and word-retrieval in patients with localized cerebral lesions. *Brain, 101,* 163–185.

Cranberg, L.D., Filley, C.M., Hart, E.J., & Alexander, M.P. (1987). Acquired aphasia in childhood: Clinical and CT investigations. *Neurology, 37,* 1165–1172.

Critchley, E.M.R. (1991). Speech and the right hemisphere. *Behavioural Neurology, 4,* 143–151.

Critchley, M. (1964). The neurology of psychotic speech. *British Journal of Psychiatry, 110,* 353–364.

Crockett, D.J. (1977). A comparison of empirically derived groups of aphasics on the Neurosensory Center Comprehensive Examination for Aphasia. *Journal of Clinical Psychology, 33,* 194–198.

Croisile, B., Trillet, M., Hibert, O., Cinotti, L., Le Bars, D., Mauguière, F., & Aimard, G. (1991). Désorders visuo-constructifs et alexie-abraphie associés à une atrophie corticale postérieure. *Revue Neurologique, 147,* 138–143.

Crosson, B. (1985). Subcortical functions in language: A working model *Brain and Language, 25,* 257–292.

Cummings, J.L. (1993). Frontal-subcortical circuits and human behavior. *Archives of Neurology, 50,* 873–880.

Cummings, J.L., Benson, D.F., Hill, M.A., & Read, S. (1985). Aphasia in dementia of the Alzheimer type. *Neurology, 35,* 394–397.

Cummings, J.L., & Duchen, L.W. (1981). Klüver–Bucy syndrome in Pick disease: Clinical and pathological correlations. *Neurology, 31,* 1415–1422.

Damasio, A.R. (1990). Category-related recognition defects as a clue to the neural substrates of knowledge. *Trends in Neuroscience, 13,* 95–98.

Damasio, A.R. (1991). Signs of aphasia. In M. Taylor Sarno (Ed.), *Acquired aphasia* (2nd ed., pp. 27–43). New York: Academic Press.

Damasio, A.R. (1992). Aphasia. *New England Journal of Medicine, 326,* 531–539.

Damasio, A.R., & Anderson, S.W. (1993). The frontal lobes. In K.M. Heilman & E. Valenstein (Eds), *Clinical neuropsychology* (3rd ed., pp. 409–460). New York: Oxford University Press.

Damasio, A.R., & van Hoesen, G.W. (1980). Structure and function of the supplementary motor area. *Neurology, 30,* 359.

Damasio, H. (1991). Neuroanatomical correlates of the aphasias. In M. Taylor Sarno (Ed.), *Acquired aphasia* (pp. 45–71). New York: Academic Press.

Damasio, H., & Damasio, A.R. (1979). "Paradoxic" ear extinction in dichotic listening: Possible anatomic significance. *Neurology, 29,* 644–653.

Danly, M., & Shapiro, B. (1982). Speech prosody in Broca's aphasia. *Brain and Language, 16,* 171–190.

Davis, G.A. (1983). *A survey of adult aphasia.* Englewood Cliffs, NJ: Prentice-Hall.

Davis, L., Foldi, N.S., Gardner, H., & Zurif, E.B. (1978). Repetition in the transcortical aphasias. *Brain and Language, 6,* 226–238.

Deacon, T. (1990). Brain language co-evolution. In J.A. Hawkins & M. Gell-Mahn (Eds), *The evolution of human languages: SFI studies in the science of complexity*. New York: Addison-Wesley.

Degos, J.-D., da Fonseca, N., Gray, F., & Cesaro, P. (1993). Severe frontal syndrome associated with infarcts of the anterior cingulate gyrus and the head of the right caudate nucleus. *Brain, 116*, 1541–1548.

De Keyser, J., Herregodts, P., & Ebinger, G. (1990). The mesoneocortical dopamine neuron system. *Neurology, 40*, 1660–1662.

De La Sayette, V., Le Doze, F., Bouvard, G., Morin, I., Eustache, F., Fiorelli, M., Viader, F., & Morin, P. (1992). Right motor neglect associated with dynamic aphasia, loss of drive and amnesia: Case report and cerebral blood flow study. *Neuropsychologia, 30*, 109–121.

Della Sala, S., Marchetti, C., & Spinnler, H. (1991). Right-sided anarchic (alien) hand: A longitudinal study. *Neuropsychologia, 29*, 1113–1127.

Demeurisse, G., Capon, A., Verhas, M., & Attig, E. (1990). Pathogenesis of aphasia in deep-seated lesions: Likely role of cortical diaschisis. *European Neurology, 30*, 67–74.

Démonet, J.-F., Chollet, F., Ramsay, S., Cardebat, D., Nespoulous, J.-L., Wise, R., Rascol, A., Frackowiak, R. (1992). The anatomy of phonological and semantic processing in normal subjects. *Brain, 115*, 1753–1768.

Démonet, J.F., Puel, M., Celsis, P., & Cardebat, D. (1991). "Subcortical" aphasia: Some proposed pathophysiological mechanism and their CBF correlates revealed by SPECT. *Journal of Neurolinguistics, 6*, 319–344.

Denny-Brown, D. (1956). Positive and negative aspects of cerebral cortical function. *North Carolina Medical Journal, 17*, 295–303.

De Renzi, E., Cavalleri, F., & Facchini, S. (1996). Imitation and utilization behaviour. *Journal of Neurology, Neurosurgery, and Psychiatry, 61*, 396–400.

De Renzi, E., & Faglioni, P. (1978). Normative data and screening power of a shortened version of the Token test. *Cortex, 14*, 41–49.

De Renzi, E., & Vignolo, L.A. (1962). The token test: A sensitive test to detect receptive disturbances in aphasics. *Brain, 85*, 665–678.

Diesfeldt, H.F.A. (1989). Semantic impairment in senile dementia of the Alzheimer type. *Aphasiology, 3*(1), 41–54.

Diesfeldt, H.F.A. (1991). Impaired phonological reading in primary degenerative dementia. *Brain, 114*, 1631–1646.

Dobkin, J.A., Levine, R.L., Lagreze, H.L., Dulli, D.A., Nickles, R.J., & Rowe, B.R. (1989). Evidence for transhemispheric diaschisis in unilateral stroke. *Archives of Neurology, 46*, 1333–1336.

Dogil, G., Haider, H., Schaner-Wolles, C., & Husmann, R. (1995). Radical autonomy of syntax: Evidence from transcortical sensory aphasia. *Aphasiology, 9*, 577–602.

Duhamel, J.R., & Poncet, M. (1986). Deep dysphasia in a case of phonemic deafness: Role of the right hemisphere in auditory language comprehension. *Neuropsychologia, 24*, 769–779.

Ellis, A.W. (1984). Introduction to Byron Bramwell's (1897) case of word-meaning deafness. *Cognitive Neuropsychology, 1*, 245–258.

Ellis, A.W. (1985). The production of spoken words: A cognitive neuropsychological perspective. In A.W. Ellis (Ed.), *Progress in the psychology of language*, (Vol. 2, pp. 107–145). Hove, UK: Lawrence Erlbaum Associates Ltd.

Ellis, A.W., & Young, A.W. (1988). *Human cognitive neuropsychology*. Hove, UK: Lawrence Erlbaum Associates Ltd.

Ellis, A.W., Young, A.W., & Critchley, E.M.R. (1989). Intrusive automatic or nonpropositional inner speech following bilateral cerebral injury. *Aphasiology, 3*, 581–585.

Erickson, T.J., & Woosley, C.N. (1951). Observations of the supplementary motor area of man. *Transactions of the American Neurological Association, 76*, 50–56.

Eslinger, P.J., Warner, G.C., Grattan, L.M., & Easton, J.D. (1991). "Frontal lobe" utilization behavior associated with paramedian thalamic infarction. *Neurology, 41*, 450–452.

Esmonde, T., Giles, E., Xuereb, J., & Hodges, J. (1996). Progressive supranuclear palsy presenting with dynamic aphasia. *Journal of Neurology, Neurosurgery, and Psychiatry, 61*, 403–410.

Fay, W.H. (1967). Childhood echolalia: A group study of late abatement. *Folio-Phoniat, 19*, 297–506.

Ferro, J.M. (1984). Transient inaccuracy in reaching caused by a posterior parietal lobe lesion. *Journal of Neurology, Neurosurgery, and Psychiatry, 47*, 1016–1019.

Ford, R.A. (1989). The psychopathology of echophenomena. *Psychological Medicine, 19*, 627–635.

Fournet, F., Virat-Brassaud, M.E., Guard, O., Dumas, R., Auplat, P., & Marchal, G. (1987). Alexie-agraphie croisée chez un droitier. *Revue Neurologique, 143*, 214–219.

Frackowiak, R.S.J. (1994). Functional mapping of verbal memory and language. *Trends in Neurosciences, 17*, 109–115.

Freedman, M., Alexander, M.P., & Naeser, M.A. (1984). Anatomic basis of transcortical motor aphasia. *Neurology, 34*, 409–417.

Freud, S. (1953). *On aphasia: A critical study*. Zur Auffassung der Aphasien. Eine kritische Studie. (E. Stengel, Trans.). New York: International Universities Press. (Original work published 1891)

Fried, I., Katz, A., McCarthy, G., Sass, K.J., Williamson, P., Spencer, S.S., & Spencer, D.D. (1991). Functional organization of human supplementary motor cortex studied by electrical stimulation. *Journal of Neuroscience, 11*(11), 3656–3666.

Friedman, R.F., Ween, J.E., & Albert, M.L. (1993). Alexia. In K.M. Heilman & E. Valenstein (Eds), *Clinical neuropsychology* (2nd ed., pp. 37–62). New York: Oxford University Press.

Frith, C.D., Friston, K.J., Liddle, P.F., & Frackowiak, R.S.J. (1991). A PET study of word finding. *Neuropsychologia, 29*, 1137–1148.

Fujii, T., Yamadori, A., Fukatsu, R., Ogawa, T., & Suzuki, K. (1997). Crossed mixed transcortical aphasia with hypernomia. *European Neurology, 37*, 193–194.

Gainotti, G. (1987). The status of semantic lexical structures in anomia. *Aphasiology, 1*, 449–461.

Gainotti, G. (1993). The role of the right hemisphere in recovery from aphasia. *European Journal of Disorders of Communication, 28*, 227–246.

Gandour, J., Holasult-Petty, S.H., & Dardarananda, R. (1989). Dysprosody in Broca's aphasia: A case study. *Brain and Language, 37*, 232–257.

Gardner H., & Winner, E. (1978). A study of repetition in aphasic patients. *Brain and Language, 6*, 168–178.

Garrard, P., Perry, R., & Hodges, J.R. (1997). Editorial. Disorders of semantic memory. *Journal of Neurology, Neurosurgery, and Psychiatry, 62*, 431–435.

Gasquoine, P.G. (1993). Alien hand sign. *Journal of Clinical and Experimental Neuropsychology, 15*, 653–667.

Gazzaniga, M.S., Eliassen, J.C., Nisenson, L., Wessinger, C.M., Frendrich, R., & Baynes, K. (1996). Collaboration between the hemispheres of a callosotomy patient. Emerging right hemisphere speech and the left hemisphere interpreter. *Brain, 119*, 1255–1262.

Geschwind, N. (1963). Carl Wernicke, the Breslau School and the history of aphasia. In E.C. Carterette (Ed.), *Brain function: Vol. III. Speech, language, and communication* (pp. 1–16). Berkeley: University of California Press.

Geschwind, N. (1964a). "Non-aphasic disorders of speech". *International Journal of Neurology, 4*, 207–214.

Geschwind, N. (1964b). The paradoxical position of Kurt Goldstein in the history of aphasia. *Cortex, 1*, 214–224.

Geschwind, N. (1965). Disconnexion syndromes in animals and man. Parts I and II. *Brain, 88*, 237–294, 585–644.

Geschwind, N., Quadfasel, F.A., & Segarra, J.M. (1968). Isolation of the speech area. *Neuropsychologia, 6*, 327–340.

Ghika, J., Bogousslavsky, J., Ghika-Schmid, F., & Regli, F. (1996). "Echoing approval": A new speech disorder. *Journal of Neurology, 243*, 633–637.

Glosser, G., Kaplan, E., & LoVerme, S. (1982). Longitudinal neuropsychological report of aphasia following left subcortical hemorrhage. *Brain and Language, 15*, 95–116.

Glosser, G., Kohn, S.E., Friedman, R.B., Sands, L., & Grugan, P. (1997). Repetition of single words and nonwords in Alzheimer's disease. *Cortex, 23*, 653–666.

Gold, M., Nadeau, S.E., Jacobs, D.H., Adair, J.C., Gonzalez Rothi, L., & Heilman, K.M. (1997). Adynamic aphasia: A transcortical motor aphasia with defective semantic strategy formation. *Brain and Language, 57*, 374–393.

Goldberg, G. (1985). Supplementary motor area structure and function: Review and hypothesis. *The Behavioral and Brain Sciences, 8*, 567–616.

Goldberg, G., Mayer, N.H., & Toglia, J.U. (1981). Medial frontal cortex infarction and the alien hand sign. *Archives of Neurology, 38*, 683–686.

Goldstein, K. (1915). *Die Transkortikalen Aphasien*. Ergebnisse Neurologie und Psychiatrie. Jena: G. Fischer.

Goldstein, K. (1917). *Die Transkortikalen Aphasien*. Ergebnisse Neurologie und Psychiatrie. Jena: G. Fischer.

Goldstein, K. (1948). Pictures of speech disturbances due to impairment of the non-language mental performances. In *Language and language disturbances* (pp. 292–309). New York: Grune & Stratton.

Gonzalez Rothi, L.J. (1997). Afasias transcorticales motoras, sensoriales y mixtas. In L.L. LaPointe (Ed.), *Afasia y trastornos neurógenos del lenguaje, Vol. 4* (2nd ed., pp. 103–125). Barcelona, Spain: Doyma.

Goodglass, H. (1980). Disorders of naming following brain injury. *American Scientist, 68*, 647–655.

Goodglass, H. (1992). Diagnosis of conduction aphasia. In S. Kohn (Ed.), *Conduction aphasia* (pp. 39–49). Hillsdale, NJ: Lawrence Erlbaum Associates Inc.

Goodglass, H., & Budin, C. (1988). Category and modality specific dissociations in word comprehension and concurrent phonological dyslexia. *Neuropsychologia, 26*, 67–78.

Goodglass, H., & Kaplan, E. (1983). *Boston Diagnostic Aphasia Examination (BDAE)*. Philadelphia: Lea & Febiger. Distributed by Psychological Assessment Resources, Odessa, FL.

Goodglass, H., Wingfield, A., Hyde, M.R., & Theurkauf, J.C. (1986). Category specific dissociation—in naming and recognition by aphasic patients. *Cortex, 22*, 87–102.

Gordon, B., Hart, J., Lesser, R., Schwerdt, P., Bare, M., Fisher, R., Krauss, G., Uematsu, S., & Selnes, O. (1990). Individual variations in perisylvian language representation. *Neurology, 40*, 172.

Graff-Radford, N.R., Cooper, W.E., Colsher, P.L., & Damasio, A.R. (1986). An unlearned foreign "accent" in a patient with aphasia. *Brain and Language, 28*, 86–94.

Graves, R., Goodglass, H., & Landis, T. (1982). Mouth asymmetry during spontaneous speech. *Neuropsychologia, 20*, 371–381.

Graves, R., & Landis, T. (1985). Hemispheric control of speech expression in aphasia: A mouth asymmetry study. *Archives of Neurology, 42*, 249–251.

Gregory, C.A., & Hodges, J.R. (1996). Frontotemporal dementia: Use of consensus criteria and prevalence of psychiatric features. *Neuropsychiatry, Neuropsychology, and Behavioral Neurology, 9*, 145–153.

Grossi, D., Trojano, L., Chiacchio, L., Soricelli, A., Mansi, L., Postiglione, A., & Salvatore, M. (1991). Mixed transcortical aphasia: Clinical features and neuroanatomical correlates. A possible role of the right hemisphere. *European Neurology, 31*, 204–211.

Grossman, M., D'Esposito, M., Hughes, E., Onishi, K., Biassou, N., White-Devine, T., & Robinson, K.M. (1996). Language comprehension profiles in Alzheimer's disease, multi-infarct dementia, and frontotemporal degeneration. *Neurology, 47*, 183–189.

Grossman, M., Mickaning, J., Onishi, K., Peltzer, L., Ding, X.S., Alavi, A., & Reivich, M. (1993). The cerebral substrate for partial recovery in a fluent aphasic following stroke: A positron emission tomography activation study. *Annals of Neurology, 34*, 248.

Gupta, S.R., & Mlcoch, A.G. (1992). Bromocriptine treatment of nonfluent aphasia. *Archives of Physical Medical Rehabilitation, 73,* 373–376.

Gupta, S.R., Mlcoch, A.G., Scolaro, C., & Moritz, T. (1995). Bromocriptine treatment of nonfluent aphasia. *Neurology, 45,* 2170–2173.

Habib, M., Démonet, J.F., & Frackowiak, R. (1996). Neuroanatomie cognitive du language: contribution del'imagerie fonctionnelle cérébrale. *Revue Neurologique (Paris), 152,* 249–260.

Hadano, K., Tanaka, H., Miyake, T., Tsuji, A., Ishiguro, S., Hashizume, S.M., & Hamanaka, T. (1992). Transcortical sensory aphasia caused by ischemic lesion of the left frontal lobe. *Journal of Clinical and Experimental Neuropsychology, 14,* 374.

Hadano, K., Nakamura, H., & Hamanaka, T. (1998). Effortful echolalia. *Cortex, 34,* 67–82.

Hadar, U., Jones, C., & Mate-Kole, C. (1987). The disconnection in anomic aphasia between semantic and phonological lexicons. *Cortex, 23,* 505–517.

Hadar, U., Ticehurst, S., & Wade, J.P. (1991). Crossed anomic aphasia: Mild naming deficits following right brain damage in a dextral. *Cortex, 27,* 459–468.

Hammond, A. (1882). *A treatise on the diseases of the nervous system* (7th ed.). London.

Hart, J., & Gordon, B. (1990). Delineation of single word semantic comprehension deficits in aphasia with anatomical correlation. *Annals of Neurology, 27,* 226–231.

Hart, S. (1989). Language and dementia: A review. *Psychological Medicine, 18,* 99–112.

Head, H. (1920). Aphasia and kindred disorders of speech. *Brain, 43,* 355–528.

Head, H. (1926). *Aphasia and kindred disorders of speech.* London: Cambridge University Press.

Hécaen, H., De Agostini, M., & Monzon-Montes, A. (1981). Cerebral organization in left-handers. *Brain and Language, 12,* 261–284.

Heilman, K.M. (1985). *Transcortical sensory aphasia.* Paper presented the 37th meeting of the American Academy of Neurology, Dallas, Texas. *Neurology, 35,* (Suppl. 1) 48–49.

Heilman, K.M. (1993). A response to Van Lancker and Sidtis (1992). *Journal of Speech and Hearing Research, 36,* 1191.

Heilman, K.M., Bowers, D., Speedie, L., & Coslett, H.B. (1984). Comprehension of affective and nonaffective prosody. *Neurology, 34,* 917–921.

Heilman, K.M., & Gonzalez Rothi, L.J. (1993). Apraxia. In K.M. Heilman & E. Valenstein (Eds), *Clinical neuropsychology* (pp. 141–163). New York: Oxford University Press.

Heilman, K.M., Rothi, L., McFarling, D., & Rottmann, A.L. (1981). Transcortical sensory aphasia with relatively spared spontaneous speech and naming. *Archives of Neurology, 38,* 236–239.

Heilman, K.M., Tucker, D.M., & Valenstein E. (1976). A case of mixed transcortical aphasia with intact naming. *Brain, 99,* 415–426.

Heiss, W.-D., Kessler, J., Karbe, H.S., Fink, G.R., & Pawlik, G. (1993). Cerebral glucose metabolism as a predictor of recovery from aphasia in ischemic stroke. *Archives of Neurology, 50,* 958–964.

Henderson, V.W. (1992). Early concepts of conduction aphasia. In S.E. Kohn (Ed.), *Conduction aphasia* (pp. 23–38). Hillsdale, NJ: Lawrence Erlbaum Associates Inc.

Henschen, S.E. (1920–1922). *Klinische und Anatomische Beitrage zur Pathologie des Gehirns, Vols. 5–7.* Stockholm: Nordisik Bokhandeln.

Hier, D.B., Hangelocker, K., & Shindler, A.G. (1985). Language disintegration in dementia: Effects of etiology and severity. *Brain and Language, 25,* 117–133.

Hier, D.B., Mogil, S.I., Rubin, N.P., & Komros, G.R. (1980). Semantic aphasia: A neglected entity. *Brain and Language, 10,* 120–131.

Hier, D.B., & Mohr, J.P. (1977). Incongruous oral and written naming: Evidence for a subdivision of the syndrome of Wernicke's aphasia. *Brain and Language, 4,* 115–126.

Hodges, J.R., Patterson, K., Oxbury, S., & Funnell, E. (1992). Semantic dementia: Progressive fluent aphasia with temporal lobe atrophy, *Brain, 115,* 1783–1806.

Hodges, J.R., Patterson, K., & Tyler, L.K. (1994). Loss of semantic memory: Implications for the modularity of mind. *Cognitive Neuropsychology, 11,* 505–542.

Holland, A.L., Boller, F., & Bourgeois, M. (1986). Repetition in Alzheimer's disease: A longitudinal study. *Journal of Neurolinguistics, 2,* 163–177.

Howard, D., & Orchard-Lisle, V. (1984). On the origin of semantic errors in naming: Evidence from a case of a global aphasic. *Cognitive Neuropsychology, 1,* 163–190.

Howard, D., Patterson, K., Wise, R., Brown, W.D., Friston, K., Weiller, C., & Frackowiak, R. (1992). The cortical localization of lexicons: Positron emission tomography evidence. *Brain, 115,* 1769–1782.

Howard, R., & Ford, R. (1992). From the jumping Frenchmen of Maine to post-traumatic stress disorder: The startle response in neuropsychiatry. *Psychological Medicine, 22,* 695–707.

Howlin, P. (1982). Echolalic and spontaneous phrase speech in autistic children. *Journal of Child Psychology and Psychiatry, 23,* 281–293.

Huber, W., Poeck, K., Weniger, D., & Willmes, K. (1983). *Der Aachener Aphasie Test (AAT).* Göttingen: Hogrefe Verlag.

Huber, W., Poeck, K., & Willmes, K. (1984). The Aachen Aphasia test. In F. Clifford Rose (Ed.), *Advances in neurology: Vol. 42. Progress in aphasiology* (pp. 291–303). New York: Raven Press.

Hübner, O. (1889). Über Aphasie. *Schmidt's Jahrbucher, Leipzig, 224,* 220–222.

Humphreys, G.H., & Riddoch, M.J. (1987). On telling your fruits from your vegetables: A consideration of category-specific deficits after brain damage. *Trends in Neurosciences, 10,* 145–148.

Ibayashi, K., Tanaka, R., Joanette, Y., & Lecours, A.R. (1992). Neuropsychological study in patients with thalamic and putamenal hemorrhage. *Journal of Neurolinguistics, 7,* 217–240.

Imura, T. (1943). Aphasia: Characteristic symptoms in Japanese. *Psychiatria et Neurologia Japonica, 47,* 605–633.

Ingvar, D.H., & Schwartz, M.S. (1974). Blood flow patterns induced in the dominant hemisphere by speech and reading. *Brain, 97,* 273–288.

Insausti, R., Amaral, D.G., & Cowan, W.M. (1987). The entorhinal cortex of the monkey: Pt. II. Cortical afferents. *Journal of Comparative Neurology, 264,* 356–395.

Irigaray, L. (1973). *Le language des déments.* The Hague: Mouton.

Jackson, J.H. (1958). On the nature of the duality of the brain. In J. Taylor (Ed.), *Selected writings of John Hughlings Jackson, Vol. 2.* New York: Basic Books. (Original work published 1874)

Jacome, D.E. (1984). Aphasia with elation, hypermusia, musicophilia and compulsive whistling. *Journal of Neurology, Neurosurgery, and Psychiatry, 47,* 308–310.

Janicek, M.L., Schwartz, R.B., Carvalho, P.A., Garada, B., & Holman, B.L. (1993). Tc-99 HMPAO brain perfusion in acute aphasia: Correlation with clinical and structural findings. *Clinical Nuclear Medicine, 18,* 1032–1038.

Joanette, Y., Gouler, P., & LeDorze, G. (1988). Impaired word naming in right-brain-damaged right-handers: Error types and time-course analysis. *Brain and Language, 34,* 54–64.

Joanette, Y., Lecours, A.R., Lepage, Y., & Lamoureux, M. (1983). Language in right-handers with right-hemisphere lesions: A preliminary study including anatomical, genetic, and social factors. *Brain and Language, 20,* 217–284.

Jonas, S. (1981). The supplementary motor region and speech emission. *Journal of Communication Disorders, 14,* 349–373.

Jones, E.G., & Powell, T.P.S. (1970). An anatomical study of converging sensory pathways within the cerebral cortex of the monkey. *Brain, 93,* 793–820.

Joseph, A.B. (1986). A hypergraphic syndrome of automatic writing, affective disorder, and temporal lobe epilepsy in two patients. *Journal of Clinical Psychiatry, 47,* 255–257.

Juilland, A., & Chang-Rodriguez, E. (1964). *Frequency dictionary of Spanish words.* The Hague/London: Mouton.

Jürgens, U., Kirzinger, A., & von Cramon, D. (1982). The effects of deep reaching lesions in the cortical face area on phonation: A combined case report and experimental monkey study. *Cortex, 18,* 125–140.

Jürgens, U., & von Cramon, D. (1982). On the role of the anterior cingulate cortex on phonation: A case report. *Brain and Language, 15,* 234–248.

Kanner, L. (1946). Irrelevant and metaphorical language in early infantile autism. *American Journal of Psychiatry, 103*, 242–246.

Kaplan, E., Goodglass, H., & Weintraub, S. (1983). *The Boston naming test.* New York: Lea & Febiger.

Kapur, N., & Dunkley, B. (1984). Neuropsychological analysis of a case of crossed dysphasia verified at postmortem. *Brain and Language, 23*, 134–147.

Kataki, M., Winikates, J., Kirkpatrick, J., & Doody, R. (1996). Longitudinal study of aphasia in Creutzfeld-Jakob disease. *Neuropsychiatry, Neuropsychology, and Behavioral Neurology, 9*, 284–287.

Katz, R., & Goodglass, H. (1990). Deep dysphasia: Analysis of a rare for of repetition disorder. *Brain and Language, 39*, 153–185.

Kay, J., & Ellis, A.W. (1987). A cognitive neuropsychological case study of anomia: Implications for psychological models of word retrieval. *Brain, 110*, 613–629.

Kay, J., Lesser, R., & Coltheart, M. (1992). *Psycholinguistic assessment of language processing in aphasia.* Hove, UK: Lawrence Erlbaum Associates Ltd.

Kemper, S., LaBarge, E., Ferraro, R., Cheung, H., & Storandt, M. (1993). On the preservation of syntax in Alzheimer's disease. *Archives of Neurology, 50*, 81–86.

Kempler, D., Curtiss, S., & Jackson, C. (1987). Syntactic comprehension in Alzheimer's disease. *Journal of Speech and Hearing Research, 30*, 343–350.

Kempler, D., Metter, J., Jackson, C.A., Hanson, W.R., Riege, W.M., Mazziotta, J.C., & Phelps, M.E. (1988). Disconnection of cerebral metabolism: The case of conduction aphasia. *Archives of Neurology, 45*, 275–279.

Kent, R.D., & Rosenbek, J.C. (1982). Prosodic disturbance and neurologic lesion. *Brain and Language, 15*, 259–291.

Kertesz, A. (1979). *Aphasia and associated disorders: Taxonomy, localization, and recovery.* New York: Grune & Stratton.

Kertesz, A. (1982). *The Western aphasia battery.* New York: Grune & Stratton.

Kertesz, A. (1984). Recovery from aphasia. In F.C. Rose (Ed.), *Advances in neurology: Vol. 42. Progress in Aphasiology* (pp. 23–39). New York: Raven Press.

Kertesz, A. (1993). *Primary progessive aphasia and other focal progressive disorders of cognition.* Paper presented at the International Neuropsychological Society workshop, Madeira, Portugal, 23 June.

Kertesz, A., & Benson, D.F. (1970). Neologistic jargon: A clinicopathological study. *Cortex, 6*, 362–386.

Kertesz, A., & Ferro, J.M. (1984). Lesion size and location in ideomotor apraxia. *Brain, 107*, 921–933.

Kertesz, A., Harlock, W., & Coates, R. (1979). Computer-tomographic localization, lesion size and prognosis in aphasia and non-verbal impairment. *Brain and Language, 8*, 34–50.

Kertesz, A., Lesk, D., & McCabe, P. (1977). Isotope localization of infarcts in aphasia. *Archives of Neurology, 34*, 590–601.

Kertesz, A., Polk, M., & Kirk, A. (1992). Visuoverbal dissociation and semantic deficit in dementia. *Journal of Clinical and Experimental Neuropsychology, 14*, 374.

Kertesz, A., Sheppard, A., & MacKenzie, R. (1982). Localization in transcortical sensory aphasia. *Archives of Neurology, 39*, 475–478.

Kinsbourne, M. (1971). The minor hemisphere as a source of aphasic speech. *Archives of Neurology, 25*, 302–306.

Kleist, K. (1934). *Gehirnpathologie.* Liepzig: Barth.

Klipper, M., & Trénaunay, P. (1900). Du naevus variqueux ostéo-hypertrophique. *Archives General Medicine (Paris), 3*, 641–672.

Klüver, H., & Bucy, P. (1937). "Psychic blindness" and other symptoms following bilateral temporal lobectomy in rhesus monkeys. *American Journal of Physiology, 119*, 352–353.

Knopman, D.S., Selnes, O.A., Niccum, N., & Rubens, A.B. (1984). Recovery of naming in aphasia: relationship to fluency, comprehension and CT findings. *Neurology, 34*, 1461–1470.

Kohn, S.E. (1992). Toward a working definition of conduction aphasia. In S.E. Kohn (Ed.), *Conduction aphasia* (pp. 151–156). Hillsdale, NJ: Lawrence Erlbaum Associates Inc.

Kohn, S.E., & Friedman, R.B. (1986). Word-meaning deafness: A phonological–semantic dissociation. *Cognitive Neuropsychology, 3*(3), 291–308.

Kornhuber, H.H., & Deecke, L. (1985). The starting function of the SMA. Commentary to G. Golberg, Supplementary motor area structure and function: Review and hypothesis. *Behavioral and Brain Sciences, 8*, 567–616.

Körney, É. (1975). Aphasie transcorticale et écholalie: le problème de l'initiative de la parole. *Revue Neurologique, 131*, 347–363.

Kramer, W. (1972). Kippel–Trenaunay syndrome. In P.J. Vinken & G.W. Bruyn (Eds), *Handbook of clinical neurology: The phakomatoses* (Vol. 14, pp. 390–404). New York: Elsevier.

Kremin, H. (1986). Spared naming without comprehension. *Journal of Neurolinguistics, 2*, 131–150.

Kurata, K. (1992). Somatotopy in the human supplementary motor area. *Trends in Neurosciences, 15*, 159–160.

Kussmaul, A. (1877). *Die Storungen der Sprache* (pp. 581–875). Leipzig: Vogel.

Ladd, D.R., Silverman, K.E.A., Tolkmitt, F., Bergmann, G., & Scherer, K.R. (1985). Evidence for the independent function of intonation contour type, voice quality, and fundamental frequency range in signaling speaker affect. *Journal of the Acoustical Society of America, 78*, 435–444.

Lanoe, Y., Pedetti, L., Lanoe, A., Mayer, J.M., & Evrard, S. (1994). Aphasie par lésion isolée du centre semi-ovale: apport de la mesure du débit sanguin cérébral. *Revue Neurologique, 150*, 430–434.

Larsen, B., Skinhoj, E., & Lassen, N.A. (1978). Variation in regional cortical blood flow in the right and left hemisphere during automatic speech. *Brain, 101*, 193–209.

Lazar, R.M., Marshall, R.S., Pile-Spellman, J., Hacein-Bey, L., Young, W.L., & Mohr, J.P. (1997). Unpredicted redistribution of higher cognitive function in patients with AVM. *Neurology, 48*, A292.

Lebrun, Y. (1987). Anosognosia in aphasia. *Cortex, 23*, 251–263.

Lebrun, Y. (1993). Repetitive phenomena in aphasia. In G. Blanken, J. Dittmann, H. Grimm, J.C. Marshall, & C.-W. Wallesch (Eds), *Linguistic disorders and pathologies: An international handbook*. Berlin/New York: Walter de Gruyter.

Lebrun, Y. (1995). Luria's notion of (frontal) dynamic aphasia. *Aphasiology, 9*, 171–180.

Lebrun, Y., Lessinnes, A., De Vresse, L., & Leleux, C. (1985). Dysprosody and the non-dominant hemisphere. *Language and Sciences, 7*, 41–52.

Lebrun, Y., Rubio, S., Jongen, E., & Demol, O. (1971). On echolalia, echo-answer, and contamination. *Acta Neurologica Belgica, 71*, 301–308.

Leckman, J.F., Walker, D.E., & Cohen, D.J. (1993). Premonitory urges in Tourette's syndrome. *American Journal of Psychiatry, 150*, 98–102.

Lecours, A.R., Osborn, E., Travis, L., Rouillon, F., & Lavallée-Huynh, G. (1981). Jargons. In J. Brown (Ed.), *Jargonaphasia* (pp. 9–38). New York: Academic Press.

Lecours, A.R., & Rouillon, F. (1976). Neurolinguistic analysis of jargonaphasia and jargonagraphia. In H. Whitaker & H.A. Whitaker (Eds), *Studies in neurolinguistics* (Vol. 2, pp. 95–144). New York: Academic Press.

Lecours, A.R., & Vanier-Clément, M. (1976). Schizophasia and jargonaphasia: A comparative description with comments on Chaika's and Fromkin's looks at "schizophrenic language". *Brain and Language, 3*, 516–565.

Lees, A.J. (1985). Tics and related disorders. *Clinical neurology and neurosurgery monographs, Vol 7*. New York: Churchill Livingstone.

Leiguarda, R., Berthier, M., & Rubio, S. (1984). Afasia transcortical sensorial producida por hemorragia talámica. *Revista Neurológica Argentina, 10*(2), 131–132.

Leiguarda, R., Lees, A.J., Merello, M., Starkstein, S., & Marsden, C.D. (1994). The nature of apraxia in corticobasal degeneration. *Journal of Neurology, Neurosurgery, and Psychiatry, 57*, 455–459.

Leiguarda, R., Merello, M., Sabe, L., & Starkstein, S. (1993). Bromocriptine-induced dystonia in patients with aphasia and hemiparesis. *Neurology, 43*, 2319–2322.

Leiguarda, R., Starkstein, S., & Berthier, M. (1989). Anterior callosal haemorrhage: A partial interhemispheric disconnection syndrome. *Brain, 112*, 1019–1037.

Lesser, R. (1989). Selective preservation of oral spelling without semantics in a case of multi-infarct dementia. *Cortex, 25*, 239–250.

Levine, D.N., Lee, J.M., & Fisher, C.M. (1993). The visual variant of Alzheimer's disease: A clinicopathological case study. *Neurology, 43*, 305–313.

Lezak, M. (1995). *Neuropsychological assessment* (3rd ed.). New York: Oxford University Press.

Lhermitte, F. (1983). "Utilization behaviour" and its relation to lesions of the frontal lobes. *Brain, 106*, 237–255.

Lhermitte, F. (1984). Language disorders and their relationship to thalamic lesions. In F.C. Rose (Ed.), *Advances in neurology: Vol. 42. Progress in aphasiology* (pp. 99–113). New York: Raven Press.

Lhermitte, F., Pillon, B., & Serdaru, M. (1986). Human autonomy and the frontal lobes. Part I: Imitation and utilization behavior: A neuropsychological study of 75 patients. *Annals of Neurology, 19*, 326–334.

Lichtheim, L. (1885). On aphasia. *Brain, 7*, 433–484.

Lieberman, P., & Michaels, S.B. (1962). Some aspects of fundamental frequency and amplitude as related to the emotional content of speech. *Journal of the Acoustical Society of America, 34*, 922–927.

Liebson, E., Walsh, M.J. Jankowiak, J., & Albert, M.L. (1994). Pharmacotherapy for posttraumatic dysarthria. *Neuropsychiatry, Neuropsychology, and Behavioral Neurology, 7*, 122–124.

Lilly, R., Cummings, J.L., Benson, F., & Frankel, M. (1983). The human Klüver–Bucy syndrome. *Neurology, 33*, 1141–1145.

Lippa, C.F., Cohen, R., Smith, T.W., & Drachman, D.A. (1991). Primary progressive aphasia with focal neural achromasia. *Neurology, 41*, 882–886.

Locke, J.L. (1997). A theory of neurolinguistic development. *Brain and Language, 58*, 265–326.

Lund and Manchester Groups. (1994). Clinical and neuropsychological criteria for frontotemporal dementia. *Journal of Neurology, Neurosurgery, and Psychiatry, 57*, 416–418.

Luria, A.R. (1970). *Traumatic aphasia*. The Hague: Mouton.

Luria, A.R., & Hutton, J.T. (1977). A modern assessment of the basic forms of aphasia. *Brain and Language, 4*, 129–151.

Luria, A.R., & Tsvetkova, L.S. (1968). The mechanism of "dynamic aphasia". *Foundations of Language, 4*, 296–307.

Lytton, W.W., & Brust, J.C.M. (1989). Direct dyslexia: Preserved oral reading of real words in Wernicke's aphasia. *Brain, 112*, 583–594.

Mackenzie Ross, S.J., Graham, N., Stuart-Green, L., Prins, M., Xuereb, J., Patterson, K., & Hodges, J.R. (1996). Progressive biparietal atrophy: An atypical presentation of Alzheimer's disease. *Journal of Neurology, Neurosurgery, and Psychiatry, 61*, 388–395.

MacLennan, D.L., Nicholas, L.E., Morley, G.K., & Brookshire, R.H. (1991). The effects of bromocriptine on speech and language function in a patient with transcortical motor aphasia. In T.E. Prescott (Ed.), *Clinical aphasiology, Vol. 20*. Boston: College Hill.

Maeshima, S., Komai, N., Kinoshita, Y., Ueno, M., Nakai, E., Naka, Y., Tsuji, N., & Imai, H. (1992). Transcortical sensory aphasia following the unilateral left thalamic infarction—a case report. *Journal of Neurolinguistics, 7*, 251–259.

Magnan, H. (1880). On simple aphasia, and aphasia with incoherence. *Brain, 2*(1), 112–123.

Margolin, D.I. (1991). Cognitive neuropsychology: Resolving enigmas about Wernicke's aphasia and other higher cortical disorders. *Archives of Neurology, 48*, 751–765.

Marie, P. (1906). Révision de la question de l'aphasie: La troisième convolution frontale gauche ne joue aucun role speciale dans la fonction du language. *Semaine Medicale, 21*, 241–247.

Martin, N., & Saffran, E.M. (1990). Repetition and verbal STM in transcortical sensory aphasia. *Brain and Language, 39,* 254–288.

Martin, N., & Saffran, E.M. (1992). A connectionist account of deep dysphasia: Evidence from a single case study. *Brain and Language, 43,* 240–274.

Martin, N., Saffran, E.M., & Dell, G.S. (1996). Recovery in deep dysphasia: Evidence for a relation between auditory–verbal STM capacity and lexical errors in repetition. *Brain and Language, 52,* 83–113.

Martins, I.P., Antunes, N.L., Castro-Caldas, A., & Antunes, J.L. (1995). Atypical dominance for language in developmental dysphasia. *Developmental Medicine and Child Neurology, 37,* 85–90.

Masdeu, J.C., Schoene, W.C., & Funkenstein, H. (1978). Aphasia following infarction of the left supplementary motor area: A clinicopathological study. *Neurology, 28,* 1220–1223.

Mateer, C.A., & Dodrill, C.B. (1983). Neuropsychological and linguistic correlates of atypical language lateralization: Evidence from sodium amytal studies. *Human Neurobiology, 2,* 135–142.

McCarthy, R., & Warrington, E.K. (1984). A two-route model for speech production: Evidence from aphasia. *Brain, 107,* 463–485.

McCarthy, R., & Warrington, E.K. (1987). The double dissociation of short-term memory for lists and sentences: Evidence from aphasia. *Brain, 110,* 1545–1563.

McCarthy, R., & Warrington, E.K. (1990). *Cognitive neuropsychology: A clinical introduction.* San Diego, CA: Academic Press.

McCleod, P., & Posner, M. (1984). Privileged loops from percept to act. In H. Bouma & D. Bouwhuis (Eds), *Attention and Performance X.* Hove, UK: Lawrence Erlbaum Associates Ltd.

McFarling, D., Rothi, L.J., & Heilman, K.M. (1982). Transcortical aphasia from ischaemic infarcts of the thalamus: A report of two cases. *Journal of Neurology, Neurosurgery, and Psychiatry, 45,* 107–112.

McNabb, A.W., Carroll, W.M., & Mastaglia, F.L. (1988). "Alien hand" and loss of bimanual coordination after dominant anterior cerebral artery territory infarction. *Journal of Neurology, Neurosurgery, and Psychiatry, 51,* 218–222.

Mehler, M.F. (1987). Visuo-imitative apraxia. *Neurology, 37,* 129.

Mehler, M.F. (1988). Mixed transcortical aphasia in nonfamilial dysphasic dementia. *Cortex, 24,* 545–554.

Mehler, M.F., & Rabinowich, L. (1990). Heterogeneity in mixed transcortical aphasia: Differential alterations in lexical, semantic and phonological processing define three distinct subgroups. *Journal of Clinical and Experimental Neuropsychology, 12,* 80–81.

Mendez, M.F., & Benson, D.F. (1985). Atypical conduction aphasia: A disconnection syndrome. *Archives of Neurology, 42,* 886–891.

Mendez, M.F., Selwood, A., Mastri, A.R., & Frey II, W.H. (1993). Pick's disease versus Alzheimer's disease: A comparison of clinical characteristics. *Neurology, 34,* 289–292.

Mesulam, M.M. (1986). Frontal cortex and behavior. *Annals of Neurology, 19,* 320–325.

Mesulam, M.M. (1990). Large-scale neurocognitive networks and distributed processing for attention, language, and memory. *Annals of Neurology, 28,* 597–613.

Metter, E.J., Hanson, W.R., & Jackson, C.A., Kempler, D., van Lancker, D., Mazziota, J.C., & Phelps, M.E. (1990). Temporoparietal cortex in aphasia: Evidence from positron emission tomography. *Archives of Neurology, 47,* 1235–1238.

Metter, E.J., Jackson, C., Kempler, D., Riege, W.H., Hanson, W.R., Mazziota, J.C., Phelps, M.E. (1986). Left hemisphere intracerebral hemorrhages studied by (F-18)-fluorodeoxyglucose PET. *Neurology, 36,* 1155–1162.

Metter, E.J., Kempler, D., Jackson, C., Hanson, W.R., Mazziota, J.C., & Phelps, M.E. (1989). Cerebral glucose metabolism in Wernicke's, Broca's, and conduction aphasia. *Archives of Neurology, 46,* 27–34.

Miceli, G., Caltagirone, C., Gainotti, G., Masullo, C., & Silveri, M.C. (1981). Neuropsychological correlates of localized cerebral lesions in nonaphasic brain damaged patients. *Journal of Clinical Neuropsychology, 3*, 53–63.

Michel, F., & Andreewsky, F. (1983). Deep dysphasia: An analogue of deep dyslexia in the auditory modality. *Brain and Language, 18*, 212–223.

Miller, G.A. (1956). The magical number seven, plus or minus two: Some limits of our capacity for processing information. *Psychological Review, 63*, 81–97.

Milner, B. (1964). Some effects of frontal lobectomy in man. In. J.M. Warren & K. Akert (Eds), *The frontal granular cortex and behavior* (pp. 313–324). New York: McGraw-Hill.

Mlcoch, A.G., Bushnell, D.L., & Gupta, S., et al. (1994). Speech fluency in aphasia. *Journal of Neuroimaging, 4*, 6–10.

Mohr, J.P. (1973). Rapid amelioration of motor aphasia. *Archives of Neurology, 28*, 77–82.

Monrad-Krohn, G. (1947). The quality of speech and its disorders. *Acta Psychiatrica Scandinavica, 22*, 225–265.

Monrad-Krohn, G.H. (1963). The third element of speech: Prosody and its disorders. In L. Halpern (Ed.), *Problems of dynamic neurology* (pp. 101–117). Jerusalem: Hebrew University Press.

Moore Jr., W.H. (1989). Language recovery in aphasia: A right hemisphere perspective. *Aphasiology, 3*, 101–110.

Morton, J. (1970). A functional model for memory. In D.A. Norman (Ed.), *A functional model for memory*. New York: Academic Press.

Morton, J. (1979). Word recognition. In J. Morton & J. Marshall (Eds), *Psycholinguistics series*. London: Elek Science.

Morton, J. (1980). The logogen model and orthographic structure. In U. Frith (Ed.), *Cognitive processes in spelling* (pp. 117–133). London: Academic Press.

Nadeau, S.E., & Crosson, B. (1997). Subcortical aphasia. *Brain and Language, 58*, 355–402.

Naeser, M.A., & Borod, J.C. (1986). Aphasia in left-handers: Lesion site, lesion side, and hemispheric asymmetries on CT. *Neurology, 36*, 471–488.

Naeser, M.A., & Hayward, R.W. (1978). Lesion localization in aphasia with cranial computed tomography and the Boston Diagnostic Aphasia Exam. *Neurology, 28*, 545–551.

Naeser, M.A., Hayward, R.W., Laughlin, S., & Zats, L.M. (1981). Quantitative CT scan studies in aphasia: Infarct sized and CT numbers. *Brain and Language, 12*, 140–164.

Naeser, M.A., Palumbo, C.L., Helm-Estabrooks, N., Stiassny-Eder, D., & Albert, M.L. (1989). Severe nonfluency in aphasia: Role of the medial subcallosal fasciculus and other white matter pathways in recovery of spontaneous speech. *Brain, 112*, 1–38.

Nakagawa, Y., Tanabe, H., Ikeda, M., Kazui, H., Ito, K., Inoue, N., Hatakenaba, Y., Sawada, T., Ikeda, H., & Shiraishi, J. (1993). Completion phenomenon in transcortical sensory aphasia. *Behavioural Neurology, 6*, 135–142.

Neary, D. (1990). Editorial. Non Alzheimer's disease forms of cerebral atrophy. *Journal of Neurology, Neurosurgery, and Psychiatry, 53*, 929–931.

Neary, D., Snowden, J.S., Northen, B., & Goulding, P. (1988). Dementia of frontal lobe type. *Journal of Neurology, Neurosurgery, and Psychiatry, 51*, 353–361.

Newcombe, F., & Marshall, J.C. (1981). On psycholinguistic classifications of the acquired aphasias. *Bulletin of the Orton Society, 31*, 29–46.

Nicholas, L.E., & Brookshire, R.H. (1993). A system for quantifying the informativeness and efficiency of the connected speech of adults with aphasia. *Journal of Speech and Hearing Research, 36*, 338–350.

Nicholas, M., Obler, L., Albert, M., & Goodglass, H. (1985). Lexical retrieval in normal aging. *Cortex, 21*, 595–606.

Niessl von Mayendorf, E. (1911). *Die aphasischen Symptome und ihre corticale Lokalisation*. Leipzig: Barth.

Obler, L.K., & Albert, M.L. (1984). Language in aging. In M.L. Albert (Ed.), *Clinical neurology of aging*. New York: Oxford University Press.

Ohyama, M., Senda, M., Kitamura, S., Ishii K., Mishina, M., & Terashi, A. (1996). Role of the nondominant hemisphere and undamaged area during word repetition poststroke aphasics: A PET activation study. *Stroke, 27*, 897–903.

Ojemann, G.A. (1975). Language and the thalamus: Object naming and recall during and after thalamic stimulation. *Brain and Language, 2*, 101–120.

Ojemann, G., Ojemann, J., Lettich, E., & Berger, M. (1989). Cortical language localization in the left, dominant hemisphere. *Journal of Neurosurgery, 71*, 316–326.

Palumbo, C.L., Alexander, M.P., & Naeser, M.A. (1992). CT scan lesion sites associated with conduction aphasia. In S.E. Kohn (Ed.), *Conduction aphasia* (pp. 51–75). Hillsdale, NJ: Lawrence Erlbaum Associates Inc.

Pandya, D.N., & Kuypers, H.G.J.M. (1969). Cortico-cortical connections in the rhesus monkey. *Brain Research, 13*, 13–36.

Papagno, C., & Basso, A. (1996). Perseveration in two aphasic patients. *Cortex, 32*, 67–82.

Pappata, S., Mazoyer, B., Tran Dinh, S., Cambon, H., Levasseur, M., & Baron, J.C. (1990). Effects of capsular and thalamic stroke on metabolism in the cerebral cortex and cerebellum: A positron tomography study. *Stroke, 21*, 519–524.

Patterson, K., & Hodges, J.R. (1992). Deterioration of word meaning: Implications for reading. *Neuropsychologia, 30*, 1025–1040.

Patterson, K., & Shewell, C. (1987). Speak and spell: and word-class effect. In M. Coltheart, G. Sartori, & R. Job (Eds), *The cognitive neuropsychology of language* (pp. 273–294). Hove, UK: Lawrence Erlbaum Associates Ltd.

Patterson, K., Vargha-Khadem, F., & Polkey, C.H. (1989). Reading with one hemisphere. *Brain, 112*, 39–63.

Paulesu, E., Frith, C.D., & Frackowiak, R.S.J. (1993). The neural correlates of the verbal component of working memory. *Nature, 362*, 342–345.

Penfield, W., & Rasmussen, T. (1949). Vocalization and arrest of speech. *Archives of Neurology and Psychiatry, 61*, 21–27.

Penfield, W., & Roberts, L. (1959). *Speech and brain mechanism* (pp. 119–137). Princeton, NJ: Princeton University Press.

Penfield, W., & Welch, K. (1949). The supplementary motor area in the cerebral cortex of man. *Transactions of the American Neurological Association, 74*, 179–184.

Penfield, W., & Welch, K. (1951). The supplementary motor area of the cerebral cortex: A clinical and experimental study. *AMA Archives of Neurology and Psychiatry, 66*, 289–317.

Perani, D., Pappagno, C., Cappa, S., Gerundini, P., & Fazio, F. (1988). Crossed aphasia: Functional studies with single photon emission computerized tomography. *Cortex, 24*, 171–178.

Perani, D., Vallar, G., Cappa, S., Messa, C., & Fazio, F. (1987). Aphasia and neglect after subcortical stroke: A clinical/cerebral perfusion correlation study. *Brain, 110*, 1211–1229.

Perret, E. (1974). The left frontal lobe of man and the suppression of habitual responses in verbal categorical behaviour. *Neuropsychologia, 12*, 323–330.

Petrides, M., & Pandya, D.N. (1988). Association fiber pathways to the frontal cortex from the superior temporal region in the rhesus monkey. *Journal of Comparative Neurology, 310*, 507–549.

Pick, A. (1924). On the pathology of echographia. *Brain, 47*, 417–429.

Pirozzolo, J.F., Kerr, K.L., Obrzut, J.E., Morley, G.K., Haxby, J.V., & Lundgren, S. (1981). Neurolinguisitc analysis of the language abilities of a patient with a "double disconnection syndrome": A case of subangular alexia in the presence of mixed transcortical aphasia. *Journal of Neurology, Neurosurgery, and Psychiatry, 44*, 152–155.

Poeck, K., de Blesser, R., & von Keyserlingk, D.G. (1984). Computed tomography localization of standard aphasic syndromes. In F.C. Rose (Ed.), *Advances in neurology: Vol. 42. Progress in aphasiology* (pp. 71–89). New York: Raven Press.

Powell, A.L., Cummings, J.L., Hill, M.A., & Benson, D.F. (1988). Speech and language alterations in multi-infarct dementia. *Neurology, 38*, 717–719.

Powell, J.H., Al-Adawi, J., Morgan, J., & Greenwood, R.J. (1996). Motivational deficits after brain injury: Effects of bromocriptine in 11 patients. *Journal of Neurology, Neurosurgery, and Psychiatry, 60*, 416–421.

Price, B.H., Gurvit, H., Weintraub, S., Geula, C., Leimkuhler, E., & Mesulam, M. (1993). Neuropsychological patterns and language deficits in 20 consecutive cases of autopsy-confirmed Alzheimer's disease. *Archives of Neurology, 50*, 931–937.

Puel, M.J., Démonet, J.F., Cardebat, D., Bonafé, A., Gazounaud, B., Guiraud-Chaumeil, B., & Rascol, A. (1984). Aphasies sous-corticales. Etude linguistique avec scanner X, á propos de 25 observations. *Revue Neurologique, 140*, 695–710.

Pulvermüller, F., & Preiβl, H. (1994). Explaining aphasias in neuronal terms. *Journal of Neurolinguistics, 8*, 75–81.

Pulvermüller, F., & Schönle, P.W. (1993). Behavioral and neuronal changes during treatment of mixed transcortical aphasia: A case study. *Cognition, 48*, 139–161.

Racy, A., Jannotta, F., & Lehner, L. (1979). Aphasia resulting from occlusion of the left anterior cerebral artery: Report of a case with an old infarct in the left Rolandic region. *Archives of Neurology, 36*, 221–224.

Ramier, A.M., & Hécaen, H. (1970). Role respect if des atteintes frontales et de la latéralisation lésionnelle dans les déficits de la fluence verbale. *Revue Neurologique, 123*, 17–22.

Rapcsak, S.Z., Arthur, S.A., Bliklen, D.A., & Rubens, A.B. (1989). Lexical agraphia in Alzheimer's disease. *Archives of Neurology, 46*, 65–68.

Rapcsak, S.Z., Beeson, P.M., & Rubens, A.B. (1991). Writing with the right hemisphere. *Brain and Language, 41*, 510–530.

Rapcsak, S.Z., Gonzalez Rothi, L.J., & Heilman, K.M. (1987). Phonological alexia with optic and tactile anomia: A neuropsychological and anatomical study. *Brain and Language, 31*, 109–121.

Rapcsak, S.Z., Krupp, L.B., Rubens, A.B., & Reim, J. (1990). Mixed transcortical aphasia without anatomical isolation of the speech area. *Stroke, 21*, 953–956.

Rapcsak, S.Z., & Rubens, A.B. (1994). Localization of lesions in transcortical aphasias. In A. Kertesz (Ed.), *Localization and neuroimaging in neuropsychology* (Ch. 10, pp. 297–329). New York: Academic Press.

Rapp, B.C., & Caramazza, A. (1989). General to specific access to word meaning: A claim re-examined. *Cognitive Neuropsychology, 6*, 251–272.

Rasmussen, T., & Milner, B. (1977). The role of early left-brain injury in determining lateralization of cerebral speech functions. *Annals of the New York Academy of Sciences, 299*, 355–369.

Ratcliff, G., & Newcombe, F. (1982). Object recognition: Some deductions from the clinical evidence. In A.W. Ellis (Ed.), *Normality and pathology in cognitive function* (pp. 147–171). London: Academic Press.

Rauch, R.A., Viñuela, F., Dion, J., Duckwiler, G., Amos E.C., Jordan, S.E., Martin, N., Jensen, M.E., Bentson, J., & Thibault, L. (1992). Preembolization functional evaluation in brain arteriovenous malformations: The superselective amytal test. *American Journal of Neuroradiology, 13*, 303–308.

Raymer, A., Moberg, P.J., Crosson, B., Nadeau, S.E., & Gonzalez Rothi, L.J. (1997). Lexical-semantic deficits in patients with dominant thalamic infarction. *Neuropsychologia, 35*, 211–219.

Reinvang, I. (1987). Crossed aphasia and apraxia in an artist. *Aphasiology, 1*, 423–434.

Reis, A., Guerreiro, M., & Castro-Caldas, A. (1996). The illiterate brain: The influence of an untrained phonological input buffer in oral repetition and digit span of transcortical aphasics. *Journal of the International Neuropsychological Society, 2*(3), 187.

Rey, A. (1964). *L'Examen Clinique en Psychologie*. Paris: Presses Universitaires de France.

Riedel, K. (1981). Auditory comprehension in aphasia. In M. Taylor Sarno (Ed.), *Acquired aphasia* (pp. 215–269). New York: Academic Press.

Robinson, G., Blair, J., & Cipolotti, L. (1998). Dynamic aphasia: an inability to select between competing verbal responses? *Brain*, *121*, 77–89.

Robinson, K.M., Grossman, M., White-Devine, T., & D'Esposito, M. (1996). Category-specific difficulty naming with verbs in Alzheimer's disease. *Neurology*, *47*, 178–182.

Roeltgen, D.P. (1993). Agraphia. In K.M. Heilman & E. Valenstein (Eds), *Clinical neuropsychology* (3rd ed., pp. 63–89). New York: Oxford University Press.

Ross, E.D. (1980). Left medial parietal lobe and receptive language functions: Mixed transcortical aphasia after left anterior cerebral artery infarction. *Neurology*, *30*, 144–151.

Ross, E.D. (1981). The aprosodias: Functional-anatomic organization of the affective components of language in the right hemisphere. *Archives of Neurology*, *38*, 561–569.

Ross, E.D. (1988). Prosody and brain organization: Facts vs fantasy or is it all just semantics? *Archives of Neurology*, *45*, 338–339.

Ross, E.D. (1992). Lateralization of affective prosody in the brain. *Neurology*, *42* (Suppl. 3), 411.

Ross, E.D., Harney, J.H., deLacoste, C., & Purdy, P. (1981). How the brain integrates affective and propositional language into a unified brain function: Hypotheses based on clinicopathological correlations. *Archives of Neurology*, *38*, 745–748.

Ross, E.D., & Mesulam, M.M. (1979). Dominant language functions of the right hemisphere? Prosody and emotional gesturing. *Archives of Neurology*, *36*, 144–148.

Ross, E.D., Thompson, R.D., & Yenkosky, J. (1997). Lateralization of affective prosody in brain and the callosal integration of hemispheric language functions. *Brain and Language*, *56*, 27–54.

Rothman, M. (1906). Lichtheimische motorische Aphasie. *Zeitschrift für Klinische Medizin*, *60*, 87–121.

Rubens, A.B. (1975). Aphasia with infarction in the territory of the anterior cerebral artery. *Cortex*, *11*, 239–250.

Rubens, A.B., & Kertesz, A. (1983). The localization of lesions in transcortical aphasias. In A. Kertesz (Ed.), *Localization in neuropsychology* (pp. 245–268). New York: Academic Press.

Ryalls, J.H. (1982). Intonation in Broca's aphasia. *Neuropsychologia*, *20*, 355–360.

Ryalls, J.H. (1988). Concerning right-hemisphere dominance for affective language. *Archives of Neurology*, *45*, 337–338.

Ryalls, J.H., Joanette, Y., & Feldman, L. (1987). An acoustic comparison of normal and right-hemisphere-damaged speech prosody. *Cortex*, *23*, 685–694.

Ryalls, J., Valdois, S., & Lecours, A.R. (1988). Paraphasia and jargon. In F. Boller & J. Grafman (Eds), *Handbook of clinical neuropsychology* (Vol. 1, pp. 367–376). Amsterdam/Oxford: Elsevier Science Publishers.

Ryding, E., Bradvik, B., & Ingvar, D.H. (1987). Changes in regional cerebral blood flow measured simultaneously in the right and left hemisphere during automatic speech and humming. *Brain*, *110*, 1345–1358.

Sabe, L., Leiguarda, R., & Starkstein, S.E. (1992). An open-label trial of bromocriptine in nonfluent aphasia. *Neurology*, *42*, 1637–1638.

Sabe, L., Salvarezza, F., Cuerva, A.G., Leiguarda, R., & Starkstein, S. (1995). A randomized, double-blind, placebo-controlled study of bromocriptine in nonfluent aphasia. *Neurology*, *45*, 2272–2274.

Salmon, E., Van de Linder, M., Collette, F., Delfiore, G., Maquet, P., Degueldre, C., Luxen, A., & Franck, G. (1996). Regional brain activity during working memory tasks. *Brain*, *119*, 1617–1625.

Sandson, J., & Albert, M.L. (1987). Perseveration in behavioral neurology. *Neurology*, *37*, 1736–1741.

Sandson, J., Obler, L.K., & Albert, M.L. (1987). Language changes in healthy aging and dementia. In R. Rosenberg (Ed.), *Advances in applied psycholinguistics, Vol. 1*. New York: Cambridge University Press.

Sanides, F. (1970). Functional architecture of motor and sensory cortices in primates in the light of a new concept of neocortex evolution. In R.C. Noback & W. Montagna (Eds), *The primate brain* (pp. 137–208). New York: Appleton.

Sartori, G., Barry, C., & Job, R. (1984). Phonological dyslexia: A review. In R.M. Malatesha & H. Whitaker (Eds), *Dyslexia: A global issue* (pp. 339–356). The Hague: Nijhoff.

Sartori, G., Masterson, J., & Job, R. (1987). Direct-route reading and locus of lexical decision. In M. Coltheart, G. Sartori, & R. Job (Eds), *The cognitive neuropsychology of language* (pp. 59–77). Hove, UK: Lawrence Erlbaum Associates Ltd.

Sasanuma, S., & Monoi, H. (1975). The syndrome of Gogi (word-meaning) aphasia: Selective impairment of kanji processing. *Neurology, 25*, 627–632.

Schäffler, L., Lüders, H.O., Dinner, D.S., Lesser, R.P., & Chelune, G.J. (1993). Comprehension deficits elicited by electrical stimulation of Broca's area. *Brain, 116*, 695–715.

Schiff, H.B., Alexander, M.P., Naeser, M.A., & Galaburda, A.M. (1983). Aphemia: Clinical-anatomic correlations. *Archives of Neurology, 40*, 720–727.

Schneider, D. (1938). The clinical syndrome of echolalia, echopraxia, grasping and sucking. *Journal of Nervous and Mental Disease, 88*, 18–35.

Schuell, H. (1957). *Minnesota test for the differential diagnosis of aphasia.* Minneapolis, MN: University of Minnesota Press.

Schulte, E., & Brandt, S.D. (1989). Auditory verbal comprehension impairment. In C. Code (Ed.), *The characterisitcs of aphasia* (pp. 53–74). Hove, UK: Lawrence Erlbaum Associates Ltd.

Schwartz, M.F., Marin, O.S.M., & Saffran, E.M. (1979). Dissociations of language function in dementia: A case study. *Brain and Language, 7*, 277–306.

Schweiger, A., Wechsler, A.F., & Mazziotta, J.C. (1987). Metabolic correlates of linguistic functions in a patient with crossed aphasia: A case study. *Aphasiology, 1*, 415–421.

Selnes, O.A., Carson, K., Rovner, B., & Gordon, B. (1988). Language dysfunction in early- and late-onset possible Alzheimer's disease. *Neurology, 38*, 1053–1056.

Selnes, O.A., Knopman, D.S., Niccum, N., & Rubens, A.B. (1985). The critical role of Wernicke's area in sentence repetition. *Annals of Neurology, 17*, 549–557.

Selnes, O.A., Rubens, A.B., Risse, G.L., & Levy, R.S. (1982). Transient aphasia with persistent apraxia: Uncommon sequela of massive left-hemisphere stroke. *Archives of Neurology, 39*, 122–126.

Sergent, J. (1994). Brain imaging studies of cognitive functions. *Trends in Neurosciences, 17*, 221–227.

Servan, J., Verstichel, P., Catala, M., Yakovleff, A., & Rancurel, G. (1995). Aphasia and infarction of the posterior cerebral artery territory. *Journal of Neurology, 242*, 87–92.

Sevush, S., & Heilman, K.M. (1984). A case of literal alexia: Evidence for a disconnection syndrome. *Brain and Language, 22*, 92–108.

Shallice, T. (1987). Impairments of semantic processing: Multiple dissociations. In M. Coltheart, G. Sartori, & R. Job (Eds), *The cognitive neuropsychology of language* (pp. 111–127). Hove, UK: Lawrence Erlbaum Associates Ltd.

Shallice, T. (1988). *From neuropsychology to mental structure.* Cambridge, UK: Cambridge University Press.

Shallice, T., Burgess, P.W., Schon, F., & Baxter, D.M. (1989). The origins of utilization behaviour. *Brain, 112*, 1587–1598.

Shallice, T., & Vallar, G. (1990). The impairment of auditory-verbal short-term storage. In G. Vallar & T. Shallice (Eds), *Neuropsychological impairments of short-term memory.* Cambridge, UK: Cambridge University Press.

Shallice, T., & Warrington, E.K. (1970). Independent functioning of verbal memory stores: A neuropsychological study. *Quarterly Journal of Experimental Psychology, 22*, 261–273.

Shapiro, A.K., Shapiro, E.S., Young, J.G., & Feinberg, T.E. (1988). *Gilles de la Tourette* (2nd ed.). New York: Raven Press.

Shewan, C., & Kertesz, A. (1980). Reliability and validity characteristics of the Western Aphasia Battery (WAB). *Journal of Speech and Hearing Disorders, 45*, 308–324.

Shipley-Brown, F., Dingwall, W.O., Berlin, C.I., Yeni-Komshian, G., & Gordon Salant, S. (1988). Hemispheric processing of affective and linguistic intonation contours in normal subjects. *Brain and Language, 33*, 16–26.

Shuren, J., Geldmacher, D., & Heilman, K.M. (1993). Nonoptic aphasia: Aphasia with preserved confrontation naming in Alzheimer's disease. *Neurology, 43*, 1900–1907.

Shuren, J.E., Greenwald, M., & Heilman, K.M. (1996). Spontaneous grammatical corrections in an anomic aphasic. *Neurology, 47*, 845–846.

Shutterworth, E.C., Yates, A.J., & Paltan-Ortiz, J.D. (1985). Creutzfeldt–Jakob disease presenting as progressive aphasia. *J Natl Med Assoc, 77*, 649–655.

Silveri, M.C., Daniele, A., Giustolisi, L., & Gainotti, G. (1991). Dissociation between knowledge of living and nonliving things in dementia of the Alzheimer's type. *Neurology, 41*, 545–546.

Simon, N. (1975). Echolalic speech in childhood autism: Consideration of possible underlying loci of brain damage. *Archives of General Psychiatry, 32*, 1439–1446.

Small, S.L. (1994). Pharmacotherapy of aphasia: A critical review. *Stroke, 25*, 1282–1289.

Smirniotopoulos, J.G., & Murphy, R.M. (1992). The phakomatoses. *American Journal of Neuroradiology, 13*, 725–746.

Snowden, J.S., Goulding, P.J., & Neary, D. (1989). Semantic dementia: A form of circumscribed cerebral atrophy. *Behavioural Neurology, 2*, 167–182.

Snowden, J.S., Neary, D., Mann, D.M.A., Goulding, P.J., & Testa, H.J. (1992). Progressive language disorder due to lobar atrophy. *Annals of Neurology, 31*, 174–183.

Snyder, P.J., Novelly, R.A., & Harris, L.J. (1990). Mixed speech dominance in the intracarotid sodium amytal procedure: Validity and criteria issues. *Journal of Clinical and Experimental Neuropsychology, 12*, 629–643.

Speedie, L.J., Coslett, H.B., & Heilman, K.M. (1984). Repetition of affective prosody in mixed transcortical aphasia. *Archives of Neurology, 41*, 268–270.

Speedie, L.J., Wertman, E., Ta'ir, J., & Heilman, K.M. (1993). Disruption of automatic speech following a right basal ganglia lesion. *Neurology, 43*, 1768–1774.

Spreen, O., & Benton, A.L. (1977). *Neurosensory Center Comprehensive Examination for Aphasia (NCCEA)* (rev. ed.). Victoria: University of Victoria, Neuropsychology Laboratory.

Spreen, O., & Risser, A. (1991). Assessment of aphasia. In M. Taylor Sarno (Ed.), *Acquired aphasia* (2nd ed., pp. 73–150). New York: Academic Press.

Spreen, O., & Strauss, E. (1991). *A compendium of neuropsychological tests: Administration, norms, and commentary*. New York: Oxford University Press.

Starkstein, S.E., Berthier, M.L., & Leiguarda, R. (1988). Disconnection syndrome in a right-handed patient with right hemispheric speech dominance. *European Neurology, 28*, 187–190.

Stengel, E. (1936). Zur Lehre von den transcorticalen Aphasien. *Zeitschrift für die Gesamte Neurologie und Psychiatrie, 154*, 778–782.

Stengel, E. (1947). A clinical and psychological study of echo-reactions. *Journal of Mental Science, 93*, 598–612.

Stengel, E. (1964). Speech disorders and mental disorders. In A.V.S. Reuck & M. O'Connor (Eds), *Disorders of language*. London: Churchill.

Stickler, G.B. (1987). Klippel–Trénaunay syndrome. In M.R. Gomez (Ed.), *Neurocutaneous disorders: A practical approach* (pp. 368–375). Boston: Butterworths.

Stuss, D.M., Alexander, M.P., Hamer, L., Palumbo, C., Dempster, R., Binns, M., Levine, B., & Izukawa, D. (1998). The effects of focal anterior and posterior brain lesions in verbal fluency. *Journal of the International Neuropsychological Society, 4*, 265–278.

Stuss, D.T., & Benson, D.F. (1986). *The frontal lobes*. New York: Raven Press.

Swinney, D., Zurif, E., & Nicol, J. (1989). The effects of focal brain damage on sentence process-ing: An examination of the neurological organization of a mental module. *Journal of Cognitive Neuroscience, 1*, 25–37.

Symonds, C. (1953). Aphasia. *Journal of Neurology, Neurosurgery, and Psychiatry, 16*, 1–6.

Talairach, J., Bancaud, J., & Geier, S. (1973). The cingulate gyrus and human behavior. *Electroencephalography and Clinical Neurophysiology, 34*, 42–52.

Talland, C.A. (1965). Three estimates of the word span an their stability over the adult years. *Quarterly Journal of Experimental Psychology, 17*, 301–307.

Tanabe, H., Nakagawa, Y., Ikeda, M., Zazui, H., Yamamoto, H., Ikejiri, Y., & Hashikawa, K. (1993). Neural substrates of the semantic memory for words. *Journal of Clinical and Experi-mental Neuropsychology, 15*, 395.

Tanridag, O., & Ongel, C. (1989). Transcortical motor aphasia due to a right hemisphere lesion in a right-handed man. *Aphasiology, 3*, 717–721.

Taylor, M.A. (1990). Catatonia: A review of a behavioral neurologic syndrome. *Neuropsychiatry, Neuropsychology and Behavioral Neurology, 3*, 48–72.

Thorndike, E.L., & Lorge, I. (1968). *The teacher's word book of 30,000 words.* New York: Teachers College Press, Columbia University.

Tolosa, E., & Peña, J. (1988). Involuntary vocalizations in movement disorders. In J. Jankovic & E. Tolosa (Eds), *Advances in neurology* (Vol. 49, pp. 343–363). New York: Raven Press.

Tonkonogy, J.M. (1986). *Vascular aphasia.* Cambridge, MA: MIT Press.

Trimble, M.R. (1981). *Neuropsychiatry.* Chichester, UK: John Wiley.

Trojano, L., Fragassi, N.A., Postiglione, A., & Grossi, D. (1988). Mixed transcortical aphasia: On relative sparing of phonological short-term store in a case. *Neuropsychologia, 26*, 633–638.

Tyrrell, P.J., Warrington, E.K., Frackowiak, R.S.J., & Rossor, M.N. (1990). Heterogeneity in pro-gressive aphasia due to focal cortical atrophy: A clinical and PET study. *Brain, 113*, 1321–1336.

Van Gorp, W.G., Satz, P., Kiersch, M.E., & Henry, R. (1986). Normative data on the Boston naming test for a group of normal older adults. *Journal of Clinical and Experimental Neuropsychology, 8*, 702–705.

Van Hoesen, G.W. (1985). Neural systems of the non-human primate forebrain implicated in memory. *Annals of the New York Academy of Sciences, 444*, 97–112.

Van Hoesen, G.W., Pandya, D.N., & Butters, N. (1972). Cortical afferents to the entorhinal cortex of the rhesus monkey. *Science, 175*, 1471–1473.

Van Lancker, D., & Sidtis, J.J. (1992). The identification of affective-prosodic stimuli by left- and right-hemisphere-damaged subjects: All errors are not created equal. *Journal of Speech and Hearing Research, 35*, 863–870.

Van Vugt, P., Paquier, P., Kees, L., & Cras, P. (1996). Increased writing activity in neurological conditions: A review and clinical study. *Journal of Neurology, Neurosurgery, and Psychiatry, 61*, 510–514.

Victoroff, J., Webster Ross, G., Benson, D.F., Verity, A., & Vinters, H.V. (1994). Posterior cortical atrophy: Neuropathological correlations. *Archives of Neurology, 51*, 269–274.

Vignolo, L.A. (1984). Aphasias associated with computed tomography scan lesions outside Broca's and Wernicke's areas. In F.C. Rose (Ed.), *Advances in Neurology: Vol. 42. Progress in aphasiology* (pp. 91–98). New York: Raven Press.

Viñuela, F., & Fox, A.J. (1992). Interventional neuroradiology. In H.J.M. Barnett, J.P. Mohr, B.M. Stein, & F.M. Yatsu (Eds), *Stroke: Pathophysiology, diagnosis, and management, Vol. III* (2nd ed., pp. 1145–1167). New York: Churchill Livingstone.

Vix, E. (1910). Anatomischer Befund zu dem in Band 37 dieses Archivs veröffentlichten Fall von transkortikaler sensorischer Aphasie. *Archiv für Psychiatrie und Nervenkrankheiten, 47*, 200–212.

Von Stockert, T.R. (1974). Aphasia sine aphasia. *Brain and Language, 1*, 277–282.

Walsh, K.W. (1985). *Understanding brain damage*. Edinburgh, UK: Churchill-Livingstone.

Wallesch, C.W. (1990). Repetitive verbal behaviour: Functional and neurological considerations. *Aphasiology*, *4*, 133–154.

Wallesch, C.W., Kornhuber, H.H., Brunner, R.J., Kunz, T., Hollerbach, B., & Suger, G. (1983). Lesions of the basal ganglia, thalamus, and deep white matter: Differential effects on language functions. *Brain and Language*, *20*, 286–304.

Warrington, E.K. (1975). The selective impairment of semantic memory. *Quarterly Journal of Experimental Psychology*, *27*, 635–657.

Warrington, E.K. (1981). Concrete word dyslexia. *British Journal of Psychology*, *72*, 175–196.

Warrington, E.K., Logue, V., & Pratt, R.T.C. (1971). The anatomical localisation of selective impairment of auditory verbal short-term memory. *Neuropsychologia*, *9*, 377–387.

Warrington, E.K., & McCarthy, R. (1983). Category specific access dysphasia. *Brain*, *106*, 859–878.

Warrington, E.K., & Shallice, T. (1969). The selective impairment of auditory verbal short-term memory. *Brain*, *92*, 885–896.

Warrington, E.K., & Shallice, T. (1979). Semantic access dyslexia. *Brain*, *102*, 43–63.

Waters, G.S., Caplan, D., & Hildebrandt, N. (1991). On the structure of verbal short-term memory and nature and its functional role in sentence comprehension: A case study. *Cognitive Neuropsychology*, *2*, 81–126.

Watson, R.T., Fleet, W.S., Gonzalez Rothi, L., & Heilman, K.M. (1986). Apraxia and the supplementary motor area. *Archives of Neurology*, *43*, 787–792.

Wechsler, D. (1945). A standardized memory scale for clinical use. *Journal of Psychology*, *19*, 87–95.

Wechsler, D. (1955). *Wechsler adult intelligence scale*. New York: Psychological Corporation.

Weiller, C., Isensee, C., Rijntjes, M., Huber, W., Müller, S., Bier, D., Dutschka, K., Woods, R.P., Noth, J., & Diener, H.C. (1995). Recovery from Wernicke's aphasia: A positron emission tomographic study. *Annals of Neurology*, *37*, 723–732.

Weinberg, J., Diller, L., Gerstman, L., & Schulman, P. (1972). Digit span in right and left hemiplegics. *Journal of Clinical Psychology*, *28*, 361.

Weinberger, D.R., Berman, K.F., & Chase, T.N. (1988). Mesocortical dopaminergic function and human cognition. *Annals of the New York Academy of Sciences*, *537*, 330–338.

Weintraub, S., Mesulam, M.M., & Kramer, L. (1981). Disturbances in prosody: A right-hemisphere contribution to language. *Archives of Neurology*, *38*, 742–744.

Weisenburg, T., & McBride, K.E. (1935). *Aphasia: A clinical and psychological study*. New York: The Commonwealth Fund.

Wernicke, C. *Die neuren Arbeiten über Aphasie*. Fortschritte d. Medicin, 1885, p. 824; 1886, p. 371, 463.

Wernicke, C. (1977). *Wernicke's works on aphasia: A sourcebook and review* (pp. 91–145). [Der aphasische Symptomencomplex. Eine psychologische Studie auf anatomischer Basis]. (G.H. Eggert, Trans.). New York: Mouton. (Original work published 1874)

Whitaker, H. (1976). A case of isolation of language function. In H. Whitaker & H.A. Whitaker (Eds), *Studies in neurolinguistics* (Vol. 1, pp. 1–58). New York: Academic Press.

Wiig, E.H., & Semel, E.M. (1974). Development of comprehensions of logical-grammatical sentences by grade school children. *Perceptual and Motor Skills*, *38*, 171–176.

Williams III, D.W., & Elster, A.D. (1992). Cranial CT and MRI in the Klippel–Trénaunay–Weber syndrome. *American Journal of Neuroradiology*, *13*, 291–294.

Willmes, K., & Poeck, K. (1993). To what extent can aphasic syndromes be localized? *Brain*, *116*, 1527–1540.

Wise, R., Chollet, F., Hadar, U., Friston, K., Hoffner, E., & Frackowiak, R. (1991). Distribution of cortical neural networks involved in word comprehnsion and word retrieval. *Brain*, *114*, 1803–1817.

Yamadori, A., & Albert, M.L. (1973). Word category aphasia. *Cortex*, *9*, 112–125.

Yamadori, A., Mori, E., Tabuchi, M., Kudo, Y., & Mitani, Y. (1986). Hypergraphia: A right hemisphere syndrome. *Journal of Neurology, Neurosurgery, and Psychiatry*, *49*, 1160–1164.

Yamadori, A., Osumi, Y, Masuhara, S., & Okubo, M. (1977). Preservation of singing in Broca's aphasia. *Journal of Neurology, Neurosurgery, and Psychiatry*, *40*, 221–224.

Yarnell, P.R. (1981). Crossed dextral aphasia: A clinical radiological correlation. *Brain and Language*, *12*, 128–139.

Zingezer, L.B., & Berndt, R.S. (1988). Grammatical class and context effects in a case of pure anomia: Implications for models of language production. *Cognitive Neuropsychology*, *5*, 473–516.

Zurif, E.B., & Caramazza, A. (1976). Psycholinguistic structures in aphasia: studies in syntax and semantics. In H. Whitaker & H.A. Whitaker (Eds), *Studies in neurolinguistics* (Vol. 1, pp. 261–292). New York: Academic Press.

Author index

Subject index